PEACE AND CONFLICT STUDIES

To My Parents –

Whose life has shaped my visions and thinking about peace

Peace and Conflict Studies

An introduction

HO-WON JEONG
Institute for Conflict Analysis and Resolution
George Mason University, USA

ASHGATE

© Ho-Won Jeong 2000

Published by
Ashgate Publishing Limited
Gower House
Croft Road
Aldershot
Hants GU11 3HR
England

Ashgate Publishing Company
Suite 420
101 Cherry Street
Burlington, VT 05401-4405
USA

Ashgate website:http://www.ashgate.com

British Library Cataloguing in Publication Data
Jeong, Ho-Won
    Peace and conflict studies : an introduction
    1.Peace 2.Peace - Philosophy 3.Conflict management
    4.International cooperation 5.Security, International
    I.Title
    327.1'72

Library of Congress Control Number: 00-134022

ISBN 1 84014 095 X (HB)
ISBN 1 84014 098 4 (PB)

Reprinted 2002, 2003

Printed and bound in Great Britain by MPG Books Ltd, Bodmin, Cornwall

Contents

Foreword to the Series

On first encountering this three-volume series, the potential reader may at first wonder: Why do we need three volumes on peace and conflict? We will attempt to offer a succinct response to this question.

The broad scope of the three volumes reflects the tremendous progress that has been made in peace research in the last half of the Twentieth Century. Most significantly, our paradigms now include not only negative peace (stopping the shooting and bombing) but also positive peace, including economic well-being, human rights and environmental issues. In other words, we have now acquired a more global perspective on the causes of peacelessness. At the same time, we have broadened our concerns beyond peacemaking (i.e. conflict resolution and conflict management) to include peacekeeping, and most important, peace building.

Recently, I attempted to identify the major peace research trends in the last decade (Alger, 2000, 2) and proposed these seven: (1) Increasing efforts to combine a number of peace tools into comprehensive peace strategies, (2) Growing attention to the importance of pursuing multiple peace tracks simultaneously, (3) The growing tendency to take a long-term perspective, (4) Numerous recent works endeavoring to bridge theory building and practice, (5) Special attention given to efforts to cope with violent conflict between ethnic groups, (6) Growing literature on the need for what is often referred to as "post conflict" strategies, so as to sustain peace settlements, and (7) Increased emphasis on long-term strategies for prevention of extremely disruptive and violent conflict.

Unfortunately, most actions of those who are attempting to reduce disruptive conflict do not reflect recent advancements in knowledge. One problem is that recent research is widely scattered, often appearing in academic journals and books that are not widely accessible. Another difficulty is that peace building is a far more complicated task than most of us had earlier assumed. Relevant government roles extend far beyond foreign offices and the military, including departments concerned with economic and social issues. Furthermore, roles must be performed not only by government officials, but also by professions and groups in what we customarily refer to as 'civil society'. Recent research has identified peace roles in diverse societal domains, including business, religion, education, media, ethnic communities, development assistance and local governance.

Coordinating these various roles, or at least making them more compatible, presents an overwhelming challenge to peace builders. On the other hand, there is a positive side to a multiplicity of peace roles in that peace builders now have many more options and resources than they did in times past. Certainly there are also significant implications for peace education. There is obviously a need for peace education curricula that takes a broad, systemic view of peace building. Although most involved in peace building will tend to perform only one role in a complicated social network, it is necessary for all involved to know the nature of the entire network, where they fit in the network, and how they are linked to, and interdependent with, other roles.

By bringing together widely scattered contributions to peace research, this series will make them more accessible. By assembling information on the activities, achievements and problems encountered by a diversity of peace roles, these volumes not only offer information on the latest research on the performance of these roles, but inform those actively engaged in these roles, as well as the general reader, of the ways in which these roles are interdependent.

Finally, this series provides rich resources for peace education courses. *Peace and Conflict Studies: An Introduction* can be used as a basic textbook in introducing peace studies to students with backgrounds in a diversity of disciplines. The other two volumes, *Conflict Resolution: Dynamics, Process and Structure,* as well as *The New Agenda for Peace Research* offer a diversity of supplementary readings in topics on which the instructor may wish to offer special emphasis. The readings in these two volumes, written from leading experts around the world, offer a feast of differing perspectives and emphases.

Chadwick F. Alger
May 2000

Foreword

We have in this book probably the first comprehensive exposition of peace and conflict studies. The sub-title *Introduction* to this 400-page book is misleading in the size context, but it is an important pointer to the fact that peace and conflict studies embrace all social studies, including economics and others that focus on institutions and structures with a view to their preservation. *Peace and Conflict Studies* seek to inject into these specialisations a human element that has been pushed aside as being of less importance than institutional preservation. This book points to the need for a more comprehensive study of human needs and aspirations.

In his writing, the author reflects his experience of teaching at the Institute for Conflict Analysis and Resolution, which, as 'Analysis' in the title indicates, was established in an academic setting to bring attention to the nature of conflict resolution process. Conflict resolution and peace building are different from official interventions. Parties are brought together in an off-the-record, private setting, and discussions go on until all parties wholly understand the motivations and concerns of all the others. It is an extension of a psychoanalysis process. All parties begin to introspect and in due course can finally identify with each other, when they find that they share the same human needs and concerns. Negotiation, compromise, the threat of the use of power and enforcement processes become irrelevant. It is hard to believe without experiencing a conflict analysis process that parties meet each other, communicate, ask questions and get down to the real issues not previously articulated.

Being analytical in dealing with human behaviour applies to all social levels; from the family, to the work place, to community relations, to religious conflicts and to the global society. In the workplace, for instance, there can be conflict followed by an adversarial bargaining process. Wage levels are the usual subject for negotiation. An analytical approach would find that the usual demand for wages increases is a means of compensation for employees feeling that they are treated as non-human robots. In ordinary bargaining, agreement is reached, but another conflict can be anticipated. An analysis of the basic issues and appropriate changes in management can resolve such conflicts and also lead to increased work output. So it is with conflicts at other levels.

This extensive and comprehensive book is, therefore, an important '*Introduction*' and will be a most valuable text, not merely for students in conflict analysis and resolution, but for international relations specialists, economists and sociologists generally. The book provides the substantive knowledge needed for conflict analysis and peace. Its emphasis on basic needs and non-adversarial problem solving framework provide the frame in which texts can be written for school children, parents, managers, lawyers and police, so-called 'intelligence' agencies, defence strategists and others who are at work within contemporary adversarial institutions and structures.

John W. Burton
Bruce, Australia
May 2000

Preface

The goal of this book is to reinterpret various theoretical approaches in peace and conflict studies as our knowledge and experience accumulate. During the Cold War period, the prevention of nuclear war attracted much attention, as conflict between the United States and Russia could have resulted in the annihilation of human civilisation. Despite the end of animosities between the two major nuclear powers, significant progress toward nuclear disarmament has not been made, with China, India and Pakistan strengthening their weapons capabilities. Violent ethnic conflicts in former Yugoslavia, Rwanda, Somalia, Angola and other parts of the world have caused many deaths and destruction over the last decade.

In addition, extreme poverty and economic disparities have been seriously undermining the well-being of the underprivileged majority of the global population. This issue remains true despite the celebration of recent economic gains for the middle class in the U.S. and other industrialised countries. In some societies, women and children continue to be victims of social oppression and economic exploitation. Concerns for the environment that captured the public imagination in the 1970s have been obscured by the emphasis on free trade and economic growth.

Given the dominant interests of political elites and the superficial nature of public discourse, dramatic measures are not likely to be taken to mitigate the sufferings of those marginalised groups in the foreseeable future. Beyond minimal institutional adjustment and technical re-orientation, fundamental rethinking is required to develop an enlarged vision of peace to meet the above challenges. In revealing and assessing human practice, the old issues wait for re-conceptualisation, reflecting on our time and space. This book has been prepared in the hope of providing a knowledge base to critically analyse the deep causes of violence and conflict across social, political, economic and environmental dimensions. Most importantly, diverse strategies for peace building are illustrated and examined.

The book can be located in the rich intellectual traditions relevant to peace studies. Peace touches upon many different aspects of our life, and the realisation of peace is affected by a complex social environment. The pursuit of a nonviolent and just society is grounded in the empirical understanding of existing problems. Peace theories have specific implications and meanings in interpreting a contemporary world, and they are less abstract and more pragmatic than traditional international relations theories which heavily focus on foreign policy decision making behaviour or the structure of an inter-state system.

The beginning of the new century is the quintessential moment to present a new book on peace and conflict studies which looks beyond a limited understanding of history. This volume can be used for peace and conflict studies courses at universities, seminars and workshops for peace activists and policy makers. It attempts to reflects the past achievement in our conceptual thinking, illustrate practice and explain many of the key concepts discussed in the field.

In preparing for this book, I owe great intellectual debts and personal encouragement to the previous generation of many distinguished peace scholars. In particular, this book benefited from the inspiration of Chadwick F. Alger who has been a role model of both intellectual humility and great scholarship. John W. Burton, whose thoughts laid a foundation for conflict resolution research, has been kind and generous to share new ideas and old wisdom. I am also very grateful to Hayward Alker and Anatol Rapoport for lending their insight and support to *Peace and Conflict Studies Series*. The late Paul Smoker, Elise Boulding, Louis Kriesberg, Michael Nagler, Glenn Paige, Michael True, Linda Groff, Luc Reychler and Juergen Dedring have been supportive of my endeavour for peace research. Discussion with Christopher Mitchell and Richard Rubenstein has helped me gain the insight much needed for writing this volume.

Charles Snare made selfless efforts and provided critical comments throughout the book. I also appreciate editorial comments made in various parts of the manuscript by Charles Lerche, Karen Andrews and Brenda Lindsay. Gloria Rhodes invested her skills and talent for copy editing. Mary was a devoted helper and without her tolerance, I could not have found time to complete this project. Nimmy's warm and peace loving nature has been inspirational to me. This book is dedicated to my parents Woo-Yang Jeong and Phil-Soon Cha whose vision, enthusiasm and unconditional support led to the production of this work.

Ho-Won Jeong
January 2000

Introduction

Our small planet faces various threats to human survival. Militarism, human rights abuses, poverty and economic inequity, the rapid growth in the world population, environmental degradation -- all have become our major concerns. Over the past two decades, peace studies themes have emerged from the search for an alternative world order, an emphasis on sustainable development and the promotion of human rights as well as the prevention of war. More specifically, peace research interests lie in uncovering the relationships between inequality, injustice and power asymmetry on the one hand and violence on the other.

The search for knowledge has to be linked to the exploration of new social and political practices at various policy-making levels. Systemic crisis can be handled by collaborative problem solving mechanisms in an interdependent world. Conflict resolution and nonviolence have been applied to many conflict situations from interpersonal to global levels.

In developing a coherent research programme, it is essential to conceptualise the meanings of peace in a way that will help the accumulation of knowledge in the field. The relevance of institutions and social relations to peace has to be examined in the context of historical evidence. For that purpose, strategies that have been adopted and practiced in the past need to be critically analysed and evaluated.

Peace research has not always been successful in the conceptual integration of human experiences. The reason for diverse approaches is ascribed, in part, to the existence of different perceptions of the world and to a lack of comparative evaluation of research paradigms. This book not only reviews and assesses various theoretical understandings but also helps formulate new interpretations of the changing world.

The Framework of the Book

In responding to challenges to synthesise different conceptions of peace and various theoretical approaches, this book consists of four sections. In Part One, meanings of peace are re-conceptualised in the context of what has been broadly understood in the field. Peace studies have engendered a new perspective that safeguarding national interests is not related to peace. Universal and global peace is not enhanced by the ambitions of national political elite, goals of state actors and policy objectives of international financial institutions. Conventional views of the world do not help us examine the nature of conflict that emerges from poverty and marginalisation. The unwillingness and incapacity of state institutions to respond to the basic needs of the population is one of major obstacles to peace. In dealing with threats to international security, the global community is required to take a fresh look at the range of collaborative actions, which would help transform the existing order.

The second part of this book identifies five approaches to understanding causes of conflict and violence. It includes organised violence such as war, violence against women, group conflict based on identity differences and dissatisfaction of basic needs, economic inequities and environmental degradation. Certain social and political settings operate in ways that aggravate economic and environmental sources of conflict.

In the third part, this volume looks at various strategies for achieving peace, and how these strategies have been applied to the real world. The conditions for overcoming violence can be improved by peace keeping, making and building. In order to reduce and prevent international violence, we need to look for alternative security mechanisms, non-adversarial methods of conflict resolution, sustainable development strategies and nonviolent action for policy changes. This section also illustrates that human life would not be improved without realising human rights, economic well-being, self-determination and ecological security.

Peace theories cover various kinds of problems in inter-personal, inter-group and international relations. In the last part, we will examine the integration of peace strategies at different levels of human society. In addition, primary inquiries will be directed toward integrating practices, policies and paths to alternative social order. Overall, we are looking for life-enhancing choices and actions in transition to a nonviolent world.

PART I

MEANINGS, CONCEPTS AND DISCOURSE

In addition to the prevention of warfare among states, peace ought to be based on justice within and between societies, a guarantee of basic individual and group rights and the non-use of violence to resolve conflict. Peace is not something alien to our everyday life. Peace is achieved, in essence, through a social process. To a certain extent, neighbourhood violence can be understood in the same logic as nations prepare for war. Family violence is tolerated by the maintenance of patriarchal social and political systems. An adversarial process may well be found in labour disputes as well as international conflict. The accepted values of hierarchy help sustain the very system that generates repression. The cessation of violence has to be accompanied by social and cultural transformations.

After examining both historical and contemporary contexts of struggle for peace, this first part defines the concept of peace and examines various meanings of security and violence. It is generally agreed that peace must be understood as more than just the absence of war. It has to be based on economic and social conditions that eliminate injustice and human misery. The holistic phenomenon of peace is contrasted with the existence of both manifest and latent violence. The new conceptualisation of peace derives from the theoretical examination of structural and behavioural conditions that reduce violent conflict.

1   Challenges for Peace

In the real world, there are only a few examples that satisfy all the elements of peace. What we usually find is the negation of peace: war and other forms of violence. The understanding of a peaceful world is also juxtaposed against the experiences of marginalisation and alienation in history. The ideals of peace are influenced by value systems of a particular society. Continuation of violence suggests that humans have not achieved the political, emotional and spiritual maturity needed for the realisation of peace.

Visions of Peace

In our age, many people still conceive of peace as equivalent to the absence of manifest violence, largely major wars between states. Preventing a nuclear war between superpowers was, in particular, a dominant concern in the second half of the twentieth century. However, the concepts of peace have been rich in content across various religious and philosophical traditions. The search for inner and communal peace derives from the ideal sought in the spiritual life. From the early period of human thinking, there has been a clear understanding that war is neither a natural phenomenon nor the irreversible will of the gods. A peaceful world belongs to a society where people can work and live together in harmony and friendship. The domination of one group over another is a major obstacle to peace.

Negative Peace vs. Positive Peace

In Eastern religions, there is a strong emphasis on links between a spiritual life and action for social justice (Smoker and Groff, 1996, p. 105). The Buddhist traditions emphasise justice, equity, nonviolence, concern for the well-being of others and compassion among living beings. They also reflect a well-ordered state of mind, inner peace and harmony within a culture. Tranquillity in the inner state of mind and harmonious interpersonal relationships contribute to universal peace.

Positive peace

The practice of non-exploitation of nature exists in Native American and African tribal cultures. Peace with the planet represents the need for humans to live in harmony with nature rather than conquer it. The notion of ecological peace from indigenous tribal traditions enables us to understand that the earth, too, is the object of violence. The earth constitutes a web in which humans are part, and by destroying living and non-living forms of existence on the planet humans threaten even their own survival.

The messages of mutual good will, unconditional love, wholeness and individual well-being as well as cessation of hostilities have been delivered in many Western religious traditions. The passages of the Old Testament of the Bible state that swords shall be beaten into ploughshares and their spears into pruning hooks. In early Christian social utopia, there was a strong emphasis on a community of love. Harmony and fullness of joy can be achieved by spiritual enlightenment.

Greek philosophers conceptualised a peaceful world in terms of a lack of civil disturbances (Nussbaum, 1997, p. 32). These philosophical traditions are also linked to unity based on the moral substance of humanity in each person and the principle of world citizenship. The vision of a world without war was embraced as the core approach to peace in the Hellenic civilisation (Chatfield and Ilukhina, 1994, p. 5). In the Roman and Medieval periods, peace implied stable relationships among units of society that lead to the control of organised violence. Peace can be brought about by order that may be imposed by a powerful coalition or even an empire.

In Enlightenment thinking, violence and conflict, seen as the greatest evil in history, are ascribed to a disorderly world. Political philosophers such as John Locke in the 17th century and Jean-Jacques Rousseau in the 18th century viewed war as unnecessary and believed that social contracts could prevent violence. Liberal reformists in the 19th century proposed institutionalised mechanisms that are necessary for the conquest of organised violence, namely inter-state war.

The idea of creating a large array of international agreements and institutions was supported by the assumption that achieving peace would be easy by defining the rights of sovereign states in an international system and preventing one state from intervening with the government of another state (Kant, 1970). Conflict should be handled through negotiation rather than resorting to war, and broadening popular influence is critical to stopping war. Educating political leaders to transform international systems was believed to be an important initial step in outlawing war and enhancing international cooperation.

* Peace understood in terms of maintaining social order does not reside in the dimensions of social and political justice. The notion of an order within and between sovereign states relegates peace to conditions of the status quo. According to the nineteenth century Russian thinker Tolstoy and other pacifist anarchists who considered peace as a cherished human value, the state power apparatus is responsible for the organisation of both oppression and violence. War can be abolished with the elimination of a political structure attributed to social oppression and exploitation. Given their focus on individual autonomy and freedom, ideas in anarchist utopias oppose government and legal institutions that impose an artificial order (Smoker, 1972, p. 63).

In response to the realisation that purposeful changes have to be made in improving human conditions, socialist movements in the 19th and early 20th century stipulated that peace could be obtained in a classless society. The primary causes of human misery are economic inequality and a repressive political system associated with social injustice. Monopoly of economic resources and power held by a few helps maintain a social system that exploits underprivileged people. Building solidarities among the human race is important in the fight for liberation from exploitation and war. Peace has a firm social dimension in which equity and consideration of others' well-being are crucial for a harmonious community life. People from different cultural and political traditions would be united by the achievement of equal society.

The ideal of equality among humans played a decisive role from old religious traditions to early socialism. For thousands of years, this vision of peace from religious traditions to modern philosophical ideas encouraged a lifestyle based on nonviolence and communal living. In modern thinking peace is no longer simply a utopia to be realised by abstract religious moral codes or principles. Rather it is a goal that can be obtained by conscious efforts to build a harmonious social order. Since warfare is considered as a means to promote the interests of the powerful, challenges to the dominant power are necessary to put a definite end to human suffering. If there were no dominant groups of people associated with oppressive states, then conflict and war would disappear. Though the visions of peace remained scarcely more than a vague hope in reality, the ideals have played an important role in maintaining hopes of establishing peace for the future generations.

Historical Experiences

Contrary to the visions of peace, human history is full of many examples of violent conflict and oppression along with the rise and fall of civilisations. Before weapons became sophisticated, the scale of violence was manageable. Faced with hostile natural environments, human ancestors had to learn how to live together to meet their survival needs. In a hunting and gathering society, one person did not exercise control over the community wealth. Few dominant patterns existed in egalitarian band society.

The construct of social domination is based on a set of behavioural norms and political structures supporting exploitative relations. In a stratified society, status coincides with the ability for social control over wealth produced by others (Boulding, 1976, p. 37). The history of organised violence and domination started with the replacement of simple subsistence farming communities by hierarchical social structures based on the concentration of power in the hands of patriarchal rulers.

In the early European civilisations, Greek city states were engaged in hegemonic rivalry, and it was a major form of violence. In addition, the alliance of Greek city states fought Persia for control of the Mediterranean. Stable order was eventually imposed by the emergence of the hegemonic power of the Macedonian and Roman empires following numerous military conquests. In the medieval period, both the Roman Catholic Church and the Holy Roman Empire maintained order within Europe. However, religious zeal along with power and profit motives led to the Crusades; military expeditions were directed against Muslim control of Jerusalem. The Thirty Years' War, fought several centuries later, resulted from the attempt of three Christian religious doctrines to vie for dominance on the European continent.

Competition between states in the modern international system was fuelled by the attempts of absolute monarchies to expand their territory and economic bases. Inter-state conflict was often related to part of the process resulting in the creation of a dominant social, political structure. Bureaucracies and armies were needed in completing the project of establishing an efficient modern state system. Populations under its sovereign jurisdictions were oppressed to satisfy the ambitions of a newly emerging state. Events in eighteenth and nineteenth century Europe reflect the surge of nationalism and efforts to consolidate the power and symbols of a nation-state. Aspirations for new national identities culminated in the French Revolution and the Napoleonic War.

The modern form of organising political space is characterised by the system of territorial states and concentration of power in specific classes. Sharp division of class relations resulted from a capitalist mode of development. Economic exploitation and miserable living conditions for the marginalised class in a capitalist system inevitably brought about a struggle to achieve equality in a modern industrial society. The nature of conflict in a modern society has become more complex with the establishment of highly stratified social systems.

The forms of interaction between different cultural systems were significantly changed by the industrial revolution and scientific and technological advances. The spatial and temporal implosion of the globe since the Renaissance extended a dominant social order to the global arena. Before the arrival of technological revolution, each civilisation enjoyed a relatively autonomous social facticity and operated under its own laws of historicity. However, the subjugation of non-European civilisations through conquest created a singular post-Colombian world (Wolf, 1997). The integration of separate and coexisting cultural systems was completed by the early 20th century.

The two world wars, which left long lasting memories of genocide and atrocities, reflect the structural characteristics of conflicts between dominant colonial powers. The hierarchical international order represented by a bipolar world system during the Cold War period coincided with threats of nuclear weapons. The characteristics of post-Cold War order are not radically different from previous ones in terms of the maintenance of relations of subordination and domination through threats and violence.

The current transformation in a world order affected by globalisation is merely one specific expression of a reconfiguration in social space and time. In structural changes of the global political economy, new material conditions have awakened both a need and a desire for broad transformation in the prevailing social epistemology and spatial forms. Global capitalism today internalises relationships and values that previously did not exist in many parts of the world. The collapse of former socialist countries in Eastern Europe can be ascribed to the powerful appeal of the symbols of affluence of Western capitalist society.

Interpretation In the legacies of human history filled with war and oppression, the desires and ambitions of political elites have always outweighed the prospect for peace. Violence has been part of an historical process that created a dominant social order. In this context, the absence of war associated with the extension of hegemonic power is simply a reflection of imposition of a hierarchical order by the use of arms and an elite-dominated political structure.

Historical conditions for peace, which can be more easily found in egalitarian social relations, would remain a dream to be realised within the existing political and economic structure. Long struggles have been waged to achieve basic rights to freedom, autonomy and equity. Domination and exploitation have been more systematic and endemic in hierarchical societies with concentration of wealth and power. Social ideology reflects basic value judgements about political and economic order. Lower-status social groups are put in disadvantageous positions by birth, skill, education or occupations (Boulding, 1976, p. 38).

While now weapons have the capability of destroying the entire population on the earth, knowledge and skills were not sufficiently developed to cope with the means of mass destruction and the level of poverty in many parts of the world. The survival of the human species is further threatened by newly emerging concerns with environmental pollution and resource depletion.

Culture and Social Values

Peace is interpreted differently across cultures and social values with varying degrees of priority given to individual and communal well-being. In most industrialised societies, providing fair political and legal procedures for competition is seen as an important condition for individual achievement, thus contributing to social progress. On the other hand, indigenous people's culture with primordial ties and face-to-face interaction is closely attached to nature, and there is more emphasis on a community's well-being than individual pursuit of wealth. Within indigenous societies inheriting a holistic vision of peace, we would be more likely to observe the preservation of communal traditions of sharing and interconnectedness. Many tribal groups living on a small island in the South Pacific, the aboriginal tribes of Australia, Northern African desert, Himalayan hillside or Amazon jungles isolated from any modern technology are found maintaining a more egalitarian social structure than those who live in Western industrialised societies.

There are certainly places on the planet where social values oriented toward enhancing opportunities for fulfilling human needs and solidarity still prevail. On the other hand, transformation of traditional decentralised societies into a homogeneous life style has occurred in many parts of the world, with modernisation replacing the community norms and networks of collective responsibility and concerns with the disadvantaged. In a modern economic system that stresses free market mechanisms, income gaps are inevitable along with the emergence of new social hierarchies resulting from concentration of wealth. It generates conditions for communal conflicts in combination with a struggle between different forces that advocate opposing value systems and social structures. To provide a stable environment for rapid economic growth, governments in countries like China maintain a tight control over society. Sovereignty rights are often claimed for justifying the oppression of minority groups as well as limiting the freedom of association and expression.

Scandinavia and other European countries, influenced by the social democratic traditions of the early 20th century, have achieved progress by guaranteeing a reliable welfare system based on free education, medicare, job training and other programmes. The principles of equity are supported by mechanisms to enhance social and economic opportunities for low income groups. Externally, welfare-oriented societies such as Switzerland and Sweden opted not to participate in any kind of international conflict. Instead, they became involved in peacemaking activities while remaining neutral in major wars. The experiences of these countries demonstrate that the commitment to human welfare is incompatible with allowing economic disparities and expensive military build-up.

The unfolding drama of social transformation influenced by the modernisation and globalisation process has an important impact on structural and psychological conditions for peace. Communal networks have broken down with social fragmentation. Traditional social values are replaced by competitive behavioural norms. Restructuring of national economies to be adaptable to international economic competition reduced the commitment to a welfare society. Social protests against government cut backs in programmes for the unemployed, students, labour union members and farmers represent challenges to market based efficiency.

Peace is most fulfilled in a place where opportunities for both psychological and material self-realisation are provided. Cultural, ethnic and racial differences are more likely to be tolerated in communities where people are entitled to freedom and autonomy. In addition, harmony and cooperation can be better maintained in a society that is supportive of economic equity and well-being. The quest for peace is linked to how to create a society that reflects such values and ideals as the elimination of economic exploitation and political repression as well as physical violence between groups of people and between nations. Horizontal communication patterns are geared toward promoting a better understanding of people with diverse cultural and educational backgrounds.

When Peace becomes Actualized

Continuity and Discontinuity

In most of the latter half of the twentieth century, identities of groups and countries in their struggle for independence were defined in terms of their ideological and political links to either Moscow or Washington. Geostrategic interests were largely determined in terms of U.S.-Soviet rivalry. During the Cold War period, enemy perceptions and mistrust hampered efforts to significantly reduce arms. The Vietnam War was based on the misunderstanding of nationalist aspirations. While the huge budget deficit was created by the expansion of military programmes in the Reagan era, Moscow's efforts to keep up with the U.S. military expenditure crippled the Soviet economy in the 1980s. Transformation of political and economic systems in Russia effectively ended a bitter battle between the two antagonistic value systems.

The end of the Cold War, brought about by the dissolution of the Soviet Union and the transition of Eastern Europe toward capitalism, generated certain euphoria. More countries have been pressed to adopt Western style democratic political systems since the late 1980s. Some suggest modern history ended with the triumph of Western pluralistic democratic systems and free market economic reform (Fukuyama, 1992). The proclamation of the new world order rests on the thesis of victory by pluralistic democracy. In line with the new triumph of the West, it has been argued that democracies do not go to war with each other (Brown, et al., 1996). This view largely represents the emerging Western hegemonic order with the demise of socialist systems in Eastern Europe and Russia. Recent structural changes between major powers replaced the international system that used to be dominated by the two superpowers since the Second World War.

In the midst of general optimism for a stable international order between major international powers, some illustrate the replacement of old ideological tension by hostilities between different cultures. The so-called 'civilisational clashes' thesis argues that fundamental cultural and religious differences would be a source of conflict between Western industrialised countries and other countries which have Muslim or Confucian values. To protect geostrategic interests, the West should maintain its alliance and be prepared militarily for future threats from other civilisations (Huntington, 1993).

In the sense that maintaining stability still largely depends on power, the post-Cold War order is not much different from the previous systems. Obviously, the dangers of global nuclear annihilation posed by rivalry between the former super powers were significantly reduced. In considering that the new world order has not changed the perceptions and behaviours of states, nevertheless, the very idea and possibility of war has not been eliminated. Many political leaders pursued war instead of peaceful settlement as illustrated in the Chechen and Persian Gulf wars as well as by the fighting in the Balkans. Under these conditions, military power remains as a tool to maintain a hierarchical world order.

Traditional security strategies that stress deterrence remain an obstacle for the path to demilitarisation. The threat of nuclear weapons proliferation has not been diminished due to the insistence of nuclear powers to hold on to their military hegemony with the deadly weapons. The French nuclear testing in the South Pacific in 1995 demonstrated the arrogance of nuclear powers. India and Pakistan boasted their national pride with development of nuclear weapons while China expanded its strike capabilities to the global arena. Russia is threatening to rebuild its massive nuclear arsenal to counter the U.S. plan to design a missile defence system.

In addition to the failure of global disarmament, the end of the Cold War did not bring about great improvement in human well-being nor liberation of oppressed people. Despite its hegemonic power and affluence, close to 20 percent of the U.S. population lives below the poverty line. The movements for self-determination in Tibet, Kurdistan and other areas continue to be brutally repressed. The assertion of differences in values contributes to inter-group conflict within a state. Fundamental religious belief systems and ethno-nationalism have become a driving force behind new violent conflicts.

In some parts of the world, the struggle between opposing ethnic and racial groups is moving toward peaceful settlement. Conflicts in the Middle East, Northern Ireland and South Africa are based on political, economic and psychological divisions. Efforts have been made to deal with these century old conflicts peacefully. The successful negotiations between the white minority government and the majority of black populations in South Africa in the early 1990s produced hopes for racial co-existence. The prospects for peace have been broadened by a series of negotiations for peaceful settlements between Israel and Jordan and other Arab countries.

In the twenty first century, the presence of both new and old issues provides a complex picture for realising peace. Institutionalised efforts to deal with manifest violence and poverty have largely been unsuccessful despite new opportunities derived from the elimination of the old Cold War order. Developing new policy perspectives requires the replacement of power politics paradigms. The global security risk now includes more than military dimensions. The impact of globalisation on individual well-being is severely felt in many poor areas of the world. The homogenising effects of globalisation integrate local economies in the global market controlled by multinational corporations (Lerche III, 1998). The new century embraces a combination of a crisis in development, continued militarisation, environmental limits and grossly unequal distribution of wealth as indicated by various reports of the United Nations and other organisations.

Zones of Instability

Conflict is endemic and systematic in many countries divided by class, ethnicity, religion and language. Severe violence was experienced in multi-ethnic states of former Yugoslavia, Somalia, Rwanda, Sri Lanka, India and other places. Political and social instability does not exist in a society that has intolerance toward other ethnic and racial groups and monopoly of power by one group.

Many violent conflicts reflect the instability or delegitimisation of a nation-state system. We saw the disintegration of the state system in Somalia, Sierra Leone and Liberia. No legitimate government emerged from factional wars in Afghanistan. Though civil wars ended in Guatemala, El Salvador and Nicaragua, continuing instabilities exist. Many governments face challenges from rebel forces as in the Sudan, Colombia and Peru among others. Whereas superpower rivalry in regional conflict was replaced by disorder in the periphery, its legacy still influences efforts to bring peace to Angola, Cambodia and Afghanistan. In fact, many of these inter-ethnic wars in the zones of conflict can be traced back to the support of local militia groups by the two superpowers during the Cold War period.

According to some observers, the post-Cold War world is clearly divided into the zones of prosperity and turmoil (Singer and Wildavsky, 1993). The term 'zone' can be described as networks of states that may be distant geographically but have high levels of interaction and share similar attributes. In the ideologically less divided international order, stability and prosperity exist in the zones of peace, comprised of Western industrialised societies. The instability in the periphery is characterised by the multitude of ethnic conflicts and failing states. A centralised modern state structure in multi-ethnic societies has faltered, and lawless violence is an every day experience. Stateless conditions were visible in Somalia, Afghanistan and Sierra Leon following civil war.

The prosperity in the West is not affected by violent conflict limited to the peripheral zones of international power and economic structure. Genocide in Rwanda and the former Yugoslavia is parallel to the atrocities committed against civilian populations during the World War II. In addition, poverty, repression and human rights violations deprive many people of decent human life. Political elites in many authoritarian states such as Egypt, Syria and Burma lack political accountabilities. State institutions in Turkey, Iraq and Iran are used as tools to repress minority ethnic groups as well as the majority population. The de-legitimisation of state power in many poor countries comes from a lack of state capacity to deal with deteriorating life conditions. Given that the Western democracies have predominant economic and military power, the events in the zones of turmoil would not spill over to the zones of peace (Singer and Wildavsky, 1993, p. 5).

2   Concepts of Peace and Violence

Peace implies many different things to different people. Some may identify peace as a lack of conflict of any serious kind. More often, the term peace making is associated with conflict resolution without the use of violence. Peace can also mean coexistence of different cultures and societies to be obtained by improved communication with others, common understanding and the ability to tolerate one another. Individual rights are guaranteed by the absence of racism and sexism. Nonviolent living creates a state of trust, harmony and cooperation. These descriptions reveal understandings of various dimensions and issues involved in peace but are not integrative conceptually. Diverse meanings of peace are related to the process to create a nonviolent world. The concept of peace is more clearly understood in comparison with the concept of violence.

Direct and Structural Violence

The most obvious form of violence is an act to do physical harm to other people. As various conditions exist to cause human suffering, the structural and institutional conditions for violence began to draw attention from peace researchers. As an opposite concept of peace, therefore, there are two types of violence, direct and structural. Both forms of violence are present in various social relations.

Direct Violence

Direct violence, the popularly understood meaning of violence, is referred to physical injuries and the infliction of pain that is caused by a specific person. Thus killing and beating, whether they happen in war or inter-personal situations, represent direct violence. Direct violence may also take the form of verbal and psychological abuse (Bulhan, 1985). In direct

19

violence, clear subject-action-object relationships are established, as we observe someone who hurts other people by a violent act. Direct violence generally works fast and dramatically. It is personal, visible, manifest and non-structural. It is carried over time by traumas left behind by its effects of harming the body, mind and spirit (Galtung, 1996, p. 31).

The use of physical force happens either randomly or intentionally in diverse types of social setting. Whereas violence in inter-personal relations may be employed as an instrument for robbery, revenge or honour, states use organised violence to achieve foreign policy goals (Nicolson, 1992, p. 17). Mass violence such as war and revolution brings about social change and a power imbalance. At a group level, the infliction of physical injury or death on other people is a deliberate policy that serves particular interests. Such physical violence as imprisonment and torture is often used for political purposes. The capacity for violence is institutionalised in prison systems, concentration camps, military forces and militia.

Recent history is filled with various forms of genocide in which one group carefully applies violent tactics to eliminate another. Nazi Germany killed millions of European Jews and other ethnic minority groups. More than one million Indonesians were accused of being communists and were executed or tortured by the Suharto regime in the mid-1960s. Pol Pot decimated at least a million Cambodians in the late 1970s to consolidate his rule by imposing fear. The majority of indigenous populations in America have been wiped out for the last several centuries by systematic policies to occupy their land. Genocide, one of the major types of direct violence, features, as illustrated above, that 'the violence is inflicted on one group by the other with very little reciprocal violence by the weaker side' (Nicholson, 1992, p. 21).

Structural Violence

Poverty, hunger, repression and social alienation constitute another way to characterise situations causing human misery. Quality of life is reduced by denial of educational opportunities, free speech and freedom of association. These conditions are associated with uneven life chances, inequitable distribution of resources and unequal decision-making power. Given its indirect and insidious nature, structural violence most often works slowly in eroding human values and shortening life spans. It is typically built into the very structure of society and cultural institutions

(Galtung, 1969). Inegalitarian and discriminatory practices can be imposed on individuals or groups in systematic and organised ways by political institutions (Wenden, 1995, p. 3). Structural violence is apparent in social systems maintained by exploitative means (e.g., slavery) throughout human history.

Oppression is embedded in a 'situation in which one person exploits another person or hinders his or her pursuit of self-affirmation as a responsible person. Such a situation in itself constitutes violence, even when sweetened by false generosity, because it interferes with the individual's ontological and historical vocation to be more fully human' (Freire, 1998, p. 37). Thus oppression, as a form of structural violence, can be maintained by manipulation of relations.

Discrimination results in denying people important rights such as economic opportunities, social and political equality and a sense of autonomy and freedom. The gross violation of human rights and dignity prevents the optimum development of each human being. The lack of an opportunity for self-fulfilment can be based on race, religion, gender, sexual preference, economic status or age. If a young female's need for education is not provided adequately because of gender differences, it constitutes inequitable life conditions. When people starve to death because of a lack of food (which is abundant to others), an exploitative economic system contributing to the monopoly of wealth by a few becomes a source of structural violence.

Certain types of economic structure perpetuate a situation where most basic standards necessary for staying alive are not met. According to some statistics, the loss of life attributed to malnutrition and starvation exceeds the number of people who have been killed by war (Fischer, 1993, p. 7). In many societies, some people are dying from a lack of protein or health care while a few enjoy a luxurious way of life. Obviously, death by starvation is no better than being killed by a gun. Social stability based on law and order without providing the means for survival is regarded as only a privilege for a select few.

If human beings are denied decent education, housing, an opportunity to work and freedom to express themselves, they become marginalised. Conditions for social fragmentation are created by a lack of equity and freedom. In some societies, an oppressive structure is maintained simply by its ability to put down revolts and other types of challenges. Organised struggle against political repression is very difficult under tight social control and fear of prosecution. At an international level, a lack of war for extended periods does not mean the existence of harmonious relations in the sense that it can be sustained by hegemonic order imposed by an empire or a powerful state.

The Relationship between Structural and Direct Violence

Various forms of violence are entailed in peacelessness that denies human dignity. Causes of peacelessness, other than war, gradually produce more deaths, psychological damage, cultural oppression and human incapacity than war. As war is but one kind of peaceless condition, the opposite of peace is more than the existence of manifest violence. Overall, the distinction between overt and structural violence is the presence of an identifiable actor who causes physical harm. Nevertheless, in its effect, violence, regardless of types, reduces an individual's or group's potential for self-realisation.

The absence of direct violence does not necessarily mean the satisfaction of conditions for maintaining decent human life. The concept of structural violence helps us understand deep causes of conflict ingrained in political oppression and economic despair. Given that gross social injustice can be maintained by personal violence, structural violence is more easily noticed in a society that is governed by fear and repression. When coercive mechanisms are effective, structural violence is not challenged for a long time. However, prolonging exploitative conditions eventually produces violent resistance like liberation movements during the Western colonial domination in Africa and Asia.

Dominant relationships are often established as a result of military conquest. Destructive means are employed to force other people to accept unjust conditions or economic inequality. At the same time, coercion can be sustained by a psychological process. Threats of injury may bring complacency and repress a demand for change. The asymmetric power relationship can become latent, impersonal, subtle and unintentional once the will of one side is imposed on the other by the organised use of force.

Cultural Violence

Cultural violence is seen as the source of other types of violence through its production of hatred, fear and suspicion. Religion, ideology, art, empirical science, as they touch upon 'the symbolic sphere of our existence', can be pointed out as possible sources of cultural violence (Galtung, 1990, p. 291). More specifically, crosses, crescents, military parades, flags, inflammatory speeches and posters have instigated certain groups of people to kill and harm those who belong to other groups. In many societies, these symbols or events have also been used to create barriers to discriminate against people who do not share them.

Certain cultural elements are linked to direct and structural violence through their value justification and the legitimisation of their instruments. In religion, there is a sharp distinction between chosen people and outsiders beyond its accepted boundaries. Nationalism justified through state ideology or ethnicity has been promoted for war. Limitations of someone's rights may derive from cultural principles of marginalisation imposed by oppressors (MacGregor and Rubio, 1994, p. 53). Some rules of structural violence such as authoritarianism or discrimination based on gender and race are typically condoned by cultural norms. In the hierarchical social values of a modern industrial society, some people are more valued because of their class or professional qualifications.

These elements do not necessarily represent the entire culture but are particular aspects of the culture. Distortion of knowledge and images about other people is maintained by a socialisation process. As both manifest and latent violence have a cultural layer, cultural practice is not strictly separated from the two main types of violence. Minimisation of cultural violence goes along with reduction in structural and direct violence.

Negative and Positive Peace

Contrary to the traditional definition of peace as absence of war, the concept of peace is now broadly understood to include many situations that guarantee positive human conditions. The realisation of peace prevents the loss of life and human capacity. Thus, peace ultimately has to be obtained by changing social structures that are responsible for death, poverty and malnutrition.

Negative Peace

Negative peace focuses on the absence of direct violence such as war. It can be brought about by various approaches. The prevention and elimination of manifest use of violence require resolving differences through negotiation or mediation rather than resorting to physical force. Nonviolent means foster the avoidance of physical violence. Total disarmament reduces the potential for future armed struggle. Social and economic interdependence discourages the use of force in conflict situations.

The notion of a stable social order is a form of negative peace (Wenden, 1995, p. 5). In real politik, international stability and order are often brought about by dominant military force. The idea of imposing peace has also been reflected in many international arrangements. The mechanisms of collective security included in the League of Nations and the United Nations reflect the notion of guaranteeing peace by dominant power. In a negative peace approach, preventing war also requires a large array of international agreements and institutions that can support stable relations among nations.

Given that imposed order contributes to sustaining the status quo, it does not seriously question the causes of recurring violence in existing social relations. Negative peace policies may focus on a present, short or near future term. Due to the fact that stability and order can be maintained by an oppressive system, negative peace is compatible with structural violence. In this situation, the absence of physical violence can derive from deterrence strategies to punish enemies. Lasting conditions of peace are not synonymous with the preservation of intervals between outbreaks of warfare. War cannot be eradicated as long as militarism remains a prevalent value. The system that prepares society for war has to be changed in such a way to construct a more humane world order.

Positive Peace

As the absence of direct violence does not explain how to deal with unacceptable social order, changing human conditions has become an important goal of peace. Peace is not only concerned about the overt control or reduction of violence but also about vertical social developments that are responsible for hierarchical relationships between people. The concept of positive peace, based on a broad understanding of social conditions, means the removal of structural violence beyond the absence of direct violence.

Positive peace would not be obtained without the development of just and equitable conditions associated with the elimination of inegalitarian social structures (Galtung, 1969). Equality is an essential element of peace because its absence perpetuates tensions of all types. The elimination of various forms of discrimination (based on class, ethnic, tribal, age, religion, racism and sexism) is a precondition for human realisation. Equality, as social and legal rights, is both a means and a goal of positive peace for individuals and groups.

All groups of people also ought to have equitable access to the economic benefits of society as well as enjoying social, cultural and political development. For marginalised groups of people, equality means overcoming obstacles related to institutional, cultural, attitudinal and behavioural discrimination. The elimination of repression and poverty is an essential element of peace (Boutros-Ghali, 1992, pp. 7-8). Equal opportunities allow people to develop their talents and skills so that they can participate in various aspects of development. Economic obstacles for the poor both at national and international levels must be overcome to obtain viable and just peace.

The goals of positive peace touch upon many issues that influence quality of life, including personal growth, freedom, social equality, economic equity, solidarity, autonomy and participation (Galtung, 1973). This comprehensive notion of peace is widely accepted internationally; peace entails, beyond violence and hostilities at the national and international levels, 'the enjoyment of economic and social justice, equality and the entire range of human rights and fundamental freedoms within society' (United Nations, 1996, p. 313). Conditions for harmonious relations derive from minimisation of all forms of exploitation. As the earth is recognised as the object of exploitation, positive peace is now extended to embrace the notion of respect for nature.

Priorities in Positive and Negative Peace

Realist critiques of positive peace argue that, in considering human nature and the power structure of the world, it is unrealistic and, thus, meaningless to equate peace with social justice. The emphasis on social justice can lead us to murky issues concerning an ideal society. It is more expedient to minimise the issues of equity by accepting the ways in which peace has been normally used in political science and other academic disciplinary areas. In this view, a narrow focus on the control of symptoms of violence has a more tangible effect than struggle for improving the quality of living. Thus, the inclusive nature of positive peace research does not have any legitimacy for the field of inquiry (Nieburg, 1989).

During the Cold War, some peace researchers raised concerns that a broadened notion of peace would divert attention away from problems of disarmament toward 'a grand, vague study of world development' (Boulding, 1978). Those who are mainly interested in the reduction and elimination of warfare consider justice a less essential requirement for peace. The first priority for peace research is to pursue knowledge that will enhance ability to manage and prevent violent conflict. Thus, popular topics in this research tradition have been control of violent social behaviour and the arms race. Priority was given to investigating various methods relevant to reduction of the risks of war, disarmament, prevention of accidental war, non-proliferation of nuclear weapons and negotiated settlement of international conflicts.

In decision analysis, the causes of wars are mainly attributed to misperceptions, enemy images and distorted values of political elites. The psychological process of war decision making can easily fall within the traditional power frame. The focus on elite decision making tends to brush aside the fact that the reality of international conflict is often derived from neglecting human needs elements and the spill-over of domestic problems (Burton, 1984). Scholars in the positive peace research tradition assert that the structural roots of violent conflict have to be more seriously studied than particular cases of avoiding and limiting war or such narrow issues as reduction in particular weapons systems (Galtung, 1969). Knowledge for conditions to achieve peace has to explain strategies to overcome institutional forms of violence. The occurrence of war is ascribed to institutions in support of violence such as military industrial complexes rather than individual or group socio-psychological war decision-making behaviour.

Positive peace studies have lengthened the list of conditions threatening human survival to include environmental issues as well as poverty and economic disparity. Given that these problems are not likely to be solved in the world's current economic and political structure, the analysis of shortcomings of the present system naturally leads to a search for policy and institutional changes that can serve human welfare. Social transformation requires alternative political space in which politics of gender and identity are important. Setting up priorities in strategies for peace building is guided by an implicit set of normative assumptions about social order.

The debate on positive and negative peace influenced the way knowledge and skills for practicing peace have been developed. In the areas of nonviolence, some people are mainly concerned with logistics and tactical issues involved in unarmed struggle against enemies, and its effectiveness is measured in terms of cost-benefit perspectives without much regard to changes in structural conditions for oppression (Sharp, 1973). In this view, nonviolent action is merely seen as an effective strategic instrument to achieve specific political objectives and score victories with non-lethal means. Others who follow the traditions of Gandhi emphasise nonviolence as a principle to remove a dominant social, economic system (Ostergaard, 1986). Nonviolent social structure can be acquired by establishing egalitarian social relations.

In the analysis of social conflict, the proponents of basic needs approaches suggest that institutional changes are inevitable in dealing with root causes of problems (Burton, 1990a). The analysis of identity and security needs is essential to conflict resolution, and the empowerment of the marginalised can help reduce oppression. On the other hand, others focus on techniques and processes without considering their role in inhibiting or promoting certain social conditions. They believe that intervenors should take neutral positions and that moral values and power positions of parties in conflicts should not get involved in process oriented problem solving. When conflict resolution and nonviolence are used only as tools for minimising manifest violence, the development of particular skills that have been tested in limited social settings is more crucial than ideas and values that can lay foundations for building a peaceful society. While controlling violent conflict is no doubt an important task, skill oriented conflict resolution practice can contribute simply to maintaining a system that is the very source of problem.

Integration of Positive and Negative Peace

During the Cold War period, anti-war movements were devoted to preventing the worst scenario of having a nuclear war. Many peace groups working in the negative peace traditions, at the same time, shared the ideal of pacifist communities that a peaceful order requires social justice. If peace research is designed for policy changes and action, its ultimate goal is to create social conditions for the betterment of the life of all humanity.

In considering the very nature of violence, building positive peace can and has to be complementary to practicing negative peace. Preventing the use of physical, manifest violence is more successful under certain social structural conditions. There is no need for the use of violence if there is justice in society. Institutions of war are based on domination, and they play an important role in maintaining the culture of violence. In that sense, peace is synonymous with the elimination of the institution of war (Lentz, 1961, p. 5).

Some pursue social justice at the expense of open acceptance and use of personal violence. The example would be the use of military tactics by organised armed groups that fight against political repression and foreign occupations. Some wars like World War II were justified in the name of protecting democracy. Class warfare was used by Marxist revolutionaries as a means to bring about economic justice. Terrorist groups depend on direct physical attacks to promote certain causes and express their grievances. The use of violence, regardless of its goals, is not considered constructive.

In pacifist views, no matter the circumstance, the means for making peace should be nonviolent. In the use of violence, there is no differentiation between good and evil. As observed in revolutionary and early Soviet Russia in the 1920s, social change acquired by violent means cannot embrace peaceful human relations. In that sense, social justice and the rejection of manifest violence cannot be easily separated from each other. Threats of physical violence provoke reciprocal actions. Efforts to change the behaviour of an enemy without resorting to violence contain fundamental moral and political values.

Peace does not necessarily mean repression of conflict especially in unjust social situations. Some degree of conflict is inevitable in any social system. Transforming protracted social conflict requires patience and time. To prevent conflict from turning it into mass destruction is a goal of a civilised society (Kelman, 1981, p. 108). In reality, however, one's choice of means in the fight against structural violence in a highly repressive society is limited, and the application of non-use of violent means would be more difficult in a ruthless political system.

Holistic Conceptions of Peace

By understanding their connections to the outside world, individuals recognise a more peaceful way of being. Concern with personal peace is not separated from universal change. In holism, the individual is directly linked to the wider environment rather than through stages of forming hierarchical relationships (Zohar, 1991). Violence against nature, inherent in the prevailing paradigm, is the source of alienation (Nagler, 1999, p. 235). Recently, some researchers have begun to understand the meaning of peace from more holistic perspectives by focusing on inner peace and its reflections in human relations as well as by shedding light on the connections between humans and bioenvironmental systems (Smoker, 1994; Macy, 1991). Whereas this new conception can resonate with world spiritual and religious traditions, the founders of general systems theory such as biologist Ludwig von Bertalanffy also demonstrate how all self-organising systems are created and sustained by the dynamics at play in the larger systems of our universe (Macy, 1991, p. 12).

In general systems analysis, the desire to destroy and possess forms a deviation-amplifying feedback loop. We can see this example in ecological destruction. To satisfy our demand for the raw materials that we want, we threaten the very foundation of our life support systems. Modern sciences have increased human capacity to subdue and control other human beings and the environment as a means to promote material and physical security of a few. Technological capacity to destroy is sustained and further developed by human greed and endless desire to conquer. The vicious circle of destruction supported by modern sciences continues exponentially (Macy, 1991, p. 7).

Despite technological advances, the emotional and spiritual maturity of human beings has not been advanced from the ancient period when people lived in caves in fear of natural phenomena (Forcey, 1989). The process of seeking security through control has endangered many life forms on the planet to the point of the destruction of ecological balance. The total destruction of the ecological system that has recently been recognised as a new form of violence is based on the persistent notion that humans are independent of the world they are destroying. Through various forms of ecocide, violence inflicted on the earth produces imbalanced relations not only between humans and nature but also between people. If humans hold themselves aloof from other species and remain immune to their impact on the natural world, they are prevented from shifting into more encompassing ideas of what it means to be human. Human survival itself would be hampered by this arbitrary way of defining and delimiting self (Naess, 1989).

Holistic views of peace oppose efforts to control and manage life rather than to live it by reducing everything to its simple form. Search for inner or communal peace means more than the absence of organised violence. If conflict is seen as a source of change, peace cannot be modelled in static terms. It is a source of energy that impels action. Peace recognised as social harmony, stability or order in the universe can be promoted by spiritual awakening. A holistic conception of peace links the ideal of the human spirit to the harmony between different components of the earth system and even universe.

3   Conflict Analysis

While they are often attributed to miscommunication and misperception of the other party's goals and intentions, many serious communal conflicts are rooted in value differences and the repression of the need for autonomy and identity. The pursuit of incompatible goals can intensify struggle between opposing forces especially in the absence of collaborative problem solving mechanisms. Antagonistic feelings and frustration deepen adversarial enemy images, making negotiated solutions to the problems difficult. In conflict situations, resources are mobilised to force the other party to change their behaviour according to one's own wishes. Mismanaged conflict erupts in violence, consequently resulting in the destruction of a community. While the control or reduction of the overall use of violence can be achieved by conflict management strategies, lasting solutions to conflict would not be provided without the elimination of social conditions that generate adversarial relations.

Structural Conditions

Conflict relations reveal the structure of a family, a community and an international system. Power differentials in conflict situations are based on the ability to mobilise both material and symbolic resources that are critical to determining the outcome of the conflict. The actors do not have the same resources as revealed in various economic and social relationships. The influence of one actor over another can be exerted through gaps in military power, economic wealth, or education. In a modern political economy, social status and wealth translate into decision making power, creating unbalanced relationships.

Many lasting internal and international conflicts have their roots in structural injustice. Serious conflict is embedded in an inequitable social and economic system, reflecting prolonged exploitation supported by coercion. The destruction of cultural identities, political autonomy and economic sustainability for the weak has been associated with the imposition of dominant power relations. This was reflected in the rule of European empires in many colonies in Africa and Asia with their superior military power in the past centuries.

Structural conditions for the emergence of serious social conflict are related to unequal access to political power and cultural marginalisation of certain groups. The uneven ability to control events produces asymmetric power relations. Hierarchical social relations are institutionalised in ways that alienate subordinate parties through denial of effective participation. Inequitable distribution of wealth and power is often justified by the privileged position of a dominant group's cultural norms.

Due to their different power status, parties have opposing interests in maintaining the system. The dominant group wants to maintain stability whereas the subordinate group challenges the status quo (Dahrendorf, 1959). Those in a disadvantaged position demand a new set of relationships when they begin to perceive the situation as unjust and exploitative. Dominant groups fear unpredictable political change that may be unleashed by challenges to the existing system. Changes are resisted by the party who benefits from unequal relations, and the structure is often maintained at the expense of the other group.

The existence of dominant relations would not necessarily translate into a struggle for change without the organisation of subordinate groups and their social mobilisation (Tilly, 1978). Demand for new policy or structural change is intensified by a weaker party's articulation of issues and expression of their frustration. Until some form of serious challenges is made either violently or nonviolently, those benefiting from the status quo have little incentive for taking the issues raised by the underprivileged seriously. While reform may be proposed to meet some of the concerns, conflict can also be suppressed by the use of physical violence, consequently reinforcing one party's will over another. Repression of resistance from challenging groups requires a sustained level of destructive violence.

Conflict and Social Order

In many instances, conflict in a contemporary political system reveals policy failures and public insecurities. It is evident in the fact that policy inadequacies are blamed for minority groups that do not accept existing values and norms. It is also clearly manifested in legitimising the maintenance of coercive instruments of a contemporary state by manipulating public fear of disorder (Burton, 1997). Given that a law making and enforcement process is dominated by the interests of those who have resources to influence the system, the government is usually not a neutral arbitrator. Institutions of economic decision making often reflect the overall distribution of political power. Threats of punishment and adversarial institutions become major characteristics of an elite-controlled society, suppressing the collective identities of marginalised peoples who attempt to pursue self-esteem and autonomy.

Rules and commands are enforced through not only negative but also positive sanctions. As many people are willing to trade autonomy for economic security, the perpetuation of material values provides the basis of self-esteem in capitalist societies (Burton, 1990b). The compliance of subjects is required in return for maintaining the material and physical security from the perceived threat of enemies. Because of a lack of an alternative order, people in a given society tend to be compelled to accept a particular order under ordinary circumstances. Domination is constituted in the large-scale disciplining needs of modern society (Foucault, 1977).

Hegemonic interests are articulated through institutionalisation of power relations supported by the imposition of general norms of behaviour (Gramsci, 1971). Hegemony is maintained by legitimising a regularised method of conflict. Continued submission is enhanced by the willingness of a ruling class to make concessions and implement policy adjustment to the extent that the use of force is obviated. Consent to dominant norms and rules results from socialisation and voluntary internalisation. Populations are manipulated in formulating and maintaining values which serve the interests of elites (Sites, 1990, p. 121).

Restlessness in modern society arises out of various forms of alienation derived from social control in everyday life. Despite continued dependence on material rewards and socialisation, the perpetuation of power breeds resistance from marginalised groups. Not only reducing inequity but also overcoming alienation resulting from exclusion would resolve conflict originating in class antagonisms.

The absence of legitimised structures and policies, along with increasing inequalities of income and opportunity, serves as the primary source of conflict. Once basic assumptions about the traditional concepts of law and order as the common good are questioned, the right of the government to rule and to expect obedience is at the root of the conflict. The articulation of collective need for dignity and purpose cannot be suppressed any longer by elite control and threats (Burton, 1990b).

Traditional Management Strategies

In the traditional management of conflict, a judicial system and public administration are mostly concerned with the preservation of the status quo and the maintenance of existing institutions. Because those in power tend to interpret challenges to their authority in terms of enforcement of order, conflict management is largely seen in terms of social control designed to minimise the challenges to the core values of the system.

Problems of adjustment and tension reduction are a main concern to decision makers in public or private bureaucracies whose main interest lies in the maintenance of existing structures (Coser, 1956, p. 20). As disruptive behaviour disturbs orderly social function, it needs to be controlled. Public education, in addition to deterrent strategies, is employed to prevent escalation of the conflict. Efforts are made to frame conflict behaviour within the recognised sets of rules of social order. The existence of underlying conflicts can even be effectively denied by legitimising power inequality (Kriesberg, 1998, p. 52).

Conflict management in a traditional setting helps reinforce coercive policy by conforming to dominant social norms. Though tension reduction measures may make the conflict more bearable in the short term, forced compromise sometimes generates serious conflict that will need to be resolved in the future. The management process is not effective in surfacing and addressing the core concerns with survival and dignity that are root causes of identity-based conflict. As differences over values cannot be solved within an existing order, conflict can be protracted. By favouring the status quo, tension reduction mechanisms only put off changes essential in directly dealing with basic issues at stake. Conflict can be terminated by reasserting dominant power relations.

In politically oppressive societies, demands for autonomy are answered by coercive responses rather than negotiation of new relationships. The legitimacy of the existing order is eventually challenged by the refusal to accommodate alienated communities whose participation is denied because of social categories. In the long run, deterrent strategies relying on threats and punishment have limited value in maintaining social control with resistance triggered by the repression of aspirations for cultural identity, security and recognition.

Dispute Settlement and Conflict Resolution

A dispute does not involve serious institutional problems, and it can be handled through bargaining or arbitration (Burton, 1996, p. 8). People can disagree on room temperature, salaries, education of children and other matters in ordinary social space. This type of problems occurring in a normal relationship can be settled by finding compromise solutions. Mediation techniques help reduce differences in opinions and contending interests. Behavioural problems in many areas of human relations have also been managed by family counselling and psychological therapy.

Competition between different groups can be handled by the existing rules of decision making as long as it does not directly challenge the existing norms of the authority relationship. Individuals may argue about implementation of specific policies without questioning the fundamental nature of the system, and an agreement can be reached over particular issues. Solving concrete problems related to the demand for more material resources in clearly defined relationships is relatively easy. The outcome of interest-based disputes is bound by the resources at stake.

By sorting out differences within an existing system, dispute settlement contributes to the stability of society with the confirmation of legitimate roles of accepted norms, values and institutions in every day life. In order to reduce the cost of and burden on the traditional legal practice, alternative dispute resolution mechanisms were introduced to solve material interests out of court or before a court settlement. The processes of dispute resolution, not connected to conflict resolution theories, have been developed out of the idiosyncratic expertise of institutionally approved practitioners (Scimecca, 1991, p. 34).

It is inappropriate to apply settlement approaches based on legal mechanisms and conventional negotiation to value and identity conflict. It is entirely 'possible to resolve an incompatibility without touching the actors and their relations'. Compromise can be accomplished without regard to examining the conflict formation. 'The actors are still there, with their structure basically untouched. But conflict is settled because both parties can now relax their conception of what is acceptable to them so that their modified goals become compatible' (Galtung, 1996, p. 114).

Conventional conflict settlement methods have clearly proved insufficient in many intractable conflicts where relative power differentials do not prevent the weaker party from resisting the unacceptable conditions of status quo. Deep rooted conflict is embedded in interpretative dynamics of past history, psychological relationships, cultural norms, social values and belief systems of identity groups. The basis of resolving ethnic and other identity based communal conflict lies in recognising the fact that freedom, autonomy and recognition are not in short supply and the fact that each group's needs can be satisfied in such a manner not to threaten the other party's security (Burton, 1996, p. 9). Dominant parties need to be convinced that maintaining oppressive policies and institutions does not actually serve their long-term interests. The high cost of the fight, in practice, makes continuing conflict a loss to them.

In contrast to settlement that focuses on reducing suspicion and distrust between adversaries, conflict resolution goes through a far more complex process. In adversarial bargaining, conflict is often considered by antagonists as a zero-sum situation in which the gain of the one is the loss of the other. Collaborative problem solving approaches can be adopted to find a solution that benefits both parties. Conventional settlement approaches are not able to change structural dynamics that lead to competitive situations.

The process of dealing with basic concerns cannot be separated from the social context associated with substantive problems (Kriesberg, 1998). The satisfaction of such psychological needs as a sense of belongings cannot be met in a certain political system (Ronen, 1998, p. 18). Changing antagonistic feelings and hostile emotions has to be accompanied by eliminating coercive, power based relationships. The conflict can become more intractable by attempting to reach an early compromise without fully defining the nature of problems.

The roots of complex behavioural relationships are revealed by analysing the roots of problems. Discovering the substantive matters beneath underlying issues can be an initial step toward collaborative problem solving. Resolution prevents the recurrence of future conflict by satisfying conditions to be acceptable to all parties. Most importantly, conflict seen as inherent in the social system can be eliminated only through structural changes (Coser, 1956, p. 19).

Conflict Transformation and Peace Building

New situations can be created in the dynamics of conflict with or without intervention of external influence. Issues, perceptions, relationships, and communication patterns continue to change along the path of conflict dynamics. Transformation can be regarded as 'the movement from latent conflict to confrontation to negotiation' in achieving the peaceful relationships of a secure community (Lederach, 1994). Conflict structure can be transformed by focusing on long-term relationships rather than immediate concerns.

Subjective and objective contexts for a constructive transformation of conflicts can be changed by a shift in power relations and attitudes. Conflict situations need to be transformed in such a way to identify and support structures that tend to consolidate peace (Boutros-Ghali, 1992, p. 61). Positive opportunities can be enhanced through the awareness of mutual dependence on one another. Resolving the issues requires the replacement of violent tactics with nonviolent action in achieving desired outcomes.

Strategies for transforming conflict dynamics cannot simply rely on the assumption that improved communication and changed perceptions would put parties on an equal basis. Changing psychological dimensions of adversarial relationships supported by the opportunities to understand different views is undoubtedly an inevitable part of the movement toward conflict de-escalation (Mitchell, 1999). At the same time, it is also critical to note that framing differences in opinions and redefining contending interests do not necessarily result in changes in oppressive relations. Efforts to end hostile, competitive and coercive processes would be fruitless if one party's domination continues to be allowed. Newly forged relationships have to be supported by structural transformation of social conditions.

In a transformative framework, identity and power relations continue to be re-negotiated in an on-going process of resolving conflict (Jeong and Väyrynen, 1999). Dynamics of conflict are not likely to be transformed toward resolution by an attempt to protect existing interests. Conflict relations would not be dramatically changed by re-establishing a status quo. In transformative perspectives, roles and relationships have to be redesigned in the process of re-structuring the patterns of transactions and interactions.

Resolving conflict in transformative perspectives has to be geared toward helping the underprivileged break out of the discriminatory social roles assigned to them within the status quo (Jeong, 1999a, pp. 27-31). The existence of injustice in asymmetric conflict structures requires strategies to deal with power imbalanced situations. Social change for promoting justice (by which conditions for decent human life can be established) is an appropriate means for peace building.

Peace building is largely equated with the construction of a new social environment that advances a sense of confidence and improves conditions of life. Leaving an abusive and dependent relationship intact is incompatible with peace building. Conflict transformation can underscore the goal of peace building through empowering a marginalised population exposed to extreme vulnerability in such a way to achieve self-sufficiency and well-being. Thus, the successful outcome of conflict transformation contributes to eliminating structural violence.

In a power imbalanced situation, the promotion of peace requires a social basis for autonomy, participation and solidarity of the marginalised. Promoting functional interdependence would not lead to a non-exploitative relationship in power asymmetry. Institution building designed to serve the interest of elites pays little attention to hidden power differences and coercive mechanisms. Reviving indigenous cultural, social and political forces is essential to expanding democratic social space.

4   Peace Research

Early efforts to study peace systematically were generated by reaction to war and other types of armed conflict. It was soon recognised that these problems originated in deep-rooted social structures. This enrichment of peace research traditions was a response to the challenge of achieving practical solutions to real world problems. While its policy orientation has normative underpinnings for improving human well-being, the method of peace research has been influenced by debate about the diverse epistemological foundations of modern social science.

Social Environment

Peace and conflict studies are not confined to traditional educational settings but are more directly connected to the activities of many ordinary people who want to change the world. The growing diversity of the knowledge base reflects new practices. Peace studies are inclusive of a vast range of approaches and experiments. Many innovative ways of thinking have been developed out of ordinary citizens' endeavours to make the world become a more peaceful place. This movement was motivated by the realisation that the existing policies of the national government would not bring about peace.

Concerned citizens began to challenge government foreign and military policies that directly affected them. The fear of destruction by nuclear weapons was real following the 1961 Cuban missile crisis that brought the U.S. and the Soviet Union close to a nuclear war. It was very clear to many by the end of the 1960s that national interests and security defined by a few experts in established policy-making circles do not promote peace and justice at home and abroad (Alger, 1987).

Various events stimulated a growing array of movements at the grassroots. While there always have been groups engaged in conscious social struggle, perceptions of the U.S. involvement of the war in Vietnam led critics to question U.S. military intervention in other parts of the world. Turmoil on the streets and campuses in the 1960s was also instigated by urban poverty and discrimination against minority groups. The concerns that generated social consciousness have had a lasting impact on the way we perceive, conceptualise and educate for peace.

Also influential was a new approach to handling conflict with the adoption of citizen diplomacy and problem solving workshops. Peaceful management and resolution of conflict have been advocated as an alternative to deterrence methods based on punishment and threats. In the United States, community programmes were established to promote dialogue among antagonistic social group members. Practitioner/scholars applied problem solving approaches to inter-ethnic communal conflict in Cyprus, Sudan and other parts of the world.

The challenges from ordinary citizens to old security paradigms were manifested in the establishment of nuclear zones in towns and cities. In the 1980s, thousands of people visited Central America and other critical areas to prevent U.S. military intervention in support of the authoritarian regimes. The movements of citizens concerned about international conflict laid an early foundation for the negotiated settlement of civil wars in Nicaragua, El Salvador and South Africa as well as nonviolent political transition in Eastern Europe.

Government policies in various parts of the world were challenged since World War II by diverse social groups. Human rights were grossly violated by authoritarian governments in Africa, Latin America and Asia. More than a million people disappeared in Chile and Argentina in the 1970s under the military dictatorships. The world also observed famine in Africa and civil wars in Angola, Afghanistan and other countries. In response to these problems, nongovernmental organisations became engaged in activities involving the release of political prisoners, the improvement of economic and social life in poor countries and the prevention of war by working directly with victims of violence and poverty. With the emergence of ethnic conflict at the end of the Cold War, such Western NGOs as Oxfam and Doctors without Borders were also engaged in humanitarian assistance and post-conflict peace building.

Grassroots challenges to state power highlight the resistance against militarisation and illustrate problems with state centric definitions of security and development (Alger, 1989). People's endeavours to improve their lives created informal political space for the empowerment of the marginalised. In Third World countries, people assert local self-reliance in overcoming economic exploitation and destruction of local culture created by both the manufactured goods and the communications products of the industrialised countries.

In response to grassroots movements for social change, peace research has been broadened to include the causes of economic and social disparities as well as political inequality beyond the traditional analysis of violent conflict. In addition, the significance of education for social justice and peaceful transformation of society was recognised by the efforts to reduce the gap between peace research, education and action. In a new peace research paradigm, nongovernmental organisations and grassroots struggles are no longer seen as separated from peace making and building activities. The recognition that events at the grassroots are deemed worthy of scholarly attention has promoted a dialogue among activists, researchers and educators.

Evolution of Peace Research

Earlier forms of conflict studies and peace education focused on arms race, disarmament and deadly conflict and war. Given that peace was largely seen as the absence of war, the purpose of research was oriented toward the prevention of war. The study of arms control and the management and prevention of violent conflict has remained the most traditional area of peace research. Systematic research on war in the modern social science tradition started with Quincy Wright (1942) who identified war as a problem to be studied separately from other social issues. Lewis F. Richardson (1960) developed mathematical models of arms race and war focused on dynamic interactive processes leading to war. Statistical data on war were systematically gathered and analysed by David Singer's Correlates of War Project (Singer, 1979).

In an early stage of peace research, the main concern was the analysis of conflictual behaviour and effective crisis management. Since the overriding problem was how to prevent nuclear warfare, the institutionalised academic endeavour was a response to the fear of nuclear annihilation during the Cold War period. It attempted to find alternatives to destabilising superpower policies that increase mutual suspicion and hostilities. Therefore, the early study of violent inter-state conflict based on methodological empiricism was tinged with ideological voluntarism affected by the reality of nuclear horror and the Vietnam War.

Conflict analysis and resolution have become a popular area of academic investigation for the last several decades. The processes of conflict interactions were illuminated by game theoretical analysis of Anatol Rapaport (1960) and his associates (1965). In understanding the movements toward de-escalation and resolution, conflict dynamics have been conceptualised by Christopher Mitchell (1981) and Louis Kriesberg (1982). The philosophical foundations for research on conflict resolution were laid out by a widely shared belief that the cause of conflictual behaviour is not inherent human instinct but a response to an actor's perception of surrounding social environments (Groom, 1990, p. 85). Conflicts cannot be resolved by efforts to defeat or annihilate an opponent. Common interests can be forged even in a serious conflict situation by exploring a non-zero-sum solution. Collaborative problem solving based on the satisfaction of basic needs proposed by John W. Burton (1987) and adopted as a major research paradigm in the field is distinguished from bargaining theories developed in business and other fields.

The realisation that the causes of war are related to oppressive systems led to building positive peace research traditions. In particular, Johan Galtung attributed violence and poverty to oppressive social and economic conditions (1975). Development and human rights became a critical field of peace research with the recognition of the fact that life diminishing effects can be inflicted by forces other than deadly weaponry (Senghaas, 1974). Sustainable development was widely accepted as a new strategy to improve living conditions in many poor communities around the world.

Political and economic structures of the international system create conditions for inequitable distribution of wealth among and within nations. Serious attention was drawn to the structural domination of capitalism and exploitation of the impoverished by the rich (Senghaas, 1974). Despite the decolonisation process, economic exploitation continued and indigenous cultural values were undermined. Self-determination has been integrated into the analysis of violence and conflict in many divided societies. In search of peaceful change, the significance of grassroots movements in development and peace making was recognised by Chadwick Alger (1987, 1990).

Feminist peace researchers have brought our attention to various forms of violence to which women are exposed. The notion of structural violence was extended to the examination of discrimination and unequal treatment faced by women (Brock-Utne, 1989). Unequal power relations among humans have been attributed to the system of patriarchy (Boulding, 1976). Culture of violence at various levels of society is sustained in terms of a masculine value system. Some women peace scholars convincingly linked the origin of war to a social system that perpetuates hierarchies among human beings (Reardon, 1985).

Harm done to the earth cannot be excluded from investigating conditions for peace (Conca, 1994). The total destruction of the ecosphere is caused by ecocide. The integration of environmental concerns into peace research helps point out that the unbalanced relationship of humans to bioenvironmental systems is a source of threat to human survival. Human beings have a unique capacity to damage the planet that supports life support systems of all species. In the recent decade, growing attention was also paid to the scarcity of environmental resources as a source of violent conflict (Homer-Dixon, 1994).

Nature of Peace Research

Peace research is an endeavour that searches for knowledge to end violence and domination. Theoretical work is necessary both for the enhancement of empirical understanding and for the reproduction of the discipline itself (Jeong, 1999b). The majority of peace researchers retain primary identities in diverse disciplinary areas. However, the substantive themes of peace research have provided lasting intellectual ties for a field that is still evolving.

A network of peace research institutions throughout the world has developed specific areas of study in the social science traditions. They cut across different specialty areas in understanding human nature, decision making, conflict analysis, disarmament and nonviolent social change. Philosophy and linguistics provide metaphors and discourse on violence and moral debates about war. Historians have studied past peace movements and their roles in opposing war. Theories based on economic reasoning can reveal concrete choices by computing the costs of war and the benefit of disarmament in dollars.

Peace and conflict studies emerged as a substance worth learning. Many of the problems, which we face today, are too complex to be studied by one disciplinary area such as psychology, sociology and political science. Peace research is 'transdisciplinary in the sense of breaking down and breaking through disciplinary barriers' (Eckhardt, 1974). The challenge remains how to find linkages between different approaches to peace. An important issue has been not only the areas to be studied but also the methods to accumulate knowledge.

Methods for Inquiry

As happened with many disciplinary areas of social science, different traditions for inquiry have influenced the directions of peace research. Peace research methods have been sensitive to helping us understand the meanings of events relevant to the causes of violence and conditions for a peaceful world. Establishing a systematic knowledge base has always been considered important for bringing about changes in the real world. It is based on the belief that the more we know, the better policy makers are prepared for peace.

Scientific Approaches

In *Toward a Science of Peace*, Theodore Lentz (1961, p. 6) emphasises the study of human attitudes, especially subjective and emotional factors, are essential in understanding the phenomena of war and peace. Some of the early empirical research was focused on exploring mathematical equations for predicting when an arms race will end in war (Richardson, 1960). Empirical study stresses observable reality in an attempt to unearth the laws of nature. Thus, scientific approaches to peace research aspire to find interconnections between facts by using mathematics, formal modelling and statistical analysis.

Simulations and cognitive analysis were applied to understanding crisis decision making. Statistical studies correlating the outbreak of war with other factors were popular in the behavioural tradition of peace research. In this endeavour, empirical collection of data has great significance, and efforts to collect data involving deadly violence have been supported by various academic and government funded institutes.

Causal analysis of human behaviour requires the examination of the impact of social, cultural, economic and political systems on people's motivations and perceptions. Through establishing a causal relationship, data analysis can be used to project future trends. Statistical analysis would be useful to predict the frequency and intensity of international and domestic violence, identify such environmental parameters as population explosion and investigate the continuing gaps between the rich and the poor. It has long been accepted by many social scientists that scientifically gathered data can be used to produce positive effects on human well-being.

Interpretative Analysis

While empirical analysis has been an important concern for those who develop peace research in the modern scientific tradition, there is also a growing recognition that interpretative understanding of social action is more helpful in analysing intentions of actors and meanings of events. The positions of actors dramatically alter the views and interpretations of the same social phenomena. Regularities in the social world are not independent of time and space and intersubjective meanings are context specific (Neufeld, 1995, p. 79). Objects of social studies cannot be simply reduced to their observable properties, and the causal laws that govern actors' behaviour are not easy to quantify.

In interpretative analysis, the meaning of peace must be investigated in the context of wider social and cultural structures, relations and processes. Diverse images of reality need to be understood intersubjectively. The degrees to which values and norms are applied to the reality vary cross-culturally (Avruch, 1998). In addition, the way meaning is attached to the world is influenced by power (Foucault, 1971). The research on violence has to be able to reveal how oppressive social practices and events arise out of privileged discourse positions within and across cultural norms.

Indeed analysis of grassroots people's struggle for achieving peace has to be based on understanding the meanings of peace from the perspectives of people who are most affected by violence. On the other hand, holistic meanings of everyday existence derive from common human experience and shared identity. Some of these ideas and values were recognised centuries ago; others have played a significant role only in recent years. The nature of peace research cannot be separated from a dialogical process between local meanings and global perspectives.

Epistemological Foundations

The nature of peace research can be defined by its objective of existence --
study of issues related to building peace and preventing war. The
knowledge base of peace research is not bound by any particular
methodology. In particular, the questions concerning the general problems
of social theory and moral philosophy cannot be answered by scientific
research methodology (Krippendorff, 1973). Compared with pure science,
peace research is an applied and normative discipline to the extent that
motivations behind theoretical analysis are associated with a commitment
to change.

Research interest and impulse cannot be easily depoliticised. The
choice of topics is affected by the researchers' desire to improve the
human and physical environment for peace. 'Knowledge of the value(s) of
peace ... is a condition for doing and understanding peace studies, and for
assessing correctly a situation and a process' (Galtung, 1996, p. 14).
Normative concerns play an important role in guiding the agenda and
exploring new directions of research trends. Normative goals of peace
research are different from those of national security or war studies.

Peace researchers look for causes of war and conditions for achieving
peace rather than studying military strategies to win the war. Critical
evaluation of such realities as poverty and death leads to the development
of policy proposals and strategies to prevent them. Active engagement of
researchers with problems is an inevitable part of the peace research
tradition. Indeed, a constitutive role of human consciousness is a defining
characteristic of critical theory (Neufeld, 1995, p. 87). History continues to
reshape a researcher's agenda, but it is basic values that are not changed.

Troubled by war, the centralisation of power and the diminishing
quality of life, some social scientists come to terms with critical theory
oriented toward political change and social justice. Peace research
promotes the analysis of ways in which a harmonious world can be
achieved by peaceful means. Analysis and praxis promoted by peace
researchers suggest practical implications for social justice, though this
position is also found in critical sociology, political economy, cultural
studies and women's studies.

Despite the impact of values on the choice of subject areas, the
structure of theory in peace research is independent of researchers' value
orientation (Nicholson, 1996, p. 177). The conscious pursuit of research

objectives to achieve peace does not necessarily intervene in the process of analysis. Indeed, strategies for effective change cannot be found without developing an explanatory theory of existing conditions that demand change.

Policy Orientation

The abolition of war and violent structures as a policy goal has practical implications for peace researchers. The research outcome should help come up with credible suggestions as to how and which aspects of the world have to be changed. Given that peace research is influenced not only by the tradition of causal analysis but also by a normative orientation, the question of policy issues cannot be left out in theoretical analysis. Strengthening the elements that support peace is an important policy question. The value based inquiries can easily translate into policy goals of establishing equitable social and economic structures and preserving an ecosystem.

The research on peace provides knowledge needed for judgment about the efficacy of various forms of action. While peace research has to be relevant to practice with a focus on existing conditions, it should be able to invoke visionary universal peace in an uncertain future (Dedring, 1999, p. 20). Policy issues cannot be separated from value issues given that scientific analysis does not itself offer clear answers to how to solve the social problems of today. The foundation of peace has to lie in recognising the worth and dignity of all human beings, and it helps identify factors that not only facilitate but also inhibit the conditions for peace. At the same time, policy formulation based on normative prescriptions can be supported by data gathering and systematic research.

If the principle that all human beings have to be free and equal is adopted as a policy goal, researchers may be able to observe empirically the existence of civic liberties by such indicators as freedom of expression and association as well as the degree of income distribution. The extent of economic, social and cultural rights can be measured in terms of the right to education, decent wages and the use of minority languages. In the same manner, progress in disarmament can be evaluated in terms of reductions in the total military budget, demobilisation of the world's military research laboratories and other indicators related to demilitarisation.

Levels of Analysis

Peace research attempts to link the levels of analysis as well as to integrate different problem areas. The level of analysis is important to understanding how peace can be achieved in practice. The degree of violence can be investigated at four different levels, including a planetary ecosystem, international, social and interpersonal (Hutchison, 1992). We can also study the effects of peace activities at transnational, international, national and local levels.

The individual level of analysis can focus on human nature. Given their varying power status in a given system, individuals have different capacities to influence the same events. The personalities and belief systems of top political leaders have been the subject of investigation in research on war decision making. The behaviour of individual units is the most important factor if we believe that social transformation proceeds from changes in individual motivation and value systems. At a personal level, peace can mean the inner tranquillity of the human spirit. Perception of threats is interpreted in terms of subjective fears as well as the absence of objective criteria for violence.

The pursuit of political, economic and social rights can be examined at a community level as well as individual. Identity and other types of social needs are more meaningfully applied to understanding the aspirations for self-determination at a group level. In most instances, 'contemporary nation states are culturally diverse, made up of many religious, ethnic and value-oriented subcultures'. Thus, when we think of peace cultures, it is perhaps most useful to consider both culturally specific social groups and potentially cross-cutting themes of a society as a whole (Boulding, 1992, p. 108). Discrimination based on ethnicity, nationalism, race, language and religion are relevant to the analysis of a communal level conflict. Groups within states pursue their rights to political autonomy, and interaction between groups is a critical factor to be studied.

At an international level, military alliance, trade surplus, political systems and industrial capabilities often determine the power status of different states. In a dominant world order, decision making power in international affairs is unequally distributed. The degree of power distribution among states affects the nature of inter-state political and economic relations. Some believe that international systems have their own inherent dynamics. Once international politics is viewed as a struggle between states to protect and defend national interests, human rights and other group and individual issues are not seriously considered.

Peace research is concerned with international cooperation to promote the well-being of individuals and groups. At the same time, individual welfare is significantly affected by environmental pollution and other problems that have to be considered at a global level. Global governance involves the active participation of subnational and transnational actors in policy coordination. Consensus building and knowledge sharing are important in policy making, as cooperation is required for policy formulation and implementation. Civil society begins to play a more important role in a global political space.

Priorities in security vary at different levels. An international level focuses on the survival of states, whereas the right to a decent life is more important at an individual level. Political or economic coercion at a national level have a negative impact on personal and group's needs for security. The stress on territorial sovereignty in an international system undermines the aspiration of various ethnic and minority groups for political independence and cultural autonomy. While a market economy and free trade help expand the international economic system, they undermine the capacities of the poor who depend on subsistence farming to survive. Unregulated industrialisation at a national level endangers global ecological security.

The concept of common security is based on the assumption that security needs for people are shared regardless of territorial boundaries. Peace and security can not be truly understood solely on an international or national level. As illustrated above, different levels are not strictly separated. Personal growth and fulfilment are promoted or inhibited by a certain social process. Particular events at a local level can be understood in connection to other similar events produced by the same national policies. At the same time, local acts can have an impact on national and global level policy making.

PART II

ISSUES

Peace issues have become more complex, and we need to understand the diverse problems that we face in the world. These problems range from inter-state and intra-state war and various types of identity based conflict to violence against women. In addition, a new level of environmental degradation and economic disparity offers new challenges. These are the causes of direct and structural violence. Human well-being in the future depends on how we solve these problems. While examining the causes of these problems in Part II, we also review theoretical understandings of violent conflict, feminist concepts of peace, economic equity and ecological security.

5   Understanding War

Human history is full of stories of war and violent conflict. War has been waged for all purposes, including preservation of territories from attack, expansion of empires, punishment of enemies and defence of allies. Since the 19th century, the size and expense of war machines and uncertainty about the consequences of war for society, as a whole, have made violence an increasingly unsustainable means for conducting international affairs. Despite its costs and the availability of non-coercive methods of diplomacy, war has been institutionalised to handle conflict. The use of violence remains among states as an accepted instrument for the extension or protection of their power. Organised military violence is persistently used in pursuit of the social goals of domination.

Resources, skills and technology have been developed to prepare for war. Maintenance of strong military power is presupposed to be the normal conduct of sovereign state business. The decision making power is concentrated in a small group of leaders and advisors whose judgement is distorted by misperceptions, enemy images and inadequate information processing. This chapter examines the nature of war and its human and material costs. It will also look at various types and causes of war as well as normative positions on war.

Nature of War

War can be defined as an extreme form of contention conducted by a violent struggle on a mass scale often measured by at least 1,000 deaths (Small and Singer, 1982). In war, even though violence is seldom the most effective way of managing differences, it is allowed 'to resolve a conflict of wills' (Glossop, 1993, p. 2). Purposeful acts of force are designed to compel the other party to yield to one's own desires. The actual use of force may be preceded by application of a variety of other coercive strategies such as economic sanctions and psychological pressure. Compared with withholding benefits or imposing penalties, the use of military force is the most direct form of effort to impose one country's will on the other.

In contrast with random violence, war is highly organised. The use of violence against specific targets is well planned with particular objectives. It is 'a highly social activity' demanding 'from the groups which engage in it a unique intensity of societal organisation and control. It involves the reciprocal use of organised force between two or more social groups, directed according to an overall plan or series of plans for the achievement of a political object' (Howard, 1979, p. 1).

Decisions and orders explicitly made to kill other people during wartime are accepted as legitimate by members of the armed forces and supported by society. Physical violence is carried out by the military with great deliberation and precision, and it is not concerned about emotional sensitivity and moral judgement. Horrifying consequences resulting from acts of force are justified by victory in the armed struggle. Uncontrolled hostility toward enemies is manifested in atrocities.

In war, 'we treat our enemies, neither as people to love, nor as human beings with rights to respect, but as things' (Woito, 1982, p. xv). Suffering, death and destruction are inflicted in order to attain political objectives. Members of armed forces are engaged in the 'legitimate' killing of members of opposing armed forces in battle. Killing in a war is justified and distinguished from murder in an ordinary setting. Enemy nationals in the occupied areas are put under severe constraints by military rule.

In the classic view, war is a business settled by bloodshed, and the goal of winning legitimises the means. Armed struggle, as an organised duel, is conceived as an extension of power politics. In the sense that a violent form of struggle is simply the continuation of political intercourse, war cannot be divorced from political life (von Clausewitz, 1977, p. 605). In the absence of interdependent decision-making, violent interactions replace governance (Vasquez, 1993, p. 35).

The outcome of war, which serves as the final arbiter of disputes, is determined not by who is right but whose will prevails. Decisions made through armed struggle theoretically have no limits (von Clausewitz, 1977). Coercive force is regarded as the ultimate and most effective mechanism for maintaining social control, pursuing vital interests and obtaining other desirable conditions. New power relations representing domination of one party over the other are rearranged with a decisive military victory.

Many consider that military power is indispensable for the survival of a state given the nature of international relations. Recourse to a violent showdown is designed to gain diplomatic advantage. As the possibility of use of violence is inherent in many international situations, a weak state often has to compromise their interests. In the existing structure of international power relations, military threat and the possibility of organised war continue to persist.

War as Organised Violence

Since effective war efforts are not conceivable without social organisations, individuals initiate or prepare organised military campaigns as members of a state or a comparable social organism. Mobilisation of resources for war is justified in terms of promotion of national interests. People willingly or unwillingly accept the call of their leaders to participate in war. People are required to cling exclusively to the state by war (Woito, 1982, p. xv). 'The institution of war exploits the propensities of soldiers and workers to cooperate with each other and obey their superiors'. In that sense, modern war 'is properly considered as a human institution in which individuals have specific roles' (Hinde, 1990, pp. 176-7).

The necessities of an effective war campaign require social control. In human history, the organisation of society in preparation for war contributed to the development of hierarchical state structures. Material resources are directed toward the destruction of enemy countries that are seen as a threat to national security. In war making efforts, a state monopolises violence and builds a capacity to destroy other societies. The whole process of preparing for and waging war reflects systematic and deliberate attempts to kill people who belong to another society.

During the period of war, authoritative control is imposed on every level of government and society. The freedom of expression, communication and movement is strictly restricted. Exclusive decision-making power over the production and allocation of resources serves the objective of winning a war. Orders are transmitted through a highly structured hierarchy because the implementation of a planned strategy requires a coherent command structure. Conducting war requires dominant and submissive relations between groups of people and their leaders. The enforcement of obedience is made possible by an authoritative hierarchy that carries out sanctions against those who do not support war activities.

Military-Industrial Complexes War preparation relies on social, economic, political and ideological mobilisation of society. Military-industrial complexes (MICs), with intricate social structures consisting of high-ranking military officers, industrialists, scientists and bureaucrats, are devoted to promoting militarism. Development in science, technology and industries is oriented toward building a new military weaponry system. Moral values, emotional appeals and behavioural expectations are manipulated to shape mass attitudes and policy toward war. Weapons of mass destruction are symbols of power status, and that helps military organisations rationalise larger military budgets. The cultural system is affected by the militarisation of society. Fear creates large public anxiety, and that allows the control of immense destructive power by a few state elites.

Military values and corresponding patterns of behaviour cut across many governments both in rich and poor countries. Militarism is a product of state policy made possible by modern bureaucratic machinery prepared for the efficient mobilisation of a large number of people who carry out violence and atrocities. In order to win a war, states want to have strong military power at their disposal supported by economic and industrial capabilities. As human competitiveness demands highly organised structures, the social and political structures of the states are transformed by preparation for war. In his farewell address in 1961, U.S. President Dwight Eisenhower warned of the uncontrollable impact of an immense military establishment and a large arms industry on economic, political and even spiritual aspects of life in American society.

Human Costs of War

Throughout history, war has caused great suffering to many who were subject to an extreme level of violence. Total destruction even resulted from primitive weapons. The level of destruction inflicted by war was well demonstrated by the great Peloponnesian War of 431-404 B.C. between rival Athenian and Spartan alliances. The Thirty Years War (1618-48) sparked by religious differences devastated Central Europe. Mercenary armies pillaged villages and burned peasant properties. The inhabitants in towns of Catholics and Protestants were slaughtered. Universal and self-perpetuating violence resulted in attrition and financial exhaustion.

The growth in the number of wars since the 17th century is reflected in an increase in the number of deaths. In the 20th century, there were more war-related deaths than in all the previous centuries combined. In wars from 1900 to 1990, 107.8 million lives were lost (Sivard, 1991, p. 20). Twice as many people were killed during World War I as had been killed in all wars combined from 1790-1913. The Second World War brought about more than 50 million fatalities. Nearly 35 million of those were civilians. Between the end of World War II and 1991, 21.8 million people were killed in 127 observed wars. Comparatively, five and half a million lost their lives in violent conflicts between 1990 and 1995. Civilians constitute between 75 and 90 percent of those victims (Smith, 1997, p. 13).

As was dramatically demonstrated in World War I and World War II, the development of military technology has contributed to a rapid increase in human casualties and the severity of economic destruction. In modern warfare, missile attacks and bombings do not differentiate between soldiers on a war front and women and children. In fact, more civilians have been killed in wars than have soldiers. Furthermore, the destruction of war caused by nuclear weapons touches every corner of human civilisation.

Mass destruction is random, as when 100 to 200 thousand Japanese civilians were killed in a few seconds by the atomic bombs dropped on Hiroshima and Nagasaki. The results of that act changed our perceptions of major wars involving nuclear weapons. Nuclear weapons, with their capacity to overkill, generated fear of human annihilation during the Cold War period. Most experts agree that compared with past conventional wars, there would be no return to normal life after a nuclear war.

Compared with the pre-modern wars between princes where soldiers killed each other to win a battle, civilians are not excluded as the object of destruction and abuse in modern warfare. In colonial wars, European troops slaughtered native populations. During World War II, massive bombing, motivated by revenge, was targeted at civilian population centres as is well illustrated in the Allied bombing raids on Dresden, Germany that left 100 thousand civilian fatalities. Massacre, rape and eviction are common especially in ethnic warfare (e.g., Serb atrocities in Bosnia, Hutu killings of Tutsis in Rwanda). In contemporary wars, half of the innocent civilian victims killed by bullets, bombs and landmines are children. In addition, children have been coercively recruited to be combatants in Angola, Liberia, Sierra Leone and other internal wars.

Civilian populations are targeted to destroy the support base of opposition forces by inflicting physical and psychological damage. Modern problems with war are not limited to the fatalities and injuries. People die due to the indirect impact of war as well as direct injuries. Warfare destroys the means of subsistence by disrupting economic transactions and social activities. Health care centres and water supplies are bombed in order to destroy the social infrastructure. Loss of crops and livestock leads to the destruction of family and community livelihoods.

Scarcity of resources can cause social collapse as well exemplified by the Iraqi society that endured the effects of bombing and an economic embargo on hospitals, health care services, schools and the entire infrastructure. Huge damage to power plants resulted in the long-term shutdown of sewage treatment and water purification plants. Many died because of unsanitary conditions. Among the victims were thousands of infants.

Types of War

The incidence of war has risen dramatically over the years, and the majority of wars have taken place with the establishment of a modern state system. During the period of 1816-1980, 67 inter-state wars, 51 imperial wars and 106 civil wars occurred. Given their ability to utilise expanded resources, the great powers were especially active in armed conflicts. For the period between 1816 and 1976, the United States, for example, was an initiator or a major target in 118 militarised inter-state conflicts. In sixty-seven of these, it initiated armed action (Gochman and Maoz, 1984).

A small-scale war, which is fought to achieve limited goals, normally ends quickly after specific objectives are satisfied. Armed units of two countries are locked in combat in a restricted area for a very short period. Protagonists refrain from resorting to highly destructive weapon systems that can provoke retaliation. In a low intensity military conflict, clashes can happen under various circumstances. In 1982, Great Britain and Argentina fought over the ownership of the small Falkland/Malvinas Islands, which have a population of less than 2,000. The invasion of the islands by Argentine forces led to an immediate military response from England. Britain drove out the Argentinean forces in order to reclaim its land. However, it did not attack mainland Argentina. The brief Chinese invasion of Vietnam in 1979 reflects the Chinese discomfort with expanded Vietnamese influence in the region. However, the two countries did not engage in a full-scale war and Chinese forces quickly withdrew.

In total wars intended to overpower enemies, the purpose of military campaigns is to annihilate the adversaries. The resources of opposing states are mobilised to the full scale in order to obtain victory at any cost. Intensive fighting takes place over an extended period until one side has no more ability or will to fight. Massive destruction is inflicted on the population and economic facilities of the enemy territory. The terms of ending war are unilaterally imposed on the defeated side. Given its scale, the motivation of war is geared toward the complete subjugation of the enemy.

The early patterns of modern military campaigns were demonstrated during the Napoleonic war. The old rules of warfare were broken as a mass army replaced the small professional corps of officers and soldiers that played an important role in seventeenth and eighteenth century aristocratic warfare. Conscription and national taxation increased the ability to deploy manpower and financial means for achieving the aims of political elites. The creation of a vastly increased modern army was supported by instigating patriotic zeal and nationalist sentiments.

Modern total wars entail massive military operations, with their destructive capability being supported by industrialisation. During World War I, military campaigns began to feature long-distance artillery. Political and military leaders deliberately chose civilians as their target for attacks during World War II. Severe casualties are impersonally imposed on civilian populations by weapons that instantly kill a large number of people. This is done without direct personal contact or the involvement of emotions on the side of military strategists and operators. Terror and fear inflicted upon civilian populations were used to destroy the national morale of adversaries. The defence of national territory has become obsolete due to the power of advanced weapons well represented by the increasing range, speed and sophistication of precision-guided high technology missiles.

Modern wars waged at the global level such as World War I and II show dramatic geographic expansion. War activities have reached every corner of the planet, and human life has been negatively affected by the intense military mobilisation and activities. The global reach of major wars derives from the nature of the modern international system as well as the development of new weapons technology. The twentieth century global wars differ from their earlier counterparts such as the military conquest by the Macedonian warrior King Alexander the Great over Persia and parts of India between 334 and 326 B.C. and the war campaign by the Mongol Empire of Genghis Khan in the 12th and 13th century, which stretched from Asia to part of Europe. These wars achieved territorial conquest but their destructive power was limited to the areas within their physical reach.

The historical examples of regional wars include the Peloponnesian Wars won by Sparta in 5th century B. C. and the 13th century Crusades between Europe and the Muslim world. In the 19th century, rivalry between major European powers produced several regional wars. The Crimean War (1853-56) involved Russia, Britain and France. The war between Prussia and France (1871) resulted from their quest for hegemony in continental Europe. The most notable regional war since World War II took place between Arab states and Israel. The war between Iran and Iraq, which started in 1980 and continued until 1988, was initiated by the ambition of the Iraqis who wanted to expand their political and military influence in the Persian Gulf area. The Iran-Iraq war represented a long-term rivalry between Sunni and Shiite Moslems for hegemonic influence over the region. The 20th century has experienced growth in the number of inter-state wars along with the increased number of new states.

In the past two centuries, many wars have been waged for the purpose of modern state building. Civil wars are conducted between two or more parties within a single state over contradictory claims to legitimacy and power of a state. There were wars that started with an ambition to unify politically divided countries with opposing regimes claiming the legitimacy to represent the nation. North Korea invaded the South for the purpose of national unification in 1950, and the Korean War ended in three years without changing internal divisions. In another case, North Vietnam militarily integrated South Vietnam in 1975.

Internal wars can lead to the collapse or division of a central political regime. Fighting in Afghanistan and Somalia brought about political and social anarchy. Truces and negotiations among different warring factions do not endure, and violence further intensifies a lack of order and morality. Internal wars in collapsed states are similar to thirteenth century European wars which were chaotic and created social disorder. In modern Europe, war served state making by drawing clear territorial boundaries. A monopoly of force within the state was established by the creation of a centralised power centre. The state's failure in monopolising and concentrating the means of coercion in the territory prolongs civil war. The internal war in Angola started in 1976 and lasted over more than two decades with the involvement of outside military assistance.

Post-Colonial Context

In the second half of the twentieth century, numerous ethnic wars were fought in former European colonies. Intolerable and unjust situations such as colonial repression and foreign domination, if negotiated solutions were not found, also provoked war. Liberation wars in Indochina, Algeria, Angola and other parts of Africa and Asia represented struggle against domination, exclusion and repression. Armed resistance waged in the form of guerrilla warfare with sporadic fighting was employed as one of the means to achieve independence from colonial rule. Its cause was popular among a sympathetic civilian population that provided logistical support such as food and hiding places.

Liberation movements aspiring for independence against colonial powers later evolved into armed struggles between rival ethno-political groups over the control of newly independent states. Many violent conflicts in the Third World illustrate difficulties in the political integration of diverse ethnic groups into the same territorial boundaries. The eruption of civil war derives from inter-ethnic rivalry. The Christian population in Sudan wanted to seek independence from the Muslim state. In order to achieve self-rule, Tamils have waged guerrilla warfare against the government of Sri Lanka, and Sikhs have used terrorist attacks in India. Other examples include the armed Kurdish struggles for the creation of their independent state, Kurdistan.

Structural origins of many wars in new post-colonial states emerged from the paradoxes of redrawing new political boundaries but were fuelled by regional and international alliance systems. During the Cold War period, some of these ethnic wars were tinged with political and ideological rivalry between superpowers. In the late 1970s and early 1980s, the U.S. and Soviet governments supported opposing factions in the Angolan civil war, which eventually involved Cuban and South African troops. Since the communist takeover of the Ethiopian government in 1974, Moscow was allied with Ethiopia in its war against Somalia supported by the U.S.

The U.S. and the Soviet Union were also directly engaged in Third World wars in order to diminish the political and military influence of the other side while expanding their own. The Vietnam War originally started with the struggle between opposing domestic political forces. However, the war included regional and international dimensions with the involvement of U.S. troops. American forces were sent to Vietnam in the late 1960s to prevent the domination of communist forces in the region that was viewed as harmful to U.S. strategic interests. In the same manner, Soviet military intervention in Afghanistan in the early 1980s was made to maintain their military, strategic influence along their border in Central Asia.

The intolerance of religious and ethnic differences between states intensified the struggle for regional hegemony. The denial of each other's needs for identity and security is considered as a primary factor in intense regional wars between Arabs and Israelis in 1956 (fighting over the Sinai peninsula), 1967 (Six Day War) and 1973 (Yom Kippur War). The underlying source of a war between India and Pakistan in 1971, which ended up with the victory of India and the creation of Bangladesh, was ethnic hostilities between Hindus and Muslims. Turkey intervened to protect their minority ethnic groups after the 1974 military coup by Greek military officers. The intervention against the Greek majority in Cyprus created military tension between the Turkish and Greek governments. Libya and Chad were engaged in territorial disputes. In 1980, the insurgencies of Muslim separatists in Northern Chad resulted in the military intervention of Libya and French support for Chad.

The dramatic increase in the number of violent ethnic and religious conflict in the 1990s is associated with aspirations for group autonomy. The collapse of multi-ethnic states unleashed military fights between different ethnic groups as we observed in former Yugoslavia and Rwanda. The creation of new states in the Balkans followed inter-ethnic violence. In Rwanda, a former Belgian colony, ethnic strife between majority Hutus and minority Tutsis contributed to the killing of half a million people over a few months.

In understanding the causes of war, it is important to note that the struggle for liberation, territorial disputes and ideological differences are often associated with cultural and religious animosities. Additionally, beneath simmering tensions and violence, political rivalries and historical hostilities play important roles in the initiation of inter-state and inter-group wars.

Just War Theory

Recourse to war for a solution to international conflict is condemned in several key international treaties. Whereas the United Nations Charter and the League of Nations Covenant denounce war as a national policy, war remains lawful in international law if it is conducted for self-defence. Though most states do not consider decisions on war in terms of moral or legal codes, efforts were made to identify circumstances in which war can be morally and legally justified as an instrument of international and national policy.

Just war traditions were established in the medieval period of Christian history and were further developed in the seventeenth century by Hugo Grotius, the father of modern international law. The theory includes two sets of criteria that restrict warfare as an instrument of maintaining social order (Peach, 1996, p. 194). One category of the doctrine governs the morality of becoming involved in the violence of war (in Latin, *jus ad bellum*; the justice of a war). The other category focuses on the actual conduct of war (*jus in bello*; justice in a war).

The just war theory espouses that there are right or just circumstances under which going to war is considered morally acceptable. Just war may be undertaken by a legitimate authority for a reasonable cause and with an ethical purpose. In just war theory, decisions on war ought to be made and legitimised by duly constituted authority, and war has to be conducted by a competent authority. The principle of right intention allows fighting war for self-defence but not for the purpose of revenge or desire for territorial expansion. War should have the goals of restoring just order, and its outcome needs to produce peaceful conditions.

A reasonable chance should exist that war will be won at a tolerable cost of life. The damage caused by fighting should be less than the harm that would be sustained if force were not used. In the principle of last resort, war should not be taken because it is easier than negotiation or other types of peaceful settlements. Even when there is a just cause, all means other than war must have been tried to reverse the wrong.

The conduct of war doctrine specifies the conditions under which the conduct of war may be ethical. *Jus in bello* determines the types of permissible military actions during a war. According to the proportionality principle, particular battles and strategies have to be chosen based on an acceptable balance between means and ends. Permitted destruction must be proportionate to the importance of the objective. The amount of force should not exceed the value and necessity of accomplishing the military objective. Benefits of conducting a particular strategy within the war must not outweigh its harms.

The notion of justice in the conduct of war also includes non-combatant immunity from killing. There are specific restrictions on the use of force with discrimination between combatants and noncombatants. It is immoral to kill innocent civilians, and deliberate targeting of children, the elderly or women is not permissible. Any costs to civilians should only be unintentional. Justifiable use of violence in war is limited to a morally defensible cause. The above principles were clearly violated in the incineration of Hiroshima and Nagasaki during World War II although U.S. military strategists justified

Nagasaki during World War II although U.S. military strategists justified attacking the population centres on the basis of destroying the enemy's will to fight.

As opposed to realism, which accepts war as a legitimate tool of power politics, just war doctrine stresses that warfare should be at least limited based on the presumption that it is not possible to abolish warfare. 'At the core of the just war tradition is the conviction that the taking of human life may be sanctioned' or even necessary to prevent aggression (Kegley, Jr. and Wittkopf, 1995, p. 515). Thus, unlike pacifism, in just war theory, some wars are viewed as a remedy for immoral or sinful human behaviour. According to the critics of just war theory, 'the argument that if war can be limited and if the belligerents can be reasonable enough to accept extraneous limitations on their conduct, they should be reasonable enough to avoid fighting altogether' (Howard, 1979, p. 6). Overall, the criteria for the moral justification of war have not been applied to most wars, and its ignorance is often justified by strategic military efficiency or ideological absolutes.

6   Sources of Social Conflict

There are different explanations about the causes of violent conflict. According to those who believe in genetic sources of violence, aggressive behaviour is rooted in human instinct. The origin of interpersonal and inter-group violence is traced to biologically determined factors. Others propose that experiences of frustration produce a tendency to attack other people. In contrast with psychological interpretations, basic needs theorists attribute protracted social conflict to dissatisfaction of both physical and psychological needs. The denial of elements required in human development is inherent to many oppressive societies, and conflict often derives from a malfunctioning system. Sources of group violence can be attributed to a lack of security, suppression of autonomy and identity and an unequal distribution of life chances.

Human Nature and Violence

Several well-known psychologists point to unconscious human urges in explaining innate potential and drive for violent behaviour. Sigmund Freud theorised the role of the unconscious in the manifestation of destructive behaviour (1961). The impulse of human aggression and destructiveness is generated by a death instinct. The energy of the death instinct, when thwarted by the life instinct, is displaced into outward aggression. Thus, a powerful desire for violence has to be reckoned with as part of a human drive toward destruction.

Some extend their arguments further to the point that violent behaviour is genetically programmed into human nature. It is even suggested that savage human behaviour originates in our animal past. Irresistible outbreaks of violent impulses are ascribed to fixed biological propensities. Given its autonomous nature, a drive to aggression cannot be easily controlled. In the view of one of the foremost ethnologists, Konrad Lorenz (1966), aggressive human behaviour reflects a survival-enhancing instinct. Humans, like other animals, are endowed with fixed patterns of behaviour oriented toward species preservation. The eruption of violence recurs rhythmically and regularly without external stimulation. Theories on genetic sources of human behaviour attempt to illustrate that aggression is expressed spontaneously and thus is independent of learning.

Repression of the innate aggressive propensities leads to seeking increased outlets in inter-group or inter-state violence. For those who accept the views of instinctive behaviour, the inability to check genetically based mechanisms of violence is perilous and fatal given the availability of the means of mass destruction. It is thus suggested that in order to prevent its discharge by aggressive behaviour, the destructive energy needs to be channelled into socially useful competition.

As opposed to the view that humans are, by instinct, aggressive creatures, biological observation has been used to demonstrate that the predatory behaviour of animals is driven by biological needs for survival rather than inter-species aggression. Predation is an inter-species phenomenon, and many mammals tend to avoid physical harm to the same species. Fighting within the same species results from rivalry over resources such as breeding space, and it does not necessarily ends up with killing (Harcourt, 1991). Human beings are one of very few species that kill each other.

In response to the arguments that 'humans have a violent brain' and that 'war is caused by instinct', the 1986 Seville Statement sponsored by UNESCO concludes that war is a learned trait reflected in cultural heritage. Theories of aggression, which link the problems of fighting and war to inherently violent human genes, have been challenged by the fact that social experience has a dominant impact on individual behaviour and that cooperation is as common as competition in social relations. Human behaviour is socially learned, and war is largely unknown in some societies.

If human beings are innately evil and biologically aggressive, mechanisms for control are likely to be seen as necessary. Tendencies toward destructive behaviour will be repressed by disciplinary control of human behaviour. Authoritarian political control may even be required (Freud, 1961). If conflict is not considered inherent to human nature, training and social change will be appropriate means to prevent violence. Most importantly, building a more caring world would help better reduce aggressive behaviour derived from the struggle for survival.

Perspectives on biological and instinctive origins of violence ignore problems rooted in organisation and development of society. Human behaviour has profound social roots. Political, economic, ideological and military structures have an impact on human interaction. Adversarial relationships among classes, nations and states do not arise simply from a deep individual psychological environment.

Frustration-Aggression Hypothesis

An excessive level of frustration is accumulated when an organism is blocked in its pursuit of a goal. According to the frustration-aggression hypothesis, human beings, as goal-oriented organisms, naturally become aggravated when they are prevented from achieving what they desire. A natural build-up of blocked energy seeks release, and aggressive action is directed to the source of one's frustration.

Given that violence is induced by frustration associated with certain situations, an external stimulation releases inherent tendencies of the frustrated agent to attack (Dollard et al., 1939). The expression of hostilities and violent behaviour are attributed to the interference with a propensity to aggression. If aggressiveness cannot be expressed against the real source of frustration, displaced hostilities can be targeted to substitutive objects. Antagonistic behaviour may be reduced by finding an alternative means to release frustration. Feelings of frustration under authoritarian political regimes are often satisfied by such means as wit, humour and drama in ordinary life.

Obviously widespread frustration among the population can be manipulated by political leaders in directing hostilities toward minority groups within a society or foreign countries. Some may argue that Hitler's attacks on Jews and other ethnic minorities were used to divert the public's attention away from bad economic conditions in the early 1930s. To reduce domestic opposition, political leaders may start a crisis abroad. The 1982 Argentinean attack on the Falkland/ Malvinas Islands was motivated by the military dictatorship's efforts to stay in power.

Societal stress and violence can be generated by frustrated expectations related to rapid urbanisation or economic depression. However, the extent to which frustration generates aggression is uncertain (Glossop, 1993, p. 55). Human behaviour is affected by a social environment, and frustrated feelings can be controlled through various adaptation mechanisms. People can be educated to behave differently. Cultural settings also influence patterns of behaviour as demonstrated by the experiences of non-aggressive societies.

Psychoanalytic Perspectives

A perceived threat produces a narrow definition of group boundaries and sharp distinctions between friends and enemies. Unthinkable actions can be induced by a dehumanised image of the enemy reinforced by nationalistic propaganda. From the psychoanalytic perspective, the perception of an enemy is formulated in a way to protect oneself from contamination by the possible boomeranging of psychic content. Another group member is perceived as a 'container' of unacceptable psychic content previously built into unconscious mechanisms (Volkan, 1990, p. 82).

In this theory, one group becomes an enemy of another through an unconscious psychological process. Stereotypical images of our enemy are created by projecting our own unwanted psychic material on the opposing groups. In group dynamics, the most-hated aspects of ourselves and our own group are transferred to other groups who are depicted as an enemy (Mack, 1990, p. 122). The likeness between enemies and ourselves, which is perceived unconsciously, 'must be denied and never permitted to enter our consciousness in order to keep our projections, externalisation and displacement stable and the identity of ourselves cohesive' (Volkan, 1990, p. 88).

The process by which an opposing group becomes a reservoir for all bad characteristics is explained by early childhood psychological experiences. New encounters are interpreted in terms of attitudes learned from childhood development experiences. Feelings of group affiliations and differentiations are affected by positive and negative polarities of the early sense of self. A childhood psychological process of constructing a self-image and a sense of others contributes to dehumanisation of an enemy at a later stage.

According to psychoanalytic understanding, the sense of self is formed in the first few months of life and is more firmly established in early childhood. A child develops a positive attitude in response to rewarding experiences with the outside world but a negative attitude after having disappointing experiences. Those feelings associated with pain and fear are attributed to a relationship to the outside world, more specifically, other groups (Mack, 1990, p. 122).

The analysis of intergroup hatred may be helped by a focus on a psychological process of creating group distinctiveness. However, it is a simplistic assumption that in-group solidarity and out-group hostility are based on the fear generated by psychic mechanisms. All group dynamics cannot be easily attributed to an unconscious psychological experience during infanthood. Our images of the outside world are maintained or changed by learning and other types of adulthood socialisation processes. The psychological aspects of struggle between groups such as misperception and enemy images have been better explained by cognitive theories that are more complex.

Relative Deprivation

Relative deprivation results from the combined effect of rising expectations and a lack of progress toward demands for a better life. Relative deprivation is 'defined as actors' perception of discrepancy between their value expectations and their value capabilities'. Value expectations lead people to believe that they are rightfully entitled to certain goods and conditions of life. 'Value capabilities are the goods and conditions they think they are capable of getting and keeping' (Gurr, 1970, p. 24). An intolerable gap between anticipated reality and the manifest reality of life conditions serves as a precondition for widespread unrest.

Subjective factors are important in understanding the perceptions of deprivation. Revolutions and revolts do not generally occur in impoverished societies. People have a varying sense of entitlement in their pursuit of available welfare or status. It is 'the dissatisfied state of mind' rather than the tangible supply of goods or social conditions (such as freedom) that produce political instability and violence (Davies, 1971, p. 136). When people do not have hope or expectations for more than they can achieve, they tend to be less discontented with what they have. However, rising expectations increase the intensity of feelings of deprivation.

An individual or collective sense of entitlement tends to rise faster than can be fulfilled. In general, the expected ability to satisfy basic material and social needs rises disproportionately to what society is able to and does deliver. Disproportionate allocation of benefits combined with poor economic performance generates further anger and emotional frustration. A reference to what other groups have brings about a more intense level of dissatisfaction. Unequal opportunities can be blamed for socially inferior status and inadequate material well-being.

Rapid social change, especially coupled with uneven distribution of wealth and power, tends to generate feelings of a growing gap between unmaterialised expectations and perceptions about existing economic, social and political conditions. In particular, the discrepancy in anticipated and actual need satisfaction increases during a short period of sharp reversal following economic and social development. Resentment results from a belief that the government suppresses opportunities to maintain legitimate gains. Violent uprisings are likely to take place when people's desires and wants grow further away from what they obtain.

Basic Needs

The satisfaction of basic needs is required for human development as well as the survival of human beings in both physical and social terms. The real source of conflict is deep rooted in the lives and ontological being of those concerned. Basic needs theories reject the *a priori* assumption that violence originates in the very nature (i.e. evil, aggressive) of humans or unconscious psychological dynamics. Needs provide factual, objective and rational criteria for analysing and evaluating an emergent social situation that may contain in its womb the potential for generating conflict. The lack of biological needs causes an imbalance in the individual's life supporting systems and causes death. Food and shelter are important for physical survival, and the satisfaction of the needs does not require large amounts of marketable goods and services.

Biological and physical needs are intertwined with mental requirements in the satisfaction of other needs. Basic needs contain more than physiological dimensions and include such primary emotions as fear, anger, depression and happiness. Psychological needs are linked to socially produced wants, desires or preferences. Thus, people can suffer from damage to self-esteem as much as from a lack of food. Fear, violence, unemployment and marginalisation generate conditions for human misery.

Human emotions are constructed within the framework of social life, and people's self-esteem is important in finding meaning in life. The source of individual identity can be found in association with the collectivity. The need for security is met with social recognition of identity and effective participation in the decision making processes. More specifically, social needs such as security, self-identity and self-esteem can be satisfied by intellectual achievement, emotional interaction with other people, physical contact, autonomy and participation in community life. Given that humans are social creatures, needs are gratified only in interaction with others (Sites, 1990, p. 136). Certain social and economic conditions are essential to the fulfilment of human needs.

The struggle to satisfy basic needs is a key motivational factor behind human behaviour and social interaction. The human being becomes the most appropriate unit of analysis (Ronen, 1998, p. 15). The satisfaction of basic needs, which is crucial for development as human beings, is universally demanded. The needs of individuals are precedent to the requisites of the system. Basic needs are ontological while interests and values are temporal and historically determined. Since the pursuit of ontological needs places power on individuals and groups, basic needs cannot be curbed nor negotiated (Burton, 1990a).

A group's ontological needs that cannot be bargained away have to be treated differently from negotiable interests. Satisfying one group's needs is not incompatible with the realisation of the other group's needs. It does not need to be considered in competitive or exclusive terms. The legitimacy of authority can be established by the creation of institutions that serve the needs of everyone. Poverty, economic inequity and social injustice need to be reduced to overcome obstacles to basic needs. Leftist insurgents in El Salvador, Guatemala, Mexico and Peru were facilitated by the denial of opportunities for decent economic and social life. Causes of many other violent conflicts in the 20th century can also be found in the suppression of human needs.

Identity Formation

Primordialism and social constructivism explain the process of group identity formation as well as forces driving the need for identity. In primordial theories, a group is turned into a natural community by the common bonds shared by the group members. Individuals belong to a group through primordial ties of blood, kinship, language and customs. As ethnic division is relegated to predetermined (ascriptive) characteristics, group membership is considered the given of human existence. The sense of self is interwoven with the identity of the group at primitive levels. Belonging to ethnic groups is tinged with raw and primitive affects that pertain to one's sense of self and its protection.

According to primordialism, common history, traditions, language, beliefs and values are objective cultural criteria that distinguish one group from another. Historical continuity is maintained by a shared culture transmitted over generations. Claims of an identity group to an autonomous status are supported by their cultural and religious concerns. Such elements as myths, memories, values and symbols are used to close ethnic group boundaries. On the other hand, identity boundaries between in-groups and out-groups are established by a subjective group consciousness. A wider self-awareness of their common history and destiny is awakened by social change such as modernisation that often leads to competition with other communities. Identity itself can be reformulated under modernisation (Rupesinghe, 1994, p. 21). Even such well known ethnic groups as the Kurds and Ibo knew little unity and cohesion until after the Second World War.

Constructivists regard identity as manufactured rather than given. Identity emerges from a dialectic between similarity and difference in group interaction. Owing to its socially constructed nature, the significance attached to a particular identity varies in situations (Jenkins, 1997, p. 11). Because identity is produced and reproduced by the social processes, constructivists do not consider ethnic identity fixed as suggested by primodialists. Though communal identity is, to a certain extent, rooted in culture and shared meanings of life, it is also the outcome of social interaction (Anderson, 1993). Ethnicity can be regarded as a cleavage splitting groups between us and them in a politicised setting.

Motivational forces behind the mobilisation of ethnic groups can be explained by instrumentalism. Identity can be used 'instrumentally' to promote individual or collective interests. In their struggle for power, competing elites use ethnicity as a tool to mobilise popular support. Ethnic categories can also be manipulated to maintain the power of a dominant group and justify discrimination against other groups in education and employment. The instrumentalist idea is not exclusive from or incompatible with primordialism in the sense that the primordial elements such as race, kinship, religion, language and regionalism can be used as manipulative instruments by elites (Gashaw, 1993).

Ethnic and religious differences are not in themselves causes of conflict, and ethnic communities may remain passive and unmobilised for long periods. The salience of group identity is awakened by socially derived inequalities in material well-being or political access. Racial or ethnic distinctions are deepened by the denial of political participation as well as a lack of physical and economic security. Discriminatory treatment along with repressive state control generates group grievances. Political and material demands reflect their efforts to seek justice for members of their group.

Conflict Dynamics in Divided Societies

In deep rooted conflict, inequity in political and economic power between different groups as well as the existence of incompatible religious or ideological convictions generates conditions for polarisation and violence. The security of communal identity is affected by antagonistic perceptions and interactions. Intractable conflicts entail disagreement over values and perception of threat to collective identity. In particular, conflict evolving around identity is always more protracted and contentious than those over resources alone.

Group conflicts erupt with the mobilisation of people by 'political entrepreneurs' against another group to remove perceived threats (Ronen, 1998, p. 13). In activating a shared identity in an opposition to the identity of other groups, past hostilities are utilised to accentuate polarisation and render conflict more violent. Mobilisation by one community activates responsive counter mobilisation by other groups that attempt to defend their interests (Esman, 1990a, p. 54). The group may perceive that their identity is threatened by the demand of the other group for the recognition of cultural rights and political status. Group competition is more intense especially during an economic decline that weakens social fabric. Thus, the threat to the expectations or interests of one community would be felt more sharply following uneven economic development. As people rally around the issues that express their grievances, previous experiences of exploitation and victimisation strengthen the group's identity.

Insurgent movements may arise when a government identified with one ethnic group attempts to impose its own values. For instance, the decision to enforce Islamic law on non-Islamic areas contributed to the civil war in Sudan. The efforts of the Ethiopian government to impose its dominant national identity and language in Eritrea provoked armed resistance that eventually led to the creation of a separate state. The struggle to control state institutions can also be a source of violent conflict between opposing ethnic groups that have significant organisational capabilities. The Nigerian Civil War was brought about by the exclusion of the Ibos following the capture of the government by a coalition of parties from the North and West.

The increase in ethno-political conflicts is related to the resurgence of ethnic identity accompanied by political instability as seen in Azerbaijan, Armenia and Georgia during and after the breakup of the Soviet Union. Especially in a society undergoing rapid changes, uncertainties grow and the demand for self-realisation becomes very vocal. The quest for well-being and power is organised around their self-identities. As we saw in many indigenous movements, groups can draw their strength from cultural bonds not associated with specific interests.

Fragmentation and strains on the social fabric derive from the imposed incorporation of distinctive communities within one political entity. *De facto* paralysis of political institutions results from a vicious cycle of fear and hostile interactions among the communal contestants. At the same time, states fail to provide the symbolic and material needs for individuals and groups. The perception of victimisation is strengthened by the denial of separate identity and repression of cultural autonomy by dominant groups. Conflict in multiethnic societies is sustained by discrimination against culturally distinctive groups.

Irrational and pathological expression of ethnic and other types of socio-political violence are well illustrated by its destructiveness and indiscriminate killings. However, communal violence is not ascribed to intra-personal psychological attributes, and it cannot be overcome by mere psychoanalytic treatments. The absence of social space for facilitating dialogue between diverse identities and values facilitates violent struggles. To prevent unrestrained violence against innocent victims, members of different communities need assistance in recognising shared interests in survival and long-term prosperity. Solutions to the conflict would eventually have to be grounded in structural arrangements that respect cultural and political autonomy of different members of society.

7 Feminist Understandings of Violence

Women all over the world are subject to various types of violence. Many sources of oppression prohibit the realisation of freedom for women. Violence against women represents a form of social control that limits their ability in every aspect of life. Oppression of women and other marginalised groups has been explained by the feminist critique of a hierarchical world order. The occurrence of both manifest and latent violence against women has emerged as an important concern in peace studies for the last three decades. Images of women have been historically associated with pacifism. Feminine values of caring, compassion and nurturing have enriched the conceptions of peace. Most importantly, the application of feminine values to the radical transformation of an oppressive social order (as a source of many forms of violence) serves as an important principle in the struggle for achieving peace.

Violence against Women

While both women and men are victims of sexism, racism, human rights abuses and poverty, there are particular types of violence that afflict women more than men. Family violence and sexual and emotional abuse of women are major concerns in many parts of the world. Direct violence against women includes rape and unorganised random physical abuse as well as attacks on women in organised war. Women and their young children currently constitute the vast majority of the world refugee population.

The abuse of women during wartime has been common. In World War II, the Japanese Army forced young women from Korea, the Philippines and other places in Asia to serve Japanese soldiers as so called 'comfort women'. Some of them were 16 or younger when they were sexually assaulted by Japanese soldiers at the war fronts. In July 1992, the

Japanese government finally admitted that tens of thousands of women were sent to military bases to provide sex for the soldiers. However, compensation for the suffering of the women was refused.

Rape and other forms of ill treatment of women have been employed as tools of a military strategy. The rape and deliberate impregnating of thousands of women, mostly Muslims in Bosnia-Herzegovina, was a form of ethnic cleansing conducted by Serb nationalists. Many documents report the assault of women by internal security forces in Peru, Colombia and other countries that have anti-government insurgencies. However, most governments failed to condemn or punish those who committed rape and killings.

Structural violence hits women severely in many impoverished countries. Among the poorest of the poor are young widows and elderly individuals with little capacity to manage household economies. The high level of poverty as well as harsh working conditions has put a particularly heavy burden on female heads of households who do not have adult males to help them. Many poor women have difficulty in getting out of the cycle of poverty that includes malnutrition, inadequate food availability and poor sanitation and water supplies as well as poor health and lack of education. Women's struggle for survival is made more difficult by the scarcity of renewable resources and other effects of environmental degradation.

The status of women in the Third World has not improved much due to the feminisation of poverty and continuing job discrimination. Young women provide a hard working labour force for multinational corporations but are paid low wages (Tickner, 1994, p. 49). Women in certain regions of the world form the majority of subsistence farmers. In particular, women in Africa produce 80 percent of the food. However, the introduction of a market oriented economic system deprives women's income by assigning low monetary value to their economic activities.

Construction of Gender Identities

It is often considered that gender roles are socially constructed rather than a natural part of social life. Individuals born into the biological categories of male or female are assigned to the social categories of men and women through the acquisition of locally-defined attributes of masculinity and femininity. Sexual roles and stereotypes are enforced by social norms, laws and education. Thus, gender has something to do with the social behaviours and characteristics. Males are expected to demonstrate masculine behaviour while females conform to models of femininity.

Masculinity and femininity are defined in relation to each other. The feminine principle is associated with giving qualities such as mercy, supportiveness, compassion and sensitivity to others. Feminine features are related to life; nature and love are of the highest value. On the other hand, masculine experiences associated with aggressiveness and physical skills are 'rooted in power-in-the world, with its epitomising act: to kill'. Law, authority, rank and status that demonstrate control belong to masculinity; 'any failure in control is seen as unmanly' (French, 1985, pp. 91-93). Hierarchy is maintained by obedient norms and structure.

The construction of masculine and feminine categories is linked to power relations arising from the practice of attaching meanings to gender identities. Emotion, body and nature have been historically associated with the identity of female gender. It has been regarded as inferior to the male gender identity characterised by reason and mind. 'One glaring example of how the dominant cultural outlook manifests this (patriarchal) oppressive conceptual framework is seen in macho, polarised, dichotomised attitudes toward war and peace. Pacifists are dismissed as naive, soft wimps; warriors are realistic, hard heroes' (Warren and Cady, 1996, pp. 3-4).

The dichotomy has been drawn between men and women in the historical context of Western cultural traditions. This dichotomy was used to create a value hierarchy in terms of status and prestige. The dominant masculinity in Western culture is produced by qualities of rationality and strength. The marginalised are excluded from the interests of privileged groups. Women, children, the poor and indigenous populations are exposed to environmental destruction and various forms of violence.

The construct of social domination is based on a set of behaviours, social structures and an ideology reflecting basic value judgements about the nature of the social order and of sex differentiation (Boulding, 1976, p. 35). As dominance systems organise most of our political and economic life, men and women alike are being rewarded for doing what society values. Whereas unquestioned adherence to rules is essential to authoritarianism, feminine values such as care and concern tend to be oriented toward relationships and respect for persons (Reardon, 1985, p. 30).

Masculine and Feminine Values

Gender can be used as an essential element in understanding social structure and the origin of violence. The root of violence is found in privileging masculine values in the process of establishing social and cultural distinctions between different gender roles (Reardon, 1985). Disregard for feminine values attached to the vision of a just and nonviolent world is seen as a cause of war and violence. Feminism is one component of a wider humanism conceived as an opposition to oppression.

Feminine views recognise the existing inegalitarian human relationships and suggest how human needs can be fulfilled. These ideas are based on a kinship model of a less structured organisation designed to promote everyone's human well-being. It reveals an innate human capacity for great sensitivity or moral behaviour. Feminine values and characteristics can be adopted and applied regardless of biological sex differences.

Competitive, organisational and exclusive masculine values support a model of hierarchical human relationships. These values are often reflected in the bureaucracies of states, churches, corporations, political parties and the military. Order is a function of control by masculine institutions. A masculine view of the world emphasises the goals of hierarchical organisations, legitimises the power of certain groups and particular political ideologies, and protects the interests of big corporations.

State building is a masculine project that encourages a willingness to engage in violence. Men considered as an aggressive biological class are given licence for engaging in wars and are motivated to fight. 'A legend of heroically violent manliness is taught in patriotic homes, neighbourhood movies, schools and boot camps' (Ruddick, 1989, p. 84). The glamorisation of violence in warfare is encouraged by continued socialisation in patriarchal societies. The arms race and other national security priorities are the main factors in the subordination of women. Social welfare is traded for military spending, and it further exacerbates female poverty. Demilitarisation requires the process to undo the masculine identity created by a modernisation process.

Growing entry of women entry into the public sector (traditionally known as the men's world) has been enhanced by women's adoption of masculine values as a strategy to be accepted for an authority role. Margaret Thatcher played down feminine qualities to appear more appropriate to a masculine political structure. As the prime minister of

Britain, she undermined social services for women and children. Her rule ended social welfare that protected the poor and vulnerable. Several prominent women who held the highest governmental decision making positions do not remain as peacemakers, but as war heroines (Vickers, 1993). Golda Meir won the Six Day War against the Arabs; Indira Gandhi initiated a war with Pakistan; Thatcher sent military forces to re-occupy the Falkland/Malvinas islands in the dispute with Argentina.

Success in politics and other institutional arenas, regarded as evidence of masculinity, demands a high degree of ferocity (Reardon, 1985, p. 33). The masculinisation of women is an attempt to prove that women can perform most tasks reserved for men. Doing the job as well as a man means accepting masculine standards and thus reinforcing dominant masculine values. By internalising 'the image and values of the oppressor, many women seem almost eager to adopt masculine characteristics and criteria in order to succeed' (Reardon. 1985, p. 56). This supports the small masculine elite groups who control institutions that run the corporate world and conduct state affairs. Women's efforts to meet these competitive and aggressive criteria of success disable their and society's ability to question the standards and the systems that have long despised feminine values.

Maintenance of violence can be understood in terms of the construction of dominance in a gendered institution and state. Greater value assigned to masculinity reinforces hierarchical and unequal relations. Women are applauded for achieving success in previously male dominated activities such as politics, military service, business and administration. However, little social respect is shown to men who enter traditionally female arenas such as nursing and childcare.

Patriarchy and Domination

Patriarchy is the central concept that determines virtually all human enterprises while illustrating the historical and social dimensions of women's exploitation and oppression. It represents a set of beliefs and values supported by dominant social and political institutions and backed by the threat of punishment. Competitive social order is compatible with authoritarian principles (underscored by coercive power), which assume human beings are not of equal value (Reardon, 1985, p. 10). Beyond the literal meaning of patriarchy as the rule of fathers, the concept of patriarchy reveals the prevalence of male dominant, competitive values at various types of institutions.

The patriarchal system is entrenched in the state's control over coercive capabilities and unequal social and economic structures. It lays down relations between men and men as well as between men and women by imposing a hierarchical structure. It gives more value to masculine tasks while demeaning feminine oriented work. In a patriarchal system, men are taught to be masculine, to compete with each other, and to hide their fears and compassion from one another. All these dimensions are crystallised in the military -- the most patriarchal institution in an already patriarchal society.

Authoritarian patriarchies originate in the major elements of civilisation--human settlement, organised agriculture, the state and male domination. In fact, the origin of a war oriented society can be traced back to a patriarchal system that depends on violence to hold in place the social order it spawned. Military concepts and values are upheld by patriarchy; its structures and practices have been embodied in the state, forming the basic paradigm for the nation-state system. Thus, there is in all aspects of that system an inevitable sexist bias that is especially acute in matters related to national security.

Feminist Critique of the World Order

The current world order represents a patriarchal system that perpetuates oppression and exploitation through exerting violence. Global systems maintained by military order are based on the traditional stratifications of social class, gender and the domination of centre countries over those in the periphery. Capitalism has transformed various forms of violence into economic coercion (Mies, 1986, p. 27). Violence against women is not accidental but part of modern capitalist patriarchy. Thus, peace is incompatible with a patriarchal system that sustains war and exploitation.

Institutions, controlled by a small number of elites, operate the global political economy and conduct the affairs of state. These elites are, for the most part, dedicated to thinking in Western, analytical terms. Although their relationship is competitive within the elite structures, the common objective that holds the elites together is the maintenance of their own control and domination.

The world, which is based on a competitive social order guided by authoritarian principles, is held in place by coercive force. This system pervades our lives and affects every aspect of society from the structural to the interpersonal. Thus, the system of domination throughout its existence in history has continued to devote large quantities of resources to war and the capacity to conduct warfare. Nation-states (the system which produces war) maintain sexist policies by taking away resources from the production of basic needs for the production of military weapons. In the contemporary capitalist world order, some privileged women have been co-opted as allies of dominant political and economic forces. However, women are discriminated against and punished when they oppose the system.

Women and the Military

Traditionally state institutions yield a variety of tools to militarise gender so that men will be ready to defend a national interest defined by government elites. In traditional attitudes and culture, men are willing to earn their manhood credentials by soldiering. Men are supposed to kill and die on the behalf of the state to prove their manhood (Ruddick, 1989, p. 77). On the other hand, women have to be properly subservient to satisfy the demand of the military comprised largely of men. Women have been integrated into the modern war system by serving in non-combat functions. During war time, many women worked in plants that produced parts for destructive weapons and supported the operations that decimated the population and social fabric of other countries.

Recently, professional military careers have become one of the new frontiers open to women. Especially in the United States, women have been joining the armed services in unprecedented numbers. They proved an indispensable part of the recent U.S. military operations in various wars. About 20,000 women were involved in the Persian Gulf War, and some of them were assigned to launch Patriot missiles. Some women's groups welcome the broadened opportunity for women in the military and argue that more combat experience for women is a prerequisite for demonstrating leadership skills. Major feminist organisations in the U.S. have supported the move for women to be eligible for combat on the grounds of professional equal opportunity. The National Organization of Women even adopted the position that women and men should be subject to draft registration and conscription on the same basis, without regard to sex. This position rests on the belief that in order to realise equality, women must share social duties and responsibilities as well as being assured of their rights.

Those in support of the increased role of women in the military hold that women's subordination and dependency are perpetuated by stereotyped associations between women and pacifism. They contend that feminism should be primarily concerned with opening opportunities for women on an equal basis with men in all aspects of our society, including those related to war. Women should not refuse to support a national military policy and participate in the armed forces of nation-states. These key arenas of control and power should not be left in the hands of men. They believe that women's subordination is perpetuated by portraying them as natural peace makers. In order to change their pacifist and passive images, women have to infiltrate the military.

The opponents of a greater role for women in the military remind us that women have been victims of militarism. Joining the war system aggravates the burden of war. State militaries are organised to maintain the system of inequality. Women are more likely to be transformed by militarisation. Feminist goals can be better achieved through nonviolent practices. The military's role in today's world, and the ideals, beliefs and behaviours it encourages are contrary to the goals of democratic equality and positive global transformation. Masculine socialisation and women's participation in the armed forces promote the limited goal of exclusive national security but they are not compatible with peace.

Feminist aspirations are antithetical to the characteristics of the military represented by hierarchy, authoritarianism and violence. The military imposes its own unique forms of male chauvinism and promotes attitudes, policies and practices that are detrimental to the attainment of equality and the values of feminism. By participating in war, women become 'direct perpetrators of violence' (Vickers, 1993, p. 18). Women must realise the extent to which they contribute to sexism through the acceptance of male superiority, intimidation and force. Their willingness to buy into the system helps sustain the very system that exploits them.

Shared Goals of Peace and Feminism

Women face the issues of supporting or resisting war in a very different context from men. Women are in a position to appreciate the value of peace better through their vulnerability to the structure of violence and deprivation. They have played the role of nurturers, mothers and natural peacemakers throughout most of the history of human civilisation. It gives a special vantage point and skills with which to assess the role of weapons and war in human affairs and to offer alternative models of behaviour in dealing with conflict and social change.

Modern feminists find a logical linkage between feminism, pacifism and socialism. That linkage has formed the basis of feminism's roots of understanding peace. By challenging the inevitability of dominant social order and war, the feminine notion of peace elegantly explains the hierarchical nature of our society. Domination and violence are caused by a hierarchical system such as military institutions that depend on superior and inferior relationships between certain members. The elimination of violence in both private and public spheres is essential to achieving peace. The goal of the liberation of women from violence can be promoted by disarmament and the campaign against war. An alternative to violence can be founded on equality and sisterhood (Carroll, 1987, p.18).

The concept and logic of domination connect feminism to transformative social projects. The goals of peace can be further enhanced by the feminist agenda committed to the removal of privileged systems for the few and the rejection of coercive power in human interaction. Given the involvement of social factors such as race, ethnicity, class and age in the construction of gender, any feminist movement working to end oppression against women must support the struggle against other forms of oppression (Warren and Cady, 1996, p. 2).

Feminist conceptions of peace are extended to the conditions of social justice, economic equity and ecological balance. Equity and democracy have to be transformational values for forthcoming social changes. Equal relations between men and women can serve as the foundation for equality among all peoples and an end to racism and ecological destruction as well as sexism. The struggle against all types of violence is supported by promotion of women's rights so as to attain an equal distribution of resources and the right to express oneself freely (Brock-Utne, 1990, p. 146).

Women's access to land, education reform and other circumstances are an indicator to measure the welfare of a society. Poverty and underdevelopment cannot be overcome in a social structure that generates inequality and violence. In trying to alter power relations, women redefine their roles against their oppressors and raise consciousness of their identity. Social justice and development require the full participation of women. The Fourth World Conference on Women, held in 1995, stressed equality and development as well as the elimination of violence against women in public and private spheres.

Reconceptualisation of Security

The militarisation of society is the unchecked manifestation of patriarchy as the overt and explicit mode of governance. The elimination of violence at a personal level is seldom emphasised in a state-centric security paradigm that puts the highest priority on the protection of a territorial state. Domestic violence against women is often ignored by the militarised notion of state security. In fact, commonalities between battered women and political prisoners and between rape survivors and combat soldiers traumatised by war can reveal the links between the private domains and state security (Herman, 1992, pp. 2-3). The threats to a demonstrative use of a nuclear weapon displays the same underlying motives as those of militia groups committed to the rape and murder of women who belong to other ethnic groups. In its nature of forcing submission by the threat or use of force, the treatment of enemies is analogous to rape (Reardon, 1985, p. 39).

National security defined as the defence of sovereignty is built into the constructions of masculinity (Peterson and Runyan, 1993, p. 36). National security reflects the impulse that produces the military dominant structures of organised violence controlled by the state. The history of nuclear development is an excellent example of a few men exercising power over many. The atomic bomb project is ripe with the images of masculine power and destruction. The masculinist bias steering the development of nuclear weapons was celebrated in the wide heroisation of such scientific 'nuclear fathers' as J. Robert Oppenheimer after World War II (Caputi, 1996, p. 134). The arms race and other national security priorities are generally accepted by the public under the influence of patriarchal military culture. In the name of national security, governments are allowed to manufacture and mismanage weapons without public knowledge as exemplified in testing nuclear weapons on human populations.

Feminine values broaden the concept of security by discussing who should be included in a security system and what factors and dimensions of security are important. First, a feminist world security system would attempt to include all peoples and all nations based on a notion of kinship extended to the entire human family. Second, the conceptual framework aims to embrace a broad, holistic definition that advocates the protection of life and enhancement of the quality of life (Reardon, 1990, p. 140).

In the feminine mode of viewing the world, an adversarial state-centric security system negatively affects the conditions for protecting the most fundamental roots of survival embodied in health and a decent quality of life. The military-dependent present world security system itself is seen as a major threat to humanity. The high cost of military spending puts a strain on meeting social and economic needs. In a framework that emphasises the feminine ethic of care, the economic and social consequences are not separated from security policies.

Feminist issues illustrate how violence is built into the hierarchical nature of our society. Militarism and war can be maintained only in a hierarchical organisation in which some give orders and others must follow them (Reardon, 1990, p. 142). Feminist peace perspectives challenge government policies and general public perception shaped by traditional concepts of security. From the masculine perspective, peace has meant the prevention of violence through institutional control; security is found in deterrence against aggression and defence of the homeland. On the contrary, the feminist security agenda seeks protection from organised state violence and the fulfilment of fundamental needs (Reardon, 1990, p. 139). Security also means individual well-being and personal safety in various social relationships, including family.

8   Political Economy

Providing basic economic necessities is essential to the fulfilment of survival needs. The failure to provide the means for physical survival is caused by certain economic policies and system characteristics. Economic disparities can be created by unequal decision-making power over the allocation of resources. Material benefits should be fairly shared to prohibit unnecessary human misery. The forces of socio-economic changes and the inability of existing structures to accommodate the demand for improvement in material well-being generate divisions in society. Free market values have not been compatible with economic equity and social justice. This chapter examines the nature of the modern political economy and its implications for social and international conflict.

Economic Disparities

The world is divided by income gaps between the rich and the poor. The increasing gap has been observed in the incomes of social categories on a global basis. The share of the income for the richest 20 percent of the world population expanded from 70 percent to 85 percent between 1960 and 1991 (Crosby and Van Soest, 1997, p. 9). In the U.S. where the distribution of wealth is the most uneven among industrialised countries, the income of the bottom 40 million Americans has not improved during the past decade. Many people do not command enough income to buy the bare necessities of life. Some 1.3 billion people on the earth have incomes of less than U.S. $150 per capita a year.

Rich industrialised countries have less than a quarter of the world's population but consume over three quarters of the goods produced in the world. However, the need for food and other basic economic necessities has not been met in many parts of the world. The number of people suffering from nutritional deprivation has steadily increased. Poor nutritional status and starvation caused by famine result in disease and mental apathy (UNICEF, 1998). Inadequate sewage and insufficient supply of water as well as malnutrition are responsible for early death and disease. Twenty percent of children in sub-Saharan Africa die before they become five years old (UNDP, 1992). In many poor countries, the populations also have a high level of illiteracy and lack a proper level of education. These miserable life conditions are attributed to the failure of economic systems.

Though there are different understandings about the process that creates inequality, income gaps, in general, have been growing fast in an unregulated free market economy combined with conventional growth strategies. Equitable global economic order is essential to producing opportunities for those who have been marginalised. The argument about narrowing the gap between the poor and the rich is not whether it is desirable, but largely about how it can be achieved.

Free Market Economy and Class Relations

Economic systems influence the distribution of wealth and power within and among nations. Enduring poverty would not be relieved through the logic of a free market economy. In the classic economic liberalism, a universally valid rule is that the good of all could only be achieved by self-regarding individualism and the pursuit of wealth. Whatever serves the prosperity of individuals is good for the whole society. Market exchange is supposed to satisfy the self-interests of individuals while providing a medium for benefiting all.

Since all must be free to engage in exchange of goods and services, the role of governments is to nurture a political environment for promoting a free market society and to protect the rights of private property. The political system should prevent the social control of economic activities. Freedom both in political and economic spheres is critical in innovation of entrepreneurship. Maximum efficiency in the utilisation of resources is guided by information about availability in the market. With the control of market values over economic activities, there is no concern about exploitation in neo-liberal politics (Carley and Christie, 1993, p. 89). It is often ignored that open competition favours those who set up the rules and have the ability to influence the system. Moral dimensions are certainly rejected in the social calculus of capitalist society.

Different forms of economic systems project unique conceptions of social order and political organisations (Cox, 1996, p. 527). Evolution of a free market economy and its social logic reflect a historical path of modern political economy. In Marxist interpretation, capitalism based on a free market mechanism is not just a way of organising an economy because a dominant class controls state, cultural and religious institutions to reinforce its superior economic position. Thus, capitalism represents a distinct system of values, social relations and structure of state associated with a particular mode of production.

Marxist Class Analysis Social structure is analysed in terms of relations between two antagonist classes--the proletariat and the bourgeoisie. The proletariat is comprised of workers who earn wages for their physical work. On the other hand, the bourgeois class monopolises capital needed to make investment in production. By paying less to workers than they deserve, the capitalist class takes the surplus value created by labour. Capitalists are not interested in the welfare of the working class but only in making profit for future investment. The concentration of the means of production in a few hands puts workers in a permanently disadvantageous position.

Divisions between antagonistic social forces reveal the contradictions of capitalism. In Marxist analysis, politics and culture are not separated from the economic domain. The notion of separation of economics and politics suggested by liberal thinking only mystifies the process of capitalist exploitation. Social harmony is not provided by a market since its competitive game makes only a few get richer. The two adversarial classes are locked in a win-lose zero-sum relationship due to their opposing economic interests.

Conflict derives from a clash between different socio-economic forces. The causes and driving forces of conflict are inequality in society; violence is the manifestation of this struggle. Class antagonism can be resolved through the achievement of an equal society that does not have an exploitative economic relationship. In considering that individual actions would be ineffective in fighting against a ruling class, building solidarity among the masses is important. The proletariat is recognised as the most critical social force in the struggle for achieving a classless and harmonious society. In Marxism, the political direction for uniting the working class in an organised manner has a firm social dimension in structural change.

International Capitalism and War

Many political economists suggest that peaceful international relations have not necessarily been advanced by economic growth. Colonialism arises from the need for the extraction of resources from abroad. Rivalry between colonial powers in the 19th and early 20th centuries represents the greed of capitalist expansion and militarism supported by it. The relationship between economic growth and international conflict has been explained by the necessity of industrial states to look for foreign markets and raw materials that are crucial for continuing prosperity.

More resources are demanded by rapid industrialisation combined with an increase in consumption and growing population. Demand for resources not available in the domestic arena creates pressure for access to external raw materials. Colonial expansion proceeds from the desire of political control over overseas resources following population pressure and resource scarcity. Competition by states that pursue access to overseas territories results in a high level of military spending and the creation of alliances. Reciprocal action by adversaries initiates conflict spirals that increase the probability of war. This model was applied to the analysis of the origins of World War I and the Japanese initiation of war against the U.S. during World War II (Choucri and North, 1975).

International conflict ascribed to the internal structural conditions of capitalist states was originally explained by John Hobson, the 19th century liberal British economist. He argued that the saturation of domestic economic activities produces pressure for expansionist policies in capitalism's defence (Hobson, 1988). The imperative to find markets for surplus goods arising from uncontrolled capitalist production and the necessity to compete for increased productivity result in imperialism. Competition between colonial powers in pursuit of foreign markets and raw materials is a driving force behind international conflict. War would not be eliminated without major changes in the economic structure.

The discussion about international capitalist expansion and war was further elaborated by Marxist-Leninist theories that attribute imperialism to the economic structure of capitalist states, which is crippled by the limitation of domestic consumption. The efforts to secure external markets for surplus products and investment of capital are supported by imperialist expansionism. Imperialism is the last and highly competitive stage of capitalism. The amalgamation between banking capital and industrial capital enables capitalist exploitation to move beyond national boundaries by means of capital exports. Workers in some sectors become materially well off due to foreign expansion with the internal consequences of restructuring the working class (Waters, 1995, p. 21).

In the Leninist view, an external outlet for surplus goods and financial investments is needed for the survival of capitalism. Imperialism is thus an inevitable outcome of the expansion of capitalism to the global scale (Lenin, 1939). It established the policy and practice of extending the rule of one country over another. The contradictions are inherent in international capitalism that promotes concentration of wealth in the hands of a few states and consequently the enrichment of one state at the expense of another. According to Vladimir Lenin, war will be ended in a classless society to be created by world revolution. The liberation of colonies is essential to world peace.

Economic Integration and Globalisation

Economic liberalists believe that free trade can bring prosperity to all. They preach that an unregulated global market is good for everyone, although some may reap benefits earlier than others. Markets are supposed to facilitate the cooperation of millions of people for their mutual benefit without coercion. One of the most distinctive characteristics of the last two decades is a trend toward global economic integration. Privatisation and deregulation, free from any form of state control, have been promoted by the emphasis on free market economy at both national and international levels. The increasing integration of the global economy was generated by the internationalisation of capitalism supported by the creation of new political alignments, transformation of social values and the acceleration of scientific and technological advances.

Successful adaptation to the competitive global economy is now the ultimate challenge to economic survival. Economic globalisation reduces the role of states to adjusting national policies to the dynamics of an unregulated global economy. The state mainly remains to enforce legal and political framework for a free market mechanism. Industrialised states have supported private enterprises by enforcing contracts and using an instrument of political leverage to impose market rules worldwide. On the other hand, the vulnerable elements of society have been further marginalised by the privatisation of many public economic functions. Distribution has not been a major concern in the process of economic globalisation based on a free market system supported by the spread of formal democracy since the 1980s.

Globalisation has produced both prosperous and marginalised economic sectors. Severe competition at international levels created not only well paid jobs in some sectors but also poor working conditions in others. Technology sectors are capable of producing a great variety of value added products in a more sophisticated consumer oriented market. Skilled core work forces have secure employment with excellent payment. However, traditional economic sectors hire many unskilled, low paid labour forces located in a multitude of production units spread across the globe. Multinational corporations have relocated their factories to take advantage of low-wage labour, taxation benefit and few environmental regulations. Poor women and children are working for multinational corporations whose production facilities moved to the Third World to avoid minimum wage requirements and other labour standards in their home countries.

In the global flows of foreign direct investment, people in developing countries have been getting a smaller share. Benefit has been very uneven in different production sectors. In the production of cheap consumer goods, competition pushes wages lower. In addition, the restructuring of industries undermined the power of labour in relation to capital (Cox, 1996, p. 531). The comparative advantage of cheap labour is found in the most aggressive and repressive states such as China, Malaysia and other newly developing countries that are leading exporters of consumer goods sold in North America and Europe. In these countries, labour discipline is tightly enforced, with severe limitation on workers' rights, to maintain political stability and support capital accumulation.

Social Transition

In a world in which affluence and poverty coexist, many poor countries are former European colonies and share experiences of years of exploitation and frustration with the dominant structure of international political economy (Arnold, 1994). In bringing about modern transformation, capitalism as a dominant institutional nexus has destroyed indigenous economies. Endogenous models of social change have been undermined by market forces.

In the Third World, traditions of sufficient economies have been pushed aside, local exchange relationships dissolved and collective forms of ownership broken up. The spread of markets into the domain of traditional life increased the number of households losing control over subsistence means in the process of being integrated into new economic relations. Commodity production pushes impoverished peasants, pasturalists and women to unproductive land.

Global economic expansion created conditions of social segregation and fragmentation within countries. Economic decisions are disentangled from family, gender and racial relations as well as cultural traditions (Houweling, 1996, p. 147). The incorporation into a cash economy leads to the devaluation of traditional productive activities of women (Cammack, P., et al., 1993, p. 214; Sylvester, 1990, p. 240). The price of economic marginalisation includes social polarisation and destruction of internal linkages. The absorption of agrarian communities into market economies generated wealth for some people who were able to accumulate land and power. The establishment of new centres of wealth goes hand in hand with the loss of control over subsistence means by many.

9   Environmental Concerns

'Only when the last tree has died and the last river been
poisoned and the last fish has been caught will we realise
we cannot eat money' (Comment from a member of
the Cree Nation on the environment and materialism).

Environmental problems emerged as a social and political issue in the late 1960s when the impact of industrialisation began to be felt around the world. The quality of life in many parts of the planet has deteriorated because of global environmental degradation. Greenhouse effects, severe river and ocean pollution, soil erosion and the deterioration of the major biological systems are related to the expansion of human activities. Deforestation contributes to the loss of biological diversity as well as climate changes. Industrial growth along with population explosion contributes to the imbalance between economic activities and nature. Dealing with diverse sources of global environmental problems has become an important security issue that concerns the protection of life on the planet.

Because of the decreasing amount of oceanic fisheries, grasslands, forests and croplands, renewable resource bases are shrinking. Acid rain caused by air pollution devastates crops and forests. Such human activities as intensive agricultural production exceed the capacity of the land for its renewal. Local environmental degradation such as soil erosion and desertification is especially severe in developing countries. Global food insecurity has been created by a shift from a variety of indigenous food crops to imported food like wheat and rice following a transfer of cropland from subsistence production to cash crop production. In addition, energy and other resource bases have become a pressing issue. Oil and coal have been supplemented by the use of nuclear energy. However, nuclear accidents at Three Mile Island in the U.S. (1979) and Chernobyl in the former Soviet Union (1986) demonstrated the possibility of a catastrophic nuclear accident. On the other hand, development of renewable natural energy sources has shown to be a very time consuming process.

Unsustainable economic growth diminishes the earth's long-term capacity to support life. Examining the causes of global climate change, acid rain, air pollution and other problems is helpful for exploring strategies to deal with them. At the same time, it is important to recognise that poverty and inequality are deepened by worsening environmental conditions. Sharing and managing natural resources is critical for the future survival of various communities. Land degradation and deterioration of other resource bases can provoke conflict and war especially in a society that has deep social and political divisions.

Changes in the Environmental System

The total earth system is comprised of the geosphere (rocks, oceans, rivers, lakes, the atmosphere, soils and ice) and the biosphere constituting the earth's integrated life support system (Manshard, 1998, p. 56). The ecosystem to support human life has been threatened by global warming, ozone depletion, deforestation, distortion of bio-diversity with the elimination of species, exploitative use of land, pollution of the sea and shortage of water.

Global Warming

Increases in planetary temperature raise the sea level in some parts of the world (created by melting land ice and polar ice caps), especially coastal areas, while causing drought in other parts. Global warming, associated with greenhouse effects, is caused by an accumulation of mostly carbon dioxide and other gases such as methane and nitrogen oxide in the atmosphere. Because the increased level of carbon dioxide prohibits the earth's heat from being re-radiated into space, the earth's atmosphere functions like the glass of a greenhouse. Thus, climate change is attributed to heat trapped in the atmosphere.

Currently more carbon is released than is used by the planet. About two thirds of the planet's excess carbon comes from the burning of fossil fuels by automobiles and industry. It is also increased by the destruction of the world's forests that have the capacity to naturally remove carbon from the atmosphere. Deforestation is responsible for between one-quarter and one-third of the carbon dioxide added to the atmosphere. At the current level of atmospheric pollution, carbon dioxide levels will double before the middle of the 21st century.

Ozone Depletion

The increased levels of harmful solar rays are caused by ozone destruction. Ozone in the atmosphere, a thin gas layer between 10 and 50 kilometres above the earth's surface, protects life on earth by absorbing excessive ultraviolet radiation before it reaches the ground. Gases such as chlorofluorocarbons (CFCs) used as coolants in refrigerators, solvents in industry and propellants in aerosol sprays contribute to the destruction of stratospheric ozone. CFCs and other gases remain for 100 years or more, each molecule acting and reacting repeatedly to break down the ozone (UN Chronicle, 1992, p. 51). The ozone layer above the Antarctic has become thin and has a large hole. A higher rate of lethal mutations in humans, animals and plants is ascribed to the rapidly disappearing ozone over highly populated areas.

Loss of Biological Diversity

Bio-diversity constitutes 'the abundant variety and variability of living organisms' that have evolved over the past three million years (Manshard, 1998, p. 61). The impact of deforestation, desertification, pollution, overfishing and overgrazing on the ecosystem threatens our planetary biodiversity. The planet now loses about one species every hour whereas fewer than 10 species became extinct each year over the last six hundred thousand years (UN Chronicle, 1992, p. 52). The loss of forests directly affects the world's biological diversity, causing mass extinction of huge numbers of plants and animals. A thousand hectares of rainforest can contain up to the following number of species: 1,500 flowering plant, 750 tree, 400 bird, 150 butterfly, 125 mammal, 100 reptile and 50 amphibian (Litvinoff, 1990, p. 240).

In rural communities, people make use of the earth's bio-diversity directly, exploiting many different species for food, fuel and raw materials. Furthermore, natural vegetation protects and sustains their land and water supplies. When rural people lose species, their welfare is devastated. Local fishing communities have long lived in harmony with the environment, producing food for both themselves and towns inland. In contrast, large-scale commercial fisheries tend to over-harvest marine resources for making a profit. Whales, dolphins, seals and polar bears have all been threatened by pollution and the over-exploitation of marine resources. Protecting diverse species is important to the enrichment of human civilisation as well as the maintenance of sustainable economic life. The welfare of future generations depends on the preservation of biological diversity.

Deforestation

Forests prevent soil erosion and provide one of nature's principle means of water management. Deforestation contributes to pollution of rivers and creeks and the loss of wild species as well as global warming. It is especially alarming that since the 1950s about half of the earth's tropical rainforests along with the largest reserves of seasonal forests have disappeared. Inadequate monitoring of commercial logging has devastated rainforests in Malaysia and Indonesia that export hardwood timber to earn foreign currency. In addition, the construction of large dams and the extraction of minerals and metals lead to destruction of the forests.

Another source for the destruction of the rain forests is economic activities related to population growth and the food requirements of cattle, goats and other livestock. The conversion of forests to agricultural land and pastures has been accelerated by land resettlement schemes for poor people from overcrowded regions. Amazon forests, which represent the most ecologically complex vegetarian formulations on the planet, have been damaged by Brazilian government policies to build highways and move settlers as well as tax incentives and subsidies to engage in cattle ranching. The clearing of land for the ranching and production of export crops has also been an important cause of tropical deforestation in Central America. Over the last several decades, more than 40 percent of the forest cover was lost with the area of pastureland and the number of beef cattle being more than doubled.

Soil Erosion

Poorly managed agriculture is directly responsible for soil erosion and desertification. Over-cropping, overgrazing and vegetation destruction, combined with excessive use of water, ploughs and fires, can erode, in a few years, soil that has taken a few million years to form. The world may have lost 10 million hectares of cultivated land. Developing countries lost 40 percent of their arable land between 1970 and 1990. In particular, soil erosion and desertification are observed in large parts of Africa. The only way to ensure sustainable use of land and natural resources is through a radical rethinking of the intensive agricultural practice and the role of land in the development process.

Water Pollution and Shortage

The scarcity and misuse of fresh water pose a serious threat to human health, welfare, food security and the entire ecosystem. 'About 1.2 billion people – over a quarter of the world's population – lack clean and safe water while 1.8 billion people live without adequate sanitation' (UN Chronicle, 1992, p. 60). As much as two-thirds of Africa may be subject to drought each year. Population growth in regions of limited natural water supply such as the Middle East, parts of Central America and North Africa has resulted in serious water shortages.

Contaminated water is responsible for a third of all deaths and 80 percent of all disease in developing countries (UN Chronicle, 1992, p. 60). Toxic chemicals and waste as well as atmospheric pollution have a major impact on the quality of water, as do agricultural use and deforestation. Sewage and toxic waste are also often dumped directly into the sea. Marine pollution is further exacerbated by shipping and sea-based activities.

Population Growth

There is a tension between population growth and the ecological system. According to many observers, global environmental problems are unlikely to be solved without stabilisation of the world population (Ayres, 1998, p. 5). The world population had more than tripled from 1.6 billion to 5.3 billion between 1890 and 1990. During the increase of the world population from 2.5 billion in 1950 to 6 billion in 2000, about 95 percent of the population growth took place in the developing world. Rapid population growth puts stress on the planet's ability to renew its resources. A rising expectation of a growing world population results in more fossil fuel burning as well as increasing consumption of scarce resources. In the United States and other industrialised countries, the consumption of resources has been made as if they were unlimited.

In many Third World countries, the population increase outstrips economic growth with the consequence of declining per capita income and deteriorating living standards. Developing countries account for more than three-quarters of the world's population while only earning 15 percent of global income. The poverty related to population increase in underdeveloped countries results in severe environmental degradation. Deforestation, desertification, air pollution, soil and water degradation have contributed to the deterioration of the quality of life of the poor in the South. Hundreds of millions poor people are forced to overgraze land and plunder forests. Cutting rainforests in South America, Southeast Asia and other parts of the world for maintaining exports to support consumption for the growing population will eventually endanger global living conditions through climate changes.

Rapid population growth pushes economic and natural resource limits. Malthus argued two centuries ago that population growth would arithmetically outstrip increases in the food supply. *The Limits to Growth* (Meadows et al., 1972) sponsored by the Club of Rome predicts unstable future trends related to the impact of accelerating industrial activities along with rapid population growth on food supply and non-renewable resource bases. Intense industrial and other human activities combined with growing population will put severe strain on the environment's ability to support human economic activities and to absorb pollution. In a neo-Malthusian interpretation, the world will increasingly face crises and conflicts generated by fast-growing populations competing for declining resources as well as massive urbanization, migration pressures and reduced government capacity (Myers, 1993).

The number of people who can be supported by a territory's resource base is limited. Unless consumption level per capita is reduced, more people simply means increasing pressure on a wide variety of environmental resources (Grubb, et al., 1993, p. 30). The carrying capacity indicates the number of people an area can support without compromising its ability to do so in the future. An excessive carrying capacity is attributed to the growing population combined with limitations on the growth of natural resources. Nature's ability to satisfy the demand for more resources is limited.

The planet is gradually moving toward overloading the carrying capacity with a rapidly growing population. Dwindling natural resource bases are well indicated by the decline in global per capita production of several basic commodities since the late 1960s and the 1970s. The yields of wood peaked in 1967, fish in 1970, oil in 1973 and grains in 1978. Prevailing economic activities are averse to the efforts to reverse the trend toward resource depletion. Present consumption and production seriously hamper the long-term ability to support the region's resource bases for future generations.

Tragedy of the Commons

The movement of water and air does not differentiate between national borders. As one great, interrelated system, the environment is not under national sovereignty. The oceans and outer space have been treated as 'commons' whose ownership is shared. Anyone's claim of ownership over the global commons considered as the public good has no legitimacy. Often the irresponsible use of the commons has created damage to the environment that belongs to others. Transboundary air pollution contributes to the disappearance of aquatic life in lakes and rivers and widespread harm to forests (Soroos, 1995, p. 299). Scandinavian forests and lakes suffer from acid rain caused by industrial pollution in other parts of Europe.

The management of the oceans has been an international concern. The world's seawater, covering three quarters of the planet's surface, plays a critical role in the life-sustaining processes of our planet. For years, waste and chemicals have been dumped into the seas with very little thought about the eventual consequences (Switzer, 1994, p. 244). The oceans are also a vast source of food and mineral resources. Antarctica is believed to have abundant mineral resources. Gold, silver and uranium are said to be buried offshore and oil reserves beneath the Antarctic Peninsula. Attention has been drawn to regulating access to the common resource domain.

Unregulated resources tend to become over-utilized, and it leads to the destruction of conditions for sustainable management. This situation is often called the tragedy of the commons. The concept was originally taken from an old English village example in which herdsmen once overgrazed their cattle on the commonly owned land (Hardin, 1968). Villagers were allowed to raise privately owned cattle in a pasture open to public use. The arrangement will work only when the number of cattle is relatively small enough not to exceed the capacity of the pasture to nourish them. Without any binding agreement, herdsmen tend to increase the size of their herd (as much as possible) beyond the limited carrying capacity to maximize their personal profit. The effects of overgrazing to the point where all the herds would starve with the deterioration of the pasture result in the shared loss of the entire community.

If community members pursue their own self-interest in seeking to maximise advantage, soon nothing will be left. In this situation, individuals engage in behaviour that is to the disadvantage of everyone. Short-term selfish benefit conflicts with long-term public good that can be shared by all. The rational pursuit of economic self-interest results in overexploitation of common resources followed by the eventual destruction of the commons.

Incentives for the resource abuse to individual advantages grow with the absence of individual ownership (Hardin, 1968, p. 1244).

The depletion of natural resources and ecological pollution derive from competitive abuse not controlled by community norms. For example, the unregulated hunting of whales in the oceans until the recent decade led them to the edge of extinction. Fish swim freely beyond artificial national jurisdictions, and overfishing creates tension between coastal states that wish to utilise them. Eventually access to the commons has to be regulated to prevent conflict over their use. Definite social arrangements enable the community to put a limit on private greed to protect the common good. Part of individual rights has to be given up to maintain shared resources.

Resource Scarcity and Conflict

Violent conflict may arise from competition for limited or inequitably distributed resources. Threats to subsistent life caused by resource scarcity increase the probability of social unrest and war. The peasant majority is pushed to the most ecologically vulnerable land while the top two percent of the total population controls more than 60 percent of land in Brazil. The struggle for access to land has been one of the main causes of civil war in El Salvador and other Central American countries (Weinberg, 1991).

Especially in many regions of the world where resources are not able to support the population, efforts to assert or prevent control over fertile cropland, forests and water create conditions for inter-state conflict. The water conflict between Israelis and Arabs is related to the use of the River Jordan. In another example, Bangladesh disputed India's plan to build a dam to divert water from the upper Ganges (Miall, 1992, p. 157).

Competition for scarce resources in overcrowded regions produces a volatile social situation for group conflict (Homer-Dixon, 1994). In particular, deteriorating resource bases coupled with rapidly growing population exacerbate the existing tension. Population dislocation can be caused by such environmental changes as deforestation, desertification, drought, soil erosion and floods. In Africa, for instance, desertification has been a driving force behind the movement of ecological refugees across national borders. The population influx exceeding the capacity of the host environment contributes to group competition along with unequal access to scarce resources.

Heightened ethnic and religious tensions, therefore, can arise from social stress following environmental degradation. Political asymmetry aggravates economic marginalisation caused by declining resource bases. Political elites often seek to promote particular interests, often by manipulating the opportunities for organised violence (Macrae and Zwi, 1994, p. 8). Intense group identities are felt with the rising level of grievance. The political mobilisation of groups is one of the final steps for widespread civil violence in the long chain of environmentally induced conflict.

The weak state capacity to handle economic problems deepens fragmentation between groups. Increases in demand from various groups have put pressure on financial resources of the government. Failure or incapacity of the government to respond to demands from marginalised groups lends support to insurgencies that challenge the legitimacy of the state.

Whereas the occurrence of certain violent conflicts can be affected by group dynamics associated with resource scarcity and its unequal distribution, environmental degradation can be a necessary, but not sufficient, condition for violence (Jeong, 1999c). Resource conflict can be peacefully settled in some societies without erupting in civil strife. Political and economic structures as well as social processes are important intermediary variables in linking environmental degradation to the mobilisation of discontented social groups.

Environmental Security

Traditionally, the control of resources for strategic purposes has been an important national security concern. Recently efforts have been concentrated on identifying the types of environmental change that might present a national security threat, more specifically, internal or interstate violence. National security can obviously be enhanced by mitigating 'the social and political impacts of environmental scarcity of resources' (Moss, 1993, p. 27). However, adding an environmental pillar to a national security agenda 'does not imply that policy makers abandoned the traditional notions of security based on the use of force if necessary to preserve vital interests' (Zebich-Knos, 1998, p. 31).

Environmental degradation needs to be considered in a more integrative concept of global security. Environmental pollution has become an important common security issue with the recognition that the environment provides the fundamental life-support system. The ecological conceptions of security can be extended to structural dimensions such as environmental sustainability and societal vulnerability.

Security for the planet depends on the structure of the whole system while the conventional concept of security has exclusive concerns for the national level. Peace on the earth cannot be realised without ecological balance. Any attachment to the nation-state and the conventional doctrine of security presents an obstacle to sustainable management of the environment. In fact, the environment was brutalised by such violent tactics of warfare as scorched-earth campaigns. Resources devoted to building military capabilities can be used more productively to diminish security threats arising from environmental degradation.

The essential components of peace should lie in co-operation for the common good, based on the concept of equity and harmony among people who depend on the earth for their survival. Most importantly, ecological security can encompass the Gaia notion of the earth as a living functional unit that seeks optimal physical and chemical conditions for life through a feedback process between the biosphere, atmosphere, oceans and soil (Lovelock, 1987).

In environmental perspectives, security problems have to be interpreted by the way societies are organised and connected to the natural world. The main source of threat is the vulnerability of modern industrialism associated with dependence on foreign trade, large-scale technology, extreme urbanisation, excessive centralisation and bureaucratic control. In order to eliminate the ecological threats we must develop a sustainable society.

The protection of the local as well as the global environment must be integral to the development process throughout our increasingly interdependent world. Sustainability cannot be achieved in one country, since ecological problems do not recognise any borders. Sustainable development becomes a goal, not just for the developing nations, but for industrial ones as well.

The ecological threats are clearly related to the conventional paradigm of development that emphasises industrialisation. Concerns with ecological degradation and resource depletion raise doubt about the desirability and inevitability of economic growth. Both the consumption-oriented wealth of the industrialized world and the poverty of the developing world are leading to environmental destruction. The destroyed environment, in turn, can ruin prospects for the future development of the rich and poor alike.

Environmental security reflects the interconnectedness of various dimensions of peace issues. A demand for cheap beef to be supplied for hamburger restaurants in North America leads to clearing tropical forests for grazing cattle, consequently contributing to global warming. On the other hand, tribal groups were driven out of their land by violent means. Poverty in Central America along with unequal land distribution is thus directly connected to people in the North through their consumption patterns.

PART III

STRATEGIES
FOR PEACE

In this section, various peace strategies are introduced to explore conditions both for preventing war and eliminating other types of violence. Pursuing peace requires various means, including a reduction in the destructive capability of human society, peaceful settlement of disputes, the denial of violence, changes in political and social institutions, international cooperation in global problem solving, economic equity and ecological protection. These issues are discussed in the following chapters. In Control of Military Power, the main topics are how to avoid war, reduce violent conflict and improve security for individuals and groups. Conflict Resolution illustrates methods and techniques needed for peaceful solutions to problems.

Human Rights focuses on the protection of individuals from state repression, social discrimination and other types of oppression rooted in social and political structures. Self-Determination stresses group autonomy and protection of community life from external domination. Poverty, international debts and other economic problems have become pressing issues in the age of global economic integration. How to reduce the gap between the poor and the rich and how to guarantee human welfare are dealt with in Development. Environmental Politics explains ways to build a more ecologically sustainable society, and features the need to protect the global commons from overexploitation attributed to human greed.

Global Order and Governance illuminates diverse proposals for restructuring the existing political order, ranging from a world government to a decentralised communal structure. In Nonviolence, the use of violence is denied for moral and political reasons, but it also has some practical strategic advantages in struggle against oppressors. Peace Movements discuss the role of ordinary citizens in changing government policies on war, militarism and social injustice. The significance of orientation to peace values is recognised in many social movements.

10   Control of Military Power

The main subjects in the control of military power are how to deter aggression and what kinds of ideas for preventing war have been proposed and practiced. Political elites have long tried to diminish the uncertainty stemming from uncontrolled military competition between states. No system of world order is possible without some form of control over aggressive behaviour of one state against another. Balance of power and collective security have long been discussed as a traditional means to prevent major wars between states. Peace keeping applied widely over the last several decades is designed to control the escalation of military conflict. The priority of non-provocative defence, often supported by civilian based defence, is to protect human life in case of foreign invasion. Disarmament is to build trust and confidence in peace by reducing and eventually removing deadly weapons. Demilitarisation of economic and social systems proceeds from the conversion of military industries, research and functions to productive activities promoting human welfare.

Balance of Power

Balance of power means that the power relationship between states and groups of states resembles one of approximate or precise equilibrium so that one side does not have a decisive advantage over the other in military strength. The proponents of balance of power assume that stability in international society can exist only if there is an equal power relationship. Since predominant power increases incentives to initiate war, unbalanced power relations are dangerous to a stable international order. The stronger power may tend to dominate, conquer, oppress and destroy other countries. Carefully managed power relationships between opposing forces reduces the temptation to go to war in the hope of achieving dominance. Diplomatic manoeuvring is made along with calculations of the relative war potential of the states. The survival of a state depends on the elite's strategic decision-making capacity in building an alliance system. Social and economic aspects of security relations are neglected with the overemphasis on military power.

System Characteristics

Interstate relations are defined in terms of the distribution of national capabilities within the international system. Irrespective of the presence or absence of common values and norms, each state's behaviour and strategies in the system are driven by power maximisation. The continued expansion of one state's military power is challenged by an adversarial state's military expansion and other measures of suitable counter alliance. Order is maintained by counterbalancing acts against the efforts of other states that pursue military superiority. War can be prevented in the process of managing power relations when the action of one state is neutralised by reaction from other states.

The status quo is reinforced by competition and balancing acts which endlessly reproduce existing power relations (Miller, 1992). On the other hand, a balance of power 'is never a static phenomenon and can never be taken for granted' (Sheehan, 1996, p. 14). In order to avert the danger of unfavourable power distribution, states, in essence, seek a margin of strength to the point of destabilisation. However, international politics has, in the end, an inherent tendency to restore equilibrium regardless of the intentions of each actor. A system of checks and balances maintained by shifting alliances does not allow the emergence of a preponderant military power. Thus, an even balance of power comes into being as a by-product of competitive striving for a favourable power balance. Successful management of power relations can be attributed to the creation of an inter-state system that prevents any state from winning a war.

A balance of power is managed by an alliance system in which states can enhance their power not only by the natural method of building up their own resources but also by an artificial method of linking themselves to the strength of other states. The balance desired is one that neutralises other states, leaving the home state free to be the deciding force. Here military instruments are crucial in re-arranging a new balance in power relations.

Concerns about survival in an anarchic international order motivate a state to prevent military domination by another state. In a multi-state system, the safest rule is to confront power with countervailing power. Stability of inter-state relations based on the protection of national rights and interests demands the neutralisation of a dominant power by an equivalent power. A law of states exists only if there is equilibrium among them.

For the smooth operation of the system, actors in the international system should share the same type of assessment and perception and be aware of each other's aspirations and policy goals. Perceived power relations determine the stability or instability of the international system because a credible balance of power cannot be objectively calculated. States need to make coherent, rational, egotistic calculations in a system of strategic interdependence. A certain level of coordination reduces the risks of uncertainty. Cooperation is based on the pursuit of common interests in maintaining the status quo. As a result, violent international conflict can be controlled and managed.

Operational Principles

There are conditions under which the balance of power can be more easily formed. First, it needs a decentralised system that does not have a superior agency controlling inter-state relations. The diffusion of power among a substantial number of major states allows constituent units to have their own policy without external control. In order to be able to manipulate power relations, independent states operate autonomously. Members of a military alliance should be equal in their political influence.

Second, the flexibility of the alliance technique can be fully utilised when decision-making power remains in the hands of a small number of political leaders and strategists. National interests are prioritised in a way to enhance power and stability. In power calculations, policy makers ought to be free from public opinion and have the political will to ignore pressure from interest groups. Domestic policies are clearly separated from foreign policies by limiting the impact of the former on the latter.

Third, rational calculation takes place within the rules of the game not to undermine the fabric of a stable power system. This allows a measurable or comparable appreciation of capabilities in terms of military power as well as economic and natural resources (Doyle, 1994, pp. 139-40). Skilled professional management of the diplomatic game is largely free to manipulate alignments and adjust policy to challenges and opportunities. It requires not only competition but also cooperation. The sense of common interest in preserving the system should also moderate hegemonic ambitions.

Leaders have to be aware that a continuous drive for a preponderance of power would yield an undesirable outcome given the measures taken by other players to compensate for the aggressive move. Hegemonic ambitions can be restrained by technological impediments to universal conquest. In case any power adjustment is needed, war should be manageable and controllable.

Fourth, there should be no ideological impediments to arrangements for the adjustment of power relations. A relative homogeneity of domestic structures among the leading members of the system is helpful for building an alliance system. The balancing process was not easy in the ideological divides between capitalism and communism in the 1920s and the 1930s or in threats posed by the religious rivalry between Protestants and Catholics in the sixteenth century.

Fifth, it is desirable that a major power should be in a position to hold the balance by committing its strengths in support of weak alliances. The preferences and behaviour of states and their interactions can be explained by the sociology of the balance of power. The balancer state can be motivated to take responsibility for maintaining an equal distribution of power because of political prestige and other advantages. Allowing the emergence of preponderant power is in no one's interest, and a balancer's power can be used to frustrate the ambition of hegemonic power.

Historical Examples

Though many small wars were allowed to happen, the balance of power system during the period from 1815 to 1914 more or less sustained peace among the great powers. The Concert of Europe served as an informal institution that allowed the five great European powers, Austria, France, Great Britain, Prussia and Russia, to manage the balance of power system. The pervasive effects of anarchy that could have turned small disturbances into major wars have been moderated by the power arrangements. The alliance of France and Russia at the end of the nineteenth century was formed to prevent the domination of Germany. The balance of power discouraged any desire of Germany to dominate the whole European continent.

The stability in Europe during this period is attributed to the existence of several conditions that are essential to the maintenance of the balance of power. First, no hegemonic power dominated other countries with superior military strength, given that power relations were decentralised in nineteenth century Europe. Germany was relatively stronger than France and Russia separately, but it did not outweigh the combined power of the two. Second, each state within the alliance system was able to move freely to one side or the other. So, a calculated management of military power relations was possible.

Third, there was no ideological impediment in diplomatic relations, and different types of political rule did not affect the formation of an alliance system. Policy makers in France and Russia were willing to ignore the differences in their political systems and were free to act in accordance with the logic of balance of power. Their main foreign policy objective was to prevent German domination in Europe. Despite the differences between absolute monarchies and parliamentary monarchies, both systems rested on an aristocratic, landlord-dominated society as well as a shared transnational culture in Europe and a common heritage of Christianity and Greco-Roman civilisation that provided a shared set of assumptions about values, norms and standards of taste (Doyle, 1994, p. 142).

The balance of power system based on power calculations also worked effectively in the eighteenth century. Counter hegemonic balancing efforts were made between the Peace of Utrecht (1713) and the outbreak of the French Revolution (1789). French King Louis XIV's first bid for hegemony ended in 1713 when a coalition of Britain, Austria and Holland imposed the Peace of Utrecht. In 1756, however, Austria switched from its long tradition of enmity toward France and joined with her and Russia in a war against the upstart Prussia. Britain correspondingly shifted its traditional continental alliance from Austria to Prussia, in part to reduce the threat to her vulnerable Hanoverian dependency, but also and more importantly because Austria was no longer prepared to balance against France, Britain's major rival (Doyle, 1994, p. 151).

In spite of its success in maintaining stable relations within a traditional international system in the previous centuries, the balance of power in the European continent did not prohibit the First World War. In fact, in this case the alliance system facilitated the escalation of local conflicts into a major war. When Austria decided to go to war against Serbia, it was difficult for Russia not to support its ally Serbia, which was weaker than its adversary. To prevent Russia's domination, in turn, Germany intervened on the side of Austria. Then France, a bitter enemy of Germany, declared war to upset the German/Austrian alliance. The fear of German domination in the European continent finally brought England into the war. Though not intended, the escalation spiral of conflict between two countries in Europe, Serbia and Austria (caused by the miscalculation of political leaders) culminated in the first major war on a global scale.

Weaknesses

As long as the international system remains an anarchy where states have to provide their own device for security, some would still see the utility of balance of power, though the actual play of the game in the future would be different from the past (Snyder, 1993, pp. 16-7). Balance of power thinking reflects the realist worldview that discounts any claim to system wide international order other than that based on force or economic capabilities to strengthen military power. The balance of power system has been considered appropriate under a condition of anarchy that places all states in a warlike situation of reciprocal insecurity. The paradox is that state security must be provided by the pursuit of greater military strength that in turn makes other states insecure. It assumes that state actors differ only in military, economic and diplomatic capabilities but not in their desires for and goals of maintaining their independence and autonomy. They are functionally similar in their efforts to achieve stable power relations (Doyle, 1994, p. 140).

While balance of power is designed to keep an international order, it can be an ineffective means to prevent war. The alliance system is unstable in managing adversary relations between states. The competition between rival states can be unnecessarily fuelled by foreign intervention, arms supplies and alliances. The system may have to be maintained through the repeated resort to military force. Especially, the cost of modern war caused by advanced technology makes the balance of power outdated in the age of nuclear weapons. The relationship between peace and balance of power has been rather contradictory. Peace is considered only in terms of status quo of an existing order in balance of power. However, the former ultimately has to be obtained through the elimination of a dominant system while the latter's main concern is with system stability and maintenance through distribution of power among states (Wagner, 1993, p. 248).

Collective Security

Collective security emphasises the idea of guaranteeing international security through military domination based on the assumption that peace can be preserved by a decisive preponderance of power. The international community pledges to defend member states under attack with all necessary forces. If the force available to the possible aggressor is to be overwhelmed by collective opposition, then no country could dominate the whole system. Given the required readiness and ability to resort to collective violence, military strength is indispensable in maintaining peace.

Goals and Functions

In collective security, as opposed to making alliances in a decentralised power system, the states in an international system make an agreement in advance to deter aggression of one state against another. Collective security imposes the values of all community members on those who threaten peace. The universal coalition would punish any aggressor in defence of the victims. This can remove the vulnerability of small states in an anarchistic world order. War can be eliminated by enhancing deterrence without uncertainty; collective power needs to be mobilised in the case of any aggression. Collaboration demands a very high degree of institutionalisation of collective security measures.

Theoretically, collective security has advantages over balance of power policy under anarchy. The security mechanism relying on collective power strengthens deterrence by reducing the uncertainties of coalition formation. In balance of power, a state contemplating aggression is uncertain about the military strength of an opponent's coalition. In collective security, however, aggressors face the prospect of preponderant, rather than roughly equal, opposing force (Kupchan, 1994, p. 45). Thus, the reduction in uncertainty decreases the chances of misperceptions.

In collective security, there is no advanced designation of a putative enemy, as is the case with defensive alliances. In fact, collective security, directed against any prospective aggressor, is contrasted with alliances that have been formed to challenge particular enemies. The presumption in collective security is that any member state of the system may behave in such an aberrant manner that corrective measures would be required (Gordenker and Weiss, 1993, p. 7).

The assumptions of preponderant force as the response to a violation of international peace can be confirmed if the collective security system really represents a deterrent to unacceptable aggressive behaviour. Collective security postulates that the use of violence or other threats to peace would result in the mobilisation of forces so great that no reasonable policy makers would undertake such action. Thus, there is an expectation that given the ability of all governments to make rational calculations, a successful system would never actually need to resort to force (Gordenker and Weiss, 1993, p. 6). The logic of collective security is based on the deterrent effects of aggregate, preponderant power (Claude, 1971, p. 256).

The theory of collective security also assumes that all states share a primary interest in maintaining peace. In order for collective security to operate, peace should be viewed as inseparable, and threats to peace anywhere must be treated as the concern of the international system. All members must react promptly and effectively against threats to peace. Peace can be immediately restored through the mechanism by which the aggressor state will face overwhelming opposition from all other members of the system.

There are some necessary conditions for the effective operation of collective security. First, the states should subordinate other goals of foreign policy to collective security. To preserve peace, each state has to be ready to give up their independent control of action to support collective security arrangements. Each state must act in coordination with other states to restore peace rather than continue to maintain relationships with the state accused of any aggression. Sanctions against an aggressor state would be effective only if collective security measures are supported by every state, especially larger powers. Collective security requires states to commit themselves to an inflexible course of action that is insensitive to the context and self-interest.

Second, member states should find consensus in each situation that a threat to peace or a breach of peace does or does not exist. Furthermore, the consensus also must include the identification of the aggressor state or states against whom collective action is applied. Third, collective security, like balance of power, will work best if power is widely dispersed. No country should be able to match the combined power of member states. Military alliances of blocs of states have to dissolve in order to promote international security.

Origins and Applications

The roots of the concept of collective security are at least as old as the Amphictyonic League created by Greek city-states for protection. Over several centuries, a long series of proposals were made for preventing any state from using coercive means to gain advantage by the collective action of the governments of all states. In fact, the core concept of collective security that an attack on one is an attack on all can be found as early as 1454 in the pact for the Most Holy League of Venice and later in the 1518 Treaty of London and in the better-known Treaty of Munster of 1648 (part of the Peace of Westphalia).

The modern idea of collective security is based on the requirement of coexistence between sovereign states and the generally accepted values of the international community. Since World War I, the pitfalls of balance of power generated support for the ideas of collective security. The first attempt to build a collective security system worldwide was made by the establishment of the League of Nations in 1919. The ideas of collective security are also echoed in Chapter I, Article 1 of the United Nations Charter, which stipulates that effective collective measures are required to prevent and remove threats to peace and suppress acts of aggression.

If peace is threatened, steps can gradually escalate from the enforcement of diplomatic pressure to the imposition of economic sanctions to full fledged military action. The League of Nations Covenant and the UN Charter mention, as coercive methods to punish an aggressor, diplomatic, economic, financial and communications sanctions as well as the use of armed forces. Non-military sanctions can precede the actual use of force or accompany it to make military action more effective. Article 16 of the League covenant stipulates that the members were obligated to sever all trade and financial relations with the aggressor in accordance with recommendations of the League Council and contribute armed forces to international military actions to be undertaken against the aggressor.

The UN Charter provides the authority structure for decision-making and rules by which armed forces can be committed to collective security response. Chapter IV of the Charter accords the Security Council the role of determining the existence of aggression or other breaches of the peace and deciding measures to be taken by members of the UN. The effective system of collective security would require an executive structure. A Military Staff Committee was originally planned to assist and advise the Security Council in the organisation of international armed forces. Procedures for establishing the Committee never materialised during the early years of the Cold War. Since the UN itself does not have an institutionalised military capacity, large-scale military enforcement would not be implemented under the current organisational structure. In the absence of stand-by forces, contributions from member states are essential. Unless powerful states show interest in mobilising their own forces, the decision on military action would be ineffective.

Past Experiences

Overall, the record of collective security in the twentieth century has not been impressive. The League of Nations failed to apply collective security measures. When the Japanese invaded Manchuria in 1931, an investigation was conducted but no sanctions were taken. Italy's attack on Ethiopia in 1936 led League members to agree on an embargo on arms and on financial aid to Italy. However, these were not completely implemented, and sanctions did not have much impact on Italy's military capacity. There was no sanction on Germany's occupation of Austria and Czechoslovakia in 1938. When Japan began its further conquest of Chinese territory in 1937, the League condemned Japanese action but no wide spread sanctions were imposed.

The credibility of the League system was hurt by the fact that the United States was not even a member. On the other hand, policies and actions of other principal powers that were official members of the League were based on their geopolitical calculations. France was more concerned with supporting its Eastern European allies to deter Germany, and the United Kingdom refused to honour their collective security obligations. Priority was given to national interests rather than collective security concerns. The principle of solidarity did not exist due to deep suspicion by member states.

When the United Nations was created after World War II, key provisions were made to deal with the weaknesses of the League system. The Security Council is supposed to control military security matters. Veto power over security decisions was given to the five great powers, including Britain, the United States, Russia, France and China. However, practices of collective security have not greatly improved under the UN, either, due to a lack of great power cooperation. In many instances, the system was paralysed by Cold War rivalry.

The United Nations did agree on military intervention during the Korean War. The agreement was made possible since the Soviet Union temporarily walked out of the Security Council in protest and could not participate in voting. While the legality of the action was challenged by Russia, UN collective security measures legitimised the retaliation of the U.S. and its allies against North Korea in 1950. The Korean War was pursued as part of American foreign policy to contain the spread of communism in East Asia.

An example of the application of collective security in the post-Cold War environment was the action taken in response to Iraq's invasion of Kuwait in 1990. No major powers exercised their veto on decisions regarding the employment of coercive means to liberate Kuwait from Iraq between 1990 and 1991. The measures included economic sanctions, a territorial blockade and ultimately air, naval and ground warfare.

The United States organised and led the coalition of both Western powers and some moderate Arab states to restore the sovereignty of Kuwait. The primary motivation was the Western governments' will to maintain their geostrategic influence in the Arab region rather than genuine concern with international peace. The action was instigated to ensure the stable supply of crude oil, which is essential to protecting the economic interests of the United States and other industrialised nations. Therefore, the war over Kuwait is a misleading guide to future collective action (Lipson, 1994, p. 111).

In the past, ad hoc coalitions were formed to carry out actual warfare against 'aggressors' (North Korea and Iraq), though these actions took place under the UN authorisation and general political oversight. In the rare case of using collective security measures against internal aggression, the North Atlantic Treaty Organisation (NATO) made a unilateral decision on bombing Serbia to force them to accept international monitoring forces in Kosovo following tense ethnic relations and violence. Western allies bypassed the UN Security Council's approval, which could have been difficult to obtain owing to the opposition of Russia and China. In the above three instances of military action, other countries sent their contingents, but the majority of military forces were made up by the United States.

Collective security remains an idea that has neither been completely tested nor entirely elaborated (Gordenker and Weiss, 1993, p. 10). The experience of the League of Nations and the UN emphasises the central role of national governments in organising military actions. Neither organisation had, in fact, an executive capacity to lend itself to carrying out decisions under a collective security arrangement. No significant military advisory groups were established in such cases as the Korean War and the Gulf War, and the role of the UN Secretariat was minimal in decision-making.

Some expected that the end of the Cold War would increase the possibility of collective action against aggression. Though the idea of collective security has endured, how policies are to be adapted to changing conditions and then executed is still a central issue. The support for collective security, to a certain extent, signifies a widespread rejection of international aggression as politically acceptable. Collective security was an idea born out of need. In practical application, however, it has proven inadequate to achieve high and rather inflated hopes. Building the formal partnership of NATO with former Eastern European countries and, to a lesser extent, with Russia has been considered part of a European collective security system. The discussion of collective security serves to clarify and demonstrate the potential costs and benefits of actions that could be used by the international community as a whole or some part of it.

Shortcomings

Many major institutional weaknesses of the League of Nations' collective security system can be applied to the United Nations. Taking procedures for the enforcement of collective security has been a challenge. Before sanctions can be applied, there should be an agreement on the existence of aggression, the identification of the guilty party and unanimity among all permanent members of the Security Council that action is warranted. It is not always easy to reach consensus on what constitutes a threat to peace or an actual breach of peace. An objective concept of aggression has not been elaborated for application to various circumstances that are implicated in one state's military action against another.

There are also many other shortcomings in the collective security system. Many countries found that the single focus on peace as a primary goal conflicts with other national interests. The business of defining aggression was often intermingled with defending the action of their ally being accused of being an aggressor. Some countries refuse to join sanctions against an aggressor due to their ties to an aggressor nation. The application of partial economic sanctions against Southern Rhodesia in 1966 by the Security Council failed because of the non-cooperation of South Africa and

Portugal. The infrequent employment of collective security measures is ascribed to cleavages among the permanent members of the Security Council stemming from a lack of common interest. The consensus necessary for prompt and effective application of sanctions is not easy to build.

Indeed, the use of sanctions in the practice of the UN system has been very limited and ineffective. Non-military sanctions available at the beginning of an escalating ladder of means against an aggressor most often do not produce an expected result. In times of military crisis, general pledges of collective action, including economic and military sanctions against states guilty of aggression, are not sufficient to bring back a sense of international security. Decisive, comprehensive and preponderant military muscle, which means war, might eventually be taken to defeat an aggressor.

Restoring peace by applying military force cannot be done frequently or easily given that the immediate costs of war to all sides are too great. In addition, the spread of advanced military technology, especially the proliferation of nuclear weapons, make collective security a very costly but less effective means. The eventual establishment of a world-police and monopolising military power followed by disarmament of states, though it is not likely to be implemented in the near future, might be an essential step to building collective security.

Applying collective security against major powers would bring about a major war that should be avoided. In the UN system, the great powers are given veto power to oppose any sanctions against them at the Security Council. That eliminates any possibility of imposing collective security measures in response to the aggression of the major powers. The collective security system could not have any serious chance for further implementation in a world dominated by a few powers that pursue conflicting interests. Deterrence through collective military superiority thus further faces the question about its validity.

Economic Sanctions

Economic sanctions have been developed since the early 20th century to express the opinion or enforce the will of the international community. Economic sanctions, as traditionally defined, are the use of economic instruments to secure behaviour desired by the sanctioning authority. In order to prevent, contain or eliminate undesired behaviour, they usually involve the imposition of, or threat to impose, economic costs on the target state. It is regarded as more powerful than diplomatic pressure but less powerful than military preparations in a chain of gradual pressure.

Historically such economic sanctions as embargo and blockade have been instruments of war, as they are imposed on adversarial nations. The League of Nations made the first attempt to detach economic sanctions from war and war inducement. Instead, they promoted them as instruments for maintaining peace. Article 16 of the League Covenant introduces the concept of penalising unacceptable behaviour by measures that fall short of war. Article 39 of the UN Charter also provides the legal basis for sanctions, as an alternative to war.

In the League of Nations system, waging unlawful war was the only ground for sanctions. League sanctions were intended to deter would-be rule breakers by bringing rapid compliance through punitive effects. On the other hand, Chapter VII of the UN Charter allows a wide latitude of interpretation of situations of 'a threat to the peace' that require collective actions. The UN Charter allows economic sanctions to be applied to a domestic situation such as apartheid in South Africa.

Until the end of the Cold War, mandatory UN sanctions were imposed in only two cases: against Rhodesia and South Africa. This reflected universal detestation of the white minority rule. Recently, economic policies have been more often used to achieve political goals outside the special circumstances of war. There is an increasing interest in using economic sanctions to prevent the genesis of conflict. Pressure has been applied to governments to create positive domestic conditions for peace through promoting democracy, land reform and the protection of human rights (Skidelsky and Mortimer, 1996, p. 155).

Since the end of the Cold War, mandatory sanctions were imposed on Iraq, former Yugoslavia, Libya, Haiti, Liberia, Somalia, Rwanda and the Unita faction in Angola. In the light of constant cease-fire violations, a Security Council embargo on Serbian dominated Yugoslavia was imposed in September 1991. Though they were non-binding and ignored by some member states, the OAS recommended sanctions against the Cedras regime in Haiti which was accused of gross human rights violations.

The Security Council can define wrongdoing in the context of 'new norms of decolonisation, non-discrimination and human rights' (Skidelsky and Mortimer, 1996, p. 159). Whereas only the Security Council is allowed to mandate sanctions, the General Assembly may recommend them, too. The enforcement largely depends on agreement at least among the great powers about the standards to be upheld and the means to be used.

The early stages of sanctions may include cutting off telephone communication and suspending airline fights. Comprehensive economic sanctions can serve as the next step following arms embargo. The chief instruments of economic sanctions are boycotts, embargoes and capital controls. A boycott may restrict the demand for the exports of the target country--like the oil boycott imposed on Iraq in 1991. On the other hand, embargo can also be placed on exports to the target state--like the oil embargo against Serbia. Capital sanctions suspend lending to, and investment in, the target state and may involve the freezing of foreign assets and restrictions on international payments. The most favoured trading status can be withdrawn with the intention to change another country's policy.

Economic sanctions have many drawbacks due to the way they work. External trade sanctions can create an opposite effect from what is intended by strengthening the internal unity of a country and fostering a feeling of defiance against external pressure. The sanctions of the League of Nations in 1935 increased Mussolini's popularity and his ability to influence people to make sacrifices while they failed to force Italy to withdraw from Ethiopia. Italy traded with countries that did not adhere to League sanctions.

While it takes time to be effective, sanctions can hurt the most vulnerable but least responsible groups. On the other hand, the groups that need to be influenced by comprehensive economic sanctions are often immune from the effects. A more targeted approach such as stopping certain types of economic transactions (e.g., freezing assets abroad) might have a more desirable effect.

In considering that aggression is mostly the act of governments, not of people, theoretically speaking, sanctions have to be directed against the governments. Especially if the population of the aggressor state is not held responsible for the act of the government, an ethical judgement can be easily made that physical and psychological pains should not be inflicted on them. Humanitarian measures are needed to compensate for the loss of the vulnerable if comprehensive economic sanctions have to be taken. Depending on economic relations, sanctions may also hurt people in the countries that actively participate in the operation with high human and monetary costs. Compensation would be needed for neighbouring countries that are affected by sanctions.

Peace Keeping Operations

Peace keeping forces, interposed between hostile forces, attempt to sustain an end to fighting. The operations are temporary measures and are intended to be provisional. Rather than determining the outcome of conflict, their task is oriented toward creating conditions in which conflict can be resolved by peaceful means. Military personnel involved in a peace keeping operation do not have the enforcement power needed to restore peace. They are lightly armed for self-defence purposes and, in general, do not have a mission to stop a large-scale bloodshed.

Their mandate has commonly been to supervise and help maintain cease-fires, to assist in troop withdrawals and to provide a buffer between opposing forces. In the past, peace keeping was primarily designed for controlling violent conflicts between states. By separating adversaries, peace keeping contributes to reduced tensions in crises, though durable solutions to conflicts and war should be sought by other means. Beyond this traditional function, it has recently been adapted as policy instruments in such instances as protection and organisation of humanitarian assistance and implementation of conflict settlement.

Origins and Goals

The international security system since World War II was originally designed to promote military enforcement under the supervision of the UN Security Council against major aggression. However, differences among UN member states, especially the five permanent members in the Security Council, made it difficult to use force in restoring peace to many violent situations. Due to the Cold War and the decades-long confrontation between the two super powers, the implementation of the United Nations mandate to enforce peace as well as preventive capability was limited. As a compromise solution, peace keeping operations evolved out of the need to stop hostilities. Without any specific mandates envisioned in the UN Charter, they 'were born of necessity, largely improvised, a practical response to a problem requiring action' (United Nations, 1990, p. 4). Their functions lie somewhere in between Chapter VI of the Charter, dealing with peaceful means of settlement of disputes, and Chapter VII, authorising the use of force to restore peace. Over the last several decades, non-coercive peace keeping activities have been widely accepted as an alternative means to control urgent military conflicts.

The traditional mandate of peace keeping is to contain war so that stable conditions are provided in the search for peace. Its goal, unlike collective security, is not to impose an international community's will on an aggressor. Peace keeping forces are impartial and fight against neither side in a dispute. In ordinary settings, they are normally outgunned by the disputants. The costly and difficult option of a forceful intervention is replaced by the mechanisms of monitoring a cease-fire. Peace keeping itself does not build trust between belligerents but is employed to contain and control violent conflict. In preventing the re-emergence of escalating violence, such activities as observing and reporting any cease-fire violations are intended for localising and diffusing conflict. Conflict dynamics that perpetuate the cycle of hostilities ought to be neutralised to allow a peaceful resolution. Hostilities need to be cooled off so that negotiation can proceed for a long-term settlement.

Traditional Functions and Operations

Several conditions should be met for the deployment of peace keeping forces. First, peace keeping operations need the consent and cooperation of parties that control territories where peace keepers stay. Consent is crucial not only for an operation's establishment but also for the rules for carrying out its mandate. Parties are also involved in discussion about which countries will contribute their troops to the operation.

Since UN soldiers are sent to areas of conflict to stop fighting without being part of the conflict, UN military personnel are permitted to use force only for self-protection, as a last resort. They are restricted to exercise restraint due to a lack of authorisation to engage in any combat activities except in the above occasion. Peace keeping cannot be successful when mutually agreed rules break down. If a party chooses not to cooperate, it can effectively defy peace keeping operations. If one of the parties decides to re-initiate hostilities, peace keeping missions do not have a mandate nor the capacity to stop a new war. Before the Six Day War against Israel, for instance, Egypt compelled the UN to withdraw United Nations Emergency Force I, and a new armed conflict started within a very short period.

In principle, peace keeping operations should not intervene in the internal affairs of the host countries. More importantly, it should not favour one party over another, and this impartiality is required for ensuring the effectiveness of the operation. For their part, the parties to conflict are expected to provide continuing support to the operation by allowing it the freedom of movement.

The Security Council sets up a mandate of peace keeping operations in line with its responsibility for maintaining international peace. The authority to organise UN peace keeping forces belongs to the United Nations Secretary General. He appoints the Force Commander and selects national contingents with the approval of the Security Council. In the early Cold War period, the UN Secretary General Dag Hammarskjöld played a more dominant role in directing UN peace keeping forces. After the conflict between the Secretary General and the Security Council over the management of a crisis in the Congo in July 1960, the power of the Secretary General was curtailed. The Security Council began to have more control over such aspects of peace keeping operations as setting time limits on the deployment of forces.

The creation of new peace keeping operations requires broad international consensus. The contingents may have to be assembled in a hurry without adequate preparation and briefing. The military personnel are offered by UN member states on a voluntary basis. Before the end of the Cold War, troops were drawn mostly from neutral states to avoid the political interference of major powers. Most importantly, any country involved in the conflicts should be excluded in peace keeping operation forces.

Past Experiences (Prior to the 1990s)

While peace keeping began to be organised by regional organisations such as the Organization of Security and Cooperation in Europe (OSCE) and the Organisation of American States (OAS), the United Nations has been primarily engaged in numerous peace keeping operations for the last four decades. Early in their development, the UN operations were divided into two broad categories, including unarmed military observer missions and peace keeping missions. Observer missions consist largely of officers who are almost invariably unarmed while peace keeping forces are comprised largely of lightly armed infantry units with the necessary logistic support elements. In practice, observer missions are sometimes reinforced by infantry and/or logistic units, for a specific purpose and a brief period. At the same time, peace keeping forces are often assisted in their work by unarmed military observers (UN, 1990, p. 8).

More than two dozen missions have been undertaken since the United Nations Truce Supervising Organisation (UNTSO) was set up in Palestine in June 1948. Other observer missions include the United Nations Military Observer Group in India and Pakistan (UNMOGIP) in 1949 and the United Nations Observation Group in Lebanon (UNOGIL) in 1958. Examples that are more recent are the United Nations Iran-Iraq Military Observer Group (1988-1991) dispatched at the end of the war, which generated deep hostilities between the two countries and the UN Good Offices Mission (1988-1990) in Afghanistan, which oversaw the withdrawal of Russian troops. These missions have a varying scope, duration and degree of success. Many of these Cold War operations helped to avoid direct clashes between the U.S. and the Soviet Union whose principal interest lies in expanding their influence globally.

On several occasions, UN peace keeping has prevented the escalation of military crises by separating forces. Some of the successful cases include the first United Nations Emergency Force (UNEF I), which was dispatched to contain the Suez crisis in November 1956 when Israel, France and the United Kingdom invaded Egypt and occupied some of its territories. The resolution of the UN General Assembly required the invading forces to withdraw from Egyptian territory and to establish a buffer zone between Egypt and Israel. In order to overcome the Security Council's inaction (attributed to the involvement of two Security Council Permanent members in the armed conflict), the General Assembly stepped in to authorise the activities managed by the Secretary General. Peace keeping forces were set up in the buffer zone until they were requested to leave by Egypt on the eve of the Six Day War in 1967.

Peace keepers returned to the Middle East after the October cease-fire during the 1973 War and remained until Egypt and Israel signed their historic peace treaty in 1979. The mission called the Second United Nations Emergency Force (UNEF II) was designed to forestall the competitive intrusion of the U.S. and the Soviet Union into the regional conflicts in the Middle East, thus preventing an explosive global confrontation. The two operations are viewed as classic peace keeping examples of supporting inter-state conflict management.

The UN's second armed peace keeping mission was conducted to preserve order in the Congo and, to a great degree, helped avoid a direct U.S.-Soviet confrontation. However, the UN Operation in the Congo, known by its French initials ONUC, had a strong mandate to end an emerging civil war by controlling a major secessionist movement. It set a potential precedent for coercive UN operations elsewhere, and some consider Bosnia-Herzegovina in terms of the Congo experience.

The UN Force in Cyprus (UNFICYP) has been the longest peace keeping operation. It was placed on Cyprus in 1964 and still remains. When conflict erupted between Greeks and Turks in Cyprus in early 1964, the immediate dispatch of UN peace keeping forces eliminated the possibility of the direct military involvement of both Turkish and Greek governments. On the other hand, the unintended adverse effect of the operations has been the maintenance of the status quo without resolving the underlying causes.

The most difficult mission during the Cold War was the UN Interim Forces in Lebanon (UNIFIL). Deployed after the Israeli invasion of Lebanon in early 1978, UNIFIL was given a mandate that could not be fulfilled. It is beyond its capacity to escort the powerful Israelis out and to restore the authority of the disintegrating Lebanese government. The continuing presence, however, is due to the fear that withdrawal would cause a substantial loss of civilian life.

New Practices

Since the late 1980s, UN peace keeping missions were dispatched to the Persian Gulf, Southern Africa, Southeast Asia and Central America. In many cases, the operations were needed to supervise the implementation of an interim or final settlement that had been negotiated. The 1989 Namibian peace building process was assisted by the UN mission that oversaw the withdrawal of hostile forces and monitored the nation's first free election. The UN also, for the first time, began its mission in the Western Hemisphere by helping to disarm the Nicaraguan Contras after the Sandinista regime was voted out of office in February 1990.

Since the fall of Berlin Wall at the end of the 1980s, more than two thirds of conflicts are based on hostilities among intra-state ethnic groups. Internal conflicts in many ethnically divided societies produced millions of displaced people, devastated economies, created deep divisions and caused physical and psychological abuses with the possibilities of spilling over to other countries. By allowing the maintenance of a cease-fire between rebels and government armies, the presence of UN peace keeping forces helped stabilise conflict situations until popular elections led to new governments.

Demand for UN peace keeping operations surged with the negotiated settlement of internal conflicts in the early 1990s. At the end of the Gulf War, a monitoring operation on the Iraq-Kuwait border and a policing and relief operation for Kurdish populations in northern Iraq were needed. The two largest missions in three decades began simultaneously in early 1992, including one to oversee the rebuilding of war-torn Cambodia and one to monitor the cease-fire in the former Yugoslavia.

Monitoring elections has been very nearly an essential function in places like Namibia, El Salvador, Angola, Cambodia and Mozambique. The tasks in Mozambique and El Salvador also included disarming rebels and arranging for the return of refugees. Peace keeping missions in Namibia and Cambodia supported and were actually engaged in civil administration functions. In Cambodia, in particular, the peace keeping operation even set up transitional authority and temporarily ran the government in conjunction with UN civilian personnel before holding popular elections.

Expanded Roles

Whereas the traditional mandates consisting of separating antagonists, observing cease-fires and verifying the implementation of troop withdrawals are still important, the nature of the missions is changing as peace keeping missions sent to internal war face different situations. In the face of civil wars and ethnic rivalries, many of the traditional aspects of peace keeping cannot be applied. Peace keeping has to control unpredictable conflict situations between hostile communities within a state. An end to fighting is a prerequisite for preventing the escalation of conflict. However, simply maintaining the cease-fire has proven not adequate to cope with volatile situations. Change in the traditional roles of peace keeping has been demanded along with the new mandates' broadened scope.

Traditional rules of peace keeping have to be redefined with the initiation of complex missions. The main function of contemporary peace keeping is to assist in rebuilding political, administrative, economic and other infrastructure. The new threshold has been observed in peace keeping operations of the 1990s. Faced with the special circumstances of internal conflict, which is different from the situations created by an interstate conflict, the mandates had to exceed beyond the supervision of truces and separation of antagonists. With varying degrees of depth and breadth in different operations, it is almost inevitable for peace keepers to serve as administrators and mediators. The new generation of peace keeping is prepared to oversee political settlements and enforce law and order (Goulding, 1993).

Peace Enforcement Ensuring compliance with UN resolutions often entails direct action. Given that the task of peace keeping in civil wars is more complex than that of separating national armies, it is inevitable that the new generation of peace keeping activities deals with multiple actors, including opposing political parties and nongovernmental organisations. Interaction with untrustworthy belligerents is essential in operating in a volatile conflict zone. In the maintenance of peace and security, the arrest of war criminals has been an important function for the UN Mission in Bosnia and Herzegovina (sent after the Dayton agreement in 1995). UN Operations II in Somalia (replacing the U.S. led intervention forces in 1993) took responsibility for disarming militia factions. The failed attempt to pursue the capture of the warlord Mohamed Farah Aidid who obstructed the implementation of the UN mandate illustrates a delicate balance between enforcement and a neutral third party role.

Compared with the traditional missions, a peace enforcement function is more clearly reflected in peace keeping at present. In peace enforcement, the distinctions between peace keeping and coercive action are blurred. The rules of consent of the parties to a conflict are not strictly held as a condition for establishing and maintaining peace keeping operations. Even when consent is not endured or withdrawn, peace keepers may still have to remain to protect the victims of the new aggression. Enforcement functions are needed to prevent the spread or resumption of conflict. In the event of disintegration of consent, it is a main challenge to deal with non-cooperation. Self-defence doctrine was broadened to remove obstacles to the fulfilment of their mandate, for instance, in assisting the delivery of humanitarian relief supplies.

More complicated relationships exist between warring parties and peace keepers in peace enforcement. Controlling the behaviour of obstructive parties was the main challenge in Cambodia, Angola and Somalia. Local opposition diverts resources to the protection of the forces. Recent experiences highlight the risks of peace keeping missions in situations where deep internal divisions remain (Ratner, 1995, p. 238). Punishing a party that violates the accord sometimes causes the third party to join the conflict.

Uncontrolled escalation draws peace keepers to local conflict situations as Nigerian soldiers in Liberia and Sierra Leone.

Peace making and building Peace keeping has been integrated with effective peacemaking and prevention of renewed conflict as well as restoration of order and institution building. There is a growing consensus that peace keeping is a tool that needs to be used with other tools such as rebuilding communities that require long-term planning. Maintaining a cease-fire has to be accompanied by the measures to remove the causes of original conflicts. Peace keeping has been considered in close connection to peacemaking since mediation and other measures of conflict resolution take time. Parties need to settle their differences in an ordinary communal setting with the help of a neutral mediator (Druckman, et al., 1999). Peace keepers are engaged in negotiations for security arrangements as well as opening communication between adversaries, investigating facts and facilitating dialogue.

Beginning in the late 1980s, a peace keeping mission has been expanded to activities that facilitate transitions to stable government. Peace keepers are now engaged in providing basic functions for local communities as well as preventing the loss of life. In response to fresh demands, the new peace keeping missions over the last several years have been extended to complement activities to rebuild war torn societies. In supporting the implementation of a comprehensive settlement, peace keeping operations have to assist in the reconstruction of governmental or police functions after a civil war. The new missions typically require more sophisticated expertise and investment of vast financial resources. Expertise in such areas as human rights and public administration has been added to fulfil the supportive functions of rebuilding war torn societies.

Multi-faceted functions of peace keeping operations cover disarmament, demobilisation and reintegration of former soldiers in a civilian society and mine clearance as well as cease-fire monitoring. In collaboration with international aid agencies, peace keeping also supports such non-military functions as protection and repatriation of refugees, rehabilitation of the security and judicial apparatus and rebuilding of war-damaged infrastructure (Findlay, 1994). In assisting in the rebuilding of social and political structures, peace keepers are engaged in observing and reporting on human rights abuses, military and police training and civic administration.

Many tasks associated with assistance in the reconstruction of governmental or police functions following a civil war shed light on a unique feature of new peace keeping missions. Policing and restoring civil administration in failed states requires the support of local civilian populations. Even tactical and operational functions can have political implications. Sustaining local support depends on a lot of different factors, including perceptions of impartiality. An atmosphere of cooperation can be generated by trusting and friendly attitudes as well as openness in communication.

Non-military functions have been integrated in the mandate of many new missions. Although peace keeping operations were never purely military (as seen in the Congo operations), recently civilian personnel have played a more important role in carrying out essential political or administrative functions, sometimes on a very large scale. This was evident in such missions as the establishment of political order in Kosovo, nation-building in Somalia, democratisation in Haiti and Cambodia and the independence of Namibia. The recent resurgence of peace keeping operations led to the expectation that civilian and military undertakings should be integrated 'with overall responsibility entrusted [to] a civilian rather than a military officer' (United Nations, 1990, p. 5).

Peace keeping focuses on the complexity of problems in individual situations. Creative responses were invented to deal with new strains. The missions of peace keepers dispatched to deter factional violence prior to a peace accord can change with a new agreement. In the case of the UN Observer Mission in El Salvador (ONUSAL) established in July 1991 by the Security Council, the original mission was to protect human rights even before the official cease-fire. Their duties were later expanded to implementing a cease-fire, demobilising regular and militia forces, confiscating weapons, monitoring elections, reforming government institutions, establishing law and order and training the personnel necessary to preserve it.

Evaluation

One advantage of peace keeping is that, compared with collective security, it does not require a large commitment from participating states. Peace keeping troops are not likely to be engaged in serious fighting with heavy casualties given the consent of parties to the conflict. The effectiveness of peace keeping operations can be judged in terms of the degree of fulfilling the mandate created by the Security Council. While UNEF I was terminated by

Egypt before the Six Day War, the presence of UNEF II sustained the cease-fire until negotiated settlements were reached at Camp David. The UN Operations within the Congo (ONUC) can be considered as a successful case because they achieved stability with the aid of enforcement actions. On the other hand, it was marked with controversies over its impartiality raised by the Soviet Union and some African states.

Among the new generation of peace keeping operations, missions to El Salvador and Namibia achieved their objectives with successful transition from cease-fire to the establishment of new governments. In the case of Cambodia, the outcome is mixed. Free elections were held with the outcome of creating a new government, but fighting among political factions was not completely stopped. The experience with the UNOSOM II in Somalia is less positive. Despite some early success in protecting aid flows, disarming the militias, repatriating refugees and promoting reconciliation, the force was embattled in Mogadishu within six months of its dispatch in May 1993. By March 1995, due to the resistance of the militias, the force had withdrawn, leaving Somalia in much the same state of anarchy as it had found it. The UN Angola Verification Mission II (June 1991-February 1995) is recorded as one of the least successful operations. The mission, created to supervise the peace agreement between the government and the rebels of the National Union for the Total Independence of Angola (UNITA), had a mandate to observe national elections as well as to verify a cease-fire and demobilise the forces. Upon their loss in the elections, UNITA refused to accept the results and the civil war re-ignited. The failure can be attributed, in part, to the breakdown of early disarmament of the rebel armies.

Ideally, a peace keeping operation should be followed by a non-violent settlement, but this goal has not been always easy to obtain in practice. Major foreign intervention did not create a permissible international environment for peace keeping operations in Lebanon and Cyprus. UN missions to Cyprus are considered a partial success since stable conditions for peace between Greeks and Turks have yet to be accomplished. Despite the presence of peace keepers that halted armed conflict, over the last thirty years, political accord has become an elusive goal. Peace keeping operations can prevent a recurrence of hostilities especially in the intractable conflict. However, it can be part of the problem by 'protecting the parties from the consequences of their negotiating stands' (United Nations, 1990, p. 8). Overall, success or failure of the missions is often affected by the degree of international support and cooperation from opposing parties and the level of authority provided to perform the mandated functions as well as the appropriateness of missions to the local conflict situations.

Challenges and Future Directions

Peace keeping operations have become more popular since the end of the Cold War and the rise of ethnic conflict. Many of peace keeping's problems are caused by this growing popularity as the international community's tool for conflict containment in an age of growing violence. While peace keepers cannot do everything, they serve a niche market where states and groups are sick of conflict and want to get on with their own lives but do not trust their enemies. Since early 1992, demand for UN peace keeping has begun to outstrip the UN capacity to supply.

One of the difficulties faced by the UN peace keeping operations is a sound financial basis. The financing of the operations has been one of its most controversial and least satisfactory aspects. This has been a particularly serious problem for operations in the Congo and former Yugoslavia that have involved more than ten thousand troops. Operations cannot proceed without obligatory financial contributions levied on UN member states. If contributions are not paid fully and promptly, the Secretary-General lacks the financial resources needed to reimburse the cost of operations to the troop contributing countries. Other problems include a lack of coordination with soldiers from different countries. Regular training programmes need to include the development of social and political skills.

A regional organisation or a group of states can also conduct a military operation to secure a sustainable environment for ending a fight under the UN Security Council's mandate before the dispatch of UN forces. National government contingents can function with UN blessing but under non-UN command. Efforts to ensure access to Kurds in northern Iraq at the end of the Gulf War were authorised by the Security Council but carried out by a Western coalition. The U.S.-led coalition implemented Operation Restore Hope in Somalia, from December 1992 to May 1993, to bring order under the auspices of Chapter VII of the UN Charter.

More peace keeping operations have been undertaken, in recent years, by regional organisations' operations (as envisaged in Chapter VI and VIII of the UN Charter). In June 1992, NATO agreed to participate in peace keeping operations in Europe under the CSCE responsibility at a ministerial meeting in Oslo. The mission in Nicaragua after the end of the Contra War was a milestone for the Organisation of American States. The International Commission for Support and Verification (CIAV) first worked with the UN to demobilise 22,000 combatants during April-June 1990. The CIAV assumed sole responsibility for the reintegration, socio-economic support and protection of the resistance combatants and their family members.

Peace keeping has variations in cooperative arrangements with regional organisations. In Haiti, the authority of the operation was handed over to the United Nations at the end of the U.S. led interventions approved by the Organisation of American States (OAS). In the case of Bosnia, which involved different types of forces by regional and UN commands, NATO provided air support for the UN ground forces. As the examples of Liberia and Georgia demonstrate, regional forces may take the command over military operations while civilian aspects of the mission are overseen by United Nations observers.

Intervention by groupings of regional states could serve purely the political interests of neighbouring powers (Boutros-Ghali, 1998, p. 22). In the case of Western African intervention in Liberia, the Nigerian soldiers made up 66 per cent of the force of the Economic Community of West African States. This regional force serves the Nigerian military regime's foreign policy and commercial interests (by asserting their influence in the region). The impartiality of peace keeping was questioned by Nigeria's alliances with different local militia factions.

Peace keeping itself can also be corrupt and abusive. Nigerian forces had taken part in clandestine economic activities by buying goods from looters and reselling at a profit. They collaborated with one of the faction leaders, George Boley, in exploiting rubber resources. Some Nigerian commanders even operated their own business in Liberia.

Humanitarian Intervention

Over the last several decades the world observed genocide, ethnic cleansing and other types of violence against humanity in former Yugoslavia, Iraq, Liberia and Rwanda. The Pol Pot regime massacred as many as one million Cambodians in the late 1970s. There are other situations that entailed a substantial loss of life. The cessation of government functions in civil wars and the collapse of states create humanitarian disaster situations. Support for the delivery of humanitarian relief to endangered civilian populations has become an important international security issue as well as an ethical imperative (De Mello, 1995, p. 138). Humanitarian intervention protects suffering people from large scale violence. This type of humanitarian intervention has increased with the end of the Cold War. Force can be deployed to stop the extermination of minority groups. Protection of human lives in failed states has become more feasible with the decline in geostrategic competition and ideological differences between major powers (Damrosch, 1993, p. 6).

Objectives and Operating Principles

Interlinked political, military and social factors create a multi-dimensional humanitarian crisis often accompanied by violent internal wars. In the post-Cold War political environment, the United Nations has had to face new situations for saving human lives in internal crises. A complex humanitarian emergency situation is typically characterised by some combination of mass population movements, severe food insecurity, macro-economic collapse and acute human rights violations. Civil wars in collapsed states have begun to raise questions about the role of the international community in the protection of civilian populations caught in internal conflict. It has become popular to interweave humanitarian assistance with military protection.

Humanitarian situations often require military intervention. Maintaining security of refugees and guaranteeing the delivery of relief aid in armed conflict can become an urgent priority because it takes time to obtain a cease-fire between warring factions. External intervention is aimed at stopping expelling or killing a large part of the population. Humanitarian intervention and international assistance are needed to relieve the sufferings of civilian populations. International intervention is aimed at curbing aggression in internal conflict. Forces can be used to prevent massacre, raping, looting and driving people away from their homes. The mandates of protection forces range from guaranteeing the delivery of humanitarian aid, aiding the evacuation of displaced people to deterring attacks in towns under siege.

Compared with collective security, multinational forces are deployed to restore and maintain peace rather than punish an aggressor. International forces protect inhabitants and other humanitarian activities. Partial demilitarisation can be imposed to ensure the safety of civilians. Protective zones can be established to deliver humanitarian relief supplies. A massive military intervention provided security for the delivery of food and medicine to starvation victims in Somalia. Measures to protect civilian populations include the establishment of non-combat corridors and the enforcement of no fly zones as happened in the case of Northern Iraq since 1991 and Bosnia-Herzegovina since 1993.

Successful humanitarian intervention requires a stronger presence with fewer tasks in a smaller mission area than peace keeping operations. The United Nations approved the use of all necessary means for the delivery of humanitarian assistance in serious conflict situations. Strong military contingents from NATO or a group of countries can support humanitarian aid under the authorisation of the United Nations. If relief work is impeded by violence, then the role of armed UN troops is to protect relief convoys and dispel those who obstruct them. Forces had to be used to get through to reach the encircled towns and villages that needed aid.

Overwhelming force is needed to restore order in collapsed states. Mass starvation in Somalia has not so much been caused by the absence of food delivered but by armed obstruction of militia groups. Food was stolen at the ports and sold on the black market. Food could not simply reach the most needed people who were targeted by aid agencies. The United Nations Task Force (UNITAF) -- a multilateral force for Somalia under U.S. command that operated between December 1992 and May 1993 -- used overwhelming military power to restore order. It is contrasted with the weak peace keeping functions of the United Nations Operation in Somalia (UNOSOM I) set up earlier in 1992 whose mandate was not fulfilled due to a lack of enforcement power.

Rules for Intervention

Humanitarian imperatives override the non-intervention principle in a sovereign state. There is a need to limit a state claim to sovereignty in massive human suffering such as ethnic cleansing. It is a generally accepted norm that international communities have the right and obligation to intervene in sovereign territory in order to stop genocide. While UN Charter Article 2 prohibits the use of force against territorial integrity and political independence of a sovereign state, the international community takes responsibility to protect the victims of aggression. Fragile situations in the field have made it necessary to expand the justified use of force in humanitarian situations.

In the total anarchy often found in merciless all-out war, pure humanitarian assistance based on consent is not possible or effective. It is hard to obtain consent in the absence of a functioning government. In civil war situations, the number of parties is large. Most importantly, collapse of civil order precludes the possibility of identifying any authority capable of guaranteeing or withholding consent to international involvement. International agreements are not important for militias. Neutrality and impartiality are less a concern for humanitarian operations in order to serve the goal of protecting human life.

Ideally humanitarian intervention should be made with the consideration of human needs alone. Gross violations of human dignity shock the world's conscience. The protection of human rights can be a sufficient reason for humanitarian intervention (Arend and Beck, 1993). Humanitarian intervention can lead to restoring the will of people and accountability of the government. The 1990 document of CSCE produced by the Copenhagen Conference confirms that democracy is an inherent element of the rule of law. Enforcement actions can be legitimised by multilateral coordination. Though the interventions were internationally accepted because of their ending regimes guilty of a large scale of human rights violations, the Vietnamese overthrow of the Pol Pot regime in Cambodia in 1978 and the Tanzanian overthrow of the government of Idi Amin Dada in Uganda in 1979 were mainly motivated by the intervening countries' regional political ambitions than by ending atrocities. The rules and objectives for intervention have to be more clearly laid out.

The authorisation of the UN Security Council allows direct protection for persons such as the Kurds in northern Iraq after the end of the Gulf War. The United Nations Protection Force in the former Yugoslavia was created by UN Security Council Resolution in February 1992. The Council was acting under its responsibility for maintaining peace and security mandated by Chapter VII of the UN Charter. These forces, dispatched and maintained without a serious attempt to obtain the consent of the conflicting parties, have enforcement mandates.

Humanitarian intervention has mostly been enacted upon eliminating threats to peace presented by internal conflict situations. Disintegration of states, the spread of armed conflicts and population movements have destabilising effects on neighbouring countries. However, the moral case for intervention can also be made, and it 'does not depend on the authorisation, or even existence, of an international organisation. Where intervention is justified, the moral responsibility lies with those who have the power to undertake it' (Mortimer, 1998, p. 120). Overall, humanitarian intervention can be applied either for the direct relief of suffering among the civilians caught in a civil war or for protecting a population against genocide or other abuses with the use of force.

Safe Havens

Safe havens can be created to protect refugees with a modest number of ground forces and significant air support. Deployment of weapons has to be prohibited to protect refugees, as is the case with weapons exclusion zones around Sarajevo and five other designated cities. The Kurdish safe havens were established under the UN mandate. Unless safe havens for refugees are protected by reliable forces, it can generate a false sense of security and be responsible for more disasters. Equally important. because safe havens are a magnet to refugees, their creation may actually end up helping ethnic cleansing by encouraging people to move. Therefore, establishing safe havens is a temporary measure to protect civilians.

The will and capacity to carry out the commitment is critical to the survival of people in safe havens. The UN Security Council declared several safe havens in former Yugoslavia but did not find political will to protect them. In Bosnia, while trying to ensure the safety of its own troops, it gave no clear mandate to use force to protect civilian populations, thus consequently allowing massacres. The Serb leadership imposed a blockade on the Bosnian enclaves by putting an intolerable limit on all food and drug convoys. All six areas designated as safe zones by the UN were frequently attacked, and two actually fell to Serb militia forces. Srebrenica and Zepa, designated as safe areas, turned into killing zones in July 1995. Female refugees made up 80 percent of the inhabitants of Srebrenica. Thousands of Muslims lost their lives after UN soldiers abandoned Srebrenica.

Recent Examples

The civil war broke out in Liberia at the end of 1989 but was held in abeyance from August 1990 until August 1992 through the efforts of the West African peace keeping force. The Economic Community of West African States (ECOWAS), though it is a subregional organisation with the primary mandate of promoting economic integration, attempted political solutions of the Liberian crisis through cease-fire and eventual elections. ECOWAS intervened to stop the fighting, which took an extraordinary human toll in the conflict. The intervention led to the cease-fire and helped the work of international relief organisations. ECOWAS turned to the UN for assistance in placing an arms embargo on Liberia. Later efforts were made to establish a government through election. The humanitarian intervention was justified to prevent massive atrocities and restore civil order, and the ECOWAS action was a regional enforcement action under chapter VIII of the UN Charter. It empowers regional organisations to undertake enforcement action to address threats to international peace and security, provided that the Security Council authorises such action. The Security Council's November 1992 measures endorsed the ECOWAS initiatives and adopted sanctions complementary to those of ECOWAS.

In the case of Somalia, no African organisation came to rescue the nation as it descended into civil war and famine. Efforts at diplomatic mediation between the warring clans failed. More importantly, a small contingent of the UN Operation in Somalia I (UNOSOM I), comprised of five hundred lightly armed Pakistani soldiers, did not have adequate capacity to protect relief work The situation deteriorated further until the U.S. acted at the request of the Security Council. Resolution 794 of December 3, 1992 authorised 'all necessary means to establish as soon as possible a secure environment for humanitarian relief operations in Somalia'. The resolution identifies the 'magnitude of human tragedy in Somalia' and concludes that it constitutes a threat to international peace and security. The United Nations Task Force for Somalia (UNITAF), a well armed coalition force of 37,000 led by the U.S., was deployed in Southern Somalia with a mandate to establish a secure environment for the delivery of humanitarian assistance. The humanitarian intervention mission was soon replaced by United Nations Operations in Somalia II (UNOSOM II) with a nation-building mandate. Smaller contingents of 28,000 solders and 8,000 logistical personnel (with the participation of 5,000 U.S. soldiers) were operating throughout the country to pursue disarmament, repatriate refugees, establish a national police force and foster national reconciliation. However, the UN operation soon faltered after the U.S. and Pakistani solders were killed by a local militia group. The mission halted with the withdrawal of its forces in March 1995, in a large part, due to a lack of a political commitment of the U.S. government to the operation entailing casualties.

The international response to Iraq's treatment of its Kurdish and Shi'ite populations in 1991 was successful in achieving conflict containment. A prompt international intervention established a secure zone in which Iraqi Kurds could not only live relatively safely but even enjoy a measure of self-government for the first time. The turning point came after the successful military action to eject Iraq from Kuwait. The Kurds in northern Iraq and the Shi'ites in the south mounted popular uprisings that elicited a swift and brutal response from Saddam Hussein. Debates in the UN Security Council over what became Resolution 688 condemned Iraq's repression of its civilian populations and found that the consequences of that repression threatened international peace and security. In dealing with the massive flow of refugees and Iraq's severe human rights violations, the United Nations has taken a special responsibility derived from its previous action against Iraq to liberate Kuwait. Negotiations were subsequently held with Iraq over the terms of the UN presence in its territory for humanitarian purposes. A secure zone was created by allied forces to protect the Kurds in the north, and later a no-fly zone was established over the southern marshlands.

Due to its superior military capability vis-à-vis the UN, the North Atlantic Treaty Organisation (NATO) led the intervention forces in Bosnia. NATO, which changed its mission from deterrence against Soviet bloc countries during the Cold War to peace enforcement, embarked on a collective security mission for the first time in 1992. For more than a year, the encircled towns and villages of eastern Bosnia received little aid as the United Nations Protection Force (UNPROFOR) convoys never used force to get through (Destexhe, 1996, p. 208). The distribution of aid was subject to the acquiescence of the Serbs who opened and closed the tap to the aid pipeline as it suited them. In response to the UN force's lack of capacity to stop Serb aggression, NATO's mandate began in 1993. NATO air attacks of the Serbian military infrastructure were used to enforce peace. In February 1994 it carried out serious air strikes to protect Sarajevo, Gorazde and other safe areas after several warnings failed to constrain Serbs' aggressive behaviour. NATO aircraft also destroyed Serb positions in order to protect UN Protection Force troops.

Non-Provocative Defence

Non-provocative defence also called non-offensive defence seeks to make war less likely, not by building more military strength, but by restructuring strategic planning in order not to threaten potential enemies. It is designed to overcome the disadvantages of traditional military doctrines that instil fear in an opponent. Traditional deterrence based on the ability to inflict unbearable pain on the enemy generates mistrust and fear and thus subsequently increases the likelihood of provoking a war. The non-offensive approach opposes military strategies that have an exclusive emphasis on the development and use of military means aimed to inflict heavy losses on an enemy.

Doctrinal Principles

Non-provocative defence does not evoke fear by restraining from hostile acts and threats. Self-denial of offensive military action signals a clear intention of no aggression. Reducing the fear of attack can be achieved by eliminating the aggressive potential of military capabilities. Weapons of mass destruction are not deployed, for retaliation is not part of a defence strategy. By abiding by the international law, the defence doctrine prohibits any recourse to indiscriminate conduct of war against the opponent's population. This strategy tries to avoid war by organising armed forces in such a manner to remove military threats to others. The psychological undercurrent is that feelings of fear and anger may induce rational people to do irrational things.

The idea is a radical departure from deterrence strategies that intimidate an adversarial state by threatening retaliation against their territories in the case of an attack. Given that military offence is not planned against another state, priorities of strategic planning are given to protection of land and people rather than destruction of enemy territories. Defensive measures are oriented toward improving a country's own security without posing threats to potential enemy territories and populations.

The success of non-offensive strategies depends on convincing the opponent, through a form of non-threatening messages, that resorting to war does not yield any benefit. In contrast with deterrence by punishment with threats of striking, deterrence by denial deprives the enemy of the desired objects. An aggressor needs to be convinced that key strategic objectives will not be obtained by military attack (Butfoy, 1997, p. 42). Credible military resistance needs to be prepared to stop enemy advance in the case of being invaded. Non-military defence can be added to further deter enemy attack (Fischer, 1984, p. 113).

Potential aggressors have to be dissuaded, before taking any action, of the credibility of the defence system. The cost of defeating and occupying the target country is out of proportion to the strategic advantages that an aggressor might attain. Aggression is made less attractive by increased losses incurred from armed resistance. In addition, potential aggressors would lose benefits of economic and social cooperation rewarded through peaceful relations.

In case of attack, valuable objects are destroyed before they fall into enemy hands. It needs to be known in advance that an aggressor's gains will be reduced by the plans of demolishing anything of tactical value. During World War II Switzerland permitted the shipment of non-military goods between Germany and Italy through the railway tunnels in the Alps. However, Switzerland made it clear that if attacked, it would make tunnels, bridges and railroad useless for many years by blowing them up before being seized. That helped dissuade German attacks. Basic features of non-offensive defence are designed to work regardless of the actual intentions and capabilities of opponents.

Defence Strategies

Non-provocative defence strategies reject forward based conventional defence plans such as deep strike in enemy territory (Møller, 1996). The emphasis is on restriction of defensive strategy to one's own territory by specifically abjuring the intent or capability to strike beyond it. Non-offensive defence denies dependence on nuclear weapons by refusing both their national possession and the option of nuclear protection provided by another state.

The defence system is decentralised and dispersed to reduce vulnerability and increase the flexibility of disabling defence. Small squads of soldiers, equipped with advanced defence arms such as anti-tank weapons, are dispersed widely throughout the region. These small units of soldiers use advanced communication technologies to keep in touch with one another.

More critical roles in territorial defence are played by a militia of civilians (who maintain their regular jobs during peace time) than by a sizeable standing army. Regular armed forces are assigned to frontal defence from the border inwards. If the regular army is defeated, it would be more effective for guerrilla forces made up of highly autonomous units to organise attacks against foreign occupation forces inside the country's own territory.

In order to avoid a widespread loss of life and property, some theorists suggest declaring urban areas off limits to military resistance and confining resistance in those sites to nonviolent techniques.

If an invading army is overwhelming and brutal, it is necessary to abandon violent resistance temporarily in order to save people's lives. Civilian-based defence can be adopted either as a fallback or as an integral component of a total defence strategy. Nonviolent civilian resistance and other forms of non-military defence can replace armed struggle under extreme hardship.

The scope of military conflict may easily spill over, but a country that maintains neutrality can remain separate from disputes between other countries. In an alliance system, a country is drawn into a war without choice. Thanks to their neutrality, Sweden and Switzerland were among the few countries in Europe able to keep out of World War II. Non-provocative defence can also be supported by confidence building measures that promote mutual security reassurance.

Defence policy is combined with an active peace policy, consistently promoting disarmament and development at the UN and other international fora and generally seeking to be an exemplary global citizen. Maintaining defensive military capability is not enough to deter any aggressor in a volatile international security environment. International prestige can be achieved by playing a useful role for other countries by such actions as hosting international organisations. International sympathy and condemnation, in case of being attacked, can deter a potential aggressor.

The reduction of economic inequality both at domestic and global levels can provide a peaceful international environment. The growing disparities are a security threat, in that they undermine harmonious relations. Substantial economic aid to less developed countries is part of strategies to achieve security. Scientific, cultural, economic cooperation, humanitarian assistance and other benefits are designed to sustain peaceful relations.

Applications

The defence systems of both Sweden and Switzerland explain the major characteristics of non-provocative defence. Small states more easily start the process because they do not have ambitions to project their power and their defence strategies are already geared toward the task of dissuading aggression against regional and global powers. Though big powers are more reluctant to try the arrangement, it can be flexibly adopted by rearranging defence strategies. During the early 1980s, the British Labour Party advocated a policy of complete non-nuclear defence. The West German Social Democratic party was also interested in non-offensive military policies.

🗡 The Swiss Model of General Defence maintains a small professional corps of officers (less than one percent of the population) at modest expense. However, all physically and mentally able men between the ages of twenty and fifty are enlisted in a citizen militia. Eighty percent of the male population can be mobilised to a state of high readiness within 48 hours of an alert. Soldiers keep their small arms, ammunition and uniforms at home and participate in mandatory training exercise with their local units each year. ✓

The Swiss army has defensive armaments, including anti-aircraft systems and anti-tank defences. Their armaments are not equipped for advances deep into enemy territory, but it maintains light vehicles suited to mountain defence. A complex system of demolition points is composed of 3,000 to 6,000 bridges, roads, tunnels and other strategic assets (Hollins, et al., 1989, p. 80). In addition, by maintaining peaceful relations with other countries, Switzerland generates international support for their existence.

🗡 Sweden's defence system is based on armed neutrality. Unlike the Swiss system, the Swedes do not maintain a vast citizen militia but keep a relatively larger standing army that is still defensive in character (Hollins, et al., 1989, p. 81). The defence forces are not powerful enough to defeat any aggressor intent on conquest but sufficiently resistant to make invasion too costly for any foreign country to try. The so called marginal cost deterrence strategy makes the costs to defeat Sweden become disproportionate as compared to the strategic advantages that an aggressor might attain.

Practical Implications

In the European security context, defensive strength may rely on limited offensive capability. The advantage of non-provocative defence is that it can be implemented unilaterally. Negotiation with another state is not needed to withdraw and eliminate offensive weapons. It is a more realistic approach especially under an inequality of power.

On the other hand, a rational actor assumption can be criticised. Cost-benefit analysis may be irrelevant in understanding the motivations of potential aggressors who are less concerned about their reputation. Lack of retaliatory power can be an easy target for an aggressive state. Self-reliance defence strategy still requires armies and sophisticated weapons. The military budget is not necessarily reduced by depending on high technology weapons in pursuit of maintaining a credible defence system.

Civilian Based Defence

Resistance by military force is not the only means to deal with opponents who could apply vast amounts of military power. Non-military answers for security problems can be found in nonviolent civilian-based defence that denies an enemy victory by withholding submission. Contrary to traditional lines of thinking requiring military build-up and arms races, it is assumed that invaders can be repelled without force of arms. The control of occupational forces can be hampered by making society as ungovernable as possible. Unarmed struggle without an end deprives the aggressors of their anticipated fruits of victory. Non-military defence posits a reservoir of power within society, beyond the coercive instruments of military force, to be mobilised in defence of people's way of life, social values and institutions.

Civilian based resistance is conducted by nonviolence techniques, including strikes, boycotts and industrial sabotage. Citizens need to be trained in the techniques of nonviolent resistance to frustrate invaders who have overwhelming power (Sharp, 1990). The drill of nonviolent forms of resistance may teach self-restraint, resourcefulness, ingenuity and autonomy. Self-reliance, self-respect and autonomy can boost a voluntary will to defend.

The withdrawal of consent and cooperation cannot be effective without internal unity and sufficient belief of purpose. Social transformation is a precondition for a shift to nonviolent defence. Solidarity throughout society is achieved by promoting social justice. It helps maintain internal strength and unity needed for mobilisation of popular support.

Careful planning is needed for a transition from military to post-military defence (Vogele, 1992). Conventional forces have to be restructured for a militia without arms. Government structure is converted to meet the requirements of social defence. The needs of civilian populations have to be satisfied by economic self-sufficiency and a decentralised administrative structure. Economic defence programmes increase invulnerability against a potential cut-off of imports by stockpiling reserves of food, fuel, heating oil and other vital strategic commodities as well as the development of stand-by domestic production capacity and the exploration of possible substitutes.

Given the cost of destructiveness, the use of military power is not necessarily an effective means to defend one's country against invasion. It is true that civilian defence cannot protect geographic borders as ordinary military forces might do. However, resort to arms produces catastrophic consequences in the age of missile weaponry when even hardware will not shield borders from penetration. Capacity for ceaseless resistance is neglected in conventional military strategies that emphasise modern weapons technology. Compared with the cost to build modern military weapons system and its destructiveness, the power of nonviolent action has unlimited utility and applicability.

Historically a civilian initiative has been undertaken to support government resistance activities. The Norwegian experience under the occupation by Germany can be a modern example. Scholars and policy makers in Scandinavia have long examined the possibilities of incorporating civilian resistance into their national defence policies. However, a more systematic consideration of the application of nonviolent methods of struggle to the problems of national defence began in early 1960s (Roberts, 1967). Some European states have incorporated elements of civilian resistance into their defence planning as a backup for the military defence.

Confidence Building

To enhance its own security, a country should recognise the vital interests of its opponents and allay fears that it poses a threat to those interests. Traditional confidence building measures can be achieved by negotiations on weapons of fear, systematic exchange of military missions and inspection of military facilities. Exchanging information on forces, weapons and military exercises is designed to reduce the risk of surprise or accidental attacks. Monitoring can be undertaken regarding activities occurring not only across borders but also within borders (Davinic, 1993, p. 3). The scope of confidence building activities can be expanded from military exercises and unusual military activities to force restructuring, armament procurement and operational doctrines. Zones of peace can be created by agreement on arms reduction and limitations.

The transparency of military planning is an essential element in confidence building. Military manoeuvres have to be carried out more openly and with less secrecy (followed by advanced announcement) in order not to provoke the potential opponents' suspicion that they might be preparations for attacks. The control of local military moves can be made difficult by poorly understood operating procedures. Confidence building measures such as notification of major military movements reduce uncertainties about each other's behaviour. Preventive monitoring techniques can help to identify the factors giving rise to instability.

Confidence building contributes to crisis management by containing and ameliorating tensions. A war that no one wants can be prevented by stability in military relations, transparency of security policies and predictability of behaviour. Security policies should purely have defensive purposes. Policy makers have to refrain from inflammatory speeches and hostile actions (Fischer, 1993). Confidence building cannot be achieved in instances where a party harbours aggressive designs.

Formal agreement or tacit rules of a game reduce uncertainties. Due to miscalculation and misperception, a small confrontation can turn into a major armed conflict. Conflict is often escalated by brinkmanship to force the hand of the other side, as well underscored in the Cuban Missile Crisis (1962). The dangers of automatic escalation can be avoided by controlling the compulsion not to get involved in confrontation over the immediate issues at stake. Crisis management reduces possibilities for first preemptive or surprise attack. Crisis management mechanisms change the psychological dimensions of security relationships by making each other's intentions more clear.

The probability of misinformation and misunderstanding can be diminished by reliable channels of communication. Crisis management can be facilitated by emergency communications and information exchange to ease concerns over unusual military activities. It helps to remove some of the uncertainties surrounding the ambiguous language of formal diplomacy. Mistakes or accidents in a crisis can have unintended effects on decision making. The Hot Line Agreement in 1963, following the Cuban Missile Crisis, provided a direct communication link between the top leaders of the two superpowers with the establishment of a direct radio and telegraph communication system, and allows the maintenance of constant contact in times of crisis.

Regional conferences offer an overall framework for cooperation not only on matters directly relating to security but in the economic, social and cultural spheres as well. In order to adopt substantive regional codes of conduct, there should exist a certain level of commonality of norms and traditions (Lodgaard, 1991, p. 84). Cooperation at the sub-regional level can be promoted by a system of non-aggression pacts, renunciation of all threats or use of force, and balanced reduction of military troops in the area. Regional arrangements have played an important role in managing conflict: the Association of South-East Asian Nations in Cambodia, the Organization of American States and the Contadora Group in Central America, the European Union, NATO and CSCE in the former Yugoslavia and the Organisation of African Union in Liberia.

Rich experiences have been accumulated by the CSCE, which has a network of direct communication on a round-the-clock basis between states. Confidence building diplomacy in Europe proceeded, with the decline of the Cold War, from the first steps of the Helsinki Final Act to the achievement of Stockholm, Vienna and other negotiations in the late 1980s and early 1990s. The 1975 Helsinki Conference on Security and Cooperation in Europe (CSCE) adopted a Final Act that incorporates cooperative measures to build confidence in the peaceful intentions of all sides. The confidence building measures include a commitment to announce, twenty-one days in advance, military manoeuvres that involve the participation of more than 25,000 troops. Confidence-Building and Security-Building Measures and Disarmament in Europe Agreement (also called Stockholm Accord, 1986) entails prior notification and mandatory on-site inspection of conventional military exercises.

In resolving internal conflict in Yugoslavia and Cyprus, people-to-people contacts are recommended as confidence building measures. Peace keeping initiatives have been taken to deal with local crisis situations. By focusing on the environment, economic cooperation and the welfare of people in their member states as well as reduction in tension and conflict resolution, CSCE adopted a broad concept of security and peace. CSCE member states hold each other accountable in such matters as human rights and democracy.

Disarmament and Arms Control

Disarmament is different from collective security and balance of power in the sense that it deals directly with the elimination of arms build-up rather than the management of power relations. In order to look toward the prohibition of war, weapons have to be drastically reduced and eventually eradicated. The elimination of all weapons is a radical idea in that it 'seeks to overturn status quo' (Kruzel, 1991, p. 249). On the other hand, arms control is designed more for containing and controlling weapons competition in certain areas. Since disarmament is difficult to obtain, reduction in the power of rapid attack has been sought through the qualitative and quantitative control of mutually destructive arms. Disarmament alone will not be sufficient to guarantee peace, but the complete removal of threatening weapons is an important condition for diminishing the chances of war and improving human well-being.

Arms Control   Those who support arms control do not have faith in the complete elimination of weapons. Concerned with the impact of technology on the arms dynamic and deterrence strategies, arms control is designed to restrain the process leading to military build-up and reduce instabilities within a relationship of mutual deterrence. It is achieved through explicit or implicit agreements limiting arms growth or restricting circumstances for their use. Arms levels can be regulated either by putting limits on preferred types and numbers of weapons as well as setting ceilings and modes of deployment. Deployment of certain types of weapons systems can be prohibited to stabilise military relations. Arms control manages the status quo to prevent escalation of military tension and to discourage the resort to military power. The control over the processes of weapon acquisition, development and possession is designed to reduce the risk of war. The goal of arms control is to constrain rather than eliminate weapons. It is based on the assumption that opponents can cooperate in the military sphere. In contrast with disarmament, arms control does not rule out the possibility of armed conflict.

Goals and Objectives

Advocating disarmament can be based on the moral disapproval of the use of force as well as the desire to escape from the fear of war. Demilitarisation of society is promoted by disarmament. Disarmament can prevent competition that could be destabilising militarily. A world free of weapons is safer than a weapon-filled one. By the early nineties, contrary to the desire for global disarmament, humanity built the capacity to overkill with more than 50,000 nuclear warheads stockpiled or deployed, some 45,000 combat aircraft, 172,000 battle tanks, 2,000 major warships, more than 70,000 tons of poison gas and millions of tons of conventional ammunition and explosives (Norris et al., 1991; International Institute for Strategic Studies, 1992).

In general, one of the major goals of disarmament is to reduce insecurity and uncertainty. Certain kinds of armaments in themselves engender distrust and hostility. Nuclear weapons, in particular, seem to fit this category. Nuclear disarmament was popular amongst a significant segment of populations in the West during the cold war period. Disarmament can dramatically lessen the likelihood that war will break out by removing threatening situations or weapons. In the event of the outbreak of war, reduced military capabilities make armed conflict less destructive than it otherwise could have been (Barash, 1991, pp. 363-4).

Rivalry among autonomous sovereignties leads to arms build-ups. States that are ahead in arms competition want to maintain or advance their superiority by developing new military technology, often in anticipation of a rival state's development of new weapons' programmes. The arms build-up is not easily stopped at an equilibrium point between states since one government's perception of its own and opponent's strength is seldom the same as their rival's perception. Disarmament changes some of the basic mechanisms of the arms dynamic that pushes states to arm themselves in reaction to military build up by others. Not only the limits on existing forces but also constraints on the deployment of future forces can minimise each other's fear and perceptions of threats.

Prohibiting and eliminating weapons that are designed for the use of first strike create a political environment of increasing trust and confidence. In response to the deployment of U.S. Pershing II missiles in Western Europe, for instance, the Soviet Union built their SS-20s missiles in Eastern Europe during the early 1980s. Given their short flight time and accuracy, Pershing IIs and SS-20s can be used effectively for the first strike. Removal of these kinds of missiles was essential to building stable relations between NATO and the WARSAW Pact. The tensions created by these weapons had been eased with the U.S.-Soviet arms reduction agreements.

Significant degrees of disarmament may well be a prerequisite for positive world development. 'In 1988 at the peak of the Cold War worldwide military expenditures amounted to $923 billion a year, that is, over $2.5 billion each day' (Sivard, 1991, p. 50). The cost of one nuclear submarine is equivalent to the annual education budget of 23 developing countries with 160 million school children. The West can increase aid by releasing money used for arms. A tiny fraction of military budgets now consumed by industrialised countries could fund major programmes of public health, agriculture and education, and this can greatly improve the lives of millions of people.

Consensus accepted by the UN Government Expert Group illustrates that the arms race cannot go hand in hand with a more sustainable international political and economic order. Progress towards disarmament helps meet urgent development needs by saving military expenditure. In developing countries, military expenditure on sophisticated imported weapons threatens economic development. According to various statistics, developing countries with high military spending as a percentage of the state budget tend to have a low life expectancy. Irrespective of economic systems and levels of economic development, all countries can benefit economically from disarmament.

Motivation and Politics

Different factors motivate national leaders to agree on disarmament. In many cases, political and economic motivations initiated disarmament negotiations. One of benefits of arms control is the reduction in the costs of armaments. The agreement on the reduced level of arms helps prevent competition that could be financially ruinous (Barash, 1991, p. 363). One of main motivations behind the Anti-Ballistic Missile Treaty of 1972 between the U.S. and the Soviet Union was the economic cost of building massive defence missile systems to match each other.

In other situations, public pressure provides a momentum for negotiations on weapons reduction. Public anxiety about nuclear weapons and the fear of nuclear war engineered many U.S.-Soviet arms control talks during the 1970s. In the 1980s, the Reagan administration entered into arms negotiations with the Soviet Union, as a response to mounting political pressure both within the United States and in Europe following a more intensive military build up (Barash, 1991, p. 359).

History

Despite a long history of war since the birth of human civilisation, disarmament has not been widely implemented. There has been strong desire for general disarmament not just limited to a few types of weapons. Most efforts made for the last hundred years, however, have concentrated on eliminating certain types of weapons rather than complete disarmament. Indeed, it is easier to agree on putting limitations on specific types of weapons system. Multilateral treaties negotiated in the past restrict growth in the arsenal, cut back or eliminate certain categories of weapons.

Early international attempts at arms control were made at The Hague Peace Conference of 1899 and 1907, but disagreement on the areas of weapons freeze prevented reaching general agreement. Serious efforts to control military build-up through negotiations between countries have been mostly made since World War I. The destructive nature of modern war made some politicians realise the price for uncontrolled development of military weaponry systems. Radical proposals were made by some politicians, including American President Woodrow Wilson at the Versailles Conference held to discuss post World War I order. Wilson called for national disarmament to the minimum level consistent with national safety so that forces of any state should not threaten other states.

Between World War I and II several efforts were made to stabilise the arms race among major powers. The proportional reduction of naval forces was proposed by the Washington Naval Conference in 1922 and the London Naval Treaty of 1930. As an early example of arms control, the Washington Naval Conference produced a treaty, which determined the distribution of the number of battleships and aircraft carriers owned by the U.S., Britain, France, Japan and Italy in the ratio of 5, 5, 3, 1.67 and 1.67 respectively. In a response to World War I experiences, the 1925 Geneva Protocol banned the use of chemical weapons while not prohibiting their possession. The Protocol was not verifiable, relying mostly on the goodwill of the signatory states.

Enthusiasm for disarmament resulted in the League of Nations Disarmament Conference in 1932. The Geneva Conference of 1932 focused on the disarmament of offensive weapons. The treaty was not effective since it was utterly unenforceable. It also failed because of an inability to reach general agreement on exactly which weapons are defensive, and which weapons are offensive. In an unstable post-World War I order, it was proposed by the French government that the U.S. and France sign an agreement to outlaw war between the two countries. The U.S. enthusiasm helped expand the initiative into the Kellogg-Briand Pact, a multilateral agreement to renounce war and to settle disputes by peaceful means. As an armament process was reinitiated by political conflicts in the mid 1930s, general attempts to ban war by the Treaty of Versailles and the Kellogg-Briand Pact failed.

Following major wars, the most dramatic disarmament can be imposed typically on losers by victorious parties. Disarmament was enforced, after World War II, on those defeated by ally forces while similar demobilisation was not reciprocated by the winners. Germany and Japan, for instance, had forced disarmament after World War II. However, the U.S. government later pushed for rearming Japan to confront the Soviet Union in East Asia.

Since World War II, there have been various international conferences to discuss the deployment and use of deadly weapons (Sivard, 1993, p. 35). Some international treaties have been concluded to eliminate weapons from certain designated areas. The Antarctic Treaty of 1959 demilitarises the continent by preventing permanent military stations from being set up. The Outer Space Treaty (1967) prohibits testing or stationing any weapons or conducting military manoeuvres in orbit. The Sea Bed Treaty (1971) outlaws implanting deadly weapons on the bottom of the ocean beyond a 12 mile coastal limit.

The Limited Test Ban Treaty (1963) signed by major nuclear powers prohibited testing nuclear weapons in atmospheric, outer space and below seas. To reduce anxiety and mistrust between each other, agreements were reached on the establishment of nuclear free zones that do not permit the deployment of nuclear weapons in their territories. In 1967 several Latin American countries signed the Treaty of Tlatelolco committed to the non-deployment of nuclear weapons in the region. Testing, acquisition or deployment of nuclear weapons in the South Pacific is banned by Roratonga (South Pacific Nuclear Free Zone) Treaty.

During the nuclear age, efforts to control weapons of mass destruction were reflected in the Nonproliferation Treaty (NPT). The treaty agreed to in 1968 attempts to stop the spread of nuclear weapons to new countries by restricting access to the fissionable materials and technical know-how. Some countries such as India and Pakistan who did not sign the treaty have eventually developed and tested nuclear weapons.

Many countries also agreed on the reduction in other destructive types of weapons. The Biological Weapons Convention (1972) bans the development, production, stockpiling and acquisition of virus and bacteria weapons. Though it is 'the first multilateral convention aimed at the complete elimination of an entire category of weapons of mass destruction', it does not specifically prevent their use (Kegley and Wittkopf, 1995, p. 493). Chemical Weapons Treaty (1993) commits its signatories to destroy all chemical weapons by the year 2003. It is more advanced than other treaties in that it outlaws the use of chemical weapons as well as their production, development and accumulation. Routine monitoring of the world's chemical industry and inspection of any suspect site is expected to enhance confidence in the observation of the convention.

The Conventional Armed Forces in Europe Treaty agreed in 1990 and 1992 sets national limits for five major categories of military equipment such as tanks and combat aircrafts deployed between the Atlantic Ocean and the Urals. In addition, 'political binding' agreement did place ceilings on troop strength air force and army units in Europe (Sivard, 1993, p. 35). There are an estimated number of 100 million land-mines in over 60 countries--one for every 20 children. The international agreement on land mines provides a total ban on producing, using, stockpiling, selling and exporting anti-personnel land mines.

Obstacles to Disarmament

Numerous past negotiations, conducted with the intentions to produce a safer world, have not been so successful in seriously diminishing the threats of modern weapons. There are many obstacles to the actual reduction and destruction of existing weapons capabilities. Achieving any agreement is difficult when tensions are high. States are reluctant to accept any limitations on their weapons capabilities. Long term adversaries have ample reasons to doubt the seriousness of the other. As long as the temptation to gain unilateral advantages continues to exist, the fear of being cheated will not disappear.

The arms race is difficult to stop in a current international system where an individual state's quest for power poses a security dilemma. Every state tries to strengthen their own forces to guard against any aggressive motives. In this situation, one state's plan to become more secure by building up military strength makes another state feel suspicious and attempt to balance perceived threats. It will renew and intensify the arms build up of the other state, and the vicious cycle ensues.

It is not easy to monitor the implementation of agreements and enforce treaty compliance. Effective verification needs to be undertaken by international agencies. Dismantling warheads with a variety of toxic and radioactive wastes involves both costs and technical challenges. Disposing of surplus conventional ammunition worldwide could run as much as up to five billion U.S. dollars annually. Complying with the Chemical Weapons Convention is very costly. Dismantling costs are up to 10 times as much as producing them (Renner, 1994, p. 31). The cost of eliminating nuclear warheads in the United States alone could approach one billion U.S. dollars a year. It costs as little as three U.S. dollars to produce an anti-personnel mine which, once laid, can remain active for as long as 50 years and prevent productive use of lands and roads. One thousand U.S. dollars have to be spent for removing a land mine.

Strategies

Because general disarmament with universal applications is difficult to implement, disarmament in comprehensive areas of weapons can be a long term goal. For that reason, the pursuit of general disarmament has been substituted by arms limitations on specific areas. Selective disarmament may include biological, chemical and nuclear weapons. Success in one area hinges upon progress in preventing other areas of weapons development.

The universal adherence to disarmament equally applied to all states can be considered successful. The weapons of mass destruction that are indiscriminant and lethal to large unprotected population centres have to be eliminated. The initial step toward disarmament may start with placing limitations on specific aspects of the military competition in the numbers and types of weapons. The eventual removal of certain types of weapon systems can be achieved by gradual moves to obtain either quantitative restrictions on growth or cutbacks in the arsenal. Other easy steps include imposing limitations on developing specific types of weapons or certain methods of delivery systems. Deployment of bombers and destructive missiles can later be abandoned by mutual agreement. To prevent becoming a bombing target, a weapons free zone can be declared.

In order to overcome limitations of partial arms control measures, unilateral initiatives can be taken. Gradual unilateral reductions can initiate a dynamic of reciprocity that produces an atmosphere of trust and elicits similar cooperative measures from other states. One state can take some initial steps such as a moratorium on building new weapons within a reasonable timetable. Such an action could generate reciprocal responses from adversaries. These steps can be abandoned if several initial steps have not been successful in encouraging an adversary's response (Osgood, 1962). Overall, diffuse reciprocity can set in motion the downward dynamic in arms control.

Transarmament from offensive to defensive forces can be made by new strategic conceptions and deployment patterns (Fischer, 1993). Negotiations for mutual disarmament can easily stall over conflicting interests. However, switching to defensive weapons systems can be unilaterally taken by one country alone and does not require complicated negotiations. It departs from a conventional notion that disarmament is risk free only if it is mutual.

The demand for high technique weapons comes from the emphasis on military power as a reliable policy tool, as well illustrated in bombing campaigns against Serbia and Iraq. The process of disarmament is not likely to be supported without establishing international norms and mechanisms that enforce peaceful resolution of conflict. Disarmament can be more easily implemented in combination with other measures to build confidence. The process of mutual confidence facilitates disarmament and arms control. Enhancing trust and communication reduces the risk of being seduced into an unwanted arms race. It is important to create an international environment in which security can be achieved by reduction in arms (Fischer, 1993). The demilitarisation of the Canadian and U.S. border in 1817 resulted from trust.

International Control of Nuclear Weapons

In realising that security policy options with nuclear weapons are limited, such countries as Canada, Germany, Japan, Australia, Sweden, Austria, Switzerland and Italy chose not to own nuclear weapons despite their technological advances. Given the weapon's mutual destructiveness, Sweden, Austria and Switzerland, in particular, calculate that deterrence causes vulnerability to their security. On the other hand, some countries are trying to build nuclear weapons for various reasons. The regional political and military rivalry led to the development of nuclear weapons programmes in Pakistan and India. The ambition of leaders for strong military power motivated Iraq to be engaged in a failed attempt to obtain nuclear weapons.

Since the 1960s international efforts were made to reduce the possibility of nuclear war. The arms control negotiations between the two nuclear superpowers in the 1970s and 1980s led to the agreements that put a cap on nuclear forces available to all parties. Since the break-up of the Soviet Union in 1991, Ukraine and other former Soviet republics agreed to destroy or remove nuclear arsenals in their territories.

The nuclear non-proliferation treaty of 1969 limited the spread of nuclear weapons technology with strong control measures. The non-proliferation treaty obliges non-nuclear weapon states to reject the option of manufacturing, possessing or controlling nuclear explosives in return for access to assistance in peaceful uses of nuclear energy. It is the first treaty to establish a routine, intrusive verification regime through the International Atomic Energy Agency's (IAEA) safeguards and to require specific commitments by nuclear weapon states not to transfer nuclear material and equipment to non-nuclear weapon states. Reporting on nuclear power installations and material audits as well as on-site inspection is IAEA mechanisms to verify non-production of materials for weapons programmes.

These efforts have been short-term and not always effective. The monopoly of nuclear weapons by a few countries does not convey a convincing message for non-nuclear countries to stop making efforts to develop nuclear weapons (Thakur, 1996). It may be difficult to continue to put pressure on non-nuclear weapons states unless nuclear powers show a commitment to disarmament. Non-nuclear powers often argue against the logic of nuclear domination by a few countries. In fact, the use of nuclear and thermonuclear weapons is a direct violation of the Charter of the United Nations according to the Resolution adopted by the UN General Assembly on November 24, 1961. The Declaration pointed out that nuclear weapons cause genocide with indiscriminate and unnecessary suffering. General nuclear disarmament, however long it may take, is the only solution to avoiding the horror of a nuclear war in the future.

U.S.-Soviet Nuclear Arms Control Negotiations

To control the nuclear arms race, the U.S. and Russian governments were engaged in numerous negotiations. The efforts for nuclear arms control between the two superpowers started in the late 1950s, and the Limited Test Ban Treaty in 1963 was the first significant outcome. The Strategic Arms Limitation Talks (SALT) Treaty I in 1972, SALT II treaties in 1979 and

Strategic Arms Reduction Talks (START) treaties sought to address the limitations in the research, development and deployment of various aspects of nuclear weaponry systems. In particular, quantitative arms control drew most of the attention in these treaties.

The SALT I Interim Agreement (on Offensive Strategic Arms) established limits on the number of intercontinental or submarine ballistic missile launchers while not requiring cutbacks in the arsenal and restrictions on the number of warheads on each launcher. Although the terms of the treaty did not preclude significant growth in the offensive power of the arsenal, Washington and Moscow, for the first time, showed a serious commitment toward efforts to control nuclear weapons. The SALT II puts a ceiling of 2,250 on the total numbers of delivery vehicles (intercontinental ballistic missiles, submarines, heavy bombers and air-to-surface ballistic missiles) with specific limits within each category as well as caps on the number of missiles with multiple warheads.

The most striking arms control agreement with deep cuts in strategic arsenals was achieved in the Strategic Arms Reduction Talks (START) Treaty I (1991) and START II (1993). The START treaty signed in 1991 calls for a reduction in each side's arsenal of strategic nuclear weapons by about thirty percent (Kegley, Jr. and Wittkopf, 1995, p. 498). According to START I Treaty, both sides would reduce warhead totals to six thousand each over seven years. The goal of START II is to further cut back the deployed strategic nuclear warheads on each side to between 3,000 and 3,500 by the year 2003 along with the removal of multiple-warhead land-based missiles. START was therefore designed as a mechanism for reducing the strategic arsenals with meaningful cuts.

Compared with the above treaties on quantitative control, the Anti-Ballistic Missile (ABM) treaty and the Intermediate Nuclear Forces Treaty were designed for qualitative control. The ABM Treaty signed as part of the SALT I agreement in 1972 constrained the ability to develop, test and deploy defence systems against ballistic missiles. More specifically, it restricts the deployment of antiballistic missile defence systems to one area and prevents the development of a space-based ABM system. However, the Reagan administration severely undermined the treaty with the Strategic Defence Initiative in the 1980s. In the Intermediate Nuclear Forces Treaty signed in 1987, Washington and Moscow agreed to dismantle all ground level, intermediate and short range nuclear missiles located in the European theatre and allow on-site inspection for compliance verification.

Limitations Military competition can be regulated by limiting, eliminating and preventing the development of certain types of weapons systems. Though arms control may be able to help reduce the uncertainty and mistrust stemming from the unpredictable cycle of the arms race, it is generally conceived that arms limitation treaties are concerned with managing and stabilising the arms race instead of ending it and often stop with codifying the status quo. Increased incentives for arms control negotiations stem from the desire to maintain a favourable strategic balance. The Soviet Union was more willing to negotiate with the U.S. after achieving military parity.

Nuclear arms control agreements can fence off dangerous and destabilising areas of military competition. On the other hand, critics contend arms control did not halt the arms race. The agreement on nuclear arms control may mislead people into believing nuclear threats have been reduced. Negotiations were used to legitimise the arms race while creating a false impression of progress.

The pitfalls of those arms control agreements are numerous. The obsession with a limitation on numbers and its consequent insistence on numerical equity has resulted in the ignorance of qualitative development of weapons technology. Reaching agreements was slower than the development of new more destructive weapons. Negotiations often have to go along with development of new weapons, as some weapons are developed to obtain concessions. Giving up some weaponry systems was used as a bargaining chip for gaining advantages in other areas. Each side tried to take a unilateral advantage by ending competition in the areas of military superiority. During the Cold War, the West insisted that the superiority of the Soviet Union in conventional weapons should be compensated by nuclear weapons.

The approval of the agreement on arms control was sometimes linked to political agendas such as improvement in human rights conditions, thus limiting the significance of the issues. The SALT II treaty signed by President Carter was never ratified by the U.S. Congress due to objections from conservative senators who mistrusted Moscow. They saw the treaty as conceding too many advantages in land-based missiles to the Soviets. The arms control negotiation considerably slowed down during the early part of the Reagan administration that waged an anti-Soviet campaign. In the late 1970s and early 1980s mistrust brought about by worsening political relations between the two superpowers led to the re-emergence of deterrence ideas.

One of the most critical requirements for successful arms control is to ensure that the other side implements its obligations with on-site inspections. Satellite surveillance can also be used for verification. Sometimes agreements lead to mechanisms to deal with accusations of noncompliance. The SALT I Interim agreement created a standing Consultative Committee that resolved many accusations of noncompliance made by both sides. Mistrust can be overcome by reduced threats of nuclear war and cooperation in other areas. The biggest cuts in the nuclear arsenals occurred only after the Cold War was over. Unilateral cuts were also made possible because of the reduced fear of the other side.

Peace Conversion

Global demilitarisation can be pursued through a fundamental restructuring of the economic sectors engaged in the wholesale manufacturing of advanced weaponry. Economic conversion focuses on the alternative use of military production technology for social needs with the diversification of arms to a civilian sector. Part of the peace dividend can be diverted to compensate for short-term job loss and help arms reliant industries switch to civil production. The resources released through disarmament need to be allocated for the purpose of socio-economic development. In general, a shift in national priorities from war preparations to civilian needs is made more easily by the end of hostilities between major military rivals.

The Goals and Process

Given that the military use of resources limits the capacity for economic development, military spending is not economically neutral. Industrial decline, unemployment and a lower standard of living are, in part, attributed to the transfer of economic resources to military production. Reduced military spending on weapons production could create more jobs and strengthen more productive sectors of the economy. In addition, the transformation of a military capacity for a civil use results in the restriction of the armaments race. Thus converting the armament industry to non-military production is socially useful and needed to control the arms race.

Conversion takes many different forms at various levels. In the conceptual conversion, the focus shifts from the pursuit of narrowly defined national interests to transnational and global challenges facing humanity. The conceptions of threat and defence have to be broadened to encompass the notion of mutual common security. Development or environmental cleaning can be funded by a peace dividend. Economic conversion reduces the wasteful military spending.

In transition to civilian based defence, the military are transformed to be organisational units that are capable of performing actions short of direct physical violence. Regular military forces, if they are functionally converted for peace time tasks, perform basically civilian functions. Relief forces are dispatched for humanitarian assistance in natural catastrophes such as flood and earthquakes.

Conversion of human resources includes the re-education and job training of rank-and-file soldiers, commissioned or noncommissioned officers, technicians and scientists who need alternative employment. Military facilities such as airfields, barracks and storage sites have to be converted for civilian utility (Møller, 1993). The civilian space programme may benefit from missile technology. Military technologies have a potential to be used for environmental monitoring activities.

Armaments and other types of military hardware have to be reconfigured for civilian tasks. Tanks could become fire-fighting equipment, and helicopters and trucks may be used in non-military construction. Materials like high-strength steel, aluminium and titanium, scratched from dismantled weapons such as tanks, missiles and submarines can be processed for civilian purposes. Conventional explosives are recycled for use in mining or road construction.

National initiatives are necessary to overcome financial and political obstacles to conversion (Bischak, 1991). Powerful forces with vested interests in military industry oppose conversion. Incentives need to be provided for military contractors seeking to diversify into civilian lines. Adjustment is needed for those communities that rely on arms production for jobs and income. Income supplements, unemployment benefits and re-training assistance reduce resistance from communities affected by military programme cutbacks.

Conversion does not cause technical and economic difficulties if well prepared. Defence restructuring should not be left alone to market forces. In cooperation with industrialists and labour unions from the military sector, the government has to develop a long-term strategy. Proper planning and assistance programmes are necessary. Savings made from cancelling procurement of expensive weapons systems help communities convert weapon production plants for consumer production. Resources are freed up for civilian purposes with the creation of more jobs.

National Policies

The conversion of military factories to alternative uses is far from being accomplished. In the United States, conversion legislation has not been easily enacted at the national level. In the past, some bold initiatives were made for the conversion of the national economy. In the late 1970s, though not successful in passing the U.S. Congress, a Defence Dependency Act was discussed to provide funds to communities for conversion planning and economic diversification. Even in a post-Cold War environment, federal government subsidies for research and development of the new generation military products have not been replaced yet with support for economic conversion. Locally organised projects and experiments form the basis for the grassroots conversion movement.

The most comprehensive conversion policy was initiated by the Gorbachev leadership in the former Soviet Union. The sheer scale of the cuts in defence expenditure was noticeable at the end of the 1980s and early 1990s. By 1993 defence production was one fourth of 1988 levels, and defence research and development activities were virtually at a standstill. Conversion plans were prepared by various ministries to help overcome the major shortages in consumer goods. The issues of national security were linked to international cooperation in conversion. Western companies were encouraged to participate in joint ventures to gain assistance in technology and marketing. The goal was to facilitate the further demilitarisation of the Russian economy, enhancing confidence in the irreversibility of the disarmament process (Schofield, 1994, p. 75).

In the absence of any central government policy, local authorities have been the focal point for conversion activity in the UK, sometimes with help of European Union (EU) funding. The EU has seen the decline of defence industries and the impact on employment as a serious problem on a European scale. The assistance coming from EU structural funds is understood in much the same way conversion in coal and steel industries have been supported in the past (Schofield, 1994, p. 80). Defence restructuring cannot be left solely to market forces, and the government should develop a long-term strategy.

Economic Conversion and Labour Unions

As early as 1929, the British Transport and General Workers' Union took initiatives to create a special committee to study the economic effects of disarmament. The metal workers union had a special working group to look into conversion. In recent years, the British trade union movement has been considerably more active at the work place and factory level. In Italy, too, initiatives for conversion have been forwarded by metal workers.

One of the best known labour led conversion efforts is the Lucas Campaign. Lucas Aerospace workers in Britain initiated the product diversification campaign in the middle of the 1970s. Lucas Aerospace produced fighter planes and other components in aerospace industries. Cut backs in defence spending led to the lay off of workers. In response to that, trade union workers developed a diversification programme that outlined the conversion of the existing military weapons production into consumer products (Hollins, et al., 1989, p. 163). Workers made contracts with local community groups, hospitals and environmental groups to produce gas heat pumps, power systems, gas turbines and kidney machines.

Another well known conversion effort includes the initiatives made by labour in the Speyer plant, which belonged to a big German aerospace company. The company produced military helicopters, but they also faced job loss situations caused by a military budget cut. Workers mobilised the support for the transformation of the plant. Local social and religious pressure groups supported the fight for the protection of jobs through conversion (Lindroos, 1980).

In the U.S., the trade union movement also participated actively in conversion efforts after the Second World War. The most active U.S. trade unions in exploring the ideas of conversion have been the International Association of Machinists and Aerospace Workers and the United Automobile Workers Union. The President of the United Automobile Workers Union proposed as far back as 1943 the creation of a peacetime joint production committee consisting of employees and employer representative to oversee the transition to a post war economy. He suggested in his proposal a programme for converting the government owned arms factories into manufacturing modern railway equipment and inexpensive housing stock. Whereas the United Auto Workers and the International Association of Machinists made important commitments to economic conversion on the national level in the 1940s, no local conversion plans have grown out of those pledges.

In the early 1980s, a strong effort was made to organise conversion planning for the economically troubled Douglas Aircraft plant in Long Beach, California. Members of the United Auto Workers Union at McDonnell Douglas attempted to identify and pursue new civilian production lines for the plant. The campaign ended when the company obtained a new defence contract. In most cases, for workers, fear of unemployment rather than pacifism, was the prime motivator of their campaign. However, it helped develop the idea of economic conversion.

11 Conflict Resolution and Management

Given that conflict is inevitable in international relations, conflict prevention, management and resolution have attracted serious attention. Incompatible demands and claims made by one party can be met with refusal, counterclaim or denial by another party. Violent conflict is very destructive and expensive in terms of human lives and material resources. In considering the cost of war, peaceful settlement is a much better way to handle conflict. However, resolving conflict nonviolently requires strong commitments from all sides. Diverse methods have been applied to deal with a dispute that arises from a disagreement concerning a matter of fact, law or policy.

While various types of peaceful settlement can be found throughout history, the 20th century has observed a growing awareness of their significance and institutionalisation of the conflict management process. The League of Nations Covenant stipulates the obligation to submit disputes to arbitration, judicial settlement, or to enquiry by the Council. Chapter VI of the UN Charter also calls for peaceful settlement of disputes with the use of a wide variety of methods, including negotiation, enquiry, mediation, conciliation, arbitration and judicial settlement.

UN organs utilise most of the traditional techniques of dispute settlement. The UN Secretary General uses his offices to act as fact-finder, conciliator, or mediator in international disputes. Submission of disputes to the Security Council or the General Assembly has something in common with the procedure of conciliation. The UN General Assembly serves as a place to hear grievances. Some international agencies have functions to investigate and make decisions on economic and environmental disputes as well as human rights abuse cases.

In case negotiation is not possible or successful, adjudication, arbitration, mediation and other third party facilitation have often been applied in resolving differences arising from the pursuit of competing interests. Communication at all official levels can frequently be distorted in traditional bargaining situations. The use of a third party is popular in opening unofficial channels of communication. Negotiation dynamics can be

167

dramatically transformed by the participation of mediators or other types of third parties. Though fact finding is itself used as one of the means to resolve differences between disputants, it is also often employed in making legal judgements or determining settlement terms for conciliation. Various dispute settlement methods are not mutually exclusive, as different techniques can be applied in a complementary manner.

Conflict can be managed and resolved through mutual agreement. In peaceful settlement, a common emphasis has been placed on refraining from the threat or use of force. Since conflict cannot be resolved in a repressive environment, conflict resolution is, ideally and in principle, opposed to coerced diplomacy. A long-term solution to deep-rooted conflict involves structural changes (Jeong, 1999a, p. 3). Building new relationships between adversaries has to go beyond short-term settlement achieved by negotiations or other methods.

It has recently been realised that resolving serious conflict means more than finding agreements on contentious issues. Settlement situations may move back to a renewed conflict. Enduring outcomes can only be achieved by satisfying key elements in peace building. Reconciliation and reconstruction have been critical in overcoming a long-term hostile relationship and consequently preventing recurrent conflict. Conflict prevention is aimed at controlling the escalation or re-escalation of violent confrontation.

Negotiation

Negotiation is one of the most frequently used means of handling international disputes. Negotiation has a longer history than the existence of modern political entities. Diplomats of states have to be willing to be directly engaged in discussion to resolve differences. International negotiation is normally conducted through diplomatic channels when each side believes that the benefit of compromised solutions outweighs the losses incurring from non-negotiation. The goal of negotiation is to reach agreement through joint decision making between parties. Exchange of concessions is common in most bargains. Compromise is normally made to serve the interests of all parties in a successful negotiation. Even when each negotiating party's preferences have not been fully satisfied, the outcomes have to be acceptable to all the concerned parties.

Parties normally have different and, quite often, opposite preferences. Each side seeks to attain agreement as close to its own preferred position as possible (Hughes, 1997, p. 92). To reach an agreement, however, negotiators search for common interests and narrow the gap between the divergent positions. Successful negotiation requires a willingness to make a compromise on their interests. Initial positions are compromised for exploring minimally acceptable positions for both sides.

The precondition for negotiation is the agreement on the agenda for discussion. Its failure prevents an initial contact from moving beyond preliminary talks. Periodic negotiation initiatives in conflict reflect exploratory probes to try out fresh ideas and test the parties' interests. If one side is not interested, the actual settlement awaits changes in the underlying situations affecting the parties.

Negotiation Strategies

Negotiation is full of manoeuvres to gain as much as possible. Reaching agreements is difficult if the parties' positions grow too far apart. Negotiators may attempt to obtain maximum value for themselves and guard against too many concessions. A variety of contentious tactics can be used in order to improve the chance of achieving a favourable settlement. Negotiators may start with an extreme opening bid in belief that such a bid helps the bargaining shift in a favourable direction. This strategy is based on the calculation that even in the worst case, the final settlement will be halfway between the opposite opening bids (Princen, 1992, p. 38). However, concessions are made reluctantly, and only when necessary, to keep the negotiation moving.

In contentious bargaining, stalemates are common since negotiators do not agree on one point over another while justifying their individual claims. Each side may ignore the concerns of the other side while trying to force their positions (Fisher and Ury, 1981). As is well illustrated by the two years of negotiation on ending the Korean War, stalling tactics increase the time and cost of reaching an agreement. In addition, the frequent use of bluffs damages the credibility of negotiators.

International diplomacy is readily characterised by the complementary aspects of coercion and negotiation in the process of communication between adversaries. The settlement process can involve not only compromise but also threats. In power bargaining situations, the other side's ideas are criticised instead of seriously being evaluated. Not the merit of each side's case but rather relative power differentials determine the terms of any agreement. Power imbalance especially in adversarial bargaining situations allows a more powerful party to negotiate from the position of strength and leaves fewer options for a weaker party. Powerful parties can demand unreasonable concessions by taking advantage of their dominant positions. Weak parties are under pressure to make concessions at the table to avoid a bigger loss in a contest of power (Hughes, 1997, p. 92). On the other hand, in power-balanced situations, neither side can force the issue in its favour, and reaching an agreement would require compromised solutions. Overall, the outcome of compromise often reflects the relative negotiating power differentials and options available at the bargaining table.

When disputing parties agree upon norms and procedures for negotiating and share information, negotiation can be effective. Negotiation can be made smoother and more amicable by stressing shared interests. Interest-based negotiation requires a high investment in mutually satisfactory outcomes since interests are generally seen as interdependent or compatible. Negotiated compromise can be reached through sharing benefits and losses. In order to achieve their goals, it is important to understand the motives and values of each party through the process of analysing their priorities.

For satisfying underlying interests, each side has to acknowledge the other side's legitimate concerns. Mutual interests cannot be satisfied by pursuing unilateral gains. More information helps understand the true interests of the other side. Making and exchanging concessions can be based on mutually agreeable standards of fairness. If each side knows the other side's bottom line (reservation value), negotiations can be conducted more effectively. Accommodation is made possible by satisfying the bottom line of both sides (Lebow, 1996, p. 56).

Face saving measures help policy makers avoid the appearance of backing down in the eyes of their constituents. Since the new stand on the issue has to be reconciled with past words and deeds, concessions need to be justified to avoid an attack from internal opposition. Proposals at the table can be phrased or conceptualised differently so that it does look like a fair outcome.

From Distributive to Integrative Bargaining

In distributive bargaining, the bargaining structure is a zero sum one by which one party's gain means a loss for the other. The agreement is difficult due to the existence of no common interests for the settlement. In the

*1 party's gain is loss for Another

situation that parties are not able to trust each other enough to enter into joint problem solving, the best outcome would be to divide limited resources. In integrative bargaining, each side's interest can be satisfied without hurting the opportunity for the other side to achieve their goals (Raiffa, 1982). A fixed pie assumption can be avoided in pursuing a shared interest. The search for joint gain may also be motivated by the desire to avert joint loss.

The best outcome would be obtained by creating win-win situations in which all sides are better off than they used to be before. In non-zero sum solutions, one side's gain is not necessarily compensated by the other side's loss. The art of negotiation is then to change the bargaining structure from distributive to integrative. In order to achieve joint gains through integrative bargaining, several potential points of agreement exist where one side's benefit does not hurt or diminish the other's interest (Pruitt and Carnevale, 1993). Developing multiple options permits different combinations of exchanging concessions. In addition, outside resources can be sought to expand the possibilities of a beneficial outcome to the negotiation.

Successful bargaining is based on efforts to maximise benefits and minimise losses for both sides through rearranging their priorities. Options can be broadened by finding compatibilities between positions. In case their positions grow too far apart, the chances of successful negotiations are likely to be enhanced by the exploration of common interests to bridge the gap. The existence of different utilities for multiple issues allows forging linkages. Concessions can be made on an issue in which one side has an important stake but that the other side considers less important. In many instances, it is also possible to disaggregate single issues in the way that a trade-off across sub-categories of the issues will be made to benefit both sides.

In general, joint gains can be found with trade-offs among different priorities because many conflicts are not strictly zero-sum. During the Camp David negotiation, the major obstacle to the Israeli withdrawal from the Sinai was the Israeli concern with security. This demand was satisfied with the demilitarisation of the territory. Egyptians agreed to remove all weapons, both offensive and defensive, from the area in exchange for the dismantling of Israeli settlements. Win-win solutions generate long-term cooperative relationships.

Multilateral Negotiations

Multinational negotiations are an essential means to deal with global security, environmental and economic issues. International conferences have been organised to discuss international trade and monetary policies, climate change, ozone depletion and the prevention of nuclear proliferation. In considering multiple actors, interests, highly complex agendas and problems with coordinating relations, multilateral conferences are more complicated than bilateral negotiations. The process of consensus building to bridge competing positions is influenced by coalition politics. Coalition structures based on specific interests should be more flexible for issue trade-off and linkage than ideologically formed coalitions (Hampson, 1995, p. 20).

Multilateral negotiation is different from the classic bargaining situation where two parties fight over a single or few items. When many parties contest over multiple issues, it is often unclear who represents particular stake-holding interests. The issues change rapidly and are interpreted in many different ways. On the other hand, opportunities usually exist for integrative or mutual gains bargaining, because there are more opportunities for making trade-offs across issues. Package deals can result from the prioritisation of issues. Given the complexity of multilateral negotiation, it takes longer to reach an agreement. The negotiations for the International Atomic Agency lasted almost three years. Over a decade had passed before the agreement on the Law of the Sea.

Negotiation between the coalitions of international actors often takes place under the aegis of international organisations. They help shape pre-negotiation processes and create or define sets of rules, procedures, norms and principles around which the expectations of negotiators are shared. In the process of negotiation on pollution in the Rhine, the International Commission for the Protection of the Rhine against Pollution (ICPR) coordinated conference agendas and supported national technical experts in identifying problems, searching for compromise between opposing positions and exploring alternatives through the networks of working groups and meetings. The conferences reflect a mix of cooperative diplomacy and hard bargaining. Discussion at various levels of national government was needed for consensus building. Various positions were negotiated through bilateral and multilateral channels before being adopted as an official agenda at the conferences (Dupont, 1993).

Good Offices

When the parties are not able to resolve disputes by direct negotiation, a third party can assist settlement. The intervention of a third party is designed to break the impasse created by deep mistrust. There are situations where adversaries often do not recognise the legitimacy of the other. Good offices can be used if the two sides want to avoid direct contact despite the need to resolve serious disputes. A third party makes it possible for the parties to communicate with each other by providing secure channels of communication. While a third party provides a sounding board for both sides' positions, their role does not include the suggestion of compromise or discussion of any substantive issues.

Negotiations have to be conducted in secret through shuttle diplomacy. Intermediaries meet separately with each side in disputes and convey messages back and forth between adversaries. Proposals can be interpreted in such a way as to look inoffensive and acceptable (Berridge, 1994). Shuttle diplomacy between separate parties may provide a basis for eventual face-to-face negotiation if communication exchanged through a third party leads the protagonists to believe that the other side is sincere about seeking an agreement.

The intermediary role can be played by the United Nations Secretary General, diplomats of neutral countries or religious leaders. In releasing American hostages held by Iran, a team of Algerians functioned as message-carriers and interpreters. Given its history, cultural traditions and geographical location linking the Arabic world to the West, Algeria was a natural intermediary.

Enquiry

Tensions between states may arise from a lack of information, misinformation, contrary interpretations of data and different assessment procedures. Disagreements can be settled by referring them to a neutral third party charged to examine the factual matters. If the disputing parties are unable to agree on points of fact relating to a controversy, an impartial commission may be allowed to investigate and report on the issue. A disinterested third party can provide an objective interpretation of law, policies or impartial assessment of the object of a serious contention. The areas of disagreement can be more easily reduced if the disputed questions hinge on technical problems.

Disputed issues can be independently investigated by specific institutional arrangements. International commissions can be created for the impartial investigation of the facts and circumstances of international disputes. The International Labour Organisation has commissions of enquiry to deal with complaints relating to labour conventions. The Law of the Sea Convention also has a provision for enquiry. Traditional types of commissions of enquiry such as the one introduced by the 1899 Hague Convention handle only questions of fact but not matters related to law (Merrills, 1991, p. 44).

By focusing on disputed facts caused by incomplete information, enquiry contributes to the settlement of conflict. Enquiry manages a relatively narrow range of disputes. The enquiry is limited to findings of fact, and normally the terms of settlement are not proposed. If a solution is recommended, the parties are free to accept or reject it. The implementation of the findings is not considered obligatory. The report does not settle the dispute but can have a bearing on the consequences. In an effort to prevent the escalation of conflict between its two new members, break-away former Soviet republics Armenia and Azerbaijan, the Conference on Security and Cooperation in Europe (CSCE) dispatched fact finding missions. Their even-handed report helped reduce tension in the region.

There are, unlike arbitration, no legal implications in investigation. The outcome is presented as a report instead of an award though parties may be willing to agree on settlement terms based on the report. Thus, enquiry can be accompanied by negotiation or arbitration to decide compensation. The process of enquiry is, at the same time, performed whenever a court or other body endeavours to resolve a disputed issue of fact. Enquiry can become an operational component of other methods such as arbitration and conciliation.

Fact finding serves the purpose of both information gathering and demonstrating attention and interest on the part of the international community. Potential threats to international peace, which many governments are reluctant to admit, can be investigated by international organisations. In some instances, therefore, the commission of enquiry may operate without the consent of one of the states involved. As part of United Nations investigation, in 1984, a commission of experts from four small European countries studied the situation involving allegations on the use of chemical weapons in the Iran-Iraq war.

Over the last decade, various missions under United Nations authority have gone to trouble spots around the world, including Guatemala, Nagorno-Karabakh, the former Yugoslavia, Tajikistan, Haiti, Moldova and Georgia. These missions were undertaken either on the initiative of the Secretary General or at the request of the Security Council or a member state. Though the main function of fact finding missions lies in collecting information, it can help in the search for ways of settling conflict. A fact finding mission dispatched to Moldova in early July 1993 generated pressure to bring the parties to the negotiation table, and it led to the attainment of a cease-fire. Personal contacts and consultations with adversarial parties can provide opportunities for future negotiations.

Arbitration

Arbitration involves an adjudication procedure by which disputants agree to submit a controversy to judges of their own choosing who render a legally binding decision in the form of a majority vote. Because the third party makes a decision based on legal norms, principles and facts, the outcome of the settlement depends on legal judgement rather than political negotiation. Disputants beforehand agree to the procedure and the scope of authority of arbitration courts. Whereas submission of the dispute is voluntary in most cases, an arbitration tribunal's decision has a binding effect.

Because the panel of arbitrators have to be acceptable to disputants, commonly each side names their own choice of arbitrators. One of the essential characteristics of arbitration is thus the free choice of judges. In case the participants do not select the arbitrators, however, parties have to accept the authority of the system that appoints the arbitrator. In addition, parties can determine the proceedings to be conducted. The authority of arbitrators is limited to the questions referred to them (Merrills, 1991, pp. 86-9).

Detailed provisions on procedural matters such as the examination of evidence, oral presentations and written pleas, have to be agreed upon. Issues are narrowly defined in separation from broad relations. At a hearing, both parties have opportunities to present arguments, respond to the other side and answer the questions of arbitrators. The parties can be represented by advocates. Arbitrators are generally concerned with the content of the conflict as well as with the resolution process. A decision is rendered based on evidence presented and can focus on technical issues. The decisions in arbitration, as in judicial settlements, are legally binding to the parties that accept the settlement procedures.

Since a third party makes a decision, a spirit of commonality, good will, trust or mutual cooperation is not required. Arbitrators have to be impartial, have good conscience and respect the objectivity of the process. In making decisions, feelings have to be avoided, and the merits of the case, equity and natural justice have to be taken into serious consideration. Creative solutions are not easy due to the nature of 'win-lose' decisions. One party's win becomes the other party's loss, and the zero-sum nature of the outcome makes the process adversarial. Arbitration is applied when the parties are not willing to engage in dialogue and when the issues do not manifest deeper, underlying conflicts.

Decisions can be complicated by a number of factors, often subject to the controversial interpretation of legal and technical data. More importantly, arbitration is not effective for value conflicts that involve religion and ethnicity. Facts and law alone cannot deal with problems that may require compromised settlement. If equity is one of the main factors (requested to be considered) and cannot be determined by simply applying the relevant laws, the arbitrators have to create new rules for the case (Merrills, 1991, p. 93). A decision in favour of one party will not help build harmonious relations. The losing party may feel unfairly treated and resentful. Ignorance of underlying emotional or value differences often contributes to further deepening an irreconcilable breakdown in relations between the parties.

The most suitable cases subject to arbitration include a question of fact or legal interpretation such as commercial transactions and other business related disputes. Objective criteria are employed in expert arbitration that is centred on legal interpretation or complex questions of technical problems. International law is important in making decisions on legal matters. The absence of an international enforcement authority can be a concern if the obligatory party does not recognise the award.

The long history of arbitration goes back to handling problems between Greek city states and the Pope's involvement in disputes between European states during medieval and renaissance times (Burton and Dukes, 1990, p. 102). Modern examples of international arbitration include territorial disputes between the United Kingdom and the U.S. in the early 19th century and conflict between Sweden and Finland over the Åland Islands in 1921. In the late 18th century, King Frederick William IV of Prussia handled the case about the amount of French compensation paid to British merchants following the French blockade imposed on the Senegalese coast.

By the end of the 19th century and early 20th century, arbitration had become a wide spread international custom. The Permanent Court of Arbitration was established by the Convention for the Pacific Settlement of International Disputes following the Hague Peace Conference in 1899. The League of Nations set up commissions of prominent jurists to settle disputes between states. In addition to territorial, commercial and other types of disputes between two states, international arbitration has been popularly adopted for issues that regularly arise in an institutionalised framework such as those regarding trade and investment. The World Trade Organisation and its predecessor the General Agreement on Tariffs and Trade set up specialised dispute settlement mechanisms.

Judicial Settlement

Judicial Settlement is formal and institutionalised in many ways. In most court cases, the dispute is relatively well defined, and the questions investigated have detailed characteristics (Peck, 1998, p. 76). More specifically, the subject of the dispute, the basis for court jurisdiction, the nature of claims and their grounds are more or less clear. Judicial decisions rely on international law that consists of treaties, conventions and other formal agreements. Customary law and norms respected by international practice and standards can also be accepted as binding. Unlike negotiated means of settling disputes, the control of the outcome is in the hands of a third party.

While compulsory jurisdiction is common in national legal systems, states are not obliged, by international law, to submit their disputes to an international adjudication process contrary to their voluntary will. Thus, the jurisdiction of the Court still depends on the consent of states. Sometimes states can formally agree to refer their disputes to the Court in the event they fail to settle it by other means. As is the case with arbitration, the parties have to agree to accept the settlement voluntarily in advance. The difference is that in a judicial settlement the judges are members of international courts such as the International Court of Justice and the Court of Justice of the European Community. Parties do not have the freedom to choose their own judges.

The predecessor of the International Court of Justice is the Permanent Court of International Justice closely related to the League of Nations. The International Court is authorised to be the principal judicial organ of the UN by Article 92 of the Charter. The judges of the Court are elected by the General Assembly and the Security Council. The International Court has general and global jurisdiction while the European Court of Justice and the European Court of Human Rights have more specialised and regional functions. One of the unique features of the European courts is that cases brought by individuals are accepted for consideration under certain circumstances unlike the International Court of Justice that only hear cases relevant to disputes between states. Thus, the international judicial system has been applied mostly to managing differences between national governments.

These established international courts do not have the authority to exercise jurisdiction over individual crimes against humanity. Dealing with individuals who are responsible for gross violation of human rights or atrocities requires separate procedures. In response to genocide in Rwanda and Bosnia, international judicial procedures have been set up to prosecute those who committed the mass murder of unarmed civilians. An *ad hoc* International Tribunal for the former Yugoslavia, consisting of sixteen judges, was established by the UN Security Council in 1993 to prosecute individuals who violated international humanitarian laws in the region. An International Tribunal for Rwanda was also created in 1994. Discussion is under way at the United Nations to create a permanent International Criminal Court, with broad jurisdiction over such international crimes as acts of aggression, genocide and massive violation of human rights.

International judicial settlement is a slow process (McIntosh, 1994, p. 208). It is more protracted than domestic adjudication. The lengthy process involves a series of formal consultations, the preparation and circulation of written notes, the election of a drafting committee and the circulation of multiple draft opinions. There is a long interval between oral hearings and the delivery of judgements. After hearing the oral submissions of the parties, the Court retires to consider its judgement. The Court, constituted by the entire fifteen judges, does not consider more than one case at a time. Until that judgement is delivered, the court will not begin hearing another matter. Delays for hearings and decisions sometimes lead parties to negotiate out of court settlements.

Adversarial relationships would not be improved through adjudication. Parties are forced to oppose each other in court. The process does not help identify or deal with underlying issues. On the other hand, international courts can make decisions in favour of weak states in their challenge to stronger states. Adjudication can sometimes provide better opportunities for guaranteeing fairness in situations of power imbalance than can negotiation. In sharp contrast with their domestic counterparts, international legal instruments do not have any effective means to enforce compliance.

In the case of a border dispute between Burkina Faso and Mali, the court ruling was publicly accepted by disputants. Other cases handled by the Court include disputes over a mineral rich rectangle of land between Chad and Libya. In light of the reluctance of states to relinquish their decision making power over the outcome, the role of the international court has not been generally significant in resolving important disputes. Only a small number of states have accepted the compulsory jurisdiction of the Court. The International Court of Justice was not very active given its record that only a small number of cases have been heard. For instance, sixty-four cases between states were brought to the Court through July 1991, and judgement was made for less than half of these (Riggs and Plano, 1994, pp. 138-9).

The International Court has mostly handled the cases in which the stakes of the dispute are low and each party can afford to lose it. Many states have been hesitant to allow the Court to decide, in particular, issues which they consider vital to major national interests. For instance, the U.S. government unilaterally withdrew the case on its intervention in Central America from the Court's jurisdiction after charges were made against supplying military assistance and training to the rebel *contra* forces in Nicaragua.

Conciliation

Disputes can be investigated by a commission that presents the parties with a set of formal proposals for its solution. The task of a conciliation commission is to elucidate the question in dispute, collect information by means of enquiry and other endeavours to bring the parties to agreement. The classic functions of conciliation include identifying the sources of conflict and suggesting the terms of a possible settlement. In consultation with the parties, conciliation commissions determine their own procedures. In the proceedings, all parties have a right to be heard. Conciliation commissions are equipped with the power of investigation in examining the nature and background of disputes (Merrills, 1991, p. 68). The impartial examination of the dispute and the confidentiality of the proceedings are crucial. The commission's major responsibility is to assist parties in finding a settlement. However, the success also heavily relies on the third party's ability to structure constructive dialogue in order to secure the agreement of adversaries.

Permanent boards of conciliation can be established to formulate proposals for dispute settlement as well as to investigate facts and laws. Conciliation has been popular for the settlement of issues of a legal nature that require an equitable outcome. Parties can still have control over the outcome of a conflict since conciliation involves dialogue, and there is no obligation to accept proposals. If the proposals are rejected by the parties, the dispute may be taken to arbitration. Compared with mediation, conciliation is more institutionalised with a formal footing for third party intervention. The proposals made by a third party in conciliation, in general, are more formal than in mediation. Beyond the information supplied by the parties, conciliators may conduct their own investigations. However, these distinctions, in practice, tend to be blurred (Riggs and Plano, 1988, p. 187).

Before World War II, conciliation was favoured by many bilateral treaties (Merrills, 1991, p. 72). Treaties between Germany and Belgium and between France and Poland stipulated that all disputes are subject to conciliation except where parties agreed to refer a dispute to judicial settlement or arbitration. A dispute between Denmark and Lithuania over the construction of a railway was settled by conciliation in 1938.

In addition, conciliation is utilised under the settlement provisions of international treaties on particular topics such as trade, the environment, international security and the protection of human rights. References to conciliation are also contained in regional agreements such as the European Convention for the Peaceful Settlement of Disputes (1957), the Charter of the Organisation of African Unity (1963) and the OSCE Convention on Conciliation and Arbitration (1992). Conciliation is used in combination with other methods of settlement such as arbitration and fact finding (as is illustrated in the 1985 Vienna Convention for the Protection of the Ozone Layer).

Mediation

Numerous examples of third party assisted negotiation exist in both modern and ancient social settings. In primitive societies, tribal elders mediated differences between their community members. U.S. President Theodore Roosevelt's mediation brought about the settlement to end the war between Russia and Japan in 1904. The Organisation of African Unity, the British and the Quakers attempted to mediate the conflict between the Nigerian federal government and the secessionist eastern region of Biafra, 1967-70. Regardless of their application to different types of social relationships, there are common characteristics in mediation. Its basic format is that mutually acceptable solutions are explored under the aegis of a third party. Mediation is not aimed at helping one party but bringing about mutual agreements.

Major Characteristics

Mediation has been widely seen as an alternative to resorting to violence at both a communal and international level. The unacceptable costs of a prolonged conflict tend to make both parties ready to engage in direct and indirect dialogue. When their own efforts reach a stalemate, the impasse can be broken through the assistance of a third party. Intermediary activities are designed to bring about a compromised settlement of the issues at stake. Compromise can be more easily accepted when disputants suspect that a settlement on their own terms may no longer be feasible. Mediation is utilised 'as an alternative to arbitration and as an adjunct to more formalised negotiation processes' (Hoffman, 1992, p. 265).

Mediation is defined as 'a process in which parties to a dispute attempt to reach a mutually agreeable solution under the auspices of a third party' (Hoffman, 1992, p. 265). In essence, therefore, mediation is considered as an extended form of negotiation whereby a third party interferes to change the dynamics of a particular conflict (Bercovitch and Houston, 1996, p. 12). Conflict management efforts between two adversaries can be extended by the role of a third party which helps affect the dynamics of the adversarial relationship. Thus, mediation supports primary parties' own efforts to manage conflict but is distinct with the intervention of a third party in the negotiation process.

Turning a bilateral dispute into a triadic interaction creates a new bargaining structure. Responding positively to proposals from a neutral party helps disputing parties avoid appearing to yield to the opponent's pressure (Bercovitch, 1992, pp. 4-5). The existence of mediators can ease tension created by mutual hostilities. Making necessary concessions is politically easier in the course of mediation than in direct negotiation. For the purpose of face saving, an agreement may be presented as an outcome of mutual concessions granted to a mediator.

The function of mediation is to attempt to 'establish, or re-establish, sufficiently good communications between conflicting parties so that they can talk sensibly to each other without being blinded by such emotions as anger, fear and suspicion' (Curle, 1986, p. 9). However, the control of emotion does not necessarily resolve the conflict unless it is followed up by direct negotiation between the protagonists. The process requires a measure of mutual tolerance and determination to reach agreement.

Parties can still control the dispute in the sense that the outcome has to be appealing to all sides, and solutions are not coerced. In that sense, mediation is distinguished from such binding forms of conflict management as adjudication and arbitration that leave ultimate decision-making power with the third party. Since disputants are free to reject a third party proposal, no advance commitment to settlement is needed. In an intercommunal conflict, mediation is most likely to succeed when parties are free from the external pressures exerted by hard line political constituents.

Process

Mediation can typically take the following steps. It starts with confirming the consent and willingness of the parties to get involved in the process even though it may be initiated by outsiders. In considering that disputants have to be persuaded to accept mediation, a third party should judge the willingness of adversaries to talk. Participants ought to accept the rules of the process suggested by a third party. A mediator should be able to open quiet communication between the adversaries. This would be followed by arranging a time and conducting face-to-face negotiating sessions between the adversaries. These meetings help identify the positions of the parties. Mediators can reframe the issues and elicit further information by asking questions after different views are fully expressed by each side.

Changing parties' images and attitudes toward one another is necessary to help adversaries communicate. In the process of interpreting and transmitting each party's proposals to the other, mediators convey subtle meanings. Proposals from both sides may need to be reworded to improve the chances of acceptance. In helping formulate proposals for settlement, a mediator meets with the parties jointly though separate meetings may also be held. If necessary, the third party more actively participates in the discussion of substantive issues. Mediators assist in constructing the agreement by suggesting possible solutions for settling differences. Caucus meetings can be organised with one of the parties separately in order to overcome contentious issues.

Although the assistance of a third party in negotiation may lead to suggestions or proposals, ultimate decision-making power belongs to the disputants. Proposed settlement can be rejected if it does not serve the interests of the participants. Disputants can withdraw from discussions if they feel that the process is unfair and is not likely to produce an acceptable settlement. Given that the proposals suggested by mediators do not have any binding power, mediators attempt to bring about a mutually acceptable solution and persuade parties that compromise is inevitable. Lastly, mediated settlement often involves third party assistance in implementing the agreement and observing the terms.

Third Party Roles In principle, third parties keep confidentiality in delivering intentions, bring the reassurance of mutual sincerity, and do not advocate particular outcomes. Therefore, mediators are more concerned with the process than the content of the outcome. Since the goal is not to help one party win, the process is geared toward encouraging the parties to accept compromised solutions. Privacy permits each party to have more flexibility in negotiation by preventing unnecessary external pressure (Milburn, 1996, p. 44). The trust of both sides can be gained by the impartiality of an intermediary.

Maintaining an attitude of impartiality throughout is expected to ensure that all parties show confidence in the process. Mediators have to be non-judgemental by not allowing their prejudices, opinions and values to intervene in the process of resolving differences between the parties. Neutrality can be achieved by not taking sides. However, being neutral does not necessarily mean a lack of care or interest in the fair outcome.

In case one party has a lower status, less bargaining power and poor negotiation skills, serious consideration is needed to prevent an unfair outcome. The transformation of conflict is not normally achieved by mediation, and it largely impinges upon the inherent situation and external context. The third party role can, of course, be greatly affected by cultural meanings attached to specific rules, beliefs, attitudes, behaviour and symbols of conflict (Bercovitch and Houston, 1996, p. 15).

International Mediation

In international mediation, a third party can be a national government, an international organisation or a private intermediary. The United Nations can make a stronger claim to neutrality and impartiality than governmental actors can. Secretary General Perez de Cuellar mediated a dispute between France and New Zealand arising from the clandestine bombing of a Greenpeace ship by French agents in 1986. The dispute resolution led to 7 million dollars compensation for Greenpeace. Mediation missions by the United Nations Secretary General finally brought the Iran-Iraq war to end in the late 1980s.

The United Nations' sponsored mediations are often initiated to address member states' interests and the Security Council's concerns.

Ideally, third parties should not have a direct interest in the disputed issues. However, Washington's involvement in the Middle East peace talks and other cases suggest that the involvement of major powers in mediation derives from the influence of domestic constituencies and geo-strategic interests. Given that solidarity is important to the successful operation of the Western alliance system, the United States and Great Britain have been interested in diffusing the crisis in Cyrus between Turkey and Greece, both of whom are NATO members. The U.S. Secretary of State Alexander Haig's offer to mediate the territorial dispute between Britain and Argentina over the Falkland/Malvinas Islands in 1982 resulted from the desire to prevent a war between its two major allies. To neutral countries like Norway and Switzerland, on the other hand, their reputation as international peacemakers is a more important motivation for mediation.

In response to the humanitarian tragedy of the war in Bosnia-Herzegovina, mediations were carried out by the Western Contact Group and U.S. diplomats from the beginning of the conflict in March 1992. These failed due to Bosnian Serb's hardened bargaining position and their unreasonable demands backed by a predominant military power. The Dayton Peace Accord, which ended fighting, was eventually brokered after NATO strikes against Serb military targets. In ending violent struggles between a white minority government and guerrilla movements in Rhodesia, several mediation attempts were made by presidents, prime ministers and high ranking foreign officers from Britain, the United States, South Africa and Zambia. The third party intervention eventually brought about an agreement that gave birth to Zimbabwe with the 1980 elections.

Nongovernmental organisations, with a reputation of peacemaking, can often be a more effective channel for communication, due to their moral authority, than can official mediators. Due to their non-threatening presence and weak power status to impose agreements, the role of nongovernmental organisations can be more effectively utilised for changing the mode of interaction between adversaries with suggesting steps toward agreement. Negotiation settings can be made more acceptable by the presence of non-political actors. Unlike state mediators who are concerned with their own national interests, mediation efforts made by religious groups are made for humanitarian reasons.

The mediation efforts by the World Council of Churches, along with the All-African Council of Churches, were instrumental in a negotiated settlement that stopped fighting in the Sudanese civil war in 1972. A century-long territorial dispute between Argentina and Chile over a few islands at the tip of South America was ended in 1984 by six years of mediation efforts by the Vatican. Quakers gained a wide-ranging international reputation through mediation efforts made in the India-Pakistani War of 1965, Sri Lanka and Zimbabwe. Their reputation as honest brokers helped them gain access to high-level decision makers. Though their mediation attempts failed in the Nigerian civil war, mutual understanding generated by Quaker mediators helped prevent a victorious party from taking revenge actions. Before the U.S. government intervention, Quaker mediators attempted to build communications between Israel and Egypt by delivering messages in the 1970s. 'The land for peace' proposal formula (adopted at the Camp David Accord) actually emerged in the process of indirect communication.

Effectiveness   The nature of an intermediary's role is influenced by the context of conflict situations involving different sets of parties and problems. In addition, a mediator's influence on parties varies depending on his or her prestige and resources. In considering their genuine concerns with human well-being and peace, the integrity of nongovernmental mediators is perceived to be higher than governmental actors, and that can translate into persuasive power. Large international organisations can bring their status, resources, ideas and knowledge to mediation. United Nations mediators effectively utilised their status and expertise in advancing new proposals that narrowed differences between the parties during negotiations in El Salvador.

The degree of a mediator's power is often affected by his/her control of the means of inducing cooperation through rewards. In bringing the settlement of the Indus waters dispute in 1960, the World Bank satisfied Pakistan by providing resources to control its own water supply (Merrills, 1991, p. 37). In brokering a settlement, a third party intervener may also offer inducements to both sides. Military and economic aid can be utilised as a necessary guarantee against non-compliance. One of the primary factors behind the success of the U.S. mediation in the Arab-Israeli conflict is the U.S. government's ability to provide tangible guarantees. After Israel and Egypt reached their initial settlement in 1978, President Jimmy Carter promised foreign aid of up to four billion dollars a year to each side. The aid has been used as side-payments that continue to provide incentives for peace.

Powerful states have advantages with the ability to influence the parties' behaviour by exploiting their strength. Mediators who have leverage may take positions to influence primary parties. Explicit and implicit pressure has been exerted for settlement in violent conflict situations. Powerful intermediaries can change behaviour by employing threats and pressure on parties that are reluctant to accept compromised solutions or to cooperate in building conditions for peace negotiations. The U.S. urged Palestinians to crack down on terrorist groups in support of the Israeli demand. In the negotiation over the future of Namibia, a Contact Group consisting of representatives of five Western members of the Security Council threatened South Africa with the prospect of economic sanctions.

Problem Solving Workshop

Ethnic, communal, class, national or international conflict can be resolved by a collaborative problem solving process. In international conflicts that involve value issues, parties often deny the legitimacy, and even existence, of the other party's claims. Facilitation can be introduced to parties that have difficulty communicating with each other. When parties do not trust each other enough to enter into a joint problem solving situation, the communication patterns need to be improved through changing the perceptions of policy makers. In resolving protracted conflict, a collaborative problem solving process can be utilised to overcome deep seated mistrust and hatred. A problem solving approach conveys a view that conflict has to be treated as something to be resolved, not to be won through an adversarial process (Azar, 1990, p. 21).

The Role of Facilitation

Compared with mediation, a problem solving workshop relies on facilitation to analyse the causes of conflict and explore solutions. Proposals from a third party mostly reflect external personal interpretation of events. Externally accepted norms and value systems do not reveal the basic needs and values of the parties. Through facilitation designed to confront the emotions and other aspects of the relationship, problem solving approaches focus on the analysis of motivations, values and goals of the opposing parties. These processes help participants understand the nature of the changes that are necessary in the political structure and social relations. Successful facilitation results in practical reasoning in searching for an instrumental means that satisfies identity and security needs at stake.

In facilitation, parties are placed in a face-to-face, analytical and non-bargaining dialogue. They should directly discuss their major concerns. Presentation of each party is not interrupted by facilitators except for clarification. Shared and non-shared values should be identified by participants themselves. This is contrasted with direct bargaining from pre-determined positions. It is also different from mediation and other processes in which a third party puts forward proposals or endeavours to apply normative considerations.

In facilitated discussion, interests to be negotiated are differentiated from underlying basic motivations and values that cannot be bargained away. Non-negotiable needs have to be recognised given the costs of ignoring and suppressing them. The search for alternative structures, institutions and policies is required to fulfil the needs of those previously deprived. Changes can result from a facilitated dialogue process involving those whose interests are threatened by potential change as well as the disadvantageous groups.

Procedures and Rules

Problem-solving workshops promote direct communications under third-party auspices. Free from governmental and diplomatic protocol, informal communication in a relatively isolated setting has been used to develop a task-oriented, analytical approach. The unofficial meetings, which can range for the period of seven to ten days of the workshops, take place in the absence of official contacts. More or less unstructured discussions are conducted under the guidance of facilitators who are knowledgeable about the group process and dynamics of conflict.

The facilitated process of conflict resolution relies on certain rules for a third party. First, sponsors need to identify the parties and issues relevant to the conflict before designing the process of promoting communication. The workshop participants can be drawn from a pool of public figures who can have an impact on decision-making in their own communities. However, they attend the sessions as private citizens, not as official representatives. The meetings have to be organised in a relatively unstructured manner to allow the participants to fully explore the sources and solutions of the conflict (Azar, 1990, p. 23). Thus, facilitators do not impose a preliminary agenda. In fostering a mutual understanding between the parties, the third party consultants help members of the adversarial communities express grievances and value differences. An improved level of communication is sought to further address specific aspects of conflicts.

At the workshop, the presence of a small panel of neutral consultants enables parties to analyse and possibly resolve their conflict under conditions of confidentiality. Resolution means the satisfaction of non-negotiable basic needs. In achieving that goal, possible outcomes are deduced from the analysis made by the participants (Burton, 1987). The role of a third party in the facilitated dialogue is different from traditional ones that seek or make suggestions for compromises. The third party is not engaged in developing proposals or making recommendation but in injecting into the discussion new knowledge and information. Their role is also keeping discussions within an analytical structure. In the face-to-face sessions, the parties are encouraged to arrive at a common definition of their relationships and elaborate both their common and separate goals clearly. Based on the analysis, the parties attempt to discover options which meet the needs of all.

Features and Principles

The purpose of the workshop is to produce a sense of possibility--a belief that a peaceful solution is attainable and feasible through dialogue. Mutually reassuring actions and symbolic gestures are expressed in a de-escalatory language which does not frighten the participants. Conciliatory moves can result from the acknowledgement of the other's humanity, identity, ties to the land, history of victimisation, sense of injustice and genuine fears. Good-will efforts fostered by communication help political elites initiate a formal process. The workshops can serve as a systematic, institutionalised input into official negotiation (Burton, 1987).

The workshop approach to interactive communication provides several innovative ways of dealing with conflict. First, the main task of the workshop is to restructure conflict by identifying and understanding each other's needs. It is, as opposed to the power politics assumptions underpinning traditional management approaches, based on the recognition that enduring solutions cannot be imposed. The parties to conflict can stop adversarial relationships. The causes of conflict and conditions for its resolution should be analysed by participants themselves.

Second, the facilitated discussion based on the principle of reciprocity does not depend on the compromise and abandonment of goals by the parties but rather understanding of the underlying issues for building a new relationship. The conflicts are not interpreted in terms of material interests which may lead to win-lose outcomes. Through collaboration, not bargaining, the workshop approach can produce the outcome of mutual gain.

The capacity to determine goals and the courses of action increases by using facilitation operating in a non-directive and non-hierarchical fashion (Hoffman, 1992, p. 271).

Third, a mutual understanding that emerges through facilitated meetings fosters the realisation that satisfaction of basic needs for all parties is interdependent or compatible. Development of shared visions of a desirable future results in finding a positive-sum solution by meeting the needs of both sides. Security needs can be met in finding accommodations that can generate net advantages to all concerned. The idea of basic human needs makes human behaviour more central than institutional behaviour (Hoffman, 1992, p. 270).

Fourth, the enterprise is geared toward changing the perceptions of adversaries. The socio-psychological process cultivates the potential for producing changes in the participants' beliefs and attitudes toward creative problem solving. It also helps the participants recognise a broad range of issues in conflict relationships. Based on the analysis of causes of conflict, the participants are encouraged to develop a broader vision of their goals. Through the workshop process, those who came as adversaries are converted to collaborators who have to work out shared problems in determining their future destiny. By finding new patterns of interactions, the workshop can create the conditions for conflict resolution.

Fifth, the workshop approach builds consensus on a framework and a set of principles which can be utilised in formal negotiations. It aims at having a direct impact on the course of the conflict by initiating a process of transforming the relationship between enemies. The transformative experience serves as a feedback to others outside the workshop. Problem solving workshops establish an informal structure for future contacts based on the experience of fashioning the possibilities of solutions to seemingly intractable conflict.

Applications Transferring trust developed at the inter-personal level to the institutional level is the initial step in the efforts to affect broad adversarial relationships. Informal meetings are not substitutes for diplomatic or political negotiations but rather supplementary to formal negotiations. The workshop format can be most effectively utilised when parties are ready for communication but not for official negotiations.

Examples include workshops held in the late 1960s concerning the conflict between Singapore and Malaysia and the conflict between Turks and Greeks in Cyprus. These were conducted by former Australian diplomat and scholar John W. Burton and his colleagues. The workshop approach was also applied by others in search of solutions in the Israeli-Palestinian conflict, ethnic conflicts in Sri Lanka and Lebanon and territorial conflict between Britain and Argentina over the Falkland/Malvinas islands. At these confidential meetings, panels of academics facilitated discussions among participants composed of community leaders and public figures.

Because of their informal nature, accurate records of accomplishments have not been established, and it is difficult to assess the success rate. Nonetheless, the approach is considered the best way of dealing with protracted conflict which involves non-negotiable values (Mitchell and Banks, 1996). The workshop's unique feature is that scholar practitioners work as third party consultants. This feature reflects the ideas of action research by which researchers are not insulated from applied settings. The role of an academic researcher is not differentiated from the role of a practitioner in exploring the possibilities for conflict resolution through observation of and intervention in the processes.

Second Track Diplomacy

Traditional diplomacy is an outdated and dysfunctional institution in handling adversarial relations. Formal interactions between representatives of sovereign states are not necessarily the most reliable method for securing cooperation. Governments are afraid of admitting mistakes or failures. Officials want to look strong and indomitable in the face of the enemy. Compared with the first track of power politics where adversaries do not reveal their intentions, track two seeks for improved relations with an exchange of ideas and emotions that can be more easily achieved by methods of unofficial diplomacy outside the formal governmental system. Second track diplomacy is an 'informal interaction between members of adversary groups or nations that aims to develop strategies, influence public opinion and organise human and material resources in ways that might help resolve their conflict' (Montville, 1987, p. 7).

The proponents of unofficial diplomacy admit that informal interaction is not a substitute for government-to-government relationships on a formal footing. Track two complements an official process to the extent that progress made in informal contacts helps set an agenda for talks at the governmental level and promotes prospects for reaching an agreement. Exploring possible solutions out of the official view and without the requirements of a rigid negotiation format compensate for the constraints imposed on government leaders. Exploratory discussion in private on all matters provides a continuing means of communication between the main protagonists (Burton, 1984, p. 156).

In situations where coercive diplomacy fails, unofficial contacts can help change attitudes by lowering tension and fear. Improvement in communication and understanding lays the groundwork for reframing politics and relationships. Since politicians are slow to embrace bold initiatives, growing social consciousness shapes the overall political environment to help leaders take positive steps toward conflict resolution. Serious negotiations can follow an understanding of root causes made at a non-governmental level.

Citizen Diplomacy Non-governmental contacts and activities of private citizens or groups of individuals designed to improve broad relations may differ, in nature and process, from more focused attempts to deal with specific subject matters. In the 1980s and the 1990s, citizen diplomacy movements were joined by people from all walks of life who have a variety of backgrounds and skills. During the Cold War period, in particular, housewives, medical professionals, educators, scientists and others contributed to building personal relationships across enemy lines. Private citizens visited Russia and Central America for fact finding missions and established bonds of friendship and networks of mutual support. Their participation in nongovernmental action reflects the awareness that foreign policy problems traditionally defined by government elites are not adequate to improving relations between adversarial countries.

Having direct personal experience of one another can decrease tension, fear and misunderstanding. Informal interaction between members of opposing groups can serve the goal of changing public opinion and mobilising support for peaceful conflict resolution. Efforts have been made to reduce long-standing, inter-ethnic hostilities between Protestants and Catholics in Northern Ireland and tensions between Turks and Greeks in Cyprus -- less successful, in this case -- through the development of links between leaders from business, trade unions, youth and educators.

Reconciliation

Long-standing conflicts cannot be resolved without overcoming hatred. Rwanda, Bosnia and South Africa, which have experienced ethnic cleansing and racial discrimination, face the task of rebuilding normal communal relations. However, past psychological wounds make continued relationships difficult. During violent conflict, kinship, territorial, cultural and economic ties are broken. It is important to break the cycle of violence. Reconciliation means coming to terms with one's old adversaries and creating a new partnership.

The psychological influences of violent attack and loss of loved ones by warfare and genocide have a lasting impact on individuals, groups and nations. Conscious and unconscious anxiety about safety and survival results from lost control over forces threatening their lives. The psychological effects of traumatic loss, which endure for years, are reflected in the victim's loss of a sense of confidence in the future as well as a capacity to trust others. Victims perceive that they are vulnerable to new attack.

Therapeutic psychological intervention can provide healing for the victims of genocide. 'Appropriate subjective feelings and ways of thinking are needed to bring about and sustain reconciliation' (Kriesberg, 1999, p. 115). Each side can be invited to talk about themselves by a neutral third party who does not have a vested interest in the particular outcome of the process. Conferences and workshops offered by groups such as the Swiss Foundation for Moral Re-Armament foster reconciliation between Germany and France after World War II (Henderson, 1996).

The healing process starts with a personalised description of the traumatic events by victims or their representatives. The acknowledgement of the tragedy and injustice of losses by the aggressors is accompanied by a formal apology and request for forgiveness. As healing is under the way with a dialogue process, psychological sensitivity is provided by establishing an atmosphere of safety and respect for all parties. Change in the relationship from threats to mutual understanding and respect should be the basis of reconciliation.

Empowerment through overcoming fear will help victims transform oppressive social relations by themselves. Victims feel safe in an environment which allows them to confront their losses without fear of losing control emotionally. Sincere and complete acknowledgement and apologies by offenders will lead a victimised group to trust the good faith of the aggressors in future relations. Such a process is very important in the interactive part of reconciliation.

Reconciliation contributes to the restoration of humanity of both sides by establishing just relationships. Because reconciliation is a mutual process, acknowledgement of guilt and forgiveness are essential to the integrity of the relationship. Re-establishing the political and social relationship of the two sides is made possible by a transaction between contrition and forgiveness. The German repudiation of Hitler and Nazism after World War II as well as compensation and restitution contributed to building peaceful relations between Germany and its neighbours.

The psychological well-being of former victims would not be improved by the demand of obligatory forgiveness for the well-being of the community. Forgiveness does not always bring about reconciliation since it can be simply accomplished by the suppression of anger. Forgiveness should not be sought by sacrificing the issues of justice. It is not a duty on the part of victims especially when the aggressors never wish to express apologies or show regret for their actions. The fear is sustained by the failure of the perpetrators to acknowledge that their acts of aggression were unjust.

Reconciliation is not always possible and desired if offenders refuse to accept responsibilities for their wrong doings. The possibility of reconciliation can be assessed in terms of the signs of mutual interests. Reconciliation is not a substitute for justice, and it has to be accompanied by the acknowledgement of guilt and repair. As seen by the activities of Truth Commissions set up in South Africa and Guatemala, search for justice and confronting past crimes is needed for reconciliation.

Post-Conflict Reconstruction

Several societies, including El Salvador, Guatemala, Haiti, Cambodia and Mozambique, have been experiencing difficult phases of post-conflict reconstruction after civil wars ended. These societies face various obstacles to building sustainable peace. Fragile political and economic conditions heighten the risk of a return to a conflict and shatter hopes for mutual prosperity. At a practical level, the need for reconstruction arises from the destruction of physical infrastructure controlled by each side in the process of achieving the short-term goals of weakening enemy capacities. Peace building aims at constructing a reassuring political, economic and socio-psychological environment for people (Reychler, 1994, p. 209). Social and economic welfare as well as good governance reinforce peace and avoid the recurrence of hostilities.

Various activities for post-conflict peace building are organised to lay the foundation for social stability and harmony. Confidence building among formerly warring parties is critical to prevent renewed fighting. It can be obtained, in part, through economic and social cooperation. Given the deeply embedded nature of problems, more than a symptomatic treatment is needed. The process of recovery is long in that mending hostile relations takes time. In tackling the root causes of conflict, peace building has to bring procedural and distributive justice (Peck, 1996, p. 74). More specifically, distributive justice is supported by equitable development strategies while the institutionalisation of a participatory political process allows adequate decision making voices by all groups to be heard.

Process and Priorities Setting up an arbitrary schedule and deadline is not easy because of the diverse political and social situations emerging after conflict. There are many daunting tasks in rebuilding a society torn by violent conflict. Different priorities exist at different stages of post-conflict reconstruction since challenges encountered on the path to recovery are not the same. The immediate issue is to address the survival needs of returning refugees and local populations. In the intermediate term, along with economic development, a new institutional framework has to replace a shaken or broken political structure. In the long run, reinforcing the norms of nonviolence and respect for human rights will nurture a peace culture manifested in tolerance and solidarity through inter-cultural understanding (Parajon, et al., 1996, p. 16).

Local capacity has to be quickly restored to initiate the return to a normal community life. Many logistical issues are involved in the resettlement process with the return of refugees, as seen in Bosnia, Rwanda and other places. Institutional procedures need to be set up to handle multiple claims to land and other assets which are a continuing source of tension. Resources such as reconstruction funds would be better managed by special committees which are acceptable to all sides. In many situations, a third party plays an important role in initiating the reconstruction process. After the 1995 U.S. led military intervention ousted the military dictatorship in Haiti, for instance, the UN had to perform most of the administrative capacities before President Aristide's government was able to function.

Disarmament is critical to curbing and controlling community level violence as well as eliminating the capacity of belligerents to go back to renewed fighting. Demobilisation and demilitarisation can be achieved by a massive de-mining program and the withdrawal of foreign troops. They need to be completed at the early stage of peace building when the commitment to a peace process has not been weakened yet. Accomplishing the Paris Peace Accord in Cambodia was difficult owing to resistance from the Khmer Rouge, and the failure of the peace process in Angola is ascribed to the refusal of rebel forces to put their arms down which ultimately led to the re-initiation of fighting.

Forces that were active during the war have to be converted to their peacetime role. Militia groups have to readjust to a complex new set of circumstances brought about by a peace agreement. In reintegrating ex-combatants and guerrillas into communities, the creation of jobs in a civilian sector is essential. Employment opportunities reduce the incentives for rejoining any future conflict. The exchange of food for weapons also supports the disarmament process.

Former adversaries recognise the legitimacy of each other and form new political parties. It takes time to nurture a culture of democracy. In a post-conflict settlement, establishing new rules of competition has to accompany the replacement of armed struggle with the election process. The capacity to hold fair elections can be enhanced by the technical assistance and training programmes of the United Nations or regional organisations. Due to the lingering suspicion originating in past hostilities, many national elections in post civil war situations have been monitored, coordinated, supervised or conducted by outside groups.

Stability and security is based on the guarantee of rights to opposition groups. The regulation of human behaviour has to be legitimised by social and cultural norms acceptable to all members of society. Law and order have to contribute to bringing equity and justice to the community. The application of law requires the development of reliable judicial institutions and arrangements. Paramilitary groups and old military institutions blamed for human rights abuses have to be eliminated or seriously reformed. The incorporation of international human rights standards into training programmes for law enforcement officials improves the administration of criminal justice (Peck, 1996, p. 111).

The development of a stable political system is supported by political representation and moderation. The interests of diverse groups have to be institutionally represented. Constitutional arrangements determine the nature of coalitional politics based on power sharing. The allocation of government positions among the leaders of diverse communities is geared toward maintaining political stability. In order to build consensus, local councils must be composed of representatives from all the opposing forces. Grievances have to be addressed through participation in the newly created system. The rehabilitation of a social fabric relies on the way power relations are expressed. The building of a civil society requires the development of human capital with a focus on the empowerment of community members immersed in violence (Pugh, 1998).

Economic viability is hampered by water shortages, a lack of agricultural land and overpopulation. Investments in natural capital are needed as well as the devotion of resources to the physical infrastructure and human resources. Local resources can be mobilised to develop sustainable small-scale agriculture. International assistance programmes may provide materials for the restitution of houses and possessions destroyed during the armed struggle. Reliable banking systems are created for the vitalisation of local business initiatives.

In adjusting economic policy to peace, income inequalities have to be seriously considered. In the consolidation of peace, distributional equity should be relegated to a higher order than economic growth (Boyce, 1996, p. 5). Promoting equitable relations between community groups is incompatible with free market reform which often increases income gaps. The fruit of peace can be more evenly shared by more investment in infrastructure designed to improve living conditions in an economically backward region. In particular, traditionally underrepresented groups can have a stake in a new system through the creation of economic incentives with a preferential treatment in employment opportunities, contracts, loans and business licences. In El Salvador, Guatemala and other places, streamlining and expediting land transfer programmes has been an important component for establishing social harmony.

Joint economic ventures that are mutually beneficial contribute to interdependent relationships between former adversaries. Development agencies begin to be more aware of using aid as a peace making tool. Economic projects can be carefully designed to build trust and confidence. Aid programmes can contribute to overcoming adversarial relations. Aid can be made conditional on the demonstration of a serious commitment to the peace process. Special attention needs to be devoted to the individuals and groups who disproportionately suffered from the consequences of violent conflict. The consolidation of peace goes along with broad improvements in living standards.

Gender imbalance requires the full participation of women in reconstruction. At the end of internal wars in Cambodia, women accounted for more than two thirds of the population. The process of displacement and repopulation forces women to take on different roles. Training and education programmes for economic and social empowerment of women have been provided by UNESCO, UNDP and other international agencies. Poor women are victims of violence and social injustice. Economic responsibilities often fall on their shoulders. Projects which generate income for the widows and orphans need special attention. Equally importantly, the needs and grievances of women have to be addressed through an empowerment process. Grassroots organisations providing training and skills can be helpful in meeting the social and physical needs of women.

Social structure can be rehabilitated by revitalising indigenous economic activities. Reconstruction has to address the issues of high levels of poverty, landlessness and unemployment. Local communities play an important role in peace building. Grassroots development efforts can be supported by resource conservation and management. Human needs oriented development for education, family planning, health, sanitation, water and food production has to be the core of social and economic development programmes. National level coordination can be made to support community reconciliation and development projects.

Preventive Diplomacy and Intervention

Several centuries ago, elements of preventive diplomacy were found in the exchange of territories, treaty making and marriage relations between monarchs. In the Cold War period, as is reflected in the Annual Report of the United Nations Secretary-General Dag Hammarskjöld (June, 1960), the term was attached to UN efforts to localise regional wars in an attempt to avoid a direct confrontation between the two major powers. However, more popular concepts and practices of preventive diplomacy have been developed in the context of exploring strategies to deal with post-Cold War violence (in the 1992 report *Agenda for Peace*). Preventive diplomacy can be defined as 'action to prevent disputes from arising between parties, prevent existing disputes from escalating into conflicts and to limit the spread of the latter when they occur' (Boutros-Ghali, 1995, p. 45).

The concept describes any early action in easing tension between the parties and creating procedures for negotiations. In urging more deliberate, early international involvement in conflicts, UN Secretary General Boutros Boutros-Ghali called for early warning systems, fact finding missions, confidence building measures, preventive deployment of peacekeeping forces and the establishment of demilitarised zones.

Successful intervention contains violence at a low level by diffusing crisis situations. Proactive policies are always more effective than reactive measures responding to the violent escalation of conflict situations. Tensions are high when ordinary peace time relationships begin to crumble. Initiatives need to be taken to engage adversaries in dialogue while keeping vulnerable situations from erupting. Timely actions have to be directed to suppressing the escalation of violent conflict by modifying suspicion among parties. Control of the situation is easier to handle before the escalation of conflict. It is more difficult to manage conflict once positions are further polarised with the involvement of threats and violent tactics.

In considering options and measures for effective prevention, major questions always remain regarding types of actions, an appropriate time of intervention, rationale behind intervention, the role of the intervener, the degree of responsibility and implementation strategies. In deploying appropriate resources, goals have to be achievable within the time frame. Different time perspectives and goals have considerable implications for the operationalisation of preventive strategies (Peck, 1996, p. 132). An early attempt can be made to persuade the parties to desist taking escalatory moves (rather than depending on threats of adverse consequences).

Priorities change, however, once a violent conflict breaks out. Faced with the resistance of an aggressive party, economic sanctions and other types of pressure may have to be applied to prevent further deterioration of the situation. Peace enforcement is required to stop raging violence (Reychler, 1994, p. 7). In addition to seeking an immediate end to violent conflict, humanitarian consequences have to be addressed. Economic assistance may need to be provided for vulnerable groups.

The application of conflict intervention tools, ranging from fact finding and confidence building to preventive deployment, has to be based on a clear understanding of problems and analysis. Conflict dynamics need to be examined and evaluated in measuring the impact of conflict interventions (Gurr, 1996, pp. 127-9). Monitoring activities are crucial for seizing an opportunity for timely intervention. Fact finding missions can lead to developing vulnerability profiles of communities and refugee populations. Reports on human rights violations and flows of refugees help assess conflict situations. Fact finding missions, like those in the Baltic republics, can be accompanied by policy proposals to reduce ethnic tensions (Birckenbach, 1997).

In response to crisis situations, such measures as preventive deployment and the creation of demilitarised zones can be taken as early intervention tools before armed conflict starts. Timely deployment of preventive forces obviates violent conflict with the establishment of demilitarised zones. For instance, the Protection Force in the former Yugoslav Republic of Macedonia helped avoid a wider scale Balkan war. Aborting imminent violent situations has to be followed up by good offices, by the UN, or by regional organisations. Along with the official diplomacy, track-two diplomacy may be introduced to reduce misunderstanding and distrust. If the situation is not controlled by ordinary conflict management measures, a militarily credible international force may be required to deter the initiation of violence.

Recent Experiences

The containment of conflict in Macedonia is credited to the effective responses of the international community to early warning signs of a possible repetition of a Bosnia-type civil war. In response to threats arising from ethnic rivalries between the Macedonian majority and Albanian and Serbian minorities as well as serious economic deterioration, intense diplomatic efforts were made at both international and regional levels. In conjunction with the official level intervention, nongovernmental organisations initiated dialogue between the adversarial communities at a grassroots level. In addition, the United Nations Preventive Deployment Force (UNPREDEP) in Macedonia was dispatched to monitor activities at the country's border in an attempt to prevent the spread of conflict. The coordination of these multi-level activities at the early stage of the conflict proved successful in containing the escalation of the tense situation.

One of the new forms of UN presence for preventive purposes has been dispatching UN observers to conflict zones. The UN observer mission to Tajikistan set up in January 1993 was involved in monitoring the situation on the ground and providing the Secretary General with up-to-date information related to the conflict situation. The mission built good relations with local authorities and with the leaders of all major political groups in Tajikistan. They encouraged peace making efforts initiated by regional organisations. The international community coordinated the supply of aid to the Tajik refugees and other types of humanitarian assistance.

Compared with the above cases, the international community failed to demonstrate their concerns with some other situations. During the Rwandan genocide, which took place between April and July 1994, the UN decided to pull out peacekeeping forces instead of protecting hospitals, schools and churches where Tutsis sought refuge. This contributed to the death of over half a million people within four weeks. In a similar case, no preventive measures were taken by the international community during the early period of the Bosnian civil war in 1992 to stop Bosnian Serb forces supported by the Yugoslav federal army. That produced 200,000 victims, four million refugees and displaced persons over three years (Destexhe, 1996, p. 207). Failure resulting from inaction can be attributed to the half-hearted support of major powers for a campaign of preventive diplomacy launched under the auspices of the United Nations. On the other hand, the successes of preventive diplomacy were reported in the regions that have been subject to intensive international scrutiny and concern.

Evaluation

Whereas short-term efforts directed toward crisis management are important for saving human lives, they do not by themselves ameliorate the problems. Once crisis situations are overcome, their causes have to be identified. The ultimate goal of preventive activities should not be mere containment but resolution (Evans, 1993, p. 70). Such instruments for the peaceful settlement of disputes as mediation, conciliation and problem solving workshops have to be applied following successful crisis management.

It is often suggested that preventive diplomacy should not be equated with correcting pervasive and deeply rooted social ills (Lund, 1996, p. 35). In this view, the focus of preventive diplomacy is not on political, socio-economic or psychological conditions, but on behavioural factors. Strategies of containing conflict tend to neglect the elimination of its underlying causes associated with long-term conflict resolution. Economic, political and social trends can produce instability. Long-term prevention work has to be based on the elimination of root causes such as oppression of minority rights.

Reconstruction and development are needed in order to move beyond the crisis management framework and prevent future occurrences of similar events. A long term solution has to be based on negotiation for structural or policy changes. Economic development programmes can be designed to build trust between adversarial communities. Human rights issues have to be incorporated into program designs. Practical actions have to cover not only political and military but also social and economic aspects of the conflict. In the longer term, prevention strategies include efforts to address structural disparities as well as the promotion of understanding among people and cooperation among states (Salim, 1996, p. 102).

Regional Mechanisms

In the post-Cold War era, regional security mechanisms have played an active role in conflict prevention. Regional organisations are authorised to take collective action within the mandate of the UN Charter. Local remedies ought to be sought in accordance with Article 33 of the United Nations Charter prior to their undertaking by UN authorities (Salim, 1996, p. 101). Regional arrangements for peaceful settlement were encouraged for border disputes and other issues of regional concern.

Over the last decade or so, institutionalised mechanisms for preventive action were established by several regional organisations. In the July 1992 summit meeting in Helsinki, the Conference on Security and Cooperation in Europe -- renamed the Organization for Security and Cooperation in Europe (OSCE) -- developed a method for early warning by establishing a Conflict Prevention Center in Vienna and appointing a High Commissioner for National Minorities. The High Commissioner has responsibility for reporting on and planning diplomatic responses to emerging ethno-national conflicts (Gurr, 1996, p. 125). As part of early consultation mechanisms on emerging conflict, fact-finding and rapporteur missions were utilised in Albania, Armenia, Azerbaijan, Chechnya, Georgia, Kazakhstan, Ukraine, the former Yugoslavia and other areas (Chigas, 1996). A unique thrust of the OSCE system is the establishment of the Court of Conciliation and Arbitration in 1994 that provides both recommendatory and binding procedures to interstate problems.

The Organization of African Unity (OAU) set up the Mechanism for Conflict Prevention, Management and Resolution (MCPMR) in Cairo in June 1993, to prevent the outbreak of conflicts through early warning. Conflict management functions are ingrained in the containment of political tension to a particular locality. Taking early political action is designed to localise violence. The Commission of Mediation, Conciliation and Arbitration (CMCA), as the permanent organ of the OAU, was originally charged with dispute settlement. However, the role was dormant between 1963 and 1990 due to the fact that its jurisdiction was narrowly confined to intervention in interstate rather than intrastate conflicts (Salim, 1996, pp.

102-3). On the other hand, ad hoc committees were created by the OAU Assembly of Heads of State and Government to hold debate about complaints lodged against the organisation's other member states (Peck, 1998, p. 161). Conflicts have also been managed by the use of good offices and fact finding missions organised through the secretary general's initiatives.

Early Warning Systems

In recognition of threats to security arising from ethnic and social strife, international communities have called, from the early 1990s, for strengthening early warning systems that would help to assess the situations of a threat to peace and prepare actions based on the information about natural disasters and political indicators (Boutros-Ghali, 1995). A global system for conflict early warning is a means to efficiently monitor deadly cycles of repression and resistance. The United Nations Secretariat is constantly monitoring many regional and internal conflicts. Efforts to design and employ early warning systems for international policy planning can be undertaken by the UN Department of Humanitarian Affairs in Geneva and New York and by the Center for Documentation and Research of the UN High Commissioner for Refugees in Geneva (Gurr, 1996, p. 125). CSCE early warning systems have been used to deal with tensions involving national minority issues at an early stage. They collect and receive information regarding national minority issues from parties directly involved, the media and non-governmental organisations.

The basis for practical preventive work is information. Early warning is the first step in the planning of practical measures to prevent conflict. Early warning facilitates understanding the source of potential conflicts and addressing them in time to abort their explosion into violent confrontation. Military, political, social and economic indicators can be developed in support of a diagnosis of causes and monitoring activities. The challenge for early warning systems is to search beyond the immediate time horizon to identify latent and low-level conflicts that have not yet attracted public attention.

Early warning evaluates the probability that certain events will generate violent conflict. Early signs of instability, ranging from border disputes and human rights abuses to flow of refugees, are critical for the assessment of possible occurrences of genocide or civil wars. Such risk factors as political mobilisation of rebellious groups, radical leadership changes, polarisation of political groups, the erosion of government legitimacy, the mobilisation of paramilitary groups and increasing use of ethnic symbols by political elites can be included in designing early warning systems. The government may enact discriminatory measures. Leaders of ethnic groups may call for the expulsion of antagonistic groups and try to obtain external support. These events may follow economic hardships and the perception of unequal distribution of wealth and resources among ethnic groups.

An early warning system should be able to provide increasingly reliable information and assessments that will help decision makers answer policy questions about specific preventive measures (Gurr, 1996, p. 125). Surveillance of armed conflicts produces an assessment of the degree and kinds of dangers to which high risk groups are exposed. The probability of a conflict occurring can be predicted based on advance knowledge of conditions likely to lead to conflict. Field monitoring and indicator construction enhance analytical capabilities that provide risk assessments. Prediction of future events has to be supported by an adequate explanatory framework. However, anticipating violent conflicts is 'not a matter of forecasting the precise timing and direction of future events' (Lund, 1996, p. 108).

A Final Note

International conflicts are diverse in nature, sources and scale. The divergent approaches mentioned in this chapter can be differently applied depending on the type of the outcome sought (partial settlement, integrative resolution), the nature of the process (bargaining, leveraged mediation, facilitation and consultation, more forceful third party intervention), the level of operations (official, nongovernmental), the seriousness of problem (dispute, protracted social conflict) and the causation (interests, values, needs). Varying degrees of outside leverage are exerted in changing the conflict situation and dynamics and consequently influencing the outcome.

In contrast with third party facilitation viewed as a means for resolving the whole aspects of conflict, a process of mediated bargaining and negotiation focuses on the narrow interests of the parties. The range of possible outcomes is bounded by the ability and resources of protagonists and the contexts within which they are mobilised. Settlement approaches are a limited endeavour designed for reaching an agreement on a particular aspect of a conflict. On the other hand, conflict resolution approaches attempt to attain 'a non-hierarchical, non-coercive integrative solution from the parties themselves' by focusing on such underlying sources of conflict as identity and security needs (Hoffman, 1992, pp. 264-65).

Social complexity and human diversity require an ability to apply conflict resolution approaches critically and creatively. In resolving differences, the contingency approaches focus on adopting different methods in different circumstances. Settlement of smaller issues by negotiation can lead to the resolution of larger problems. However, conflict would not be resolved over time by simply managing its destructive aspects without tackling the underlying sources of hostility.

Given political and social implications derived from its outcome, conflict resolution is not strictly a value neutral business. It contains certain ethical as well as political imperatives. The questions of social justice, economic inequality and value differences are not separate from the approaches to resolving conflict. In addition, successful resolution entails efforts to encompass both the intellectual and emotional components of the process to overcome adversarial relationships.

12   Human Rights

Human rights have become a major concern of modern society, with violent oppression being used as a form of social control to prevent democratic participation. Many people around the world are deprived of an equal opportunity based on gender, race, religion and ethnicity. A lack of distributive justice denies adequate access to the goods and services available in society. The concept of human rights has been expanded to encompass the concerns of the oppressed and exploited. The denial of freedom and other rights to self-realisation constitutes social injustice. Despite the existence of universally acceptable legal norms and principles, human rights have not been enforced across national boundaries because of a sovereign state's resistance.

Human Rights Abuses

Root causes of human rights violations originate in not only political oppression but also deteriorating economic and social conditions. Expression or organisation of political opposition in China, Turkey, Kenya, Pakistan and other countries under an authoritarian government leads to imprisonment. Political intolerance often goes hand in hand with social discrimination against certain categories of people (Symonides, 1998, p. 12). Victims of communal violence often include indigenous populations, refugees, women, children and minority groups. Human dignity has also been violated by extreme poverty and social exclusion in many underdeveloped countries.

Prior to the 1990s, the application of Cold War logic to regional struggles legitimised the consolidation of power by rightwing military dictatorships and authoritarian rulers. Sacrifice of human rights was justified by the containment of communism and sometimes to support expansion of Western business interests. In Argentina, Brazil and Uruguay, military authoritarian regimes, which took power through military coups in the 1970s, halted the electoral process and banned political party and union activity. In Uruguay one in thirty of the population passed through prison.

205

It has been common to kill and torture suspected members of opposition groups under many authoritarian governments that are facing rising political challenges. Violence is often used to close all political space for opposition. Between 1980 and 1982, every week hundreds of brutally tortured bodies were found on the streets of Guatemala and El Salvador (Sinclair, 1995. p. 9).

In an internal war, human rights violations by the government forces have been severe. In the current and past examples from Indonesia, Peru, Guatemala and other countries, the army used terror for social control and counter-insurgency campaigns targeted civilian populations. The government death squads suppressed rural community groups and trade union movements. Children were interrogated about the suspected activities of their parents.

Some states resort to the use of extreme violence in an effort to wipe out indigenous communities. Millions of indigenous people have been displaced and killed in the modern state-building process. The principal objective is to impose models of social organisation consistent with 'national security' by destroying traditional forms of social relationships and indigenous cultures which are fundamental in the making of a people's identity (Alecio, 1995, p. 38). Indigenous peoples' struggles for the preservation of forestlands and territorial autonomy have been brutally suppressed in Malaysia and Brazil (Cultural Survival, 1993). In addition, indigenous people were often the victims of terror in a counterinsurgency policy. In Guatemala, as many as six hundred indigenous communities were destroyed in the 1980s.

Violence caused by the manipulation of religious and ethnic differences is a paramount human rights problem in many parts of the world. In Kenya, India and other societies divided by ethnic suspicion and hatred, communal violence is often encouraged or directed by the government (Human Rights Watch, 1995). The murder of unarmed ethnic group members has drawn the attention of the international community. Human rights violations create a security threat to individuals and various social groups. Mass violence and genocide are committed by the individuals of dominant social groups as well as government officials. It suggests that in the post-Cold War environment, non-state entities such as warlords have also to be fitted into the international human rights system (Tomasevski, 1995, p. 91).

In addition to political repression and violence, economic disparities serve as unfavourable conditions for human rights. Wide spread extreme poverty is no less demeaning than physically inflicted violence as a threat to the right to life and to the full and effective enjoyment of human rights (Resolution 51/97 of 12 September 1996, the UN General Assembly). Decent living standards have been denied in Africa and other indebted countries implementing harsh economic measures designed to control inflation and imbalance of payments. Stringent monetary policies contribute to deteriorating social services and a drastic fall in income levels. Low wages provide the key to developing countries' competitive edge in international markets and this means cracking down on labour movements. Trade unions and other grassroots organisations were crushed to implement neoliberal economic programs supported by foreign loans and investment.

Connections to Peace

As confirmed in many international documents, the preservation of the dignity and worth inherent in the human person is the basis of all human rights. The individuals, as the subjects of these rights, are 'the principal beneficiary and should participate actively in their realization' (The United Nations, 1995, p. 93). The ideals of human rights enshrine equal rights, self-determination, democracy and social and economic progress. The principles of human rights are constituted by their universality, objectivity, equality and interdependence. Equal dignity among human beings lies in their common heritage in such a way that it enhances a spirit of brother/sisterhood in their relations.

Human rights, in general, enhance positive conditions for human development. Individual civil and political rights such as freedom of information and expression protect individuals against the state. Security at a personal level means the prevention of physical abuse through the prohibition of torture. The right to exchange and express ideas cannot be neglected in promoting autonomy and freedom. This requires that 'the will of the people shall be the basis of the authority of government', and 'this shall be expressed ... by universal and equal suffrage' (*Universal Declaration of Human Rights*, 1948, Article 21).

Human rights are essential for achieving positive peace and development. To achieve economic and cultural rights, we need to have the conditions of social justice. Human rights are inseparable from the access to survival, self-realisation and satisfaction of other types of basic human needs (Nayar, 1996, p. 186). Education, work, cultural identity, self-expression and other means of physical and psychological subsistence are essential to fulfilling the inherent dignity and worth of all human individuals.

In considering the reciprocal relations and interdependence of respect for human rights and development, civil and political rights are indivisible from economic, social and cultural rights. Development must be based on human rights principles of non-discrimination, equity, social justice, self-sufficiency and solidarity. Political aspects of human aspirations are further fulfilled by the realisation of the right to a standard of living adequate for maintaining health and material well-being. On the other hand, the demand for decent life and equity is easily suppressed in an oppressive political environment.

The elimination of structural violence against the marginalised has its own intrinsic importance. Inequality and unfair treatment at personal and group levels stem from ethnocentrism, racism, sexism, colonialism and authoritarian political rule. Given their intrinsic value, economic justice and fair treatment of all people are important in their own right. Simultaneously it can also be said that they are an essential component of positive peace. Discrimination against ethnic and linguistic minorities builds up anger and frustration. A lack of freedom and economic inequity create conditions for political and social unrest – sometimes civil war.

Sustainable peace cannot be obtained without the existence of a civil society that guarantees human rights. Differences in political systems and cultural traditions cannot be used to impede the universal application of human rights standards. Besides political freedom and civil rights, individuals are entitled to the right of cultural autonomy and the use of the language that belongs to their own community. In culturally heterogeneous societies, the guarantee of individual civil and political rights does not necessarily satisfy the requirement of group rights. Economic, cultural and social rights include group autonomy and non-discrimination. The subjection of peoples to alien domination and exploitation constitutes a denial of rights to self-determination.

Three Generations of Human Rights Movements

Whereas human rights are considered as a claim for universal reason and an assertion of common humanity, their application undoubtedly reflects the uniqueness of each separate situation (Douzinas, 1996, p. 119). The formation and even the very existence of rights change in response to the prevailing socio-economic conditions. The aspirations for human betterment have been expressed throughout the struggle for human rights in a dynamically changing social environment. Scientific and technological developments and modifications in economic and social institutions affect the ways in which human rights are perceived.

The historical formation of three generations of human rights activism began with civil and political rights, was expanded to economic and social rights and finally incorporated collective group rights (Chadwick, 1996, p. 580). The first generation of human rights movements represents a number of entitlements that can generally be called civil and political rights. It emerged from the struggle to obtain freedom from monarchic rule in modern history. The French and American revolutions were a response to the need of the middle class interested in their individual freedom of commerce and their political role as citizens. In taking power, they instituted civil and political rights that were articulated as the rationale for the American and French revolutions at the end of the 18th century.

The first generation focuses on negative rights of non-interference with the private life of citizens (Weiss, 1994, p. 115). Their basic principles proclaim that 'all men are born and remain free and equal in their rights'. They are reflected in such rights as equality before the law, freedom from arbitrary arrest and freedom of opinion and expression (Robertson and Merrills, 1996, p. 3). The principles affirm freedom to do anything that is not harmful to other human beings. Establishing human rights standards is critical to protecting citizens against unregulated government power. In controlling the power of the state over individual citizens, major attention is paid to what the government ought not to do. Ensuring freedom and autonomy of individuals is tied to personal initiatives and responsibilities to secure the conditions of social well-being. Individuals are protected by procedural rules and have due process rights. Effective access to the suffrage and justice systems helps individuals maximise their ability and further their interests.

The second generation entails positive rights that are inherent to economic and social well-being such as access to land, respectable labour conditions, prevention of child labour and so forth. Human rights concerns cannot be fulfilled in the harsh realities of hunger, disease, illiteracy and other aspects of underdevelopment. Social revolutions in 19th century Europe were struggles to satisfy the economic and social needs of people who were economically suppressed. Following the socialist and workers' movements of the 19th century, many governments accepted the obligation to ensure their citizens economic and social well-being. The use of economic resources by the government has to be geared toward fulfilling necessities as well as a more equitable share in the goods of society.

The third generation sheds light on group well-being realised by collective rights. The rights and interests of certain groups of people can be better met by their self-identification as members of a collective entity. They take a more holistic approach embracing a brotherhood and sisterhood of humankind and their inseparable solidarity. Its emergence was influenced by a non-Western movement to end colonialism and racism in the mid twentieth century. The third generation of collective and solidarity rights was sought by groups with common identity and experience in the struggle to achieve self-determination of racial and ethnic groups. This was reflected in the adoption of the international standards condemning genocide and apartheid.

In human rights movements, there is also a growing concern with the inequitable international economic order. Economic development in the poorest countries is now considered the collective responsibility of the international community. Equitable economic relations among states are of a key concern for sustainable development of the least developed countries. 'The rights of people to self-determination in its economic, political, social and cultural dimensions lie at the heart of the recognition of the right to development' (UN, 1995. p. 77). The monetary policies of international financial institutions have adverse effects on conditions for the fulfilment of human rights. In combating widespread poverty, aid must be provided along with alleviation of external debt burdens.

As we begin the 21st century, the issues have been further broadened, with an emphasis on the unity of humankind, to include ethnocide, genocide and environmental abuse. The international community is concerned with the rise of xenophobia and other types of intolerance in ethnic conflicts. Recently condemned, the use of unilateral economic sanctions and heavy military spending impedes the ability to devote resources to human development. Industrialised countries must restrain from harming the population of other countries with the export of hazardous substances and waste. The protection of the environment, the common heritage of humankind and peace have emerged as new rights that belong to a collection of persons rather than single individuals (Weiss, 1994, p. 116).

Development of Principles and Norms

Human rights principles have to be converted into legal obligations for governments through international treaties. The efforts to develop international law in human rights date back to the early nineteenth century with the formal prohibition of slave trade by the Treaty of Vienna in 1815 and the General Act of Brussels (UN, 1995, p. 5). In 1864, the major states in Europe wrote the first Geneva Convention for victims of armed conflict. The first significant multilateral human rights treaty, arising out of war, was devoted to caring for wounded and sick soldiers and respecting the immunity of military hospitals and their staff. During the period of the League of Nations between 1919 and 1939, the concerns of human rights encompassed the protection of such categories of people as slaves, workers, minorities and the inhabitants of trust territories.

Modern human rights laws were significantly expanded in reaction to Nazi aggression and atrocities. The horror of the Second World War generated awareness of the close connection between respect for human dignity and peace. The United Nations Charter, in its Article 1, paragraph 3, stresses 'respect for human rights and fundamental freedom for all without distinction as to race, sex, language, or religion'. The Preamble to the Charter of the United Nations ranks respect for human rights second only to the need to prevent war. UN charter article 55 recognises that peaceful and friendly relations among nations have to be based on respect for the principle of equal rights and self-determination of people. It stresses a higher standard of living, full employment and economic and social development. Also emphasised is universal respect for, and observance of, fundamental freedom that is a necessary condition for the creation of social stability and well-being.

The international bill of rights is made up of three documents, including the 1948 Universal Declaration of Human Rights and the two 1966 UN covenants. The 1948 Universal Declaration of Human Rights further defines the meanings of human rights asserted in the United Nations Charter. The principles of the Declaration support inherent human dignity and the precedence of inalienable and imprescriptible rights to freedom and equality over all powers of the state. The Declaration's preamble says 'it is essential, if man is not to be compelled to have recourse, as a last resort, to rebellion against tyranny and oppression, that human rights should be protected by the rule of law'.

According to Article 2 of the Universal Declaration, the dignity of the human person should be recognised without distinction of any kind. Human rights are by nature universal and acquired by birth by all members of the human family, regardless of the political, jurisdictional or international status of the country or territory to which a person belongs. The individual is entitled to have civil and political rights to block certain government actions, hence protecting individual freedom from undesirable governmental action. The Declaration is also regarded as 'one of the very first international instruments to recognise the ethical and judicial value of economic, social and cultural rights and to affirm their equal and interdependent relationship with civil and political rights' (UN, 1995, p. 26). The obligation to implement the Declaration was later affirmed in a considerable number of international human rights instruments.

After thirty years' efforts to define the meaning of the human rights language in the UN Charter and the Declaration, two treaties on human rights were produced in 1966: the first treaty pertains to civil and political rights; the second relates to economic, social and cultural rights. The 1966 Covenant consists of thirty articles, the first twenty-one of which prohibit torture and arbitrary arrest, guarantee a fair trial and equality before the law and protect freedom of association, expression and religion. The remaining articles emphasise the right to just and favourable conditions of work, vacations with pay, rest and leisure, education, nutrition, health care, social security and an adequate standard of living. It is acknowledged that free development of individual personality and well-being is guaranteed by the right to participation in the cultural life of the community as well as the right to social security.

Social, economic and cultural rights are also well represented in the 1974 United Nations Educational, Scientific and Cultural Organisation (UNESCO) resolution on peace. Peoples and individuals have to be able to enjoy affirmative rights permitting them to do certain things. Governments are obligated to do their best in order to satisfy these rights. With the number of non-Western states increasing in the 1960s and 1970s, an emphasis shifted to positive, communal rights. The document also gives priority to the elimination of colonialism and racism by emphasising that peoples should have the rights to self-determination along with other rights.

The Declaration on the Right to Development adopted by the General Assembly in 1986 'marked a turning point in that it expressed a new way of regarding the very concept of "development" following the failure of national and international development policies' (UN, 1995, pp. 74-5). The Declaration defined development as 'a comprehensive economic, social, cultural and political process, which aims at the constant improvement of the well-being of the entire population and of all individuals on the basis of their active, free and meaningful participation in development and in the fair distribution of benefits resulting therefrom'. In the discourse on human rights, the international community, for the first time, questioned whether the primary objective of economic activities is simply achieving financial and macroeconomic balance. Foreign debt was acknowledged as an unfavourable condition for protecting decent human life by the majority vote in the UN Commission on Human Rights.

The Vienna Declaration and Programme of Action, which emerged at the World Conference on Human Rights held in 1993, notes several key areas of future focus with reaffirmation of the right to development and its interdependence on democracy and other fundamental rights. Most importantly, paragraph 5 of the Vienna Declaration confirms that every type of right has equal significance. The Vienna Conference document highlights that 'human rights are universal, indivisible and interdependent and interrelated'. Political, civil, economic, social and cultural rights should be 'treated in a fair and equal manner and with the same emphasis' (UN, 1995, p. 98).

Conventions in Specific Categories

In response to systematic mistreatment of people with marginalised political and social status, many treaties have lent significance to the elimination of racial discrimination and discrimination against women. The Declaration on Race and Racial Prejudice by the UNESCO's General Conference in 1978 denounces racist ideologies, discriminatory behaviour, prejudicial attitudes and structural arrangements and institutionalised practices resulting in racial inequality. The International Convention on the Elimination of All Forms of Racial Discrimination (accepted broadly by the international community since 1965) requires legal and educational steps to eliminate such forms of discrimination as exclusion, restriction and preference in the treatment of human beings on the grounds of race, colour and ethnic origins. In combating racism and racial discrimination, the Vienna Programme of Action in 1993 further specifies regular system-wide consultations, coordination and reporting at national, regional and international levels.

The Convention on the Prevention and Punishment of the Crime of Genocide approved at the General Assembly in 1948 identifies state responsibilities for putting an end to such practices as killing and causing serious bodily and mental harm to members of distinct national, ethnic, religious and other groups in times of both war and peace. The Genocide Convention was thus designed to protect the group identities of national, racial, ethnic and religious communities beyond the promotion of individual rights.

The rights of indigenous populations are affirmed by the international community's commitment to their economic, social and cultural well-being. In response to the indigenous movements, the Sub-commission on Prevention of Discrimination and Protection of Minorities authorised a study on discrimination against indigenous populations. Following the recommendation of the study, the Working Group on the Rights of Indigenous Populations was formed in 1982. It served as a principle forum for discussion about the concerns of indigenous people. The working group's mandate is to elaborate and develop norms for the protection of the rights of indigenous populations.

It prepared a Draft Universal Declaration on Indigenous Rights approved in 1994 by the Sub-commission on minority issues, which was further studied by the Commission on Human Rights. Later, two studies were prepared by special rapporteurs: one on treaties between indigenous populations and states, and the other on principles and guidelines for the protection of the cultural and intellectual patrimony of indigenous peoples. Indigenous authority in cultural customs, religions, education, social welfare and economic activities are recognised in the Declaration, but little effective gains were made in self-governance.

UN covenants and conventions on discrimination against women are aimed at preventing economic and political discrimination rooted in social practice or deliberate government policy. Following the Convention on the Political Rights of Women in 1952, the Convention on the Elimination of All Forms of Discrimination against Women (that entered into force in 1981) explicitly links the promotion of women's rights to global development, international security and peace. There are provisions on equality in access to education, employment, health care and other aspects of social and economic life as well as equal rights within the family. Meeting specific needs of rural women and the suppression of prostitution and trafficking in women are also stipulated. The Vienna Declaration and Programme of Action recognises that women's rights are universal and should not be subordinated to culture or religion. For the first time, the UN declared the elimination of violence against women in public and private life as a human rights obligation.

The moral framework for the rights of children was expressed in the 1959 Declaration of the Rights of the Child that affirms that 'mankind owes to the child the best it has to give'. The UN legal instrument designed to implement the Declaration was provided by the Convention on the Right of the Child (1989). The Convention is aimed at protecting the child against sexual and economic exploitation. Children should have the right to health care, education and leisure. States shall ensure to the maximum extent possible the survival and development of the child by promoting the right to preserve his or her identity. Assistance needs to be provided for those who face emergencies, abandonment and ill treatment. The Convention also outlaws the recruitment of child soldiers and other abuses against children in war and calls for special protection. The Convention was ratified by more countries than any other human rights instrument.

Though it does not cover internally displaced people, the 1951 UN Convention Relating to the Status of Refugees offers the legal protection of refugees by allowing the right to seek asylum. The awareness of problems with stateless people was critical in producing the Convention Relating to the Status of Stateless Persons (1954) and the Convention on the Reduction of Statelessness (1961). The Vienna Declaration notes that it is a state obligation to develop strategies to address the root causes of mass migrations and the internal displacement of persons.

The Convention against Discrimination in Education was sponsored by UNESCO in 1960 to recognise the right of national minorities to maintain their educational activities such as teaching their own languages, culture and history in schools. It addresses minority rights which were overlooked in the 1948 Universal Declaration of Human Rights. A more specific obligation to promote minority rights was mentioned in the 1993 Declaration on the Rights of Persons Belonging to National or Ethnic, Religious and Linguistic Minorities. Economic aspirations and conditions for enhancing ethnic and cultural identities of communal groups shall be fully guaranteed by legislative and other measures. The UN Sub-Commission on Prevention of Discrimination and Protection of Minorities helped develop an international consensus on the definition of a minority and promote the idea that protection of minority rights is essential to political stability.

International Labour Organisation (ILO) treaties have been concerned with diverse aspects of the right to work, conditions of work, social security and the protection of migrant and child workers. Most noticeably, they prohibit forced labour, strengthen the right to organise for collective bargaining and unionise workers. In 1948, the ILO produced the Convention on Freedom of Association and Protection of the Right to Organise. Later the ILO produced other basic treaties to accompany the previous ones. They include conventions on collective bargaining (1949), abolition of forced labour (1957), migrant workers and their family members (1983), discrimination in employment (1958, 1964), vocational rehabilitation and social policy (1983).

Implementation of Human Rights Policy

The international community has the collective responsibility for ensuring the conditions necessary for the enjoyment of human rights (UN, 1995, p. 93). International agencies, which are independent of states, can be an effective means to protect human rights. The United Nations General Assembly has given broad authority to initiate studies and make recommendations for assisting in the realisation of human rights and prevention of discrimination based on race, sex or religion.

The General Assembly, along with Security Council, passed recommendations on numerous subjects, ranging from sanctions against apartheid in South Africa and the rights of the Palestinian people to self-determination. Through the conclusion of international conventions and the adoption of recommendations, the ILO has pioneered advancement in such matters as the regulation of working hours, provision of adequate wages, equal pay for equal work, social security and freedom of association (Robertson and Merrills, 1996, p. 283). In consultation with the General Assembly, the ILO also made recommendations regarding the protection of trade union rights and the prohibition of forced labour. The protection of cultural rights has been of immediate interest for the work of UNESCO. Other UN specialised agencies have long been active in the human rights field. UNICEF worked actively for the ratification of the Convention on the Right of the Child and made a strong effort to promote its implementation (UN, 1995, p. 83). The United Nations High Commissioner for Refugees, charged with fact finding and technical assistance as well as delivery of humanitarian aid, responds to the problems concerning refugees and stateless persons.

The recently created office of a High Commissioner for Human Rights coordinates policies and actions of different UN organs, reinforces international cooperation and initiates a dialogue with governments (Robertson and Merrills, 1996, p. 112). Gross violations of human rights are discussed at the UN Commission on Human Rights, which meets every year for a six week session in Geneva. The Commission set up by the Economic and Social Council is empowered to formulate recommendations and provide information and other services with the input of nongovernmental organisations. The Commission conducts on-site investigations and produces valuable reports with the deployment of rapporteurs. In the 1990s, human rights field monitoring teams were deployed to El Salvador, Haiti, Rwanda and Cambodia. These missions, integrated into the human rights component of peacekeeping operations, were all sent under the direction of the UN Security Council.

The Human Rights Committee evaluates periodic reports submitted by states and produces general comments through its advisory/monitoring role for the International Covenant on Civil and Political Rights. It also has a function of inquiring and investigating complaints from other states and individuals. The same reporting and review procedure has been adopted by a committee created to facilitate the implementation of the Convention on Economic, Social and Cultural Rights. Committees have also been established by the international conventions on the rights of the child, discrimination against a particular race or gender and other major issues for the purpose of monitoring compliance and formulating general recommendations on specific issues.

In realising the goals of the Third Decade to Combat Racism and Racial Discrimination proclaimed by the UN General Assembly in 1993, the UN Commission on Human Rights appointed a Special Rapporteur on contemporary forms of racism, xenophobia and related intolerance. The process for monitoring and demanding accountability for the abuse of women's rights led to the appointment of a Special Rapporteur on Violence Against Women (Bunch and Carillo, 1998). The special rapporteur actively seeks and collects information on violence against women, its causes, and consequences; the office can recommend measures at regional, national and international levels to eliminate violence against women (UN, 1996, p. 133).

Periodic reports on government abuses can help examine human rights records. States are called upon to submit periodic reports concerning their implementation of human rights protected by the International Covenant on Civil and Political Rights and other agreements. The states that have ratified the Convention on Discrimination against Women are required to evaluate the progress made by their policies in the prevention of discrimination. The periodic reports produced by states are scrutinized by the Committee on the Elimination of Discrimination against Women for monitoring the fulfilment of state obligations to prohibit gender-based discrimination. To ensure compliance, the Committee on the Rights of the Child also considers the report submitted by states parties to the Convention.

In general, government assessments themselves are not necessarily authoritative given that they reflect their own views. However, pressure can be put on the offending governments by negative publicity though it is not linked to enforcement functions. In addition, reporting in and of itself may cause states to rectify some types of human rights violations. Another purpose of reporting is to give international organisations an authoritative source of information in making recommendations about the implementation of human rights policies.

Individuals may seek help directly from international agencies without being inhibited by states. Refugees can have a direct contact with the office of UNHCR. Prisoners in an international armed conflict have the right to communicate directly with the International Committee of the Red Cross. Many treaties contain optional provisions that allow individuals to submit complaints to supervisory committees. More than forty states, not including the United States, agreed to the right of their citizens to petition the UN Human Rights Committee (created by the 1966 UN Covenant) following recourse to national efforts, for a violation of civil/political and socio-economic cultural rights by a government. The Committee is made up of individual experts but not government representatives. The International Convention on the Elimination of All Forms of Racial Discrimination was the first UN human rights instrument to set up an international monitoring system, in particular, a procedure for individual complaints (UN, 1995, p.33).

These individual appeal procedures have rarely been used, and even in cases where a treaty violation has occurred, no legal authority exists to enforce the findings (Donnelly, 1995, p. 55). Some exceptional cases include a complaint filed against the Canadian government by the Lubicon Lake Band of Indians in northern Canada with the Human Rights Committee (dealing with violations of the Covenant on Civil and Political Rights) in 1987. The petition claimed that state-sponsored oil and gas exploration threatened the Indians' means of subsistence and thus violated their right to life and to self-determination as a minority. Three years later, the committee upheld the claim (Sachs, 1996, p. 148).

State Sovereignty and Human Rights Protection

States demonstrate their commitment to human rights protection by ratifying international conventions. The Vienna Programme of Action calls for measures ensuring ratification of the Convention on the Rights of Child and encourages states to ratify the Convention on the Elimination of All Forms of Discrimination against Women. The Subcommission on Prevention of Discrimination and Protection of Minorities has carried out special studies to overcome obstacles hindering the universal ratification of international instruments. The General Assembly, the Commission on Human Rights and various treaty bodies have made a solemn appeal for the universal acceptance of treaties, accompanied by a definitive timetable.

Traditionally, the protection of human rights has not been a major state concern. One major obstacle that the international community faces is the lack of enthusiasm of political leaders. They see international investigation as an intrusion in their internal affairs. Implementing human rights poses direct challenges to state authorities by defining and prohibiting governmental abuses against individuals and groups. International standards of human rights represent assaults on state power and sovereignty by restricting what a state can do within its own borders. Therefore, the protection of human rights cannot always be entrusted to states and to international bodies controlled by states. Governments are not likely to press human rights issues since such interests interfere with other interests and set a precedent that can be used against them in the future. In particular, the efforts to scrutinise their abuse have been criticised by some Third World government officials as imposing Western standards on their cultural traditions and political circumstances.

The UN Human Rights Committee and the committee created by the Racial Discrimination Treaty are independent of state influences but they have no authority to sanction violators of human rights. Hence, states find it easy to disregard their recommendations. Furthermore, the Universal Declaration of Human Rights is not legally binding. It is only a recommendation, but not an international treaty, and does not have any provisions for enforcement. Since there is no enforcement mechanism in international human rights issues, human rights violators have to be brought to public notice.

Governments are obliged to prevent abuses of power and to create conditions for the realisation of freedom and equality by international pressure (Tomasevski, 1995, p. 90). Donors can push for political reform by conditionally attaching economic aid to human rights protection. In 1991, foreign donors agreed that new aid had to be linked to political liberalisation in Kenya. The pressure led the regime to agree on holding multi-party elections with the legalisation of opposition parties. The Scandinavian countries employed economic aid as leverage to improve human rights conditions in other countries. Threats to withdraw assistance would only be effective if offending governments depend heavily on outside assistance.

Regional Experiences

Europe's human rights mechanisms are based on sophisticated legal mechanisms, and its experience suggests that human rights can be effectively protected by regional institutions. The Organization of American States also developed such institutional mechanisms as the American Convention on Human rights, mostly with a focus on civil and political rights, and the Inter-American Court of Human rights. The African Charter on Human and People's Rights combine both collective and individual rights. On the other hand, Asian countries have not developed any intergovernmental forum comparable to other continents.

The European Convention on Human Rights and Fundamental Freedoms defined a set of civil and political rights and established a court. All participating states have democratic political systems and voluntarily accept the legal regime. Cases of violations brought by individuals, groups and one state against another are examined by the European Commission of Human Rights. The agencies are made up of individual experts not instructed by state officials. The Council of Europe requires that new members meet criteria set up by international human rights covenants such as the European Convention on Human Rights. Without constitutional guarantees of human rights and institutional mechanisms to support individual freedom, countries are not entitled to Council membership.

The European Court of Human Rights gives binding judgements about the legality of state policies under the European Convention on Human Rights, which has been effective since 1953. All states in the Council of Europe abide by the convention and accept the supranational authority of the Court. Since October 1994, the Council moved toward giving individuals standing to sue in the European Court of Human Rights. Individuals are granted the same legal status in the court as a state accused of human rights violations. The petition of individuals of 18 European countries is allowed against the highest levels of national government without waiting for the exhaustion of national avenues. The European Commission on Human Rights can also respond to private complaints.

Nongovernmental Organisations and Grassroots Struggle

Independent nongovernmental institutions can contact the government officials of countries where human rights are denied. The International Committee of the Red Cross, organised by a group of Swiss citizens in 1864, makes prison visits in an attempt to protect victims of war from harm. The International Rescue Committee tries to find new homes for refugees. The Anti-Slavery League was involved in movements against slavery. Cultural Survival and other Western based NGOs provide assistance for indigenous people and other victims of modernisation in learning educational, technical and legal skills.

Many private groups are most active in defensive protection of human rights. They include Amnesty International (calling for the release of prisoners of conscience and the cessation of all torture and execution), Human Rights Watch (well known for its investigation and documentation of abuses of civil and political rights in diverse geographic areas) and the International Commission of Jurists (seeking to mobilise support for the rule of law). The International League for Human Rights has been engaged in assisting victims of human rights violations and networking with other agencies to promote a broad range of rights covered in international treaties. Campaigning against political arrests and torture is aimed at drawing public attention to human rights issues. Equally importantly, NGOs are often involved in drafting the resolutions of the UN human rights subcommissions.

Compared with Western based NGOs, grassroots human rights movements in many Third World countries have been fighting for the survival and well-being of their own community members. In the late 1970s and early 1980s, El Salvador, Guatemala, Argentina and other Central and Latin American countries were the staging ground for the confrontation between dynamic popular movements and repressive governments (Uclés, 1995, p. 154). Victims of government abuses formed grassroots human rights organisations in response to the military-led onslaught (Sinclair, 1995, pp. 9-10). Particularly well known are the Mothers of the Plaza de Mayo in Argentina, the Group of Relatives of the Detained-Disappeared in Chile, the Mutual Support Group in Guatemala and the Committee on the Mothers of the Disappeared in El Salvador. They held public demonstrations, organised strikes and street graffiti, arranged other types of popular mobilisation and demanded the return of their loved ones.

13   Self-Determination

Many conflicts around the world are attributed to a lack of self-determination. The increase in the number of intrastate conflicts during recent decades has been dramatic, especially in considering the relative decline in the number of interstate conflicts. Intense, often violent, inter-ethnic conflict has been accompanied by the struggle between different forces to maintain and break up multi-nation states. New independent states such as Croatia, Eritrea and Bangladesh were created with significant human cost resulting from armed struggle. Kurds, Tibetans, Palestinians and Kosovar Albanians have been struggling to achieve political autonomy and independence. Self-determination can be understood in terms of policies and practices that can manage inter-ethnic rivalries. Multi-ethnic polities have been the norm through the ages. This chapter will examine the definition, institutional mechanisms and practical application of self-determination.

Basic Principles

Self-determination is a basic principle for realising the freedom to control one's own life. It serves as the prerequisite for achieving positive human conditions for a decent life and self-fulfilment. The desire to rule one's self and to control one's own life is essential to human existence. Self-determination symbolises the aspiration of individuals to create, fashion and rule themselves and not to be dominated and moulded by others. The quest for self-determination is, therefore, not just a political ideal to be invoked in times of danger but the unchangeable aspiration of an individual human being.

Individual human beings are endlessly looking for various group identities to satisfy their aspirations for a form of social being. Personal freedom can be interpreted in the context of an individual human being's ability to have control over his or her own life. On the other hand, most importantly, the quest for self-determination is achieved through group action in a community. Self-determination can be suggested as 'a type of collective existence rather than a one-time political happening' (Stavenhagen, 1996, p. 5).

Human aggregates can pursue the goal of steering their own destiny in daily life through numerous means. Freedom to choose a form of government is a universal principle. It is of utmost concern that the goals of self-determination be compatible with a participatory political and economic system that protects the rights of individuals and group identity. Autonomy is an ethical imperative to be fulfilled in the pursuit of a right to organise fully representative and democratic political entities.

The notion that the population should govern itself but not be subjected to alien rule upholds the ideal of the equality of peoples. Desire for determining one's own destiny is especially strong for those who are victims of oppression and have a sense of their own distinctiveness. The goals of self-determination include the liberation from oppression and deprivation. It is often expressed in the claims of self-conscious territorial communities that they rule themselves.

Self-determination as a basic norm for the construction of the peaceful world provides the conception that the identity needs of individual human beings should be a more primary concern than the territorial ambition of the state. Human being's loyalty does not necessarily reside in the state system, and individuals can be reincorporated into a new socio-political framework. Every individual should be able to exercise a voluntary choice to live under a self-given constitution.

Theoretically speaking, granting self-determination to all would remove a major cause of an inter-communal conflict. However, this optimistic projection of self-determination as a force for peace has been called into question by the frequent clashes between rival ethnic communities. Being transformed into an umbrella for providing prosperity and justice to all has proven a difficult goal to achieve in many ethnically divided societies. Those who claim the right of self-determination for themselves often deny others the same right. Micro-nationalism has often been manifested in historical legacies of oppression and violence dating back many centuries. The Croatian and Bosnian Serbs' practices of ethnic cleansing represent an extreme form of exclusion and reject the notion of community that transcends ethnicity and religion.

Historical Context

The principle of self-determination was developed with the emergence of nationalism in the 18th and 19th century (Hannum, 1990, p. 27). The idea of self-determination has, since the French Revolution, spread throughout the world, unifying peoples into nations. National movements were organised for peoples whose states disappeared from the map as a sovereign entity centuries earlier. Moves to ignite the spark of national insurrection derive from a cultural thrust generated by the intelligentsia. Mass mobilisation for liberation from foreign rule has become a modern phenomenon.

In the 20th century, social crisis and institutional collapse following the destruction of multiethnic empires facilitated the resurgence of ethnic and national identity. In the aftermath of World War I, independence was granted to linguistic and other cultural minorities dissatisfied with political boundaries that were drawn across the landscapes of disintegrating Austro-Hungarian and Ottoman empires as well as the European segments of Russia. The victorious countries used the principle of self-determination to legitimise the division of defeated countries with the creation of Czechoslovakia, Yugoslavia, Finland, Poland, and the Baltic States.

However, the doctrine of liberation was not applied to European colonies around the world despite their powerful appeal to the subjugated peoples of Asia and Africa. It was considered largely as a moral but not legal principle that can be universally applied. Reflecting this tendency, the phrase about the principles of self-determination was not even contained in the Covenant of the League of Nations.

Since World War II, there has been an interest in movements toward self-government. The UN Charter recognises that the right to self-determination prohibits other states from intervening in internal affairs. The UN has been actively engaged in the decolonialisation of Asia and Africa with the retreat of colonialism and colonial powers. The Trusteeship Council was created to facilitate the independence of former European colonies (Alger, 1999a, p. 32). It is made up of government representatives whose countries are engaged in preparing people of former colonies for self-rule. The obligation of trustees is to promote the capacity of colonised people to develop social, economic, and political conditions for self-government.

Thanks to the increased membership from newly independent states, self-determination was placed in the context of the liquidation of colonialism and Third World nationalism. The UN General Assembly adopted a Declaration on the Granting of Independence to Colonial Countries and

Peoples in 1960. The subjugation and domination of any people constitute a denial of fundamental human rights and serve as an impediment to world peace and cooperation. The Declaration acknowledges that all people are entitled to self-determination by virtue of a right to freely determine their political status and pursue economic, social and cultural development.

It also emphasises that inadequacy of political, educational and economic preparedness should not serve as a pretext for delaying independence. Most states in Asia, Africa, and the Caribbean became politically independent, but economic dependence on former European colonies remains as a limitation on their self-autonomy. In further recognising the demand that repressive rule against dependent people should cease, in 1961, the General Assembly created the Special Committee on the Situation with Regard to the Implementation of the Declaration on the Granting of Independence to Colonial Countries and Peoples. Their work generated much pressure on colonial powers and influenced world opinion.

During the period of decolonisation, in many instances, little attention was given to ethnic and other divisions within colonised territories. In general, 'the national unity' or 'territorial integrity' was regarded as a respected norm with some exceptions, including the partition of British India into India and Pakistan and the single colony of Ruanda-Urundi into Rwanda and Burundi (Hannum, 1996, p. 28). However, the broad visions of struggle for self-governance have not been applied to the treatment of various groups in arbitrarily created multi-nation states, and it illustrates that the revolution ran its course (Bennet, 1991, p. 371).

Toward the end of the 20th century and after the Cold War, 'national self-consciousness' has exploded into a virtual epidemic of demands for self-rule by territorial communities based on ethnic, religious, and historical identities. Most of the demands have come from peoples perceived as nations. They have included small indigenous folk communities, obscure pockets of transplanted peoples, and large populations sharing a religion or language distinct from the state in which they are located. Ironically, the contemporary burst of nationalism and micro-nationalism has occurred in the same period that state boundaries have diminished in significance in the lives of most people.

The Basis of Claims for Self-Determination

Determining who is entitled to self-determination includes both subjective and objective components. The members of the group have to think of themselves as distinctive from others and share certain objective characteristics composed of language, religion, history and ethnicity (Hannum, 1996, p. 31). Historical traditions, common culture and ideology are used to support claims for autonomy and independence. Ethnocultural commonality provides an important basis for self-determination. In addition to the existence of a distinctive identity from the rest of the country, a claim for autonomy and independence can be sympathetically heard by the experience of systematic political and economic discrimination (Buchanan, 1991).

Self-determination has both internal and external dimensions (Shehadi, 1993). The internal dimension is explained by the relationship between the people of a given territory and those who govern them. The people are a source of state sovereignty, and it has been legitimised by a democratic process. Identity groups seek greater political autonomy to control local matters by themselves. Demands for autonomy can be satisfied by legitimising the exercise of the right to internal self-determination. Greater autonomy allows not only the preservation of their cultural identity but also the promotion of collective economic and political interests.

The external dimension involves the relationship between a self-defined territory and the outside world. International treaties recognise the freedom of all peoples to determine their political status and to pursue their economic, social and cultural development. Many of these treaties, in general, have been applied to circumstances where colonialism prevailed. The principles of decolonisation have been used to allow independence for the entities that are geographically separate from the colonising power (Alfredsson, 1996, p. 60). Translating basic principles into effective political institutions has been difficult because the nature of the peoples who own the right to self-determination has not been clearly defined. There is no consensus on standards for determining which people or communities are entitled to independence.

In particular, confusion persists due to the insufficient development of international instruments and controversial state practices as well as a lack of conceptual and policy precision. On the other hand, the right of independent statehood for minorities within existing states has not been widely supported by international law. New states were created by the agreements of the component parts of states or dissolution of federalist states. The assertions of self-determination have thus been more easily accepted by the international community especially when the demand of the people was consistent with the geopolitical interests of great powers.

Forms of Self-Determination

A minority group challenges the authority of a dominant centre to exercise the control over their territories in various ways. The expression of self-assertion, depending on its content, ranges from cultural, religious, and educational endeavours to the ultimate step of struggling for territorial or state power. Different forms of self-determination can be explained in terms of the internal regulation of a people's affairs within a country and the external regulations of people's status *vis-à-vis* the outside world. The pursuit of cultural and economic autonomy is distinct from political independence. Claims of territorial sovereignty stem from the demand for national liberalisation in a decolonising setting or they are made by separatists in multi-ethnic states.

People with culturally distinctive identities pursue their rights to self-governance by asserting their nationhood. The denial of autonomy strengthens the desire of ethnic minorities to seek their own state. Self-determination in the form of secession is better characterised by being directed against the legitimacy of an existing state rather than constituting political opposition to a particular government or constitutional regime (Lawson, 1995, p. 79). National minorities concentrated in one region of a country can easily demand separation or integration with contiguous regions of adjacent countries.

Democratic Ideals and States

Once an independent state has been established, its constituent peoples must express their aspirations through the national political system. At the same time, the political space occupied by the state has to be reconfigured to allow the expressions of cultural plurality. In reality, however, many newly created states have exclusive and non-democratic national political systems and do not represent the entire population (Daes, 1996, p. 52). As a result, political, ideological or religious differences produced an internal conflict for control over a central government in Lebanon, Afghanistan, Angola, Mozambique, Cambodia, Rwanda, El Salvador and Peru.

In the process of state formation, self-determination has not been widely accepted as a right of peoples attached to the needs, aspirations, values and goals of the social and cultural communities (Stavenhagen, 1996, p. 4). 'Self-determination, from its first enunciation as an international norm, has been chained uneasily to the state-protective ideas of national unity and territorial integrity' (Young, 1991, p. 41). The state system has not always proven to be a good unit in fulfilling economic and social needs. The statist view of international politics does not help to effectively handle the demand for autonomy. People look for identity because the existing state does not serve the needs of particular types of community. Class, ethnicity, and nationalism are competing sources of loyalty for many marginalised peoples.

This state-centric approach suppresses the desires of minorities and indigenous peoples, categorised as the nation, the people, or the ethnic group. Challenges to the legitimacy and control of established jurisdictions provoke repression by national governments. India uses coercion to entrench and consolidate its power in Punjab and Kashmir. In other places, too, authoritarian political tactics have been common in controlling ethnic tension. The right of self-determination for Kurds and Tibetans was denied by force, based on sovereignty claims to the territorial integrity of Turkey and China respectively (Stavenhagen, 1996, p. 9).

Autonomy of Minority Groups and Indigenous Peoples

Minorities have been formed by centuries of intermittent warfare accompanied by the drawing and redrawing of borders along with the disintegration of empires. Focusing on the human rights of individuals is different from the non-discriminatory treatment of a group. Diversity can be achieved by accepting the group identity of minorities. Permanent collective rights and special status for minorities are essential elements in creating a desirable process to build stable communal relations. The collective rights of ethnic minorities as distinct communities to official status for their language, separate schools and fair political representation are crucial for preserving their own cultures.

Indigenous peoples have struggled to preserve their political, economic and cultural characteristics in response to challenges by a dominant centre.

Many were killed because of their resistance against developers or decimated by disease. Despite being deprived of political representation, they organised distinctive societies with their own languages, laws and traditions. The same treatment given to those under foreign domination, however, has not been extended to indigenous peoples even though they are entitled to the right to autonomy.

Indigenous peoples, in some instances, negotiated with existing states for their political status and representation. Several indigenous tribal groups such as American Indian Nations in the United States and Canada and the Maori in New Zealand tried to gain recognition of boundaries and mutual trade relations. Through entering as equals into treaties with colonising states, they wanted to prevent the elimination of their international status without their consent (Alfredsson, 1996, p. 60). However, in the end, it made little difference in terms of discrimination and land seizures (Hannun, 1996, p. 76). The collective rights to self-determination for non-state peoples were denied under the guise of universal individual rights in the Americas. Indigenous people's movements have raised demands for restitution and greater autonomy since the 1970s (Wilmer, 1993).

State and National Boundaries

A nation is defined in reference to distinct ethnographic features and self-consciousness of a collective cultural entity. National identity is developed by a sense of political community that shares common institutions and a single code of rights and duties for its members. National political communities also encompass definite social space, a well demarcated and bounded territory, with which the members identify and to which they feel they belong.

On the other hand, a state has an international legal status with sovereignty that allows exercising exclusive control over a population within territorial boundaries. Each people is entitled to its own nation-state, thus joining sovereignty and nationalism under the concept of self-determination. The emergence of consciousness of a separate ethnic or national identity leads to the insistence on the congruence between the political and national unit (de Silva, 1996, p. 111). 'Nationalism, understood as a quest for self-government by the people, is a fundamental feature of modernity' (Veit-Brause, 1995, p. 61). In the absence of a unified nation, modern states face the task of internal nation building. 'The principle of national self-determination, once declared a universal principle of state-making, gives rise, by its own logic, to a proliferation of potential nations' (Veit-Brause, 1995, p. 65).

One of the most potent myths of contemporary social and political experience is the notion that human beings have to live in nations, and nations have to form the political edifice called sovereign states (Camilleri, 1995, p. 219). Thus, 'modern states must legitimate themselves in national and popular terms as the states of particular nations, while their content and focus are different' (Smith, 1991, p. 15). Delineating the psychological boundaries between the insider and the outsider and establishing the cultural unity within those boundaries has been one of the important functions of the national community (Camilleri, 1995, p. 220).

In an ethnically heterogeneous country, the official national culture of the state does not adequately represent the way of every person's life. The nation-state system contains the seeds of disintegration. Ethnic conflict has been instigated by an awareness of national boundaries and a perception of incompatible group interests. The growth of nationalism has been a reaction to the unresponsiveness of states to the concerns of communities (Hannum, 1990, p. 23).

Failure of Nation-State Building

Since the maintenance of a nation state is supported by a system of shared social values, the stability of a nation state requires a high degree of cultural homogeneity. A nation, in this sense, is not formed by primordial characteristics but is a social construct created by the imposition of a common language and a uniform educational system. The political unity of a multi-ethnic state is undermined by the active mobilisation of diverse cultural communities within their borders such as the Ibos in Nigeria and Christians in Southern Sudan.

The frontiers of many Eastern and Central European states such as Hungary were imposed by the post World War I and II settlements. Most African state boundaries were drawn by the colonial powers without taking into consideration ethnicity, language, or common cultural values. Many African and Asian states are therefore artificial products of imperialist rivalries. The arbitrary division of cultural groups following colonial withdrawals has generated secessionist movements.

Modernisation along with decolonisation has often unleashed ethnic and nationalist forces that challenge state authority and old territorial boundaries. Most of them were involved in conflicts whose origins can be traced to the end of colonial empires (Ghai, 1992). The divide and rule policy implemented, in part, by the manipulation of ethnic differences, serve political purposes. The need of the European colonisers to govern their vast territories with the aid of some subordinate groups justified designating members of particular ethnic groups as their agents. Colonial labour policy created the mix of different ethnic groups with migration and allowed the concentration of accumulated wealth in a few hands.

Multi-Ethnic State

The aspiration to become a mono-ethnic state with an exclusive right to territory is an unattainable dream in that very few states have ethnic homogeneity. A pure nation state is an exceptional phenomenon because the territorial frontiers of the sovereign state are rarely congruent with national boundaries. State territories are either larger or smaller than the area inhabited by the corresponding nation. Currently less than 10 percent of states could claim to be true nation states, and at least 2,000 self-conscious ethnic communities exist. Multiple nationalities are included in Russia, India and Indonesia.

Nations can be scattered over several state borders. Kurds do not have a state of their own as they are divided across Turkey, Iraq, Iran and Syria. The Palestinians are spread across Jordan, Israel, and other Middle Eastern states. Many ethnic and religious communities spanning the borders of existing states claim the right to self-determination and may decide to fight to form their own states. Especially when the loyalty of the population does not go to a sovereign state, it cannot be claimed that the nation is synonymous or mutually compatible with the state. The cohesion of a state is weakened by ethnic, class, linguistic and religious divisions.

Many multi-ethnic states turn out to be a breeding ground for growth of nationalistic manifestations. One group's success in secession leads to demands by other groups. Claims to exclusive rights to self-determination generate the domino effect of ethnic unrest. The fragmentation of multi-ethnic states produces a chain reaction of spill-over of ethnic conflict in Armenia, Georgia, the Caucasus and former Yugoslavia. A multi-nation state may fear that allowing the creation of a new state for one group would raise the expectations of other minority groups. In addition, the demand for self-determination by a national group divided by state territorial boundaries can be a source of inter-state tension. Hostilities toward the Hungarian minority in Romania provoked the call for the intervention of Hungary.

Methods for Reducing Intergroup Tension

Balancing competing claims between minorities and majorities is crucial for building a pluralistic society where various separate nationalities exist side by side with a single citizenship. The concerns of minority groups can be addressed by a variety of means that allow more control over and autonomy for their life. They include the creation of new territorial boundaries, greater access to decision-making, distributive economic policies in favour of disadvantageous groups and acceptance of cultural pluralism. Complex patterns of relationships among groups within a state defy attempts at simple theoretical generalisation of which methods are more useful. They can be applied under a great variety of conditions depending upon the balance in population growth, regional concentration of particular groups, and degrees of economic development.

Territorial Arrangements

Territorial arrangements can be made through secession, partition or integration with neighbouring states. A minority group in a newly independent state may demand autonomy or attempt to rejoin the original state or a neighbouring state with the same ethnicity. Since the disintegration of the Soviet Union, Russians in the Ukraine wanted to join the Russian federation; Armenians in Nagorno-Karabakh pushed for secession from Azerbaijan in favour of integration with Armenia.

Independence has been demanded by many minority groups around the world. Succession has been given by the majority vote in a referendum in East Timor and other places. It sometimes has also resulted from violent struggle following the failure of the majority group to accommodate a minority group's demands. Eritreans were given independence from Ethiopia in 1993 after a three-decade long civil war that ended with the seizure of power in Addis Ababa by a coalition of contending groups. The struggle for succession often provokes war and costs heavy human causalities. As seen in Nigeria and Ethiopia, hundreds of thousands of people suffered from starvation. Bangladesh's independence in 1971 was achieved by India's military intervention against Pakistan.

Partition is another arrangement for separating antagonists, where groups are territorially divided, through disintegration of a heterogeneous state into homogeneous states. Partition can happen when all attempts at self-autonomy fail. Units of a large state withdraw from and severe ties to the existing state system. The former Soviet Union dissolved into several dozen new states; Czechoslovakia separated into the Czech and Slovak Republics in the 1990s.

Creating an independent state cannot be universally applicable without massive disruption. International communities have been reluctant to approve the demands of minority groups for new territorial arrangements. In general, however, the demand for total secession is more likely to be heard sympathetically following the failure of structural reform that satisfies regional and cultural autonomy.

If the legitimate concerns of various segments of the population are met, statehood or independence can be granted. New states may result from the agreements of the component parts of the old states. In Croatia and Bosnia, on the other hand, the unilateral declaration of independence by sub-state units provoked internal wars between different ethnic groups. As the comparison between Czechoslovakia and the former Yugoslavia demonstrates, peaceful partition is obviously better than a brutal civil war.

Difficult situations are found when ethnic groups are mixed geographically with no clear boundary lines. Complexity of ethnic configurations cannot be eliminated by reordering of heterogeneity. In Northern Ireland, for instance, the majority status of Protestants could be reversed to a minority status in a united Ireland. In an ethnically divided society, in addition, the demand for secession is endless (Horowitz, 1985, p. 509). Subgroup cleavages are a continuing source of tension in the Ukraine, Georgia, Croatia, Bosnia and many other newly independent states in recent decades.

In general, homogenisation does not come from the methods of secession or partition based on separating antagonists, for the remnants of each group are still left on the wrong side of the border. Ethnic diversity within the secessionist region does not change with the creation of new territorial boundaries. Despite territorial separation, hostilities may continue now with an international dimension added to previously internal ethnic conflict. As fear about discrimination within a new state generates resistance to changes in existing political boundaries, secessionist movements can produce bitterness and hostility.

Regional Autonomy and Federalism

Not all national groups seek an independent state. Instead of insistence on full independence, minority groups can demand more autonomy within the existing political jurisdictions. Minority groups, regionally clustered, can be granted self-governance to control matters of direct relevance to them. Self-control of regional groups over their internal affairs, short of independence, allows the protection of dignity, identity and cultures by placing minority groups on an equal footing with the rest of the national society (Alfredsson, 1996, p. 72).

Regional autonomy can be obtained by proliferating state power through ethno-territorial lines. In federalism, the state devolves power to specific groups of people even though the centre still holds dominant authority. In guaranteeing greater regional autonomy, federalism can provide a primary form of power sharing. It emanates from the desire of people to form a union without losing their various identities. Autonomous or semi-autonomous regions can be created to be governed by a particular ethnicity. If a central state has to devolve more power to its subordinate members than federalism, confederalism can be suggested as a loose form of political association, which is one step before an independent statehood.

Despite variations in federal arrangements, each region or province is treated equally in a federation. Constitutional arrangements are made for appropriate regional representation in the central government. By the institutionalisation of territorial concentration, federalism allows autonomous rule for small ethnic groups. Swiss federalism is comprised of twenty-two powerful cantons, each of which is dominated by one of the country's three homogenous language groups, German, French, and Italian. In Canada's federalism, French-speaking Quebec has a substantial amount of autonomy concerning language and other cultural issues. Canada granted special privileges to Quebec to keep the province in the federation. Such arrangements however, provoke resentment from other regions.

Federal systems offer different opportunities for conflict management by avoiding the concentration of power among institutions at the centre. Power can be scattered by the separation of political functions at various levels of the government. The capture of a single office or institute does not permit one ethnic group control of power in a diffused political process. The struggle for the control of the centre becomes less intense by encouraging competition at regional levels. Compartmentalisation of conflict at a regional level has a dampening effect on ethnic conflict. Inter-ethnic conflict can be compartmentalised within limited political boundaries (Horowitz, 1985, p. 598).

Forging Inter-Group Links The emergence of a more complex pattern of group loyalties can ease tension at the centre, which serves as a focal point of political competition and power struggle. The division of the majority group can be achieved by the formation of multi-ethnic political organisations at the centre. Links between intra-ethnic divisions can be forged beyond ethnic boundaries (Horowitz, 1985, p. 598). Alternative identities can be created by political ideologies, class affiliations and religious orientations. Despite regional differences between Fleming and Walloon, religious and class divisions are more important in Belgium.

An inter-ethnic coalition diminishes political cleavages along ethnic identities. Class identity is not closed to any particular ethnic group member, with class divisions being mitigated by social mobility. The formation of cross-cutting group loyalties is encouraged by minimising the role of social and cultural differences in inter-group relations and building alignments based on mutually shared interests and universal values. Intra-ethnic group competition exacerbates inter-ethnic tensions by absorbing the energy available for conflict with external groups (Levine, 1996). Internal politics become fierce and intense if ethnic groups are fragmented along class, ideological, and other lines. The reservation of specific political offices for members of designated ethnic groups results in competition among members of the same ethnic group for the position.

Power Sharing and Consociationalism

Majority rule based on rigid boundaries between majorities and minorities carries permanent disadvantages for certain groups. The alienation of long-term minorities from the government can be overcome by consensual democracy. In power sharing, the representatives of all significant groups participate in the joint exercise of governmental power. Joint decision-making on all issues of common concern needs to be complemented by a high degree of group autonomy because decisions must be in the hands of each group (Lijphart, 1990, p. 494). In addition, consensual adjustment in the normal and ongoing pursuit of group interests can be made by proportional political representation and minority guarantees.

Consociational democracy is a rather technical term originally proposed by Arend Lijphart to denote a model of democracy that seeks to resolve political differences by techniques of consensus rather than majority rule. Because the exclusive control of power by one majority group leaves little stake in the system for minority groups, electoral systems can be re-designed to encourage forging coalitions in divided societies where political parties break along ethnic lines. A grand coalition in a parliamentary system is created with representatives from all groups in the government. Multi-party fluidity can be gained through making and remaking legislative majorities and minorities.

Cooperation can be promoted by power sharing arrangements at the centre. Austria, Belgium, and the Netherlands have developed a clear tradition of accommodating elite behaviour. Despite high social fragmentation, the Netherlands has maintained political stability due to the ability of the leaders of the contending subcultures to avoid the dangers of inter-group conflict through cooperation (Lijphart, 1984).

Electoral incentives can serve as a technique of conflict reduction by avoiding a winner-takes-all outcome. In direct democracy where political representation is important, minorities can be protected by adjusting the territories in which their votes are to be counted. Over-representation of marginalised minority ethnic or racial groups in the political process helps them feel more secure. Preferential treatment in political representation reduces the fear of minority groups.

Coalition cabinets with the representatives of different parties are supported in a parliamentary system with proportional representation. The rights of all participants are protected by a careful division of political power. The leaders of all important ethnic groups form a ruling coalition. Joint rule is based on the distribution of high level offices. Political representation and public service appointments can be based on proportionality. Positions are divided on a proportional basis for each ethnic group. Multi-ethnic societies can be maintained by an inclusive political system based on proportionality.

Joint rule by the representatives of different ethnic groups requires a collegial decision making body. A common concern is handled by joint decision making. Decisions over its own affairs are left to be made for and by each separate group. Each group has a veto power over important government policies. The ability of the minority group to veto issues of particular importance to them provides a high degree of autonomy.

The rules of consociational democracy can be more easily applied to a society segmented into vertical groups. Though groups divided by cleavages are not in constant contact, their leaders interact to bargain at the level of the state. They share overarching interests in cohesion, stability and efficiency. The key to success of consociationalism lies in the ability and willingness of elites to negotiate intergroup compromises that are acceptable to all segments. Negotiation is feasible due to a culture of compromise and accommodation.

Political stability derives from power sharing arrangements characterised by proportionality and minority veto. On the other hand, the quality of democracy in consocialism can be undermined by the supposed requirement of mass deference to elite decisions and its need for secrecy in bargaining. Extra costs or inefficiencies may recur from the need for compromise. The inflexibility of the system to a demand for change can result in a low capacity for innovation.

Distributive Policies

Conflict can be managed by social and economic policies that attempt to separate ethnic and class affiliations. Income gaps tend to be generated by the concentration of certain ethnic groups in particular sectors of the economy (Horowitz, 1985, p. 109). The economic underpinning of group hostilities increases with the ethnic division of labour and ethnic specialisation of occupations that may render certain groups in a disadvantageous position. Ethnic grievances are reduced by both sectoral and regional balances in income distribution and resource allocation. Material opportunities for disadvantaged groups are more easily provided during the period of economic growth. It will allow the demands of one group to be satisfied more easily without threatening the interests of others. On the other hand, market mechanisms of distribution 'are likely to direct wealth and income disproportionately to the already economically advantaged' (Esman, 1990b, p. 483). Economic opportunities need to be handed down to the economically underprivileged ethnic group by a government.

Distributive policies can change the ethnic balance with respect to economic rewards and political opportunities. Public funds can be allocated to reduce economic and social inequalities in income, unequal access to land or other economic resources. Ethnic representation or proportionality may be applied to opportunities for higher education, employment in both public and private sectors, ownership of business licenses, and the awards of contracts in order to help disadvantaged groups. Ethnic aspirations can be fulfilled by opportunities for social mobility. Economic self-determination allows all peoples to freely dispose of and utilise their natural resources and wealth without prejudice. Group control of its resources can help maintain its economic status.

A low degree of political participation can be compensated by economic opportunities. In order to keep alliance, Malaysia mixes political co-optation with conciliatory economic policies toward minorities. This reflects an attempt to allow balance in ethnic influence. Malays have more influence in politics but are economically in a disadvantageous position. Chinese and Indian minorities benefit economically. In Taiwan where politics is dominated by the minority of about 15 percent of mainland Chinese, economic opportunities helped control the political aspirations of indigenous populations until serious reforms incorporate the native Taiwanese majority into the political system.

Cultural Plurality

The protection of minority rights can be based on the cultural integrity of ethnic groups (Wiener, 1996). People pursue the right to maintain and develop their cultural traditions such as language, religion and customs even under the political domination of another group. Groups can be allowed to maintain the right to teach their own language and the right to practice their own religion.

Ethnic cultural autonomy can be more easily protected by the creation of autonomous regions. The French speaking population in the province of Quebec has self-governance on such matters as immigration policies as well as enjoying linguistic autonomy. In the event that cultural minorities are too small to be represented at the national level, their representation can be arranged on special councils to advise on minority issues and cultural affairs.

Traditional ways of life can be kept from an assimilation process through maintaining culture. The identity of minority groups is protected by permitting cultural rights. Examples include cultural minorities concentrated in relatively homogeneous areas: Scotland and Wales in Great Britain, South Tyrol in Italy, Swedish speakers in Finland, Corsica in France, and Catalonia, the Basque country, and Galicia in Spain.

A Final Note

Peaceful coexistence may be achieved by the negotiation and accommodation of competing demands for political autonomy. Structural and procedural arrangements can be carefully designed to prevent the competition from erupting into destructive violence. The quest for self-determination is not merely based on the rational pursuit of organised group interests but it does reflect human aspirations for self-fulfilment. In ethnically divided societies, in particular, a nation state model has proven to be inadequate in satisfying rising demands for identity and autonomy. The needs of diverse social groups would be better guaranteed in an interdependent world that makes territorial border lines less significant.

14   Development

The current international economic system emphasises free markets, open trade and foreign investment. This may offer the prospect of rapid growth and efficiency in production for advanced industrialised countries. Yet, the reality is that the great majority of people in poor countries have not had positive experiences with growth and development. The disparity between the rich and poor continues to widen in the growing world economy. This provoked dissatisfaction and demands from the world's poor for economic equity.

Originally, development was equated with economic growth and modernisation. Reflecting on the experience of failure in many Third World countries, however, a growing emphasis has been put on human welfare and aspirations. Development activities are comprised of cultural and political elements as well as material. Grassroots oriented strategies have been adopted to overcome obstacles to the marginalised in the existing structure of the political economy. The meaning of development can be cast in the context of promoting human well-being, one of the most important conditions for realising peace.

Modernisation

In modernisation theories, the quality of life is improved by the process of transition or transformation toward a modern, capitalist, industrial economy. The theories are evident in the past experiences of Western industrialised countries. Modern society is conceived to be composed of mass consumerism, high literacy rates, urbanisation and rationalism. In the 1950s and early 1960s, it was widely believed that the reason for underdevelopment in Africa, Asia and Latin America was related to a lack of modernisation that would bring rational culture and Western style institutions. Changes in not only economic factors but also social and psychological patterns (e.g. attitudes toward work and wealth) are interlinked in a mutually supporting manner to reinforce development (Brohman, 1996, p. 15).

As a result of modernisation, more specialised and complex political and economic institutions have replaced the council of elders in tribal cultures. Rationalisation of authority is made with the legitimisation of institutions run by trained bureaucracies assigned to specific functions and roles. Political parties channel popular demands and aspirations to government policy making. Decisions are based on universally applied standards, and advancement in social status is determined by merits rather than traditional ties (Handelman, 1996, p. 13). Economically, modernisation is represented by industrialisation, urbanisation and the technological transformation of agriculture.

Modernisation theory, born in the context of the creation of newly independent countries with the demise of European colonialism in the 1950s and 1960s, assumes a linear evolutionary model of development. As the path of Western development is viewed as a model for the Third World, less developed countries have been assimilated into a modern industrialised world. There is a clear distinction between traditional and modern values; traditional cultures and social institutions are seen as backward. In cultural terms, the secularisation of society has been brought about by the spread of scientific knowledge and technology. The legal and institutional reforms required for capitalist development can be achieved by modernisation

Underdevelopment is attributed to such internal obstacles as low levels of education, poor infrastructure, political control and cultural values. 'Establishing economic value requires the devaluing of all other forms of social existence' (Sachs, 1992, p. 18). By seeing tradition as a burden for progress, old wisdom has been turned into ignorance. Redefining the roles of men and women into commodified labour has led to the transformation of autonomy into dependency. Indigenous, autonomous social and economic activities embodying wants, skills, hopes and interactions with one another have to be mediated by the market.

The transformation of traditional cultures is seen as the opening step toward a modern industrial society based on universal standards rather than ethnic and family ties. New social relations have to be established by modern cultural values and economic and political institutions. The transition from a traditional society to modernity is propelled by education, urbanisation and the mass media. Schools teach modern values, scientific knowledge and technical skills that support the operation of newly introduced industries and institutions. The diffusion of modern ideas from the developed world to the developing world comes with the media. Migration from countryside to city increases exposure to urban culture. Western foreign institutions and aid agencies such as the Peace Corp have been involved in speeding this process (Handelman, 1996, p. 12).

There has been discussion about whether modernisation helps alleviate poverty or causes an increase in inequity. The emphasis on big industrial and construction projects representing the symbols of modern progress has not yet yielded improvement in the standard of living or the reduction of poverty. It has often been pointed out:

> For people on the margins, disengaging from the economic logic of the market or the plan has become the very condition for survival. They are forced to confine their economic interaction ... to realms outside the spaces where they organise their own modes of living (Sachs, 1992, p. 20).

A Growth-Oriented Development Model

In institutional thinking and the public mind of the West, development has primarily been described as 'simply growth in the income per person in economically underdeveloped areas following an increase in the per capita production of material goods' (Sachs, 1992, p. 12). Though unequal distribution is recognised as an unfortunate outcome of an economic growth model, it is stressed that everyone will eventually benefit from the trickle down effect of growth. The adoption of classic and neoclassic economic theories requires an increase in reliance on the market mechanisms and the private sector. The key to development is the elimination of market regulations. Foreign investment is an engine for the transfer of managerial and technical skills to Third World countries.

In conventional economic theory, an increase in the Gross National Product (GNP) is calculated by the monetary value of all the final goods and services. Growth relies on the expanding forces of production and consumption. Economic growth measured by the GNP is not synonymous with development since increases in the GNP simply mean more economic activities. Growth data do not indicate the direction of change in income distribution and its impact on the well-being of people. More relevant to the formulation of development policy is what is produced, how and at what social and environmental cost, and by whom and for whom. Increases in monetary flows and expenses do not necessarily have a positive impact on human well-being, progress, justice and equitable distribution of wealth. In a growth-oriented model, economic health is measured in terms of how much more a country can produce as a whole.

Growth-oriented models have not brought about improvement in nutrition, health, water, sanitation, housing and education in many resource depleted Third World countries. International donor agencies have recently expressed a growing commitment to programs for the poor but in a way to be compatible with the development of a free market oriented economy. The main goal behind World Bank loans, directed toward improvement in the productivity of farmers, is drawing them further into the market (Sen and Grown, 1987, p. 38). From past experience, however, market integration and expansion through commercialisation have not yet proven sufficient to tackle the problem of widespread poverty.

International Economic Imbalance

In a liberal economic order, trade is seen as a locomotive for growth. It has long been argued that since global competition makes everyone efficient, society will benefit from integration into a global market. Efficiency in an international economy results from specialisation in the production of goods with comparative advantages in production costs. An optimal international division of labour is supposed to be arranged through the free movement of goods and services. Trade liberalisation supported by multilateral treaties such as the General Agreement on Trade and Tariffs (GATT) attempts to eliminate barriers to import and export goods and services.

However, since the benefit is not always reciprocal, trade issues are more contentious than neoclassic economic theories suggest. The terms of trade (referred to the ratio of export prices to import prices) have been unfavourable to the producers of raw materials. The North is able to convert natural resources into final goods efficiently thanks to their greater technological sophistication. Powerful advertising machines sustain the demand for these products. In addition to more profitability in the production and export of manufactured goods than those of raw materials, the prices of raw materials are vulnerable to the wide fluctuations in global supply. Each of more than two dozen developing countries rely on just one commodity for more than one half of their export earnings, and the income of another thirteen countries comes from the export of just two. The export price of Third World commodities has gradually fallen relative to the price of the manufactured goods for which they must pay. In the long run, it has often been reported that the prices of primary product exports have experienced a general downward trend (Kegley and Wittkopf, 1995, p. 268).

The critics of free trade argue that international trade produces a value transfer from less developed countries to more advanced ones. Such transfer shows up in the form of losses for less industrialised societies through declining terms of trade for their products *vis-à-vis* the processed goods they import. Trade imbalance in Third World countries is worsened by the persisting need to import oil and machinery. Imbalanced capital flows are further aggravated by diverse forms of transferring profits, patent and licence fees and interest services. During the recession of foreign markets, export earnings crash, subsequently making interest payments on the massive foreign debt only possible by further borrowing.

Trade deficits and capital outflows cause economic imbalance and consequently put strain on living standards for the poor. Payments from the less developed countries to the developed overshadow compensation made by public and private investment and the grants of industrialised countries. Indebted governments have to turn to the IMF for credit, and the lending conditions include implementing a package of austerity measures. To repress domestic consumption, the price of food and other economic necessities are raised along with a cut in wages and social services.

Dependency Theories

In order to explain a continued lack of economic progress in the majority of poor countries, the dependency school emerged in the 1960s and became popularly accepted especially in the early 1970s. They directly challenged the major assumption of a conventional development model that the underdevelopment of the South is largely a temporary stage en route to industrialisation and modernisation. In their view, Third World poverty is attributed to the colonial past and current external linkages. The situation will not improve unless structural exploitation of industrialised countries over underdeveloped ones is terminated.

In dependency, the structure of a global economy controlled by the advanced capitalist states condition the direction of political and economic development (Cardoso, 1972). The developed countries cannot serve as a role model because their structural conditions for development were different from those faced by those countries in the periphery of the world economy which serve as external sources of demand and investment outlets.

Underdevelopment is ascribed to the historical expansion and penetration of a capitalist system in many sectors of periphery economies. Given their privileged positions, the local elite of the states in the periphery help sustain the exploitative links once the penetration of international capitalism is made.

The international division of labour establishes the terms of a centre-periphery relationship. Trade is largely seen 'as part of the capitalist process of value extraction' (Pettman, 1996, p. 126). The advanced industrial countries sell their own processed goods above their actual value while buying the commodities of the periphery societies under their value. In this relationship, underdeveloped Third World countries in the periphery of the world economy produce raw materials that are exported cheaply to economically advanced countries in the centre. On the other hand, the periphery has to import manufactured goods made of cheap materials at high prices. The South essentially provides raw materials and some simple manufactured goods to feed the continued growth of the North.

The asymmetric economic relations are ascribed to the fact that the periphery lacks the expertise, technology, management and capital owned by the centre. Dependency theorists argue that a lack of capital and entrepreneurial skills in underdeveloped countries is not internally caused but is imposed on them by an unequal international economic structure. Through the forced division of labour, Third World economies have to specialise in production with poorly skilled, cheap labour while the North concentrates on complex and often high tech industrial products (such as automobiles and computers) and services (such as banking, insurance and communication). Due to these structural limitations, the periphery countries have to accept the devaluation of their commodities on the world trading markets. The underdeveloped countries, as an unequal partner in the market, are rewarded with little benefit (UNDP, 1992, p. 68). This situation is maintained by the economic and political dependency of those states whose income largely derives from the production of raw materials.

The market set up in an exploitative manner puts many Third World countries in a position of subordination. Since the unbalanced trade relationship generates debt and drains resources from the poor, the periphery is deprived of a surplus for development. Any income coming from productive activities has to be spent for debt servicing instead of re-investment in infrastructure building or local consumption. Because of disadvantages created by the international division of labour, many countries in the South do not have an opportunity to develop industrial skills, and they are forced to continue to exchange raw materials for processed goods.

Even though there are sectors that benefit from the international economic structure, conditions for development are weakened by dependence on external economic forces. Dependency theorists point out that the Third World situation has been deteriorating vis-à-vis the industrialised world. For example, in the 1930s Third World countries essentially had a self-sufficient economy but now they even have to import food (Women's Feature Service, 1993, p. 30). It is argued that since the periphery is doomed to underdevelopment due to its linkage to the centre, it is necessary for a periphery country to dissociate itself from the world market and strive for self-reliance.

Import Substituting Industrialisation

In order to decrease external dependency and heighten self-sufficiency, several Third World countries at a more advanced level pursued industrialisation as a key to growth. Import-substituting industrialisation (ISI) was the dominant development strategy experimented in Argentina, Brazil and other large, developing countries in Latin America and South Asia in the 1950s and 1960s (Brohman, 1996, p. 53). Its goal was self-reliance, along with technological transformation, at a national level by establishing industries able to supply intermediate and final consumption goods. It was believed that increased production of manufactured goods could promote economic diversification, thus avoiding worsening terms of trade for primary products. Politically, it was driven by the desire for gaining national prestige through economic strength and the assertiveness of modernising economic forces.

More advanced stages of industrialisation can be fostered by nurturing domestic markets for the consumption of internally produced manufactured goods. By the 1960s, ISI was implemented in the areas of heavy industries such as steel and basic chemicals. In order to protect domestic industries from foreign competition, the import of numerous consumer goods was subjected to quotas and high tariffs. Main policy tools also include tax concessions for domestic industries, low interest credit and direct subsidies for domestic manufacturers. State-owned enterprises were created to carry out import-substitution directly or to support private capital. The development strategy was popularly supported by an urban-based class alliance, including the industrialists, labour and technocrats.

Manufacturing consumer goods locally requires capital equipment such as machinery and raw materials (Handelman, 1996, p. 232). Technology has to be borrowed directly from the North at a high cost. Heavy foreign borrowing for supporting industrialisation created indebtedness with a shortage of hard currencies. Due to income inequalities, a domestic market for the consumption of automobiles, household appliances, petrochemicals and other highly capital intensive goods was not fully nurtured.

Other problems include an unbalanced income distribution between sectors derived from investment in capital intensive technologies. Income inequalities are related to unfavourable internal terms of trade against agriculture. The institutional framework conducive to capital accumulation has not materialised because of inefficient economic management and the inability of the state to limit corruption. Economic instability has eventually justified military coups and authoritarian rule. Industrialisation in the South, internally oriented at the sacrifice of other sectors, has proved unfruitful.

The New International Economic Order

Based on the widely shared perception of their competitive disadvantages, Third World countries demanded closing the gap between rich and poor countries in the 1960s and the 1970s. The dissatisfaction with the existing international economic structure was eventually expressed in the Declaration of the New International Economic Order (NIEO). The Sixth Special Session of the UN General Assembly, held between 9 April and 2 May 1974, passed a resolution that demanded profound reorganisation of economic relations in favour of redistribution of wealth.

The following elements of the NIEO were elaborated in the proposals at UN meetings and other international forums. Correcting unsatisfactory terms of trade is critical in ensuring equitable economic relations. Remedies to a liberal economic order focus on redressing the disadvantages of producing primary commodities. Deteriorating terms of trade can be reversed by the redistribution of benefit and intervention in the market mechanism. Commodity prices have to be regulated to minimise the effects of the unfavourable terms of trade. Tariff barriers for products from poor countries have to be reduced to obtain open access to the domestic markets of industrial countries.

In order to help stabilise world prices of primary product exports, an international commodity agreement was proposed. Produce cartels would be capable of setting prices for such primary commodities as cocoa, coffee, tin and sugar. The stabilisation of commodity prices can also be supported by the creation of buffer stocks purchased by industrialised countries. A common fund may be established by multilateral commodity agreements.

Third World countries also demanded preferential treatment in all fields of economic co-operation. This includes transfer of advanced technology and increases in economic aid and financial support as well as the regulation of multinational corporations. Special debt relief was suggested in the form of easy repayment terms, a subsidisation of interest, renegotiation for the rescheduling of payments and forgiveness for loans by international banks and financial institutions. Industrialised countries were asked to make a commitment to economic aid to poor countries by allocating a certain portion of their GNP.

Less developed countries also wanted to see the increase in public investment in developing countries so that they would be able to produce 25 percent of the world's industrial goods by the year 2000. In addition, they sought changes in the structure of the international financial institutions whose weighted voting schemes allow the control of decision making by the North. Overall the NIEO pursued a counterhegemonic economic order against values and knowledge which permeate a structure of liberal political economy. It attempted to forge a unity in the Group of 77 comprised of Third World countries opposed to great power blocs by not only developing independent economic policies but also formulating the shared agendas and strategies of economic development.

The Outcomes The NIEO has produced modest success in a few limited areas. It has become a widely accepted international norm that every state should have sovereignty over its national resources. The oil crisis of 1973 was seen as the brief peak of the South's bargaining power. In the areas of the commodity trade, the Lome Agreements were signed between the European Community and African, Caribbean and Pacific countries in 1975. These countries were allowed preferential access to European markets for both agricultural and manufacturing goods. A commodity stabilisation system was instituted to meet emergency situations (Mingst, 1995, p. 223).

However, most demands (especially a common fund, cancellation of debt, increases in the volume and types of foreign assistance as well as changes in the weighted voting systems of the World Bank and the IMF) did not draw much reaction. Equitable management of growing global economic interdependence has not been realised due to a lack of support for reform in the main international institutions concerned with finance and trade. Industrial development in the Third World has continued to be hampered by control of multinational corporations and policies of international financial institutions (Payer, 1982).

The North-South dialogue initiated with the NIEO ended in a deadlock. The North was not interested in redressing the inequities in the distribution of income and wealth especially when they faced a recessionary economic environment following the oil crisis in the early 1970s. The North formed a common position in confronting individual developing countries on debt and other issues. The South failed to organise effective negotiations for several reasons. Individual countries do not have technical, detailed negotiation capacity at many forums and on the multitude of subjects (South Commission, 1990, p. 21). Before negotiation, the South failed to strengthen its collective bargaining positions and update its agenda. It was especially critical since the South does not have many organisations to depend on for building a common stand vis-à-vis the North. Though the secretariats of UNCTAD and a few other UN specialised agencies were sympathetic to the demands of the underdeveloped world, most key decisions have been made by Western dominated institutions such as the World Bank and the IMF.

Political success in the anti-colonial struggle was not translated into the economic gains. Despite their emphasis on neutrality in the Cold War international politics and decolonisation, developing countries have widely different levels of development with no common ideology or political system. They also differ in culture and economic organisations. Individual countries have not always sustained solidarity in the face of temptation to seek remedies for their economic problems. In addition, they were unable to withstand the pressures exerted on them by the North. Owing to different national priorities, some broke ranks with other countries of the South without realising that this would harm the broad interests of all, including their own. Even worse, certain political elites in the Third World formed collaborative relations with economic and political elites in the North.

Illusions Despite the demands of Third World countries during the 1970s, the gap with rich countries was growing for most countries of the South. Especially since the 1980s, the NIEO was marginalised with the increasing debts. Despite their challenges to neoliberal ideology, Southern political elites did not completely deny economic liberalism. The NIEO mainly served as a bargaining chip to gain concessions from the West (Cox, 1996, p. 398). The norm of free trade was modified mainly to establish new economic relations between states. The centrality of states was reflected in a claim to the sovereign monopoly over the ownership and use of natural resources. In fact, the NIEO basically meant more control of economic process by political elites in the periphery.

Equitable distribution in the South did not draw much attention. Equity within a state is another matter different from equity among states. Many of the same Third World leaders, who made a claim for equity, ignored unfair distribution of wealth in their own countries and permitted wider gaps between the rich and poor as well as disrespecting grassroots development practices. Favourable trade terms may help mainly commercial elites. More accumulation of capital can be made in the export sectors of developing countries with the growth of capitalist activities. However, this will not bring about improvement in the living conditions of the majority of the poor population in the Third World that suffer the most from the international economic integration. What the New International Economic Order means can be translated into some kind of 'capitalism for everybody' charter (Galtung, 1985). It is unclear what will happen to the economic life of the masses, how autonomous the local economy will be, and to what extent the wealth will be distributed in the margins of the global economy.

Structural Adjustment

The 1980s are known as the 'lost decade for development'. Many poor countries faced protracted balance-of-payment problems. Structural adjustment was presented as the key to debt management by the World Bank and the IMF. The new international environment for dominance of a neoclassic economic model was created by the economic crises in the South and the decline of socialist experiments. As a method of tackling a crisis in the balance of payments, the international financial institutions prescribed neoliberal economic programmes intended to stabilise the currency, reduce government spending and encourage private investment.

State intervention in the economy was blamed for the cause of economic inefficiency, and market deregulation was an answer to improve allocative efficiency and international competitiveness. The control of inflation requires the reduction of budget deficits as well as price increases. Economic liberalisation pursued by structural adjustment meant decentralisation of economic decision making to the private sector, and market mechanisms have to play a primary role in resource allocation.

The concentration on production of primary commodities was re-introduced for future economic growth in much of the South because of their weak industrial capacity and narrow internal market base. These policy changes meant reinforcing the division of labour by imposing neoliberal, free market economies on a national level as a condition for long-term growth beyond short-term economic balance. De-industrialisation and the underdevelopment of various sectors seem to be inevitable in the reorientation of economic structure toward the export sectors of agricultural and other primary goods.

Structural adjustment has been intensely applied to the economies of Latin America and Africa that experienced external indebtedness aggravated by falling commodity prices. Interest rate hikes caused deep recessions and squeezed real wages throughout the 1980s. Employment opportunities were suppressed by the economic liberalisation that included the privatisation of many public enterprises. The emphasis on efficiency and productivity resulted in the lay-offs of workers in privatised industries. The adjustment process was recessionary and regressive particularly in Africa where poverty and deprivation continued to deepen.

Austerity measures, while being designed to dismantle pre-existing economic arrangements, reduced the room for manoeuvre in balancing the economic well-being for ordinary people with improvement in macro-economic conditions (Jeong, 1995a). Household incomes suffered from economic recession. Cut-backs in public expenditure forced by international lending agencies have resulted in a reduction in social services available. Making a livelihood has become more difficult after spending on health, education and other services was the first budgetary victim. Stabilisation of macroeconomic conditions in some countries was achieved on the basis of hardship on the majority of the population especially with the further deterioration in the income levels of the poorest segments of society.

Such market induced miseries as depressed incomes in urban areas, unemployment and reduced social services have political and social implications. Structural adjustment programmes worsen political and social instability by putting burdens on the poor. Austerity programmes created stiff opposition, including mass political demonstrations, strikes and riots in urban sectors. Criticisms were raised by the UN Economic Commission for Africa and the UNCTAD. The UNICEF launched 'adjustment with human face' programmes to mitigate the adverse impact of neoliberal adjustment policies on the vulnerable.

In response to these challenges, in the 1990s, the new capitalist development orthodoxy was modified with an additional focus on development of human resources (World Bank, 1991). On the other hand, new lending programmes of the international financial institutions continue to be anchored in the overall framework of neoliberal economic policies despite their inclusion of such components as the provision of financial assistance and entrepreneurial opportunities for poor farmers and other low income groups.

Human Centred Development

It was widely known by the end of the 1960s that the high economic growth rate did not necessarily bring improvement in the economic well-being of the population. Conversely, conventional growth can worsen the levels of absolute poverty. Satisfaction of basic needs for the majority does not directly result from an increase in material production for those who have a reliable income. On the basis of this realisation, there has been a growing understanding that the aims of development have to be redefined toward encouraging local participation and fair distribution of income with the organisation of small scale projects benefiting from socially and environmentally appropriate technologies (Brohman, 1996, p. 204).

In response to a lack of progress in the elimination of poverty, in the 1970s, many international development programmes began to shift their focus to projects that can support the rural poor and small farmers. Redistribution of income has an equal footing with growth in the concept of basic needs elaborated by the ILO (1976). Investment in human resources has been considered as essential to increasing incomes for the poor. Employment opportunities for the marginalised have been the main vehicle for an equitable distribution of income and wealth among all sectors of the population (UNRISD, 1980). The concept of basic needs was further enriched by the incorporation of less tangible needs such as participation, identity and freedom (Max-Neef, 1986). Thus, a more comprehensive notion of basic needs approaches to development stresses not only the satisfaction of a minimum physical requirement but also the realisation of qualitative social and psychological needs, which are subject to change across cultures.

The development process ought to facilitate a conducive environment for people, both individually and collectively, in releasing their full capacity. The maximisation of human potential through a participatory development process is associated with a reasonable chance of leading productive and creative lives. The formation and use of human capabilities will be frustrated by the failure to realise human development described as 'a process of enlarging people's choices'. The desire for long and healthy lives can be fulfilled by the availability of resources that support a decent standard of living, self-respect and political freedom.

The purpose of development is not directed to material objects but life conditions for people. The environment, population, women, habitat and hunger were brought to the forefront of development by the early 1970s. The international development community, including United Nations agencies, recognises the interaction of physical, technical, economic processes and social change. The economic and social components need to be integrated in the formulation of a unified approach to development planning.

Since its first publication of the Human Development Report in 1990, the UNDP has measured and analysed socio-economic development with indicators composed of life expectancy, adult literacy and real GNP per capita. In these reports, internationally comparative levels of deprivation are determined by how far from the most successful national case the other countries are. Now it has become an international consensus that improvement in social conditions is tied to economic development.

Endogenous Development

Developmentalism touches upon a complex set of attitudes and value systems that affect the issues of economic scale and the relationship of the community to the land (Jeong, 1995b). Modern development strategies have discounted cultural factors. Folk knowledge in traditional practice is regarded as backward, and modernity downgrades diverse and small scale economic activities. Outside expertise replaces the wisdom of community groups. Local autonomy is surrendered to an alien culture and knowledge embodied in foreign expertise and resources.

Western development planning has led to import dependence, debt burdens and a huge resource deficit. Social cohesion has been weakened by economic practice which gives rise to divisions and tensions. Small collaborative units are overshadowed by large institutions, the state, industrial giants, banks and corporations. Slow and carefully evolving initiatives of small communities have not been able to adopt the competitive attitude required by existing market systems (Pye-Smith, 1994, p. 159). Indigenous development is more difficult to achieve with the local economy being embedded in the modern market economy.

The concept of endogenous development contradicts the conventional social science paradigms that see development as a definable path of economic growth passing through various stages. No single model of development for the whole world can be imposed on diverse cultures and different systems of values. The particularities of each society reject the necessity, possibility and suitability of mechanically imitating industrial societies. The value systems attached to close family and community support are the strength of traditional societies.

Economic resources are not detached from social relationships in indigenous culture and value systems. Indigenous knowledge, skills and culture help counteract the almighty mechanisms of patriarchal capitalism and its free market economy. Social dynamics refer to the process emerging from the combination of both technical and social creativity over time. The whole idea of technical assistance projects is antithetical to the utilisation of local expertise, as underdeveloped countries have become dependent on foreign technology. More attention needs to be devoted to the peculiar problems and opportunities of local environment (Ekins, 1992). Different populations combine natural resources, productive skills and social structures in myriad ways to reproduce their society.

Self-Reliance

If development should focus on the quality of human life but not the capacity to produce more wealth for a few people, the goal of development is not the increase of the GNP per capita or of world trade. Self-reliance has been suggested to promote the subsistence of periphery populations and to overcome regional inequalities and income disparities. Development, oriented toward the welfare of individual human beings, can only take place through autonomy. Thus, the first step is to rely on your own land, raw materials, capital and creativity, no matter how limited they are (Galtung, 1985). Economic resources and expertise can be developed at the individual, local and national level. On the other hand, self-reliance is compatible with horizontal trade; that is, exchange of resources and goods among equals.

Local economies cannot be insulated from processes, actions and decisions in the broader global setting. Especially, the ability of developing countries to control events even within their national borders is constrained by the external environment (South Commission, 1990, p. 283). To achieve self-reliance, periphery countries should opt partially or entirely out of the system for a shorter or longer period. This, in turn, means that self-reliance becomes not only a tool for individual, local and national growth but also an instrument to bring about basic structural change.

The need of societies to promote self-reliance requires a different arrangement with the capitalist core to create new conditions. Development options for the people of the South can be broadened by taking steps toward collective self-reliance, solidarity and regional integration. Building a regional socio-economic infrastructure helps a dissociation of the periphery from the capitalist dominated world economy while providing the economies of scale necessary for success in the promotion of industrial development (South Commission, 1990, p. 16). Regional markets can be created by economic diversification and participation of those societies at a similar development stage.

Collective self-reliance in the South results from mutually beneficial exchange between Third World countries with different areas of expertise and relevance of experiences. New sources of expertise, management and technical skills can be pursued by joint endeavours. Development options are widened by addressing separate and different needs more effectively at a collective level. Regional self-reliance benefits from geographical proximity, similarities in demand and tastes and availability of complementary natural and financial resources as well as shared capital and markets.

Inward looking development models are designed to overcome dissatisfaction with the international economic order. Cooperation within the South helps build a stronger bargaining position with the North. It further strengthens an interest and desire in promoting economic integration at a regional and subregional level. Cooperation has been enhanced by UNIDO and UNCTAD being devoted to the development of skills and expertise in Third World countries.

At a local level, growing self-reliance enforces a self-directed development process with the mobilisation of internal resources to meet the community's own needs. Food self-reliance is more easily achieved by grassroots programmes for the mobilisation of resources for agricultural production than large scale government projects. Priority is given to small scale agriculture over any large scale industrial scheme. Community based assessment and planning stress greater recognition of skills and knowledge of local peasants. Cooperative economic practices may complement a traditional focus on domestic food production. External assistance needs to be integrated into the purposes of those it is meant to benefit. Solidarity among grassroots movements can be built by cooperation among NGOs in the South as well as between North and South (Alger, 1990).

In many countries, production for commercial exchange has been a major concern in national and international levels of economic activities. It may need to be admitted that it is difficult to build a political and economic capacity to de-link. In Tanzania and Zimbabwe, efforts for self-reliance at the national level were curtailed by international economic forces. Land reform in Zimbabwe was not easy because of economic dependence on export crops produced by big farmers. However, self-reliance strategies can be more easily implemented at a community level deprived of resources.

Empowerment and Grassroots Strategies

Development is understood as a process of empowerment by which people make decisions concerning their own lives. In considering that the aim of people centred development is empowerment, people are taken as the point of departure and as active participants. The aspirations and desires for making life more meaningful in locally constituted contexts are transformed into political claims for empowerment. Instead of being viewed as passive recipients of external aid, the poor and other marginalised groups can redefine their own lives in the struggle to obtain the means of livelihood.

The politics of mass movements foster policies and programmes toward enhancing the basic rights of the poor. Empowerment is a multifaceted process 'to achieve collective strength to oppose elitist structures' (Brohman, 1996, p. 345). Sustainability, democratisation and other qualitative, non-material aspects of development goals would not be achieved by top-down strategies. In spite of enormous constraints, control over resources is increased by the organised efforts for popular participation. Political mobilisation based on consciousness raising and popular education supports a struggle to pursue identity and community development.

Popular movements are multiple though they share an emphasis on empowerment through action oriented participation and mobilisation. Some movements are locally based; others have evolved to build a national network. The dynamics of politics also differ as some press for transformation of the system and others want to be simply included in a decision making process. Oppressed people may be less conscious of effective organisation, but they have purposes and goals for daily survival. Peasants' struggles in many parts of the world may have little or no coordination, planning or political strategies. In many cases, they attempt to avoid any direct confrontation and use symbolic action in challenging the authority and elite norms (Scott, 1990, p. 29). However, mass movements based on passive forms of resistance, even short of collective defiance, represent a form of individual self-help.

Urban Informal Sectors

Economic activities among the poorest of the urban poor operate apart from the formal sector that does not provide income generating opportunities. Micro-enterprise, petty commodity production and self-employment constitute an informal sector that is complementary to the operation of a formal economy. A creative fusion of social and economic elements in overpopulated Third World cities is found in such informal economic sector activities as selling firewood, preparing cooked meals at construction sites, shoe shining and producing components for appliances (e.g., radio and TV). These economic activities are characterised by low productivity and inefficient management within the framework of a neo-liberal economic model. Subsistence forms of economic activities engaged in meeting family needs have long been neglected in neo-liberal economic paradigms which are mostly concerned with macroeconomic indicators such as inflation, interest rates and so forth.

Production of grassroots cooperatives is linked to the communities' well-being and local consumption, consequently contributing to social transactions. Small units of cooperatives that produce and sell bread, clothing, knitting, carpentry and other goods and services meet various economic necessities and have multiple functions and purposes (Walton and Seddon, 1994, p. 70). Small-scale entrepreneurs make use of the household labour of women and children. In this grassroots oriented development struggle, equity and solidarity are important principles beyond the pursuit of profit and consumption. Micro-enterprises supported by social and kinship relationships constitute a mode of production based on social solidarity.

In these enterprises, symbolic relations, rituals and non-productive socialising are as important as economic transactions (Simard, 1996, pp. 152-

3). These productive activities are a way of life for the marginalised in urban areas and a place for women and others to negotiate their identity. In particular, the presence of women is visible in the urban informal sector (Women's Feature Service, 1993, p. 81). Small trade is the principal occupation of many women in urban centres throughout many Third World countries. Self-employed and working women's associations spring from their informal sector activities.

New ideas and material objects can be creatively integrated into a subsistence-oriented value system. Economic activities for the satisfaction of basic needs (food, clothes, shelter, health and education) for all members of society are compatible with a high level of local autonomy. Need satisfaction and security rather than accumulation of profit are the driving force of economic activity. In Tanzania, during the economic crisis of the late 1980s, urban women relied on their networks within the informal sector to survive as small-scale entrepreneurs (Walton and Seddon, 1994, p. 66).

Communal Economic Activities Collective forms of various associations have been established in response to survival problems in deteriorating economic situations. The powerless can be empowered by ownership/operation arrangements and their own training programmes. Economic activities for the urban poor have also been organised in church groups, migrant clubs, neighbourhood associations, labour unions and many more vehicles of civil society. Since the late 1970s, neighbourhood associations in Mexico and Venezuela have been organised to improve the quality of life. Neighbourhood groups have been linked to other strands of grassroots movement that share similar interests (Walton and Seddon, 1994, p. 71). Their goals are equitable development and equal social relations. The examples of how poor urban communities get organised in overcoming the challenges of the dominant society and the local power structure are abundant in the shantytowns of the Third World. Neighbourhood and other types of popular grassroots organisations worked together around the issue of building a democratic social space.

Women's Struggle for Survival

The poor have suffered disproportionately because of market induced economic adjustment. In reaction to the economic decline, poor women were forced to rely on their own resources to ensure the survival of their families.

In overcoming the IMF economic programmes, families in many poor societies were engaged in extensive mutual aid by borrowing and lending goods and services. The costs of subsistence were reduced by coordination among local groups.

Food preparation, childcare and other activities are shared by community members. Communal kitchens and neighbourhood committees were formed for infant nutrition and basic health care. The spread of communal kitchens has coincided with the economic crisis. Groups of women pooled their resources to organise workshops for skills and self-employment.

The role of women has been important in acquiring basic resources such as water, electricity and so on. Scarce resources have been maximised through exchanges of goods and services among kin and neighbours. The poor individually appear to be marginalised, but they can together mobilise savings, diversify resources and spread costs without dependence on outsiders. The poor have cooperative responses to increasing austerity. Their self-esteem is enhanced by taking charge of their own destiny.

Economic and social activities organised for survival often serve as a women's forum for empowerment. Cooperative and collective forms of activities were developed to maintain the living conditions of their families. Mutual support with other women helps to share their difficulties, struggles and their ideas of social justice. Every form of resistance is organised against those who threaten their survival (Walton and Seddon, 1994, p. 58).

The challenges posed by a recession lend momentum to go beyond simple survival strategies. The mobilisation of poor urban women during the recession of the 1980s provided a grassroots base for the emerging women's movement in many developing countries. Women are more deeply rooted in their communities than men due to their roles as homemakers and mothers. Their groups developed into broader urban based grassroots organisations and created centres of dialogue and mutual assistance within an inchoate civil society (Walton and Seddon, 1994, p. 71). Mothers' clubs and communal dining areas are natural sites for collective action. Women's groups and other community organisations respond to the specific contexts of marginalisation and discrimination.

Credit Movements   Mutual self-help provides a collective response to poverty. Credit facilitation for women stimulates household income generating activities in the Third World. As poor people face discrimination within a financial system, an alternative banking system was developed by the credit movement. The Grameen Bank in Bangladesh that began as a private nongovernmental organisation has become a lender to poor peasants, mostly women. Rural women increase their self-respect and living standards by making an income that supports a household economy. Their near perfect record of loan repayments is a clear contrast with a national government's default in loans from the World Bank and the IMF.

Meanings of Development

Development touches all aspects of life, ranging from group consciousness and the nature of the human collective to their relations with the outside world. Development is a multi-relational process that enables human beings to fulfil their potential by building self-confidence. Democratic institutions and popular participation in decision making are essential to the genuine development. In order to enjoy lives of dignity and fulfilment, people have to be free to express, learn and organise to improve their conditions. 'It is a process which frees people from the fear of want and exploitation. It is a movement away from political, economic, or social oppression' (South Commission, 1990, p. 10).

The process of development depends on the nature of society. Thus social equations are as important as the effective utilisation of economic resources. Development is closely linked to a system of constant interaction between people and the surrounding material world. Development has to ultimately contribute to realising the human potentialities so that impoverished people can improve their social and economic well-being. Economic activities are not restricted to monetary or material domains. Economic transactions in which individual actors are engaged cannot be separated from a communal social space.

The context of social, economic and political organisation is important to development. Culture, as related to values, beliefs, attitudes, customs and patterns of behaviour in a given society, can be adopted as a vital pillar of social and economic transformation. The development process is directed at achieving a natural, complete, full-fledged form of an object and organism (Sachs, 1992, p. 8). Individuals and groups are assisted in controlling activities that affect them. Their participation conforms to a framework of rules set by themselves as a part of a large community.

Development as a social programme cannot ignore such moral principles as equity. Failure to meet the needs of the marginalised, including women, children and elderly people, is incompatible with the goal of development. Development has to be able to contribute to peace by satisfying the need for food, shelter, education, health facilities, water and other basic necessities. In considering that the denial of human dignity and equality has been a cause of alienation and social discord, inequity and discrimination cannot be justified by growth-oriented economic achievement. The material and social needs of people are more easily protected by a democratic form of government at various levels (South Commission, 1990, p. 13).

Development Discourse and Power

Many national economies are dominated by big industries, large-scale agriculture and media cartels, mostly controlled by a handful of people. The dominant power relations are reinforced in elite oriented development strategies. It is often ignored that the material needs of all the social strata cannot be met in the periphery of the capitalist system (Amin, 1990, p. 18). Economic hegemony is maintained not only by the expansion of the world market but also by epistemological justification of its system. Through a process of development discourse, the poor have to be willing to be incorporated in a production and consumption system (Schrijvers, 1993, p. 12).

The violent basis of the unequal power relationship is largely hidden from the donor's view. Development knowledge based on the dominant, reductionist epistemological bias serves the interests of control rather than the needs of liberation. In this knowledge base, the oppressed and marginalised are to be transformed for the economic growth of others. The formulation of alternative development strategies proceeds in the context of overcoming current relations of power, in that knowledge as a social construct cannot be generated independently of the political and economic conditions.

Development is not separated from economic, social, cultural and political processes of change in human societies. Development knowledge has to encompass historical and specific social contexts. For instance, obstacles to rural development in Central and Latin America cannot be resolved without considering the issues of land distribution blended into ethnic and class-based relations. In the concept of auto-centred development, peripheral social formations are restructured to support an internal base (Amin, 1990). Political and economic power would be distributed in favour of the masses through a development process that does not benefit a particular class. The forces of production have to be redirected toward serving people's needs.

Violence and the Green Revolution Subsistence agriculture maintained mainly by the work of women in many African and Asian countries has been destroyed by Western technology and expertise of the so-called Green Revolution (based on the idea of unlimited technological control over nature). Traditional agriculture that is responsive to the cycles of nature has been replaced by mechanisation. Commercial farming is introduced at the expense of subsistence farmers. Local self-reliance is undermined by political and economic dependence on modern agricultural capital and technology.

The Green Revolution destroys a peasant's traditional source of identity and security (Shiva, 1991). Promotion of profit-oriented agriculture and concentration of land contribute to political and economic conflict. The economic marginalisation process of vulnerable population groups has led to sexual violence and cultural genocide. Peasants are economically and spiritually divided from a sense of place (Curtin, 1996, p. 64). In the ideology of Western developmentalism, intensive, small-scale economic activities are treated as backward and primitive. Epistemological violence stems from the basis of science and technology (Schrijvers, 1993, p. 9).

The Green Revolution illustrates that 'violence is still inherent in the dominant development model' (Curtin, 1996, p. 63). It is well contrasted with the Third World women's traditional practice of agriculture that is structurally akin to pacifism in its commitment to ecological peacemaking. Contrary to universalistic, monolithic development thinking, women's cyclical practices illustrate a sense of appropriateness to and sustainability in a particular place. In a mode of production that is collaborative with nature, treatment of the land reveals the moral self. The community has to encompass nature as much as its people.

A Final Note

Social structures hinder efforts to overcome poverty. Growth-oriented strategies have distorted indigenous mechanisms of resource allocation. Production for domestic consumption is sacrificed at the expense of agricultural export promoted under the conditions of extreme inequality of land holdings and income (Sen and Grown, 1987, p. 34). The economic well-being of underprivileged communities is further deteriorated by sectoral and regional imbalances. Income inequalities arise from rigid class divisions, largely based on the concentration of land ownership and capital. Modern political structures modelled on those of the colonial rulers left economic control effectively in the hands of a small elite. Opposition to the dominant development model was met with repression and violence.

The sustainability and desirability of the current economic system can be questioned by its failure to provide economic security and welfare. It is widely admitted even among the established policy making circle that the benefit of economic growth has not reached the poorest. The logic of desired internal development is enhanced by alternative development outside of the global constraints. Development is not synonymous with a growth pattern that generates a polarisation between a growing number of the poor and the rich top layer. Community based development processes challenge the hierarchy and the values determining the hierarchical order.

Compared with a conventional growth-oriented approach, an alternative model is needed to promote need-oriented, endogenous, self-reliant, ecologically sound development based on structural transformation. Economic development strategies have an impact on the allocation of the means to satisfy basic needs. No universal path to development is warranted if the logic of development is derived from the traditions, values and institutions of the society. Rather, learning about other groups and cultural practices enriches the process that helps each society expand its knowledge base and discover strategies suitable to the local environment.

Development is a concrete social process with specific causes and preconditions that are liable to change. The process is highly dependent on the availability of natural resources and cultural energy motivating people to search for innovations. Some economic planning may always be necessary even in an extremely decentralised economy, and the national centre can provide a good infrastructure for any cooperation between the local units to address resource imbalances. However, self-reliance still needs to serve as a precondition for genuine cooperation based on the principle of symmetry.

Development should respect the needs of a certain group of people with their own cultural values. The goal is to improve a specific situation for people living in a certain region with a unique set of natural resources. Compared with mainstream strategies that consider development in the context of the GNP or some other abstraction, alternative approaches focus on the well-being of people and community. New forms of development based on the knowledge and needs of grassroots people reject any attempt to remould people's lives with predefined standards and universal models. Recognising the role of indigenous institutions and practices requires an intellectual emancipation from modernist development paradigms.

15   Environmental Politics

The roots of environmental deterioration are initiated by the activities of industrialised countries. They produce the largest proportions of the world's current emissions of pollutants and hazardous waste. Recently the contribution of rapidly industrialising countries such as China and India to global pollution has also drawn attention. To correct the environmental problems that follow industrialisation, it is often argued that economically advanced countries should bear the main responsibility given their financial capacity and technological prowess to lead the combat against environmental decay.

Environmental deterioration can be tackled at various levels. While local level action is important, global coordination is essential to achieve goals to prevent such problems as global warming and depletion of the ozone layer that have an impact on everyone on the planet. Management of the global commons also has important implications for the preservation of resources for humanity. Other important issues include protection of endangered species and maintenance of bio-diversity. Resolving environmental issues requires agreements on norms, and it is essential to build consensus on the nature of global action. The implementation of environmental policies requires the participation of diverse actors, ranging from non-governmental organisations and national government to international organisations.

Building Global Consensus

Since the first global environmental conference was held in 1972, the nature of international cooperation has dramatically changed. Along with the creation of new international institutions, multilateral treaties have been signed in areas ranging from reduction in global warming to the preservation of endangered species.

The Stockholm Conference

The UN Conference on the Human Environment held in Stockholm (1972) was the first initiative to put the environment on the global political agenda. The Stockholm Conference symbolically marked the coming age of the environment as a major global issue. Its significance can be found in lending legitimacy to environmental issues in international politics with an emphasis on the links between the environment and development (Thomas, 1992). More specifically, the Conference adopted the first global action plan for the environment. The United Nations Environment Programme (UNEP) was created by the UN General Assembly as an instrument to coordinate the international response to the new agenda and build environmental awareness and stewardship.

One of the other significant achievements at the conference was the establishment of international norms such as the recognition of state responsibilities for pollution. Article 21 of the Stockholm Declaration stresses the responsibility of sovereign states to 'insure that activities within their own jurisdiction or control do not cause damage to the environment of other states or areas beyond the limits of national jurisdiction'. The next article calls upon the states to cooperate in the further development of international law regarding liability and compensation for the victims of transboundary pollution.

The Rio Conference (Earth Summit)

The urgency of problems with development and the environment prompted the so called the 'Earth Summit', officially known as the United Nations Conference on Environment and Development (UNCED), which was held in Rio de Janeiro, Brazil, 3-14 June 1992. This was 20 years after the first worldwide UN conference on the Human Environment in Stockholm. The highly publicised conference brought a wide range of people. Powerful political leaders were joined by some 10,000 representatives of non-governmental organisations (NGOs) and scientific and business communities. They discussed a comprehensive action plan extending into the 21st century and provided a blueprint for integrating environmental protection with economic development.

The gathering produced global treaties on climate protection and on biodiversity as well as a set of proposed guidelines for forest management. In addition, it adopted the Rio Declaration that set principles for sustainable development. As a non-binding action plan for the Declaration, Agenda 21 attempts to reconcile conservation and economic growth. It identifies and elaborates the social and economic dimensions of environmental concerns while mentioning financial mechanisms, technology transfer and other means of implementation.

Recognising the global nature of environmental problems that face humanity, the central agreement of the Earth Summit stresses that sustainable development is not an option but a requirement increasingly imposed by the limits of nature. It includes measures and incentives to reduce the environmental impact of industrialised nations, revitalise development in the Third World, eliminate poverty worldwide and stabilise the level of the human population. To facilitate the implementation of these goals, the Commission on Sustainable Development was created. In response to the Third World demand for financial aid, Western industrialised countries agreed to establish the Global Environmental Facility.

International Policies

Environmental problems must be resolved internationally because of their interconnectedness across borders. International treaties and institutional arrangements are made to monitor problems, assess the effectiveness of agreements and facilitate policy co-ordination. The treaties are binding only on the signatories. To be effective, more importantly, multilateral agreements have to be implemented by the signatory governments. Due to a lack of enforcement mechanisms, the implementation by national governments relies heavily on public pressure and monitoring activities of both international organisations and nongovernmental organisations (Trolldalen, 1992, p. 38).

Some types of environmental issues have received much more scrutiny from international policy makers than other issues have. In particular, serious international efforts were made for establishing regulations for the protection of the atmosphere, management of the Antarctica and the sea, the preservation of biological diversity and the natural habitat and the control of air pollution. Depending on the degree of opposition from vested interests and the level of public interest, reaching international agreements to take action in some areas has been easier than others.

Protection of Ozone

In the areas of protection of the ozone layer, international initiatives resulted in the March 1985 Vienna Convention for the Protection of the Ozone Layer that was signed by twenty-one countries. Though no enforcement rules were mentioned in the convention, the agreement spells out the obligation of states to control activities that may adversely affect the ozone layer. In addition, participating states pledged cooperation in research and monitoring, information sharing on chlorofluorocarbons (CFCs) production and emissions and continued efforts to pass control protocols. The Vienna Convention also provided fact finding and non-compulsory dispute settlement systems to handle the problem of compliance.

The Montreal Protocol on Substances that Deplete the Ozone Layer signed by twenty-seven countries in September 1987 proposes plans for a gradual phase out of trade of ozone depleting chemicals with consumption control measures and reduction targets. In this commitment, production and consumption of CFCs would be reduced by 20 percent in 1994 and 50 percent by 1999 with the use of 1986 as a base year. The provisions include collecting data on production and consumption of CFCs, sharing technical information and promoting technical assistance to help Third World countries comply with the protocol. In concluding the Montreal Protocol, compromised solutions were negotiated between the United Sates and European Community, which are the major consumers and producers of CFCs. However, the refusal of developing countries, especially China and India, to sign the Protocol remains a serious concern.

The targets and timetables of the Montreal Protocol set earlier were amended in London, June 1990. The revision of control measures was affected by new scientific data that found the previously agreed measures inadequate in reducing damage to the ozone layer. In the negotiation on Protocol amendments, participating states accepted the mandate of phasing out all major ozone-depleting substances by the year 2000, with interim reductions of 85 percent in 1997, and 50 percent in 1995. The financial and technology transfer provisions specify that a fund would be created to pay the costs for developing countries to meet their control obligations (Parson, 1994, p. 50). Sanctions are supposed to be employed against non-compliance in addition to trade restrictions with non-signatory parties on controlled substances and their products.

Reduction in Global Warming

Compared with the efforts to protect the ozone layer, it has been difficult to produce agreements to specify a target and timetable for controlling emissions of greenhouse gases given the vested interests of powerful corporate groups such as industries. Since greenhouse gas emissions from the burning of fossil fuels have been much higher in the North than in the South, industrialised countries have been called to take the major responsibility. In recent years, however, dramatic increases in carbon dioxide production in rapidly industrialising countries have become a serious problem especially since those countries refuse to take any responsible actions. Though China, India and Brazil account for more than 20 percent of global emissions, they have opposed tough regulations. Whereas some countries obstructed key international efforts to establish strong rules and regulations such as mandated reductions of CO_2, the European Community assumed a lead role in the negotiations by virtue of its commitment to the reduction of joint carbon dioxide to 1990 levels by the year 2000 (Porter and Brown, 1996, p. 95). Strong support for negotiation on reduction in the emissions of green house gases has also been demonstrated by small island states that are concerned about rising sea levels.

Scientific consensus following a series of conferences on the atmosphere and general climate in the 1980s was pivotal to the conclusion of the 1992 Framework Convention on Climate Change signed by 154 countries at the Rio Environmental Summit. Its objective, as is stated in Article 2 of the convention document, is the stabilisation of atmospheric concentrations of greenhouse gases 'at a level that would prevent dangerous anthropogenic interference with the climate system'. It promotes international cooperation in greenhouse science and coordination of various domestic policies and actions on reduction in carbon dioxide and other greenhouse gas emissions. The Convention admits that given their dominant level of emission and wealth, industrialised countries are primarily responsible for addressing climate change at present and have been called upon to take responsibility for climate change prevention and mitigation policies. The provision of financial resources and transfer of technology were promised to meet the full costs incurred from the implementation of the agreement by developing countries. Most industrialised countries broadly pledged to cut down their greenhouse gas emissions to 1990 levels by the year 2000.

While the framework convention mentions the restoration of greenhouse gas emissions to earlier levels, the convention is mostly comprised of pledges to control green house gases. Whereas an emphasis was put on the need for governments to submit reports on their relevant policies and projections and meet regularly to evaluate progress (for future amendments), no legally binding commitment was made to hold emissions to a specific level by a certain date. The framework convention's action requirements for all parties specified in Article 4 were limited to preparing contingency plans in reducing the level of climate change as well as developing national inventories of anthropogenic emissions.

In recognition that the commitments made by industrialised countries would not be sufficient to achieve the convention's goals, further negotiations were held for reducing greenhouse gas emissions beyond the year 2000 (Switzer, 1994, p. 225). Eventually legally binding targets and time tables were set up by the Kyoto Protocol adopted at the Third Climate Conference held in December 1997. It produced an agreement on an aggregate 5.2 percent global cut in emissions from 1990 levels of six greenhouse gases in the period 2008-2012. However, the Protocol will not come into force until 55 states, with a combined emission aggregate of 55 percent of 1990 levels, ratify it. Overall, the negotiations on climate change have been dominated more by political and economic interests than environmental imperatives. This was clearly revealed by the U.S. government's consistent opposition to any legally binding measures for greenhouse gas reduction.

Conservation of Wildlife and Biodiversity

Balance between the species, preserved over the last seventy-five million years, has been seriously threatened by the unprecedented decimation of prime habitat in much of the tropical forests and wetlands. Special protection for the habitats of rare or endangered species, declared in the 1982 UN World Charter for Nature, has drawn growing international attention. The Biodiversity Convention signed by 157 states at the end of the United Nations Conference on Environment and Development in June 1992 takes a comprehensive approach to conservation efforts through the protection of not only the animal and plant species but also the maintenance of the habitat where they live. Its focus is on the sustainable use of biological diversity with the development of national strategies and a fair sharing of the benefits coming from the utilisation of genetic resources.

Other conventions shed light on the preservation of limited categories of wildlife with the identification of specific methods such as trade sanctions. The Convention on International Trade in Endangered Species of Wild Fauna and Flora (CITES) controls, reduces or prohibits international trade of endangered animals and plant species and their products. In order to prevent the commercial overexploitation, the convention that became effective in July 1975 completely banned commercial trade of those species whose survival is threatened by extinction in the absence of strict regulations. It also created an elaborate series of trade permits within each category of endangered species and between importing and exporting countries. Lacking a provision for sanctions in the case of non-compliance, the convention's weakness lies in ineffective or rare enforcement of restrictions.

The rapid decline in the number of elephants, blue whales, panda bears and other large animals represents human's overexploitation of nature. International concerns were raised by the dramatic decline of African elephant populations in the 1980s – from 1.3 million in 1979 to 625,000 in 1989. Elephants were killed for their tusks to be processed in Hong Kong and China. More than 80 percent of ivory products were imported by Japan. Measures to ban trade in ivory were enacted under heavy pressure from NGOs, the U.S. and the European Community at the 1989 CITES conference. The ban reduced incentives for poaching and smuggling African elephants with a resultant plunge in world raw ivory prices (Porter and Brown, 1996, p. 83).

While CITES focuses on preventing the extinction of territorial wildlife, concerns with birds and other migratory species led to such international treaties as the 1979 Convention on the Conservation of Migratory Species of Wild Animals, which was concluded in Bonn. The treaty recognises wild animals as an irreplaceable part of the earth's natural system. The Bonn Convention attempts to prevent the killing of migratory species, in general, with the removal of obstacles to their migration. States are obliged to maintain wetlands and other habitats for those migratory species. Despite its potential capacity to serve as a powerful tool for conserving migratory wildlife, only about 40 countries have acceded to the agreement due to its enforcement costs and requirements.

The International Convention for the Regulation of Whaling followed a long history of overexploitation of whales that threatened their extinction. The International Whaling Commission created by the 1946 Convention helped design quotas and minimum sizes for commercially caught whales along with the prohibition of certain species near extinction. These regulations, however, were not effective until a moratorium on all commercial whaling began to be implemented in 1986 (Oberthür, 1998, p. 29).

In 1994, the pressure from anti-whaling groups led to the creation of a whale sanctuary in the Southern Ocean and Antarctica in addition to upholding the moratorium in 1993. These measures were resisted mostly by Norway, Japan and Iceland who wanted to protect their minor economic interests. These countries began so-called 'scientific' whaling after the international convention stopped commercial whaling activities. In particular, Norway openly defied the ban by killing 226 mink whales in 1993 to satisfy whaling interest groups.

Population Issues

In recent decades, there has been a growing recognition that population policy has to be integrated with environmental concerns. In response to overpopulation in the South, an international population programme has evolved since the mid-1960s. In 1965, national policies to reduce fertility were adopted by only five developing countries. Now international population institutions such as the United Nations Population Fund (UNPFA) conduct demographic analysis and research. They provide assistance to developing countries for all phases of their programmes in policy development and training as well as offering contraceptives (Crane, 1994).

The September 1994 International Conference on Population and Development in Cairo adopted the Programme of Action whose sixteen chapters are aimed at stabilising the human population by the year 2020. The gathering discussed inputs for family planning and related social welfare programmes. Improved reproductive health care as well as the issues of migration, AIDS and teenage sexuality became part of the main strategies to control global population growth.

As well illustrated at the Cairo conference, obstacles to coordinated international actions are rooted in political and cultural fragmentation. In order to gain support for reproductive health and women's empowerment themes, women's groups actively lobbied at the three preparatory meetings and at the conference. Whereas the U.S., Germany and Japan pledged substantial increases in their funding for family planning and other population control measures, opposition to abortion and the use of contraceptives was made by the Vatican and conservative Muslim countries.

Management of the Global Commons

The global commons as biological or physical systems lie largely or wholly outside national jurisdictions, serving the welfare of humanity. The water of the oceans flows across many boundaries, and carries fish and other natural resources or pollutants with it. The use of satellites in orbit has significant economic potential, and they must be able to move without the restrictions of national airspace. The indivisible nature of the global commons along with the expansion of human activities has brought about the need for their management.

The traditional norms of open access and free use have recently been challenged by the efforts of some countries to unilaterally control proportions of the global commons. The overlapping boundaries of oil drilling sites are sources of international conflict. Another source of tension is related to the abuse of the global commons by some states. Technological changes can easily result in the depletion of resources in the global commons. Therefore, traditional ways of using the global commons acknowledged by norms of free use and unlimited access are incompatible with the resource scarcities caused by overexploitation.

Technological development also brings about issues related to the equitable distribution of human resources. Given their advanced technologies for mining the deep-sea nodules, some countries have the advantage of exploiting natural gas and oil found in the continental shelves. The allocation of resources takes place either on the basis of unilateral appropriations or an agreed method of determining rights of access and use. When resources are likely to be scarce due to a high international demand and cannot be divided among countries, the division of the global resources into national resource zones becomes a contentious issue.

The regulation on the use of resources can be made through a shared management system. In the areas of fisheries, rules on the types of nets were adopted by international commissions for preserving certain sizes and types of fisheries. In addition, international fishery commissions assigned quotas specifying the amount of fish which each country can catch every year to put the combined harvest within the limits of the renewability of resources. Regulations have to be implemented with the support of monitoring and compliance mechanisms.

The international community needs to have more independent sources of information and analysis of the growing uses of global commons and their economic and political implications. The conservation and allocation of ocean and outer space resources would be assisted by international efforts that focus on improving capabilities for gathering and assessing information about the global commons. Scientific study is needed to determine which activities are likely to affect the conditions of resources and the surrounding environment.

Expansion of international consultative processes needs to involve those who use and those who are affected by others' activities in the oceans and outer space. A material basis for new institutional links among communities has been shaped by the interests and actions in the global commons. Conflicting interests can be clarified to reduce the prospects for increasing international conflict particularly between have and have-not countries. Greater international consultation has been demanded by less developed countries.

Questions also arise when the fundamental tenets of international ocean laws are applied to polluting activities. Discharging pollutants that contaminate fish to the point that they are unfit for human consumption would be an example of the exploitative use of the oceans. There is a growing understanding that states do not have the right to use the oceans as a sink for disposing of waste under the same 'freedom of the seas' doctrine that permits the use the seas for navigation.

International policy does not recognise the right of a country to pollute areas beyond its boundaries. The Geneva Convention on the High Seas of 1958 calls upon states to prevent pollution of the ocean, in particular, with the discharge of oil from ships or pipelines and the dumping of radioactive wastes or other harmful agents. In the 1972 London Convention on ocean dumping, it was agreed that certain highly toxic types of waste should not be disposed of in the oceans. Special permits for dumping are required for a list of other chemicals. The Law of the Sea Treaty in 1982 set forth an obligation to prevent, reduce and control marine pollution. States have responsibility for preventing polluting activities, and violators will be fined. Several international treaties now also ban such uses of the commons as testing and locating nuclear weapons in the commons. The Limited Test-Ban Treaty (1963) prohibits testing nuclear weapons in the waters of the oceans, the atmosphere and outer space.

Such issues as the difficulty of dividing the global commons, the volatility of the technologies affecting the use of the global commons, and the growing conflicts over rights to the resources of the ocean and outer space require substantial international management (Brown, et al., 1977). Effective international management of the global commons relies on the networks of legal and political accountability that is consistent with the interdependencies of user and resource. Efforts are needed to limit extensions of exclusive national authority in the global commons before the build up of the needed international accountability networks.

Those who change the conditions of the global commons through pollutant materials should be responsible for their actions to the international community. The international community has the right to determine what pollutants may be introduced into the oceans or any other non-national area that is owned by all, such as outer space. This principle is based on UN resolutions on the ocean and outer space that the global commons are 'the common heritage of mankind'. The international community should have the authority to define and apply the accountability obligations, which are binding on all countries and special interest groups using the common resources.

The Antarctic Argentina, Chile, France, Japan, Norway, South Africa and Great Britain made territorial claims in the Antarctic between 1903 and 1943 based on first exploration, geographic proximity and other reasons. The rejection of these claims by the U.S., Russia and other countries as well as disputes over the use of the continent led to an international agreement in 1959. The Antarctic Treaty signed by twelve countries resolved the ownership controversies by postponing the question of sovereignty. Meanwhile, the entire Antarctic region below the 60 degree latitude is governed by the Antarctic Treaty. Through collective management arranged by the Treaty, Consultative Parties composed of thirty-eight states take measures to protect the environment and exchange scientific information. The Antarctic is preserved for research and scientific purposes. Therefore, military activities and the dumping of radioactive wastes are banned. Later other agreements, including the Canberra Convention (1980) and the Madrid Protocol (1991), were added for conservation of fauna, flora, seals and other marine living resources.

Outer Space   No sovereignty claim can be made over any part of outer space above each country since the planet is rotating. Scientific research and commercial activities in outer space have dramatically increased since Russia launched its first satellite into orbit in 1957. Now more than twenty states use outer space for telecommunications, remote scanning and weather forecasting.

The Outer Space Treaty of 1967 declared outer space as the province of all humankind. The use of outer space as a global commons is affirmed on the basis of equity. Space activities have to be conducted to improve human welfare. No weapons of mass destruction (including nuclear weapons) are allowed to be stationed. Similar rules and principles were adopted for a 1979 treaty to regulate human activities on the moon and other celestial bodies (Soroos, 1995, p. 300).

Oceans and Seabed   The oceans, which comprise about 70 percent of the earth's surface, have been traditionally used as navigation and shipping. In the doctrine of freedom of the seas traced back to the proposal of Dutch lawyer Hugo Grotius in the early 17th century, sovereignty was recognised for rights to control territorial waters. Reflecting this tradition, for centuries, international customary ocean laws accepted a three-mile zone of territorial waters in which costal states exercise exclusive sovereignty. With the accelerating scale of resource exploitation made possible by technological advances after World War II, some coastal states challenged the three-mile zone and claimed marine resources in ocean areas up to two hundred nautical miles.

After failing to reach consensus on the breadth of coastal jurisdictions at the United Nations Convention on the Law of the Sea (UNCLOS) I and II, disagreement on the width of territorial seas was eventually resolved by the Law of Sea (UNCLOS III), which was negotiated between 1973 and 1982 (Churchill and Lowe, 1988). The sovereignty of a coastal state over territorial seas has been broadened from three to twelve nautical miles. In addition, such commercial activities as fishing can be regulated in the exclusive economic zones that are extended out to two hundred miles. In case territorial claims overlap, equitable dividing lines need to be drawn by agreement between those states.

Coastal states may have a claim to resources in the continental shelf and the oceans within 200 nautical miles. The establishment of exclusive economic zones granted by the Law of the Sea Treaty is designed to prevent the decimation of the fisheries off the coasts of some countries by fleets from other countries. The concept of an economic zone, while allowing navigation, over flight and communications, recognises the primary rights of coastal states to resources that belong to the waters and seabed of the area.

The 1982 Law of the Sea Treaty also specifies the use of the oceans and seabeds with the exploitation of such principal resources as copper, cobalt, nickel and other minerals. In this area, UNCLOS III maintains overall the idea of a common heritage of humankind by approving a public monopoly. A newly created UN Seabed Authority will regulate mining on the deep seabed beneath the high seas. Profits will be fairly distributed among UN members.

Free Trade and the Environment

The Convention on the International Trade in Endangered Species, the Montreal Protocol on Substances That Deplete the Ozone Layer and other international treaties impose trade sanctions against countries that fail to comply with the rules. On the other hand, some countries like the United States, which provides the single largest market in world trade, have a unique capacity to take the lead in defending the right to use trade measures for environmental objectives. The U.S. threat to ban some Asian countries' fish products from the U.S. market and to prohibit their fishing operations in U.S. waters persuaded them to give up whaling as well as drift-net operations in the Pacific Ocean. The United States also banned wildlife-related export from Taiwan in 1994 after finding that the country failed to control trade in rhino horn and tiger bone (Porter and Brown, 1996, p. 130).

While trade policies were successfully used to improve environmental standards of trading partners in the above cases, domestic environmental standards have been challenged by multilateral trade rules in other cases. The U.S. used trade restrictions to protect dolphins and other marine mammals from the use of destructive drift nets. A GATT dispute resolution panel decided against the U.S. ban on the import of tuna from Mexico and Venezuela imposed on the grounds that their fleets did not meet U.S. standards for minimising dolphin kills in tuna fishing. The controversial decision highlights the desire for free access to markets over environmental trade restrictions.

Japan and many European Union members, except Austria and the Netherlands, have shown little interest in using trade for environmental purposes. Developing countries are concerned about the use of trade measures by industrialised countries in improving international environmental standards. They view them as barriers to their exports. India, for example, tried to incorporate a ban on unilateral trade measures into the programme on trade and environment of the World Trade Organisation.

The proponents of growth have criticised environmental regulations for prohibiting free trade and international investment. They argue that increased trade liberalisation would lead to economic growth, which will in turn lead to greater investment in environmental protection (Porter and Brown, 1996, p. 132). The World Trade Organisation can be used to challenge unilateral trade restrictions (for example, on imports of tropical timber products from the developing world) imposed for environmental reasons. On the other hand, many NGOs opposed the GATT Uruguay Round agreement in 1994, based on the absence of any environmental provisions. In the process of issue definition and agenda setting for the negotiations on trade rules, environmental groups demanded changes in GATT rules to guarantee a country's right to set environmental domestic standards. They also called for reform of the dispute resolution process to ensure that environmental experts are included. So far, there have been continuing resistance to and acrimonious debates about the use of trade instruments for environmental protection (Mather and Chapman, 1995, p. 259).

International Organisations and Coordination

International organisations are engaged in coordinating responses to growing global environmental problems. Resources are mobilised for education, training, spread of information, financing and technical cooperation by co-ordinating agencies (Thacher, 1991, p. 447). They facilitate international agreement by serving as a forum for negotiation. International secretariats have been set up to design and implement monitoring programmes stipulated by treaties and measure their effects. Technical assistance for implementing programmes is provided by several United Nations agencies.

In particular, the UNEP performed such critical functions as surveying and monitoring the global environmental situations and management (Thacher, 1991, p. 438). One of the UNEP's primary tasks has been the development of a body of knowledge on the global environment by conducting scientific assessments on rates of desertification, deforestation, ozone depletion and loss of biological diversity. These data are used in development, decision making and setting up targets for the regulation of economic activities. Scientific research on environmental management has been enhanced by the Global Resource Information Database integrates environmental information from various geographical levels. It is designed to acquire the data and information needed for environmentally sound management of the world's natural resources. The UNEP makes a contribution to harmonising different environmental standards and setting guidelines for the management of environmental resources (Trolldalen, 1992, p. 35).

The Global Environmental Monitoring Systems (GEMS) was established by the UNEP in the mid-1970s in order to obtain data essential for better management of global environmental problems. Its monitoring activities programme provide reliable data on changes in climate. The objective of GEMS is to coordinate various international environmental monitoring efforts, including those of the specialised agencies of the United Nations that focus on pollution. The exchange of information between countries is facilitated to make more efficient use of the resources available worldwide for scientific research on environmental matters.

UN technical agencies are involved in environmental protection in their own functional domains. The Food and Agricultural Organisation (FAO) works on the areas relevant to agriculture and forestry. The FAO manages the Tropical Action Plan in collaboration with the UNEP and UNESCO and coordinates, along with its regional fisheries commissions, programmes to increase fisheries management capacity in developing countries. The UNESCO has been responsible for facilitating scientific research and environmental education. It organised the first international Conference on the Biosphere in 1968 and launched in 1971 the Man and Biosphere (MAB) programme, which is designed to provide necessary information to manage the problems of conservation.

The World Meteorological Organisation (WMO), concerned with long-term climate changes, sponsored the First World Climate Conference in 1979 and the Second World Climate Conference in 1990. These meetings contributed to the consolidation of scientific consensus on global warming and drew the attention of policy makers to the issue. The World Climate Research Programme coordinated by the WMO aims to assist policy makers in planning and managing climate sensitive activities. The Intergovernmental Panel on Climate Change created under the co-sponsorship of the WMO and UNEP produced a critical assessment report in 1995 that suggests a discernable human influence on the climate (Molitor, 1999, p. 219).

The World Bank's role in global environmental management is prominent in control over financial assistance programmes such as the Global Environmental Facility (GEF). External funding is needed for developing countries implementing conventions on biodiversity and climate changes. New natural resource management strategies demand investments to ease the transition. The GEF was also institutionalised to finance the projects supported by the Commission on Sustainable Development (CSD).

Nongovernmental Organisations

The unwillingness of governments to resolve many environmental dilemmas led to the mobilisation of a worldwide network of environmental organisations that engage in global monitoring and political action. The emphasis is placed on changing public perception and behaviour in challenging prevailing international values, norms and policies. Dissatisfied with the official process, for instance, several thousand people who participated in the NGO Forum at the Rio conference negotiated unofficial treaties that offer alternative strategies.

Growth in the number of environmental NGOs has become phenomenal. Though its support base, especially in the U.S., deteriorated in the 1990s, the membership of Greenpeace substantially increased from 1.4 million to 6.8 million in the second half of the 1980s. Friends of the

Earth (FOE), whose international office is located in Amsterdam, has affiliates and local chapters in many developing countries, including Malaysia and Indonesia. In 1993, FOE offices worldwide had a total budget of approximately $15 million with 700,000 to one million contributing members worldwide (Wapner, 1996, p. 122). With their global reach, these NGOs keep abreast of developments on environmental issues.

NGOs lobby government officials, gather information, organise protests and boycotts, produce educational merchandise and carry out scientific research. Alternative science paradigms have been advocated by the Club of Rome and the Worldwatch Institute. Their research on security, food, energy and population areas is directed at scientists and decision makers at all levels. Under heavy NGO pressure, the World Bank has required environmental impact assessments on many projects since 1989. NGO pressure contributed to the agreement on key international conventions on climate changes and protection of endangered species. NGOs also support monitoring activities in the implementation of provisions of environmental treaties through their watchdog functions.

Green politics, made up of lobbyist organisations and green parties, can bring about changes in local, national and supranational levels of policy making. They even participate in the government in western Europe to ecologise existing policies. In contrast with confrontations between governments from the North and the South, NGO movements bond general concerns among people. On the other hand, NGOs employ diverse strategies and approaches to environmental problems. Groups mostly with origins in North America – the Sierra Club, National Wildlife Federation, Nature Conservancy, Audubon Society, Environmental Defense Fund and the Wilderness Society – take a conservationist approach. They seek environmental preservation compatible with a capitalist system.

Some of them have been involved in developing such strategies as Debt for Nature Swaps. In the debt-for-nature swap programme, such international NGOs as the Nature Conservancy and World Wildlife Fund purchase the debt of a country from lending institutions. In return for cancellation of the original loan, the government has to agree to set aside and preserve a huge proportion of its forests and land. Based on the understanding that the debt crisis forces many Third World countries to exploit their natural resource base, the programme is designed to ease the debt crisis and encourage natural resource conservation in developing countries (Kamieniecki, 1991, p. 354). The scheme to re-channel financial resources back into Third World countries has been targeted for wildlife conservation in Bolivia, Costa Rica, Ecuador, Zambia, Madagascar and other countries which experience economic hardships. While debt-for-nature swaps are not, in themselves, an answer to the protection of wildlife throughout a vast majority of developing countries, it is an innovative way of helping local people save endangered species.

Greenpeace, Earth First and other groups that are active in the Northern Hemisphere and attack both capitalist and socialist systems. In order to appeal to mass consciousness, they sometimes take direct action. By adopting the practice of bearing witness as related to political action originated with the Quakers, Greenpeace links moral sensitivities to political responsibility. In the past, their direct action against whaling drew media attention. A ship was sent to pursue a whaling fleet that was engaged in killing whales that were smaller than the size officially allowed by the International Whaling Commission. In documenting the fleet's activities, they positioned themselves between harpoon ships and pods of whales. The photograph of the scenes reproduced in newspapers generated a worldwide sensation (Wapner, 1996, pp. 52-3).

Influenced by their respective social structures and cultural history, environmental movements in many Third World countries are heterogeneous. In Brazil and other Latin American countries, environmental issues were embraced by intellectual circles and the middle class born in cities. Compared with other Asian countries, both the rural and urban ecological movements, concerned with occupational health and the devastation of rainforests, are relatively strong in Malaysia. The ecological movements in India, Sri Lanka, Thailand, Kenya and Tanzania have a popular profile though this does not necessarily mean significant representation in the formal political process. Indigenous communities in Brazil, Ecuador, Bolivia and other countries pursue an alternative to the present path of modernisation in seeking resources for their survival. Community networks in rural areas attempt to keep the balance between humans and nature by developing technologies of low environmental impact.

Struggles in Indigenous Communities

Tropical forests where millions of indigenous populations live are vulnerable to those who seek to exploit resources. Tribal communities lack the political and economic influence necessary to fight the system imposed on them. However, struggles against building big dams and logging of primary forests are visible in many other parts of the world. Local coalition groups have been formed in support of indigenous struggles. The Yayasan Indonesia Hijau (Indonesian Green Foundation) was organised in 1978 by local people concerned about the destruction of rainforests. The Environmental Protection Society of Malaysia has played an active role in lobbying the interests of displaced forest dwellers.

Environmental and human rights groups recognise the marginalised situations of indigenous tribal groups who live in forests and assist in mobilising public support. As part of an international campaign, the Japan Tropical Forest Action Network supported children and women of communities affected by logging and commercial agricultural schemes in Sarawak, Malaysia. They called for preventing the import of tropical timber (Asian and Pacific Women's Resource Collection Network, 1992, p. 44).

Local struggles to save rainforests often takes place between the timber industry and local environmental movements. In Costa Rica, the timber industry is responsible for 90 percent of forest destruction. The creation of the San Miguel Association for Conservation and Development in 1988 reflects an attempt to keep forests under the control of local communities by preventing logging companies from buying out small landowners. The group offers incentives to local people to hold on to their land by not only teaching sustainable ways of harvesting wood without the destruction of the forest but also developing regional markets for their products (Sachs, 1996, p. 143).

In the case of protecting the rainforests of the western Amazon, a grassroots local struggle was organised by the Xapuri Rural Workers Union. This group of rubber tappers depended on the forest for their livelihood, extracting latex from rubber trees and gathering nuts in seasons when the rubber was not flowing. They opposed the extensive clearing of trees throughout the 1980s by using such tactics as thwarting the ranchers' chain-saw crews. The struggle with rich ranchers, which eventually provoked the murder of Chico Mendes in December 1988, drew support from international environmental movements (Sachs, 1996, p. 134).

Women in many impoverished communities are also at the forefront of rehabilitation and conservation of the local environment. Modern agricultural development projects create large areas of marginal soil, which negatively influences the availability of wood, water and grass. The farmers, mostly women, suffer from poor yields on eroded soils as developers with professional training cut down trees on a subsistence farmer's land. Women have to spend several hours each day in search of food. Tree growing activities have been popular with rural women who depend on the environment for their living.

Grassroots organisations in Zimbabwe, Namibia and Kenya were involved in conservation efforts. Traditional seeds and indigenous tree species have been reintroduced to reverse local environmental degradation. They also organised tree growers' cooperatives that generated income by selling seedlings. These movements attempted to reverse desertification by planting trees for conservation of soil and water. The movements promoted traditional agroforestry techniques previously abandoned in favour of modern farming methods that rely on fertilizers, pesticides, new seed varieties and irrigation systems (Merchant, 1996, p. 21).

Women's groups in Zimbabwe began to plant drought-resistant indigenous trees. A project in Gambia sponsored by the International Fund for Agricultural Development is designed to uphold women's cultivation rights under a new land distribution scheme. The National Council of Women of Kenya planted several million trees between 1977 and 1987 throughout the country to reverse the desertification process. The Green Belt movement of Kenya, funded partly by the UN Development Fund for Women, employed about 50,000 women in tree planting projects. Kenyan women's access to fuel, wood and water for subsistence was the primary motivation underlying the women's Greenbelt Movement.

Indigenous culture and traditions are used as a means of empowerment. Traditional ecological use of forests for food, fuel, fodder, fertilizer, water and medicine is contrasted with cash cropping. Indigenous environmental organisations in Kerala, India tried to demystify science in order to save one of the last remaining rainforests in the region. India's Chipko movement, which took place over a wide area of Gujarat State, India from 1972 through 1978, represents one of the best known women's struggles around the world to save their forest based on traditional knowledge. Reflecting an ancient Indian tradition that regards trees as images of the cosmos, about 20,000 women participated in the tree-hugging movement that defended their valleys from erosion in the face of cash cropping for the market. Developed out of a women's organisational base and supported by local males, this successful movement involved direct confrontations with loggers and police by using such methods as marches, picketing and singing as well as embracing trees (Merchant, 1996, p. 20).

Large development projects are fiercely opposed by local populations. Anti-dam groups organised coalitions at local, national and international levels. Through international pressure, the World Bank and other foreign donors became more reluctant to pledge funds for dams. Local people's fights, combined with negative international publicity, sometimes result in the withdrawal of foreign funds for dam projects. The campaigns against big dams in such countries as Brazil, Indonesia, Nepal and India effectively pushed changes in World Bank policies. The independent Inspection Panel was established in 1993 to assess the impact of Bank funded dam projects after the institution was criticised by the international community. International protest forced the Bank to change policies in the areas of environmental assessment of economic projects that have a direct impact on indigenous people and resettlement.

The Narmada Campaign against the massive river valley project and displacement of thousands of tribal groups drew international attention. The Bank's dam and irrigation projects in the Narmada Valley of India were opposed by grassroots groups that wanted to save their communities. The movement against the Sardar Sarovar Dam has become a global rallying point. The local campaign was later supported by a network of committed activists around the world called the Narmada Action Committee as well as the Environmental Defense Fund based in Washington, D.C. Under pressure from environmental groups and politicians, the Bank announced its withdrawal from the project in 1993 (McCully, 1996, pp. 301-6). These movements often serve as a catalyst for resistance in other parts of the region. In the Philippines, the campaign against the Chico Dam inspired other campaigns in Malaysia and Thailand (Asia and Pacific Development Centre, 1992, p. 42). Local NGOs in Malaysia managed to gain enough support to force the abandonment of the Tembeling dam project.

Indigenous fishing communities suffered from the depletion of fisheries in their waters mainly due to the activities of foreign fleets.

Driftnet fishing and other modern forms of destructive fishing by other countries hurt people in the South Pacific Islands (Asian and Pacific Women's Resource Collection Network, 1992, p. 103). Communities of the Pacific have been waging their international campaigns at institutions such as the United Nations to persuade Japan and Taiwan to withdraw their fleets. Their campaigns were not very successful due to the high profitability of irresponsible fishing activities and the disregard of the two countries for international laws.

Sustainable Development

Sustainable development has been discussed over more than a decade as one of the possible ways to tackle environmental problems. The concept of 'sustainable development' was thrust into the mainstream of world debate by the 1987 report of the World Commission on Environment and Development (WCED), entitled 'Our Common Future', which suggests that the types and levels of production and consumption of goods on a global level must be brought into line with the finite ability of the Earth to sustain them. As repeated later in Agenda 21 (UN Chronicle, 1992, p. 49), the underlying theme is that economic development has to be compatible with environmental preservation given the fact that development will not be sustained without the resource base. On the other hand, the report rejects the notion of environmental limits to growth (Mather and Chapman, 1995, p. 248).

The concept of sustainable development is based on two central questions. First, is it possible to increase the basic standard of living of the world's expanding population without unnecessarily depleting our finite natural resources and degrading the environment upon which we all depend? Second, can humanity collectively step back from the brink of environmental collapse and, at the same time, lift its poorest members up to the level of basic human health and dignity? The strategy for sustainable development suggested by the WCED report (also called the Brundtland Report, named after the commission's chair) stresses meeting the material aspirations of the present generation without compromising the ability of those for the future. It advocates economic growth in addressing the issues of satisfying the needs of the poor as a means of solving environmental problems. Thus, the major concern is not with limitations on growth, but with strategies for resource utilisation in pursuit of that growth.

While some see the present structure as being at the crux of the environmental problems, others treat sustainable development as an adjustment within the present economic structure. A more orthodox school advocates that continuing economic growth is necessary to break the links between poverty and environmental degradation. Along with this view, the World Commission report proposes the necessity of 'more rapid economic growth in both industrial and developing countries' which 'will help developing countries mitigate the strains on the rural environment, raise productivity and consumption standards and allow nations to move beyond dependence on one or two primary products for their export earnings'. To raise living standards globally, the Commission anticipates a five to ten fold increase in world industrial output at some point in the 21st century (WCED, 1987, p. 213). Thus, the main concern remains that global economic output must continue to grow rapidly to meet the needs of the poor and to make environmental improvements affordable worldwide. There is, both technologically and economically, a fundamental question as to whether sustainability is feasible with a middle class standard of living for a stable population of 10-12 billion people (Ayres, 1998, p. 33).

The Brundtland Report is criticised for being too optimistic in reconciling environmental protection and economic growth. The report is more concerned with the redefinition of priorities nationally and internationally (WCED, 1987, p. 19). It assumes that threats to the environment can be handled within the current pattern of the economic development model. In its view, trade barriers in wealthy nations are obstacles for developing countries to export their products (and they have to be removed for facilitating economic growth). However, more pressure would be put on the environment as impoverished countries pressed by debts rely more heavily on commodity export. In redefining global development within the environmental context, the guidelines of the report are drawn from the modernisation concept. It represents a comfortable compromise with the presuppositions of the ideology of industrialisation. It is thus programmed to reinforce the existing order and pattern of development.

In capitalist development, the profit motive and government promotion of foreign investment and transnational corporations are not considered as part of the problem. The key to overcoming the environmental crisis does not lie in a growth-oriented model since technology and efficient resource management alone would not make way for a new era of both economic growth and environmental sustainability. Lower rates of growth would eventually be inevitable as pollution and other types of stress on the environment affect economic activities. The only viable option is to balance the relationship with the natural world by the development of a new organisational framework adaptable to ecological principles and changing life systems to reduce consumption of damaging industrial products and fossil fuel energy. Material values and life styles attached to overconsumption will not be changed without the transformation of mass media, industries and corporate advertisers (Henderson, 1994, p. 30).

Ecologically adaptable development projects are designed to bring back sustainable modes of life and subsequently overcome economic marginalisation. However, the strategy is based on community learning rather than conventional growth-oriented strategies. Sustainable rainforestry in many indigenous communities has been eroded by Western modernisation and science. Global environmental management has to respect innovative local practice. Traditional methods of managing water quality have been developed over many centuries of practice. Selective use of the scientific, technological innovations is compatible with interest in developing appropriate technology, for instance, to utilise non-fossil fuel energy sources. Those who seek solutions through radical social change go further to suggest the establishment of decentralised, self-sufficient communities (Goldsmith, 1972).

Prospects for Future Cooperation

The most serious problems with implementing international environmental agreements are related to the lack of an enforcement mechanism. Preventing the harmful accumulation of pollutants is an international objective that is difficult to argue against, despite a relative degree of urgency in priority. There are different interests between polluters and victims of the pollution. Many states simply refrain from becoming parties to the treaties designed to limit or reduce the negative human effects on the environment, and therefore states are not legally obliged to uphold them.

Leaving the enforcement of environmental standards to the national governments of the polluters has not proved to be a satisfactory arrangement. In most cases, the principle tools of environmental implementation are persuasion and embarrassment by the public exposure of non-compliance (Hempel, 1996, p. 123). Even the states committed to making good faith efforts to support international environmental regulations find it difficult, if not impossible, to fulfil their obligation.

There are conflicting perspectives on international pollution policy between the developed and less developed countries. The conflicts between rich and poor countries greatly hamper the adoption of global strategies. For instance, at the Stockholm conference in 1972, numerous Third World states argued that the industrialised countries are primarily responsible for the world's pollution problems. They insisted that it is unfair for less developed countries to be prevented from polluting the environment as they attempt to undergo rapid industrial growth themselves. The Third World continues to resist efforts to impose strict international pollution standards that would be expensive for them to implement. They consider it a luxury in view of the more pressing economic and social needs of their societies.

Obviously developed and developing countries face different sets of concerns and problems. There are also wide differences regarding priorities and strategies for protecting the environment. Many communities in developing countries struggle to mitigate the impact of soil erosion, desertification and rapid urbanisation. Environmental problems of developing countries arise from and contribute to poverty. Based on the recognition that some of these problems were created by industrialised countries, in recent years, there has been a growing call for financial contributions from the industrial countries to overcoming environmental degradation of the South. Pollution control and species protection are important concerns for the public in the industrialised world. On the other hand, as is well reflected in the U.S. government positions in a series of negotiations on reduction in greenhouse effects, there have been concerted efforts to oppose any serious measures that can hurt domestic economic interest groups.

Global environmental problems are a shared responsibility by the whole of humanity. These problems will be solved only by a cooperative, comprehensive global strategy. Whereas collective action is made easier by international institution building, consensus has yet to emerge on how to stop this disturbing trend for the entire planet beyond this generation. Global dialogue between different societies, beyond policy makers and scientists, would be able to help narrow the gap in our environmental thinking.

16 Global Order and Governance

Peace is difficult to achieve in the existing international system mainly dominated by sovereign states. The current state centred system has been inadequate in providing security and welfare. Interdependence in the environment and global economy increased international contact. The expansion of transnational problems requires solutions beyond the resources of a single state. In addition, the failure of a modern state system to prevent international violence has promoted a search for alternative political arrangements to a state centric model.

In traditional views, states are the main actors engaged in competition for maximising national interests. Due to a lack of overarching supranational authorities, international order has been conceived of as anarchy over a long time. Cooperative arrangements such as international regimes have emerged to overcome the lack of coordination in key international policy arenas. Functionalism does not actively envision political integration but believes in the benefit from cooperation between countries on economic, social and other policy issues.

Integration theories have long focused on the role of functional cooperation in promoting peace and human well-being. The experiences of the European Union lend validity to neo-functionalism, which advocates the gradual transition of state power to a bigger supranational authority. It has also been argued that war could only be abolished by the creation of a world government that can enforce law and order. Contrary to the world government, pacifist anarchists believe that autonomy and basic needs can be best fulfilled by a decentralised, non-bureaucratic system based on community.

Origins of a Sovereign State System

Sovereignty is defined as a political entity's externally recognised right to exercise final authority over its affairs. The legitimacy justifies political integration and control within territories. A state's claim to hold a monopoly on the 'legitimate' use of violence within its territory needs to be legally recognised by other states. Territorial concerns and interests will remain a dominant concern as long as sovereignty continues to be a major principle.

The roots of the contemporary international system go back to the middle 16th century in Europe. The concept of sovereignty formally emerged with the signing of the Peace of Westphalia that ended the Thirty Years' War and, more importantly, redrew the map of Europe into a system of legally equal states. It served as the principle of relations among the states of Europe by acknowledging no authority above them. The government of each country has sovereign rights within its fairly well defined territorial jurisdictions. Countries shall not interfere in each other's domestic affairs. It was believed that if these principles of a political-territorial order were bound, fewer wars would occur.

The construction of a modern sovereign state system was a popular trend at the end of the Napoleonic war. The modern state consists of an organisational apparatus to manage scarce resources. Civic order in a territorially demarcated jurisdiction is maintained by a set of institutions. The degree of effective control represents power relations within territorial boundaries (Murphy, 1996, p. 87). The state imposes common norms, rules and institutions on the populations within its territories.

The Covenant of the League of Nations and the United Nations Charter respect sovereign integrity by reaffirming existing territorial order. A systemic notion of sovereignty explains that individual states are equal to each other in legal status. The fact that all states have independence means order within a state but anarchy among states.

Realism and Neorealism

In realism, the constitutive actors in the international system are sovereign states. Other actors such as multi-national corporations or NGOs are subordinate to states and operate within structures created by states. International organisations and law do not have superior authority, and states determine their own policies. Given the absence of accepted international authority, states depend on self-help for their own security (Cox, 1996, p. 503). The failure to create centralised authority permits conditions of international anarchy.

In anarchy, unregulated inter-state relations generate endless struggle and sometimes war. National interest is defined in terms of power by a prominent realist thinker Hans Morgenthau. Realists see power as an end in itself as well as a means to an end (Sheehan, 1996, p. 12). International conflict is inevitable because human nature is based on a Hobbesian perpetual and restless desire for power. Continual reshuffling of power among the players in a zero-sum game is based on the power-seeking essence of human nature. In realism that sees conflict as inherent in society, the pursuit of power takes the political form of innate rules of human behaviour.

In contrast with classic realism, neorealism also called structural realism stresses that a power struggle does not stem from evil human nature, and the quest for power is not necessarily an end itself. Power is pursued as an instrument of survival. (Kegley and Wittkopf, 1995, p. 29). In neorealist perspectives, the world of inter-state relations is treated as a historically fixed framework for action that is unsusceptible to change. It is identical in its basic structure over time without changes in the nature of the system because changes take place only within the system (Cox, 1996, p. 505). In the regulation of power relations, an international system puts constraints on state behaviour.

States differ in their capabilities for mobilising strength, but all of them adopt a particular concept of national interest as a guide to their actions. States are considered rational, unified actors, and their international behaviour is marginally affected by domestic politics, the irrationality of individual leaders or intra-state organisational rivalry. As maximisation of profit is the main motivation for firms in the marketplace, so maximisation of security is sought by states in the international system. Conflict can be managed or escalated by a rationally calculated behaviour in the pursuit of national interests.

States pursue rival national interests, and cooperation is difficult due to the uncertainty of each other's motivations and actions. In general, states have a tendency to shy away from international cooperation, in part, for the fear of vulnerability arising from too much dependence on others for their well-being (Waltz, 1979). The maintenance of order in the absence of central authority is an overriding concern in the defence of state power and interests. International stability becomes a special vested interest of dominant powers in the management of the status quo.

Transnational Relations: Actors and Process

The global layer encompasses not just political relations between states or relations between state alliances. From the early 1970s, there has been growing interest in transnational relations, though real politik is still dominant in international diplomacy. Transnational phenomena consist of social, cultural and economic processes not controlled by states. Throughout modern history, aided by communication and transportation technologies, people, goods, cultural traits, values and ideas freely migrated in a vast open space. These processes have become far more significant and diverse with the emergence of new sets of issues such as environmental pollution, resource scarcity, human rights abuses, poverty and financial indebtedness.

Despite the continuing domination of states, nongovernmental organisations, multinational corporations, intergovernmental organisations and supranational institutions such as the European Union demand an increasing role in global policy making. The stage of global politics is now shared by many actors with the growing array of issues surfacing on the political agenda. Economic and political development combined with technological change affect transnational exchange and transactions. The inability for governments to manage problems arising from trans-border transactions requires cooperation even at the cost of losing autonomy.

The connections between London, New York and Tokyo are 'more extensive than the connections between any of these cities and the more distant parts of their national hinterlands' (Murphy, 1996, p. 107). Decisions and actions in one part of the world often come to have world-wide ramifications. One government's policy can easily intrude upon the interests pursued by groups and governments in other countries. Consequently, relationships and issues are readily politicised with the mobilisation of opposing political coalitions (McGrew, 1992, p. 5). In a fragmented system of competing bureaucratic agencies, an agency in one state might build a coalition with its counterparts in other states in order to enhance its domestic influence.

The world witnesses the transnationalisation of not only conflict but also cooperation with the increasing trend of global integration (Rosenau, 1997, p. 75). A diverse range of agencies or groups are involved in the political decision making processes at all levels from the local to the global. Networks, associations or interactions cut across national societies, creating more interdependent relations between individuals, groups, organisations and communities that belong to different states. Civil society's network of links circumscribes the autonomy of state action. Epistemic and policy communities are created by transnational cooperation and loyalty. Transnational networks of specialists do conceive and define global problems in particular spheres of concern.

The increasing role of many transnational actors is propelled by various motivations. It is illustrated by the following examples: multinational corporations (Ford and IBM), nongovernmental organisations (Greenpeace and Friends of the Earth), religious bodies (the World Council of Churches and the Vatican) and professional associations (the International Geological Association and the International Peace Research Association). Many kinds of non-state actors pursue different objectives such as profit and environmental preservation. The configuration of interests and capabilities of these actors change across issue areas.

Interest groups bypass governments because they operate within the societal domain and beyond direct state control. Power politics is made less important by the permeability of the state to external influences. The distinction between domestic and international politics has been less clear with the diverse range of groups involved in decision making processes. A vast array of transnational interactions cuts across national societies, and transgovernmental relations permeate the institutional structure itself.

International Regimes

In regime theories, international actors do not operate in an empty social vacuum. Patterns of stable expectations create an international political space permeated with norms and rules. The interests and power of states are still important, but formal or informal institutional practices mediate the outcome of international interaction. Individual state actors coordinate their policies, as adaptations to conditions of anarchy especially in the environment, trade and other functional areas where their mutual interests are interdependent.

Internationals regimes (different from their usage, in common parlance, referred to internal rules or a domestic government) can be defined as 'sets of implicit or explicit principles, rules and decision making procedures around which actors' expectations converge in a given area of international relations'. Principles are based on beliefs and understanding of the world. Norms are treated as standards of behaviour defined in terms of obligations and rights. Rules prescribe action with the convergence of expectations (Krasner, 1982, p.186).

Regimes enhance functional cooperation by governing the relationships of interdependence. Norms, rules and procedures regulate state behaviour and control its effects. Regimes develop implicit and explicit principles in specific issue areas to coordinate the self-interests of states. Some spheres of activity covered by regimes are maintained or amended like trade rules with GATT. The concept of an international regime has also been applied to the existence of policy co-ordination in human rights, environmental, security and other issue areas. International norms and institutions can be erected for the mutual realisation of economic welfare (Zacher, 1990, p. 141).

There are different interpretations of how regimes are created and maintained. Regimes are grounded in the perceived usefulness of facilitating collaboration among self-interested actors. Reciprocity and cooperative behaviour are mutually beneficial in a range of collective situations. Regimes can be perceived as an institutional response to collective suboptimality problems. An incentive structure surrounding behaviour are often established by rules and norms that stress rewards for those complying with rules but costs those who do not.

In the sociological interpretation, regimes derive from complex political interaction in collective action situations. Shedding light on social aspects of international relations leads to an emphasis on cooperation derived from changing expectations. Regimes are not static and can respond not only to changing perceptions and definitions of issues but also new power relations.

In hegemonic stability theory, regimes have been constituted under the protection of dominant powers. While the hegemon creates the regime out of self-interest, it benefits all states. The premise is that a hegemonic power produces desirable outcomes for all states by maintaining international order considered as a public good. Despite the decline of hegemonic power, the regime can survive because the existing forms of co-ordination continue to serve as flexible mechanisms while reducing uncertainties. Britain in the 19th century and the U.S. in the latter part of the 20th century supported open regimes for international investment and trade.

In considering that centralised decision making is not an optimal response to situations of interdependence, regimes are generally accepted as a means of managing a certain sphere of common concerns. 'International regimes are intermediary factors between the power structure of an international system and the political and economic bargaining that takes place within it' (Williams, 1994, p. 28). Regimes mediate the relationship between power distribution and the outcome of international policies.

Implicit and explicit principles about how problems can be addressed are formalised in organisational settings or international treaties.

Regimes may survive and evolve as long as they provide information and facilities for dealing with matters among their members. The challenge to the regime emerges with the failure to satisfactorily achieve its goals. Means for the communication of intentions and expectations are essential to the cooperative behaviour of actors. To ensure compliance with rules, formal international agreements include monitoring and sanctioning abilities supported by reporting procedures and performance review mechanisms.

Institutions are important to the extent that they 'shape the range of likely interactions and limit the scope of behaviour' (Daugherty, 1993, p. 76). Institutions, though not always essential, handle disputes within the given relations. International organisations have co-ordinating functions, but they are not concerned about a process of integration or creation of supranational authority. Cooperation in specific issue areas is the dominant concern (Stokke, 1997, p. 36).

Regimes and institutions facilitate the interaction of states within their spheres. Regime analysis is less concerned with the activities of sub-state actors and transnational institutions. A regime's scope is issue-specific institutionalised cooperation rather than a broad regional process. In regime theory, there is no change in the assumptions on the nature of state behaviour. States are dominant actors in international decision making and pursue their own self-interest. The main motivation for voluntary cooperation derives from the desire to satisfy self-interest. Thus, it is a conservatively adaptive attitude toward the existing structures of world order (Cox, 1996, p. 510).

Functionalism

Functionalism proposes to promote peace by elevating living standards and introducing new patterns of global cooperation beyond national territories. The theoretical validity of functionalism is based on the premise that the origin of war and conflict is attributed to deficiencies in the economic and social circumstances. Functionalism responds to challenges to overcome a new type of common enemies such as poverty and diseases. The treatment of these issues should take priority over political matters. International cooperation for social and economic development is essential to the maximisation of human welfare, but it is not ensured by the state system (Mitrany, 1975).

The conflictual sphere of 'high politics' (military and political matters) monopolised by diplomats and political leaders is minimised by the cooperative sphere of functionalism where the agreement on practical matters can be more easily reached. In the long run, low politics referred to a process of dealing with less controversial economic and social problems is more effective in changing inter-societal relations (Cox, 1996). The path to unity is found through functional cooperation, not political means. Despite divisions by national, religious, ideological and other differences, people still have shared issues such as prevention of disease. Technical cooperation in specific sectors is motivated by a common desire for prosperity. Professionals and technicians are more concerned with the practical everyday life concerns, ranging from health and education to transportation. The proliferation of functional organisations entices states to the patterns of cooperation. The efforts to promote social well-being will become focal points for cooperation between countries and serve as a device for undermining sovereignty and creating new loyalty to the international community.

In *A Working Peace System*, David Mitrany, the proponent of functionalism, envisions a world with a fertile mingling of common endeavour and achievement. 'The Community itself will acquire a living body not through a written act of faith but through active organic development' (Mitrany, 1975, p. 42). The early examples of functional organisations based on technological solutions to limited problems are the Universal Postal Union (1874) and the International Telegraphic Union (1865). Functionalism is also embodied in the specialised agencies established as component parts of the UN system working in the areas of agriculture, environmental management, health, scientific collaboration, technical assistance and economic development. In seeking technical and logistic solutions, these specialised agencies focus on specific, generally non-political problems.

Process International action in one area can eventually be generated across sectors by affecting other related areas. Co-ordination in a technical sector gives rise to pressure to extend cooperation in social and economic issues. Working with non-controversial issues will help build habits of cooperation in other areas. As functional cooperation eventually produces trust in political and security matters, the gradual integration of economic sectors and technical arenas gradually spill over into politics. Each society is less inclined to get engaged in disruptive conflict that breaks mutually beneficial ties.

Technical relations can be built first within the same group of functions such as communication and transportation. The next stage is the coordination of several groups of functional agencies with the creation of some intermediary agency as a clearing house. Then the functional agencies can be further coordinated at an international level. A network of institutions will supercede a nation state system with an increase in activities by specialised agencies. At the last stage, international action ought to have some type of overall political authority (Mitrany, 1966).

A more centralised world authority would emerge not by an artificial design but by the stealth of government control over social and economic issue areas. The eclipse in loyalty would eventually force sovereignty to be transferred to a supranational entity, although the shift of loyalties of people would take place over a long period. The intent of creating supra-state global organisations is not a reflection of the ambitious will of a few political elite but is based on the needs of humankind.

Assessment   The final form of supra-national government through an evolutionary approach can be more easily achieved than by the grand design for the world government. On the other hand, functionalism may not be easily developed in an asymmetric relationship. Although economic cooperation leads to building peace in advanced countries, sceptics may argue that functionalism can lead to the dependence of Third World countries on Western capitalist powers. Economic disparity cannot be easily beset by increased functional cooperation. Deep seated conflict would not be set aside by technical cooperation. Social and economic problems cannot be separated from a political process. Technical work has been politicised by the resurfacing of North-South political issues within specialised UN agencies.

Neofunctionalism

Neofunctionalists agree with the significance of international networks of cooperation in integration. Environmental protection, promotion of human rights, democratic governance, and other concerns can be better achieved within a larger institutional framework than a state. Policies on health, migration, law, education and culture need to be co-ordinated across national boundaries. Political spill-over would take place as a result of domestic pressures to enhance regional institutions. Inherent links between issue areas accelerate integration that serves the purpose of not only bringing about prosperity but also preventing war. Common interests are strengthened by relying on integrative institutions.

Neofunctionalism was proposed in the 1950s and 1960s primarily to explain the European Community (Haas, 1958). As a reconstructed theory of functionalism, neofunctionalism seeks to 'address directly the political factors that obtrusively dominate the process of merging formerly independent states' (Kegley, Jr. and Wittkopf, 1995, p. 541). Contrary to Mitrany's emphasis on technical, non-political dimensions of international organisation, neofunctionalists believe in the extension of these agencies into political realms. The creation of supranational institutions in one sector would help a new constellation of political forces extend the area of integration to other sectors.

Controversial areas are chosen on purpose rather than avoided so as to push for the process designed to create new supranational communities. Political pressure exerted by major proponents of integration at key decision making points can play a crucial role in convincing the public and its opponents of greater benefits emanating from the formation of a large community. The strategy for accelerating the integration process is to seek cooperation in the areas with political significance. The spill-over of group pressure into the federal sphere will strengthen the integrative impulse (Haas, 1964).

The key groups making up a pluralistic society have to accept the initiation of a deliberate scheme of political unification, but it does not require a majority consensus. In addition, the participants do not necessarily need to have identical goals and aims. Even a vague level of value sharing among political, industrial and labour groups facilitates the acceptance of a federal scheme. The existence of real or imagined threats, though not indispensable, is a helpful condition. The central institutions, once set up, will have to assert themselves in such a way as to give rise to more expectations for federalist measures.

The politicisation of certain issues can help establish international standards that affect the conduct of states. Neofunctionalists argue that non-political cooperation alone cannot lead to full political cooperation nor eliminate all causes of war and other conflicts. The process of political integration is not automatic and gradual, as functionalists suggest. Once functional competence is entrusted to an international authority, the higher levels of integration move forward with the role of elites motivated by federalist ideals (Hughes, 1997, p. 239). The scope and authority of international institutions are increased through a conscious strategy of innovative leadership that could overcome an impasse in the creation of a new political union.

A process of integration can address political issues in the efforts to bring greater cooperation. Spill-over effects are magnified with the expansion in the range of relevant actors. In establishing supranational institutions through the fusion of functional roles and administrative structures, interest groups and bureaucrats are the main actors for the integration process. Such elements of civil society as trade unions, industrial associations, consumer groups and other advocacy groups also have a positive orientation toward international institutions.

Critics argue that political integration, beyond functional cooperation, may not be needed for the benefit of people. There is fear that ordinary people's concerns can be ignored by bureaucratic decision making. In addition, the 'spill-over' process of authority from one functional sphere to another can be reversed by strong national political leaders. French President Charles de Gaulle opposed the accumulation of more authority by the European Community bureaucracy in Brussels.

A neo-functionalist approach requires certain conditions for its success, including steady economic growth and equality, the existence of pluralistic interest groups and the capacity of member states to adopt and respond to a new change. Participating units are assumed to have not only common cultural heritages and similar political institutions but also geographic proximity. Enthusiastic leaders with a shared vision have to be able to mobilise public support for integration. Similar levels of internal social and economic development are important for symmetric relations within a large community. These conditions limit the general applicability of a neo-functionalist approach for countries with different cultures as well as different types of political and economic systems.

The European Union

The European Union is a prominent example that represents an example to build an integrated political community based on neofunctionalist principles. The creation of a supra-political entity has followed a significant degree of economic integration among the member states since the first foundation of the European Union (known as the European Community prior to November 1993) was laid in the early 1950s. Federal institutions have been put in place to handle particular problems independently of their constituent governments.

From the beginning, there has been the federalist impulsion behind the integrative forces (Pinder, 1998). The process of economic integration was initially propelled by Franco-German rapprochement following World War II. Political and economic interests drove the expansion of a large supranational community. Most economic barriers have vanished with the creation of a larger market. Corporations and professionals such as lawyers have a closer association of their self-interest and identity with European institutions than those of national states.

Process Full economic integration has opened the way for a considerable degree of political integration. The process of economic integration began in 1951 with the establishment of the European Coal and Steel Community that harmonised and unified the policy sectors, central for post-war economic reconstruction. The supranational authority was allowed to make decisions without the approval of the member states. It was followed by the creation of the European Atomic Energy Community and the European Economic Community, more widely known as the Common Market, in 1957. Economic barriers were further eliminated by the formation of the European Community with the merger of the three institutions in 1968.

The Common Market was pursued by the framework of a broad economic union designed to gradually eliminate internal tariff barriers and quotas and establish uniform external barriers. This was eventually accompanied by a free flow of workers, capital, transportation and agriculture as well as the free trade of goods. A common agricultural policy was adopted in 1964 and a common fisheries policy in 1983. Other areas include the regularisation of workers' conditions.

Economies of scale with the benefits of specialisation and innovation have been achieved by the emergence of a bigger market that enhanced the opportunities for investment. An important institutional step toward the monetary union started with the operation of the European Monetary System in 1979. Further acceleration of efforts for a unified Europe was visible in the adoption of the Single European Act in 1986, which eliminated the veto power of member states in most issues needed to create an integrated market beginning in 1993. The Single Act also formalised a co-ordination system for technological and environmental policy arenas.

The agreement on the Maastricht Treaty at a summit meeting in December 1991 provided a critical juncture for forging closer political and economic unity. Based on the agreement, in 1999, the European Union (EU) finally moved toward a central monetary union with the establishment of a single currency and a regional central bank. The EU has developed a common foreign and defence policy and built Europe's identity in international politics. People in a member state are permitted to work and own property in any other member country. The integration process produced a sense of a European citizenship.

Structure The institutional structure consists of the European Council of Heads of States and the Council of Ministers as well as the Executive Commission. The Commission, whose 17 members appointed by member states, proposes legislation, administers policies and represents the Union in international negotiations. The Commission has an independent revenue source drawn from value-added sales tax and customs duties. The EU budget sustaining the high costs of subsidies is larger than the combined government expenditures of Argentina, Chile and Brazil. The heads of states meet twice a year, but the Council of Ministers (comprised of cabinet members drawn from member state governments, one representative of each government) meets more frequently and plays an important policy making role. The Council has ultimate control over key decision making issues by approving the policy recommendations of the Commission.

People in member countries have been linked to the integrated Union by directly electing representatives of the European Parliament since 1979. The Parliament discusses, through an advisory body role, the EU budget proposed by the Commission, and its power was later extended to the right to approve the appointment of the Commission and the right to make a decision with the Council on various legislative issues. Environmental issues are an important agenda with the popularity of green parties in the Parliament. The Court of Justice hears disputes airing under treaties that govern the Union, and the cases can be brought by individuals as well as states. It also rules on legal questions raised by the Commission and interprets EU law for national courts. It is distinctive from other international tribunals in that its decision is binding.

Neofunctionalist Strategies The European Community, as the terrain of unbundled territoriality, is recorded as the first multi-perspective polity since the advent of the modern era. Close political integration contributes to promoting common security concerns and stronger bargaining power in international negotiations. Before stagnation in the 1970s and early 1980s, the integration process moved smoothly in the functionalist framework. The process had to be pushed, in a neofunctionalist mode, by the intervention of political decision makers (Mingst, 1995, p. 238). Direct steps with ambitious political goals were necessary when the movement toward integration was stalled (Hughes, 1997, p. 258). Scaling up the integration was made by the adoption of the Single European Act in 1986 designed to achieve a genuine common market with the removal of the remaining restrictions in the movement of goods, services, capital and labour. Another substantial step taken by political leaders was the agreement of the Maastricht Treaty in late 1991 that created a joint currency with a single central bank and a joint security policy.

Besides moving up the scale of economic integration, the process was also expanded geographically (Hughes, 1997, p. 258). The original six members of the Common Market (Belgium, the Netherlands, Luxemburg, West Germany, France and Italy) were joined by Great Britain, the Irish Republic and Denmark in 1973; Greece in 1981; and Portugal and Spain in 1986. Portugal, Spain and Greece were accepted with the transition from a military government to a democratically elected one. Changes in an international security environment following the Cold War brought membership to the neutrals such as Austria, Finland and Sweden in 1995. The denial of Turkey's membership is related to human rights abuses and the military domination of politics. Other countries have also been rejected for membership because of their failure to meet such conditions as a democratic political system and an advanced economy.

The process leading to a political and economic union has not always been smooth with the enlargement that comes with problems of greater diversity and new interests to be accommodated (Pinder, 1998, p. 17). Due to domestic politics, some conservative governments were not willing to give up state sovereignty and attempted to avoid social commitments. More importantly, the process has been engineered without much popular input. Most treaties were negotiated with little public consultation. Public opposition was generated by fear of a central bureaucracy controlling their daily life. Before their approval of the Maastricht Treaty at the second round, for instance, the Danish public rejected the treaty in a June 1992 referendum, and the French public approved it with a very narrow margin a few months later. The target date of the single currency had to be delayed due to strict financial requirements. Most countries had to go through a reduction in debt and cut back in social programmes to meet the monetary requirement.

Regional Cooperation

Efficient resource allocation within the region was facilitated by economies of scale and shared infrastructure. The process of European integration based on similar economic objectives, common values and symmetric relations can perhaps be difficult to duplicate for other parts of the world. Nonetheless, rather loose forms of various arrangements emerged.

The North American Free Trade Agreement (NAFTA) is comprised of not only Canada and the U.S. but also Mexico at a Third World economic development stage. NAFTA went into force in 1994 and evolved out of the U.S.-Canada Trade agreement of 1988. Reduction in barriers to trade in all but a few hundred of approximately 20,000 product categories ended most restrictions on foreign investments and other financial transactions. The free flow of goods, services and investment among members goes hand in hand with the gradual elimination of most economic barriers.

The driving forces were not social or political groups, but multinational corporations that seek larger market shares and low labour costs in Mexico as they are faced with stiff international competition from Europe and Japan. The pact phased out restrictions on investment and most tariff and non-tariff barriers, facilitating mergers and acquisitions (Mingst, 1995, p. 240). Yet compared with the European Union, the free trade agreements are not aimed at achieving economic integration due to differences in economic capacity, social gaps and political systems. In addition, social, political and security dimensions are missing in the free trade relationship. Cooperation in investment and trade has not produced a free movement of labour as happened in Europe.

Regional organisations have been important in the co-ordination of economic policies. The annual meeting of the Asia-Pacific Economic Cooperation group (APEC) serves as a forum to discuss regional trade and other policies. Twelve Latin American countries and Mexico formed Latin American Integration Association in 1981 to enhance free regional trade. By creating the Southern Common Market in 1995, Brazil, Argentine, Uruguay and Paraguay eliminated internal tariffs and set common external tariffs. In order to promote economic development and integration, Dominica, Jamaica, the Bahamas, Belize and other small island countries joined to organise the Caribbean Community and the Common Market in 1973.

The Association of South East Asian Nations (created in 1967) has the primary function of economic policy coordination but recently began to raise their collective voice in response to Western criticism against human rights abuses and other policy issues. Other notable subregional organisations include the Economic Community of Western African States (ECOWAS, established in 1975) and the Southern African Development Community (1980). They focus on regional development and economic cooperation. ECOWAS has expanded its function to subregional conflict management efforts. In the above cases, regionalism plays diverse political roles beyond economic realms.

Security Community

Integration is not necessarily limited to only the merging of governmental units into a single unit. In a somewhat different fashion, integration is also defined as the formation of a 'security community' within which people can develop an expectation that change would proceed by peaceful rather than violent means. Social problems are resolved by institutionalised procedures without resort to large scale force (Deutsch, et al., 1957). Institutions and practices allow reliable modes of common understanding and communication in the absence of an authoritarian central power. On the other hand, it may need some form (even though it may be very loose) of organisation.

Security communities are divided into two types. First, the amalgamated type (e.g., the United States) means the formal merger of independent units into a single larger unit with some type of common government. Second, the pluralistic type (e.g., the combined territory of the United States and Canada) is characterised by the legal independence of separate governments that form a security community without merger (Deutsch, et al., 1957). The Organisation of American States (OAS) may also be considered as a pluralistic community since it has been engaged in the promotion of security and democracy. The OAS General assembly is allowed to suspend from membership any government that comes to power through the overthrow of a democratic government.

World Government

Its proponents argue that the centralisation of power and policy would help the maintenance of international peace and order. The causes of war are attributed to the fact that states remain the most powerful actors in world politics. The state secures its national interests in economic and political conflicts with another country. International violence is inevitable due to the absence of international law or morality.

The ideas of the world government rely on the assumptions that a multi-state system cannot serve the common goals of humanity, and that peace and welfare can be achieved through centralisation of small units. A world government could more easily force various political entities to respect peace, restrain them from fighting and find peaceful settlement.

Modern Philosophical Traditions

The world government and other types of arrangements to create supranational authority have been seen as a remedy to a disorderly world by several influential thinkers of modern time. Jean-Jacques Rousseau, Emmanuel Kant and other philosophers asserted that the civil state contributes to the possibility of a moral life. Rousseau finds a remedy for war only in such a form of federal government as shall unite states by bonds similar to those uniting their individual members. Every state is compelled to obey its common resolves by coercive power that is strong enough to constrain any member from withdrawal when their particular interest runs contrary to the general interest. The confederation should operate under the authority of the law, and any one state should not be allowed to prevail. Its legislative body must have powers to pass laws and ordinances binding upon all its members (Rousseau, 1927).

In the proposal for a peaceful federation, Kant suggests that states may learn enough from the suffering and devastation of war to accept a rule of law that can be voluntarily observed, rather than backed by power. Wars would be increasingly violent; periods of peace would become more burdened by rearmament and by hostile policies that would lead to further conflict, ending in a final war of extermination. Such a war annihilates both parties and justice itself. A war of extermination and the employment of all means for war must be prohibited by a rule of law (Kant, 1903).

In a Kantian federation, the supremacy of law would be observed by a voluntary association of sovereign states that agree not to use force. The federal league of states uses arbitration to settle all their disputes and guarantee free movement of goods and citizens. Freedom and equality guaranteed by representative governments are indispensable for citizens of states which join a federation. That would enable them to resist being drawn into the new wars upon which their rulers are otherwise all too likely to embark. Federation, not a world state, would most likely promote justice within and between states while preserving their unique characteristics and freedom vis-à-vis each other.

In his rather pessimistic letter to Albert Einstein, Sigmund Freud proposes that wars can be prohibited only if humankind unites in setting up a supreme agency to which the right to judge all conflicts of interest shall be handed (Freud, 1959). Given his views of violent human nature, endorsement of necessary power is natural to Freud. In his reply, Einstein also agrees that the cure for war is the establishment of an international legislative body whose decision will be invoked and found binding in every dispute.

Proposals for the World Government

The theory of the world government envisages the establishment of powerful central institutions for the management of relationships among states, specifically for preventing international war. Law making and enforcement capacity as well as adjudication power are given to a world government. The centralisation of power can result from disarmament of states and the creation of an international enforcement agency. Disarmament is necessary to eliminate the capacity of states to challenge the authority of the world government and to wage war against each other. Owing to the unprecedented destructiveness of nuclear weapons and the oppressive burdens of defence budgets, the imperative of survival is overcoming the barriers to general disarmament. Under the pressure of necessity, the disarmament process is not the mere reduction or limitation of weapons. Universal and complete disarmament has to be executed simultaneously. Fairness and security for all states requires equal and proportionate reductions in each major category of weapons.

The Clark/Sohn plan, introduced in *World Peace through World Law*, is the best known among various proposals for the world government (1966). The detailed scheme for the world government is based on the transformation of the current United Nations System. The issues of instability, conflict and war can be addressed by modifying voting procedures at the Security Council to restrict veto power, creating a world police force, strengthening the powers of the General Assembly and expanding agencies in the sphere of economic development. While states may be able to maintain their sovereignty, the world federal government should have adequate power to maintain law. This is the only practicable way to achieve a just and lasting peace.

One of the most comprehensive elements of the proposal is reflected in the transformation of the UN General Assembly into a popularly elected body of 744 members. The voting power of states would be proportionately allocated according to the size of their populations. Large nations will have more representatives, but the upper limit of 30 will be imposed for the Assembly (Clark and Sohn, 1973, p. 17).

The final responsibility for the enforcement of the disarmament process and the maintenance of peace would be given to two full time Standing Committees of the General Assembly. A Standing Committee on the Peace Enforcement Agencies would exercise legislative supervision over disarmament and the UN Peace Force. A Standing Committee on Budget and Finance would recommend an annual budget to the General Assembly (Clark and Sohn, 1966).

The present Security Council needs to be substituted for an Executive Council composed of seventeen representatives elected by the General Assembly. It is responsible to the Assembly, and its members would serve for the same four year term as the Representatives in the Assembly. The executive branch of the world government ought to deal with military intervention around the world. There is no veto power, but twelve of the seventeen members can approve any armed action. The Council would direct the disarmament process and other aspects of the whole system. An actual disarmament stage would cover ten years of step-by-step proportionate reduction in all categories of the national armed forces and armaments at the rate of ten percent per annum. After taking an arms census first, the proposed Inspection Commission supervised by the Executive Council would verify the disarmament process and report the implementation of the required reductions by each state.

The Economic and Social Council would be continued and strengthened with greatly increased funds in order to remove the causes of world instability attributed to economic disparity. A World Development Authority under the general direction of the Council would assist development of the underdeveloped areas of the world through grants-in-aid and interest-free-loans. This is needed since world stability and peace can be threatened by the immense economic disparity.

The International Court of Justice would make a judicial decision when conflicts occur between states. Its role is to interpret and apply law against international violence. Whenever the continuation of the disputes threatens world peace, the General Assembly would direct the submission of such case to the world judicial body. The Court has compulsory jurisdiction to decide the case, and its judgement would be enforced. The General Assembly would direct economic sanctions or action by the UN Peace Force to ensure compliance. Disputes, which do not exclusively have a legal nature, can go to the World Equity Tribunal (Clark and Sohn, 1973, p. 35).

The new institutional structure would not be completed without having enforcement power. In maintaining law and order, a World Police Force would be the only military force permitted anywhere in the world following the process of national disarmament. The force would include 200,000 to 600,000 professional volunteers. Weapons and other supplies for the army could be obtained from member states to be disarmed. The proposed Peace Force is made up of two components. A standing component (a full time force of professionals) stationed throughout the world would facilitate prompt action to keep peace. A Peace Force Reserve would enlist individuals, partially trained, that are subject to a call for service with the standing component in case of need (Clark and Sohn, 1973, pp. 28-32).

Overall, war is supposed to be prohibited under the world government. Centralised power would be used to ensure compliance with international law and suppress acts of aggression. This is an approach based on worldwide solutions to violent conflicts. The power of the world organisation is restricted to matters of maintaining peace. All other powers are reserved for nations to avoid opposition based on fear of possible interference in domestic affairs.

Obstacles

Major criticisms of the world government are related to problems and difficulties with the process to create a central government. Political arrangements are inevitable in order to get beyond the existing structure. However, it would be difficult to build a consensus on reforms. The world government proposal does not offer strategies concerning how to achieve it especially faced with opposition from national governments. Obstacles to the implementation of the disarmament process include vested interests rooted in deeply ingrained thinking habits, mutual fear and mistrust. Opposition will also be raised by the military establishment, armament industries and their employees.

People retain a strong loyalty to their nation state, and there is a general distrust of a centralised power system. Traditional bureaucrats and diplomats may continue to dominate power politics. Governments, of necessity, can become omnipresent and almost omnipotent. It can be oppressive to impose its power and decrees on everyone. A tightly integrated society would not satisfy a diverse range of demands and needs. Conflicts cannot be solved by the mere integration of diverse societies that differ in cultures, social traditions and value systems. Even more serious, the federal state may face the threat of secession, and there can be a bloody civil war. It remains a serious question how the federation could enforce its law on the states.

The fear of a dominant central power can be reduced, to a certain extent, by a less stringent form of federalism in which central authority and non-sovereign governments share power. In response to the weaknesses of world government proposals, some suggest the institutions of world cultural organisations based on the restructuring of UNESCO. In this view, an extensive intercultural transmission of ideas and their internalisation by individuals and societies is more feasible than the formation of global institutions for external control.

Anarchism

Anarchy is viewed by many people as lawlessness and disorder, yet its original meaning reflects a social order based on voluntary patterns of cooperation that renders law and its enforcement unnecessary. Anarchism emphasises the self-fulfilment of an individual human being and promises a happy life in a harmonious communal society. In its traditional anti-statism, anarchism strongly opposes large scale impersonal institutions that rely upon force and intimidation. It demands radical reform at all levels of social, economic and political organisations. The universal appeal of reason prevails in an anarchist community based in natural organic processes of mutual aid. In the view of Leo Tolstoy, the state embodies organised violence, and anarchism unites humankind in the community of love and God.

> In contrast with its popular images associated with violence, anarchism
> is not a creed of terror and destruction, of social chaos and turmoil, of
> perpetual war between the individuals within society. On the contrary, it

is the opposite of all these, a way of life and organic growth, of natural order within society, and of peace between individuals who respect their mutual freedom and integrity. It is the faith of the complete man growing to fulfilment through social, economic, and mental freedom. It is a social philosophy, but it is also a philosophy of individual aspirations (Woodcock, 1944, p. 64; originally cited in Smoker, 1972, p. 64).

The basic assumption of anarchism is that self-realisation and justice will be achieved only through the decentralisation of power and withering away of the state. Self-autonomy and justice in a communal life is the main goal of anarchism. The populist impulses can bring about changes that eliminate the established elite circle and state bureaucracy. The contemporary state system is poorly equipped to cope with ecological and economic problems. The large-scale centralisation puts limits on individual autonomy. In opposition to interference with individual freedom, anarchistic thoughts advocate the removal of the hierarchical structure of government as an obstacle to participation.

Anarchism rejects Hobbes' notion that a sovereign state is needed to protect individuals. Human beings work cooperatively, and an artificial order leads to exploitation. A state represses socially conscious, caring human spirits and innate impulses. Human society interacts better with each other as a smaller unit of organisation than a coercive, large form of government. Material needs and collective responsibilities can be satisfied spontaneously without the coercion of a hierarchical government structure. It is impossible that the government could know and foresee the needs of people. Self-regulating natural order is violated by legislating or fixing individual choice within a limited range through some external authority or socialisation process.

Meanings of Democracy

Egalitarian interactions and the even distribution of power throughout society are not necessarily guaranteed by the institutions of parliamentary democracy. It should not be naturally assumed that the hegemony of parliamentary democracies will necessarily guarantee peace (Smoker, 1992). The development of Western democratic systems in the 19th century coincided with the expansion of European colonialism. Decision making in major Western democracies on such issues as wars does not reflect informed political processes. The democratic ideal should be advanced beyond the currently primitive interpretations inherent in the parliamentary democracy paradigm.

The inadequacies in modern pluralistic democracies are not just linked to such issues as proportional representation. Rather they can be seen in terms of failure to meet fundamental concerns with participation and egalitarian interactions. The euphoria developed over events in Eastern Europe after the fall of one party political system a decade ago has masked the irreparable inadequacies in the new capitalist democratic system (Smoker, 1992). The fundamental proposition of democracy needs to focus more on an ongoing process than the structure of representation. In contrast with parliamentary democracies based on vertical hierarchies, true democracy is characterised by horizontal processes across a broad spectrum of relationships.

The realisation of participatory democracy is affected by psychological, sociological, economic, cultural, technological, political and ecological processes. Democratic interactions are not merely political as well illustrated in small-scale communes and communities. It is clear that 'the ideas and institutions of Western culture are not well adapted either to the planet's capacities ... or to the needs of either the individual or the collective human psyche' (Clark, 1998, p. 6). True democracy is characterised by an integral nature of a broad web of human interactions. A process of everyday life has to reflect an egalitarian ethos of circular complex relationships.

Egalitarian interactions have to be accepted as a new democratic principle. Humankind's universal desire for freedom of action does not derive from possessive individualism but is understood in the context of 'autonomy within community' (Clark, 1994, p. 20). Economic decentralisation is a more appropriate form of integrating nature and society. Moving toward smaller scale economic organisations and sensitivity toward the human subject in economic planning shall overcome the foundations laid down by modern economies (Schumacher, 1973). It would reduce the widespread global structural violence maintained by the political and economic elites of dominant Western powers.

Global Civil Society

The spatial boundaries of a global civil society are different from the constructed boundaries of the state system. The autonomy of a global civil society allows for the construction of new political space. The informal process is delineated by the networks of economic, social and cultural relations. Global civil society is being occupied by the conscious association of actors, in physically separated locations, who link themselves together for particular purposes.

Patterns of interaction between societies consist of the consequences and actions derived from the process whereby individuals and groups seek their goals. It is at the level of social networks comprised of nongovernmental organisations and institutions that conditions for individual need satisfaction are determined. Global civil society opens up a new potential and opportunity for progressive forces to make transnational links, and thereby to insert themselves in a multilateral world order. There exists a moral conviction that individuals belong not only to their respective sovereign states but also to a more inclusive community of humankind.

Global politics reflects 'a function of the processes of legitimisation and de-legitimisation in world society' (Rosatie, et al., 1990, p. 162). Self-regarding sovereign states are frequently pressed to defend the moral basis of their foreign policy to citizens and outsiders alike (Alger, 1987). One of the best examples would be economic and political sanctions against apartheid in South Africa organised by the world community in the mid-1980s. Due to the anti-apartheid movements and lobbies, many politicians had to press for sanctions against the white minority government, and a number of multinational corporations had to divest themselves of their South African subsidiaries. That led the minority government to give up their power and privileges in favour of popular elections.

A Final Note

It is difficult for countries to insulate their societies and economies from processes, actions and decisions in the broader global setting, since the ability of governments to control events within national borders is constrained by the external environment. At the same time, many within national borders, strictly considered as the business of a sovereign state, can have an impact on the rest of the world. Thus, the accountability of national behaviour and policy is an important issue.

The trend toward globalisation can help decentralise a political system, but economic and cultural domination may even be further accelerated. Some of these changes are fundamental enough to mark a historic departure from the past. The integration of global markets for money, finance and technology and the predominance in these markets of transnational corporations based in the North have far reaching implications for the world economy. Global interdependence is not symmetrical, and the South is in a position of subordination as an unequal partner of the North (South Commission, 1980, p. 284). The societies and economies of developing countries are more vulnerable due to their increasing dependence on external forces.

New international economic and political structures and arrangements need to be devised for dealing effectively with problems raised by growing interdependence. Equitable sharing of burdens and benefits will continue to remain an important concern. Multilateralism and international institutions are an important part of the process of building a more equitable and democratic international order. On the other hand, non-adversarial problem solving would not be promoted in a hierarchical order controlled by elitist decision making.

17   Nonviolence

The history of how people have tried to change society is often presented as a history of war and violent revolution. However, violence is not the only way to bring about dramatic social change and eliminate unjust relationships between societies. Nonviolence can be adopted as a strategy to wage struggle against social injustice and repressive political systems. The preservation of human life is an important goal of nonviolent action (Paige, 1993). In that sense, nonviolence literally means restraining from taking up arms or killing or wounding people. The institution of violence exploits the fear of social disapproval and self-assertiveness. It distorts everyday values to justify otherwise unthinkable actions.

By overcoming dominant relations, the practice of nonviolence contributes to building a more caring world where an emphasis is placed on cooperation and trust, less on competition and self-assertiveness. Nonviolent society can be created by meeting everyone's basic needs. In considering that the motivation of nonviolence derives from the desire to create a more desirable and caring world, the efforts have to be ultimately directed toward abolishing the institutions of oppression.

Meanings

The word 'nonviolence' popularly appeared in the 20th century, while this term was often equated with 'nonresistance' and 'passive resistance' between the 17th and mid-19th centuries. Compared with nonresistance, the term 'nonviolence' means more than the refusal to commit or sanction violence to include devotion to eradicating social and economic inequalities and other causes of violence. Nonviolence can be described in terms of insistence on freedom of conscience and the struggle to find a correct relationship with established authority. Since freedom is never voluntarily given by the oppressor, it must be demanded by the oppressed. It is adopted as a 'moral force' in revolutionary nonviolent struggle, in the quest for a just social order (Cooney and Michalowski, 1977, p.10).

319

Nonviolent action translates courage, dignity and assertiveness into an effective form of struggle. Nonviolent struggle is non-military, decentralist and participatory but revolutionary in its comprehensiveness of the changes sought. Its commitment is to consistent respect for and defence of the autonomy and integrity of persons. The democratic impulses embodied in the use of popular nonviolent power must be part of the transformation process. For example, resistance to military service as well as the refusal to pay taxes altogether or hold back the percentage of tax that would finance the military complex are ways of noncooperation with the state and lay the basis for a less centralist revolution.

Nonviolence confronts repressive social institutions and practices that inflict physical hurt or damage but also cause a psychological wound. Violent action by one party to a conflict 'does not justify retaliation in terms of violence'. Belief in rejection of any use of physical violence is anchored on moral grounds or 'on what might be called grounds of utility' or a combination of both (Sibley, 1963, p. 7). The aim of nonviolent struggle is not victory over the other side but mutual gain through realising an intrinsically good end. It is committed to persuading or converting an opponent to see the justice of one's cause. Thus, nonviolent peacemaking is carried out by the constructive means of resolving conflicts, reconciliation, in an ideal sense, without reliance on coercion of any kind (Nagler, 1997).

Nonviolence may also be understood as a basis for social organisation. It is based on the understanding that all forms of inequality breed more violence. A nonviolent society would prevent social hierarchies and discrimination as well as political and economic oppression and war. The organisation of violence is of itself undemocratic and inegalitarian. The removal of an elite by assassination or other types of violent means does not guarantee real change of structure. As seen in the Russian and French Revolutions, an attempt at violent social change brought about more violence and human misery.

The overt violence of physical conflict is not an effective tool for change. Since means and ends have to be just and consistent, a wrongful means cannot be adopted to secure a just end. The destruction of war and mass violence has heavy human costs, and this has an important political effect as well. Violence dehumanises and brutalises both the victim and the executioner. All proponents of nonviolence agree that the probability of reaching an agreement with an opponent is much higher with nonviolence than when violence is used (Sibley, 1963, p. 8). It drains humanity, egalitarianism and communicative politics from any situation.

Traditions

The traditions and practices in nonviolence can be traced back to religious pacifism, Leo Tolstoy's anarchism and the Gandhian struggle. Nonviolence has been embraced by many religious traditions, including Buddhism and early Christianity. There is an ample tradition of nonviolence to social evil in many societies. In American history, for instance, we can observe nonviolent opposition of the colonial America, through the abolitionists and peace crusaders of pre-Civil War years down to the anarchists of the industrial era. Nonviolent action was also adopted in the sit-down strikes of the 1930's and the conscientious objections during the two world wars.

Religious pacifism refers to the traditional belief that all killing, in particular, in war, is wrong. Quakers, Brethren, Amish, Mennonites and other peace churches are committed to justice for all but not to killing (True, 1992, p. 180). A number of religious sects believe that bearing arms was forbidden by the Christian gospels. The rejection of taking anyone's life is based on the belief in the equal worth of all persons. Their anti-authoritarianism leads to the total rejection of war with the disposition to deal with conflict through collective reasoning and consensus. Their refusal of military service is based on their demand for the rights of conscience. Most of these were primarily concerned about personal morality and salvation and so avoided a compromise with the world of politics.

In an attempt to create and maintain a just social order, most of the peace churches secluded themselves by following a program of withdrawal from the world. These churches identified civil authority with the violence state governments employ to maintain their power. They forbade wilful participation in government; for example, holding office or voting would bring an occasion when their decision has to inflict injury on others or those who would injure other people are elected.

The modern philosophical traditions of nonviolence have been established by Leo Tolstoy. He opposed the organised violence of the state expressed in war, and economic oppression associated with a few owning large amounts of land and major industrial enterprises that the majority of workers and peasants depend on. He argued if the exploited peoples refused to cooperate with their political and economic masters' tyranny, colonialism and other government hierarchies would collapse; the mass refusal to serve in the armed forces would prevent further wars (Tolstoy, 1967). Many pacifist communities are convinced that peaceful societies would be sustained over long periods without participation in war if individuals accepted the moral obligation to resist all war through nonviolent means. Their total rejection of military service stems from their opposition to military institutions as the legitimate foundation of a society and denunciation of physical violence in human relations as an organisational principle.

Nonviolence as a strategy for change was fully developed by Mahatma Gandhi in his campaign, between the 1920s and the 1940s, centred on the goal of independence from Britain. The potential of India's national self-sufficiency was explored by the efforts to develop cottage industries such as spinning and weaving. The purpose of boycotting British textile products was to remove economic benefit stemming from British colonisation of India. Although Gandhi is known for his campaign to achieve freedom for his countries, he also fought for the rights of the marginalised groups such as poor peasants, workers and the lowest Hindu caste.

Gandhi's campaigns attracted a large number of people to the commitment of non-cooperation and civil disobedience as demonstrated in the protest against the Salt Acts, which required the purchase of salt from only the government. Gandhi was imprisoned for his nonviolent resistance acts, and his arrest brought 500,000 people seeking to join him in jail. The mass resistance raised questions, among the British leaders, about the continued occupation of their largest colony and divided the public.

Nonviolence has also been used in cases of civil strife and local conflict. One of the most notable examples is protest against racial segregation at restaurants, toilets, transportation, sports events, schools and churches in the Southern U.S. during the 1950s and the 1960s. The refusal of Rosa Parks to take a seat in the back of a public bus provoked the Montgomery bus boycott in December 1955. Freedom Riders refused to ride on segregated buses in their successful struggle to desegregate interstate bus transportation (Barash, 1991, p. 566). Other boycotts, marches and nonviolent sit-ins continued in more than 100 cities until the integration of public facilities. The dimension of nonviolence was later extended from integration and other civil rights issues to social justice.

The Southern Christian Leadership Conference (formed in 1957) was pivotal to organising African American civil rights movements. Its leader Martin Luther King, Jr. adopted the Gandhian philosophy of nonviolence along with the Christian values of love and forgiveness. He preached that violence is multiplied by violent response; only love, not hatred, can drive out of violence, as darkness 'cannot drive out darkness' (King Jr., 1963).

In addition, the methods of noncooperation and civil disobedience were taken up by Western peace movements to protest against military policies, in particular nuclear testing and nuclear bases. Though defence through nonviolent methods was first proposed by Gandhi in the 1930s, this idea has gained urgency and persuasiveness since the invention of nuclear weapons. Conscientious objection opposes the justification of war. As part of civil disobedience action, war tax resistance movements rejected the payment of war taxes.

Nonviolence Theory on Power

In the theories on nonviolent action, power is not seen as something exclusively exercised by leaders of rules. The power of rulers can be effectively denied by their subjects who withdraw obedience. The power of noncooperation is different from the widely accepted notion of power regarded as relatively fixed, durable (if not indestructible), self-reinforcing and self-perpetuating. The notion of power that corresponds to the ability to inflict sanctions and physical destruction on potential enemies or disobedient subjects is often synonymous for a means of coercion. This type of power, in the last resort, can only be controlled or overwhelmed by superior physical might and it is implicit in theories of deterrence and balance of power.

In nonviolence theory, power is treated as diffuse and fragile. The power of a government emits from the few who stand at the pinnacle of command, but its sources such as human and material resources, skills, knowledge and authority are external to the rulers. Obedience is not inevitable but is essentially voluntary. Power in a relational context 'is never the property of an individual; it belongs to a group and remains in existence' only so long as it is accepted by a certain number of people. Power vanishes at the moment of the disappearance of 'the group, from which the power originated to begin with' (Arendt, 1969, p. 44). Power derives not from the barrel of a gun but from the consent or acquiescence of the ruled.

Political power is fragile because it is dependent for its strength and existence upon a replenishment of its sources by the cooperation of people (Sharp, 1973, p. 8). 'It is the people's support that lends power to the institutions of a country, and this support is but the continuation of the consent that brought the laws into existence to begin with' (Arendt, 1969, p. 41). Political power stems from the cooperation of people and social institutions. The reasons people obey include habit, fear of sanctions, moral obligation, self-interest, psychological identification with the ruler, indifference and lack of self-confidence. Thus, all government is based on consent, which is not to say that people necessarily approve of their government, but rather that in some cases at least they are not prepared to pay the price for refusal of consent.

Given the fact that the interdependence offers a source of power and pressure, one of the most important principles of nonviolence is denial of cooperation. Non-cooperation operates in such a way as to cut off the oppressor's source of power. When people lose the fear that is a traditional means of social control, the use of fear does not yield its power. The coercive power of states cannot compel individuals to act. Consent can be withdrawn by refusing to act under a given rule. The refusal may involve inconvenience, suffering or even death, but consent for a particular policy can ultimately be withdrawn by the subjects. Nonviolence actions require imagination and flexibility in responding to unexpected situations and maintaining the pressure. Sometimes it is necessary to prove the commitment. Enduring courage is grounded in a deep understanding of the goal of and commitment to nonviolence because one might have to pay with his or her own life and physical well-being.

If a ruler's power is to be controlled or thwarted by withdrawing help and obedience, non-cooperation must be widespread and sustained even in the face of repression. If all people would struggle despite the risk, they would bring the goal closer (Thompson, 1995, p. 141). Once obedience and cooperation are withheld, the sources of power are severed or restricted. Through popular participation, people's own sources of political and social power can be mobilised. In that sense, power derives from 'the human ability not just to act but to act in concert' (Arendt, 1969, p. 44). In nonviolent struggles, the greater the proportion of the population who withdraw support, the greater the probability of success.

Moral and Political Principles

There is no justification for the use of violence not only because it is immoral but also because it leads to more violence. Overall, unarmed struggle offers the hope of transcending the self-destructive character of militarised revolution. The work of fraternisation, communication and education is essential for the conversion or neutralisation of opponents. Nonviolence is not passive inaction nor a routine tactic (Kirk, 1989, p. 118).

In order to fight for a specific cause, it entails an active attempt to defend a position in conflict arising from relationships found in social life.

Given that adversaries are not viewed as enemies and criminals, in the Gandhian conceptions, nonviolent action is not aimed at destroying or hurting anyone. Nonviolence sustains and supports human qualities by separating the person from the issue. The resulting conflict dynamics and the human interaction are very different from violent conflict. The emphasis lies in communicating with the opponents who make an error instead of trying to injure or annihilate them. Nonviolence involves a task to change the opponent's course of action without causing their loss of face. Hatred and anger are carefully directed toward the very systems of evil behind certain policies but not a person.

Experiments with truth can be made through an attempt to resolve the tension between the truth one's opponent knows and the truth which one knows oneself. Conflict provides an opportunity to move to a higher level of truth, which can also mean justice and integrity. The form of mutually agreeable solutions emerges from truth judged by the realisation of human needs. A nonviolent campaign is conducted through a commitment to dialogue concerning the change desired in the opponent. Nonviolent resistance could weaken the morale of the opposite side and work through its persuasive power. It seeks to express love and support for the opposition while rejecting the evil they might do.

In Gandhi's view, truth can be achievable through love and tolerance for other people. Chaos and domination follow the failure of love (Terchek, 1998, p. 33). In addition to causing no harm, love, in more active terms, is referred to helping others grow and flourish. Thus, 'the essential spirit of nonviolence springs from a deeper, inner realisation of spiritual unity in one's own self' (Bose, 1987, p. 30). Human action is a continuous process in which ends and means are distinguishable temporarily but not morally. The relationship between the two is organic, like seeds and a tree.

The transcendental meaning of love implies 'identification with and service of all living beings' as opposed to selfishness, hatred of others and a wish to harm them (Parekh, 1989, p. 117). In a holistic sense, the nature of violence imposed on both human and non-human life is not separable since the instrumental logic of violence does not distinguish different life forms. If all life is equally sacred and revered, people should do all in their capacity to alleviate all forms of violence and suffering. The notion of nonviolent love entails reverence for life, deep respect for the opponent's humanity, and an insistence upon meeting the other with sympathy and kindness, but also with absolute firmness.

Dignity and power come from an inner conviction that people can grow and change. Gandhi did not regard nonviolent action simply as a matter of political techniques or tactics without conviction (Bose, 1987, p. 20). *Ahimsa* in Sanskrit is often referred to not only as a negative concept of doing no harm but also a positive concept of unbound love for all. This notion of overcoming violence is related to '*satyagraha*', which translates into 'relentless search for truth and a determination to search truth' (Gandhi, *Young India*, 19 March 1925). It explains the process to transform individuals and society in the struggle for freedom and justice.

The truth seeking principle is distinguished from passive acquiescence or the desire to avoid pain or death at any price. A commitment to truth counts more than numbers in a nonviolent struggle (Sibley, 1963, p. 31). Nonviolence maintains one's dignity and respect by accepting self-suffering. A willingness to accept suffering demonstrates a commitment to persist in the objective. Unless one is prepared to suffer, the depth of one's commitment can be questioned. 'The positive attributes of courage and serious thinking are imperatives for self-suffering' (Bose, 1987, p. 33). It might mean the willingness to suffer to take responsibility for reforming the planet and to defy the whole might of an unjust empire to save honour, religion and cultural traditions. Nonviolence action, as applied to real world problems, faces the inescapable constraints of political life and mass action.

The willingness to suffer for the practice of nonviolent principles of love and truth goes through continual testing, experimentation and occasional errors; it requires constant, unstinting effort (Gandhi, 1951). Refraining from violence is not born out of fear but out of courage. Thus, nonviolence can be described as outraged and strong but not passive and weak. Nor is it a comfortable compromise based on cowardice. In considering that moral ideals make 'the most exacting demand', therefore, it is crucial to overcome a common human tendency that accepts 'the limitations imposed by the established social order and the accustomed way of life'. The satisfaction of leading a moral life does not go without sacrificing any of the usual comforts (Parekh, 1989, p. 129). Nonviolent resisters accept imprisonment or physical injury without retaliation. They demonstrate courage and willingness to suffer voluntarily for their cause.

Nonviolence Principles of Social Life

Contemporary nonviolence has to concern itself with the whole social fabric in that violence breaks the sense of a community. Pervasive violence circumscribes social existence beyond physical survival. The fabric of society is composed of constantly changing relationship in 'a oneness'. It seeks to heal and bring together an inner realisation of the sense of unity (Bose, 1987, p. 19). Refusing the use of organised violence is linked to not only a short-term personal and political commitment but also a long-term search for social transformation. Nonviolence has a broad definition of what causes and constitutes violence; it takes the initiative against the existing system of dominance and privilege and gives conscious attention to the building of an alternative social structure.

The rejection of violence as a social principle is shared in nonviolent religious and political traditions. The refusal to use or condone violence may take many different forms and practices. Some withdraw from society to pursue a life of isolation from the larger society. They try to seek personal fulfilment through contemplation and non-involvement. Others are more devoted to directed action for the alleviation of other people's suffering. Whereas religious traditions of nonviolence are concerned with moral integrity in front of evil, nonviolent political action aims at the liberation of long-subjugated people.

Nonviolent social principles espoused by Tolstoy and other pacifist philosophers reject a modern state that embodies centralised, hierarchical structures. Social harmony would not be obtained by the order and security based on the institutionalised violence of a state. Fear is divisive and 'cannot be the foundation for permanent unity and strength' (Sibley, 1963, pp. 69-70). By relying on the coercive discipline and capability, states threaten one another and internally repress those who do not accept the dominant ideology and power structure. Though it is supposed to minimise and even eliminate violence, the state gives rise to new forms of violence. It creates artificial boundaries and justifies killing in defence of a few acres of land. Politicians, merchants and officers bring peasants to war either to be killed or to kill strangers in the name of patriotism (Tolstoy, 1967). Though people may not commit themselves to violence, they cannot become nonviolent by shutting their eyes to state violence. They simply transfer an inescapable moral burden to others' shoulders (Parekh, 1989, p. 128). Many pacifists believe that a cycle of violence feeds and perpetuates systems that promote sexism and authoritarianism.

The Gandhian perspective also suggests that the ultimate goal of nonviolence is to replace a violent economic and social structure. Violence is structural with its institutionalisation in economic exploitation and political coercion. Industrial civilisation 'is saturated with violence' (Naidu, 1996, p. 238). Materialism emerging from massive industrialisation prohibits the moral and spiritual development of human life, feeding individual greed and state aggression. A self-sufficient grassroots economy overcomes the marginalisation of economic life for the oppressed. The practice of sharing and caring can be promoted with the re-distribution of excessive wealth.

The realisation of a nonviolent society is dedicated to the welfare of all; nonviolent social goals are more readily achieved in a stateless society where all political and legal authority have been abrogated and where relations between people are governed only by moral authority. Each of the small communities is autonomous and self-governing but linked with others in a non-hierarchical network. The democratic ideal of nonviolent society is thus based on self-sufficiency and egalitarian principles.

As indicated above, the general principle of nonviolence is directed to restructuring the existing order. Therefore, it is not simply a strategy to obtain narrowly defined objectives. The goal of a nonviolent society is to satisfy human needs with a central emphasis on freedom. Realising oneself as an autonomous person is possible in an anarchistic and decentralised community supported by an egalitarian social structure.

Principled nonviolence based on moral rejection of a governmental practice is compatible with a doctrine for structural transformation. As a total approach to living and a philosophy of life, it serves as an ideal to aim for and a strategy for challenging institutions of war and exploitation. Principled advocates of nonviolence refuse to accept and cooperate with a system that utters contempt for human life. Nonviolence, seen as a way of life, involves every aspect of a person's existence, including education, agriculture, energy systems and economics. A nonviolence life principle resides often within the framework of an all encompassing spiritual belief that is shared by members of the community. Such community takes decisions by consensus in the framework of participatory democracy. In addition, each community pursues self-sufficiency in meeting its basic needs for food, clothing and shelter (Ostergaard, 1987). The promotion of human needs and security is attained by demilitarisation and egalitarian relations.

Economic justice for all is sought by nonviolent disciplines of social life. Without violence, development should proceed from below and not be directed from above by the state. Political domination of the colonised countries has coincided with economic exploitation. The local economies of colonised countries were either destroyed or seriously disrupted. In those situations, self-government cannot be attained or have a real meaning without the rehabilitation of self-reliant society. Gandhi believed that independence of India would be more easily achieved by recovering a traditional, self-sufficient economy.

Nonviolence can bring about change especially for groups without access to political power. An important task for nonviolent movements is to develop an overall social plan and alternative vision (Paige, 1997). For instance, peace movements against nuclear weapons may need to promote non-hierarchical social relations and a decentralised decision making structure along with the concept of a civilian based defence to replace the current nuclear and conventional force strategies.

Nonviolence develops ways to resolve conflict while building a bond and maintaining solidarity within and between communities. In order to alter people's beliefs and appeal to their universal human values, often times, nonviolent action has to go beyond simply gaining immediate political objectives. Nonviolence as a way of life has important human consequences that are in sharp contrast to the current militarism prevalent both internationally and nationally.

Technique Approach

There is a schism between different schools of nonviolence: a way of life with transformative values and a technique to accomplish specific tasks. A nonviolent means of protest or resistance can be chosen for purely tactical reasons in order to avoid taking any casualties. In the utilitarian interpretation, nonviolence does not need to be embraced as a personal way of life. The technique approach separates itself from the pacifist traditions and their structural concerns. In its framework of thought, since means are chosen for pragmatic reasons, they can be separable from ends. Action is based on operational precision rather than political construct. Strategies and tactics in nonviolent struggle are as important as in other kinds of conflict, including military.

If nonviolent action is considered as a means of combat, it needs to concentrate on the matching of forces, the waging of battles and the strategy and tactics. It requires 'soldiers' to have courage and discipline and to be prepared to make sacrifices. Strategic calculation 'must necessarily foresee an adversarial process, since the objectives in question must be achieved at the expense of opponents engaged in a similar process' (Ackerman and Kruegler, 1994, p. 7). Nonviolent struggles do not need to be connected to specific belief systems. Most leaders of nonviolent campaigns have not been pacifists, according to Sharp (1973), but have used nonviolent action as a technique primarily for practical reasons, not so much as a moral preference that most pacifists share.

Nonviolence techniques such as strikes and boycotts are recommended as weapons for both the weak and the strong. Power relations can be changed by the systematic employment of nonviolent sanctions that erode and undermine the support base of adversaries. Nonviolent sanctions are susceptible to strategic analysis that is drawn from Machiavelli, Clausewitz and other thinkers of the real politik. 'In the environment of conflict, nonviolent sanctions are the functional equivalent of tactical military manoeuvres. Their only special feature is that they may alter the calculus of conflict by one side's refusal to inflict costs in the form of human causalities' (Kruegler, 1992, p. 22). Here nonviolent sanctions are adopted as tools of strategy to obtain specific objectives with reduced costs.

Nonviolent action, examined in terms of a set of techniques for waging a struggle, is referred to as 'war without weapons' (Sharp, 1973). Any suffering short of physical injury can be inflicted upon the opponent in order to achieve the goal of defeating the enemy. The opponent is not seen as a partner who can work together to satisfy the needs of all sides. Relationships in a struggle are adversarial. A negative conception of opponents can easily produce dehumanisation that is an impediment to conflict resolution (Burrowes, 1996, p. 115).

Strategies and Tactical Decisions

Nonviolent direct action is prepared and organised like its violent counterparts in terms of strategies, tactics and logistics (Ackerman and Kruegler, 1994; Kruegler, 1992). Before the application of the techniques of struggle, waging nonviolent conflict can be planned on different levels of analysis and decision making. Concerns at a macro level are connected to long-term views of a conflict. Strategic decisions are based on the logic that determines the use of direct action and sanctions in a struggle with an opponent in determining the status or conditions of particular objects.

The choices made at a strategic level may be discussed specifically in terms of an acceptable compromise, a legitimisation of the struggle and an envisioned path to winning. The parameters of acceptable settlement may be defined at the beginning stage of strategic planning. Compelling objectives for action are clarified and counterbalanced with the calculation of acceptable costs to be borne. More specifically, the decision to use nonviolent methods derives from an acceptable balance between the imposed costs and the possibility of achieving objectives. Based on the analysis of a given conflict, a method to achieve the objectives with minimum costs is chosen. Strategic choices are made based on their predictable consequences. This 'is the same for violent, nonviolent, and mixed conflicts' (Kruegler, 1992, p. 21).

Strategic level decisions that coordinate and employ those engagements in the pursuit of objectives need to be translated into preparing ultimate and effective sanctions. Nonviolence action as sanctions attempts to create a favourable shift in the relative balance of power by bearing costs for an adversary (Ackerman and Kruegler, 1994, p. 4). Successful mobilisation of political and social support puts pressure on opponents. In an operational plan of conducting nonviolent conflict, such mechanisms as conversion, accommodation, coercion and disintegration have to be connected to strategic objectives, organisation of the fighting force, material resources and methods for sanctions (strikes, boycotts, protest and so forth).

Sanctions and resources have to be deployed in a manner so as to meet the likely response of the opponents with cost-effective principles. Since spontaneous and isolated incidents of resistance are no more effective in accomplishing substantial change than occasional rioting, organisation is critical in any struggle (Lakey, 1987, p. 66). The plan for winning a series of campaigns against a particular opponent can be carefully thought out and implemented. Crucial at this point are the political choices of how to mobilise the resources of a society for the struggle as well as the assignment of leadership responsibility and authority.

Protagonists exchange sanctions to paralyse the opponent's strategy. In an effort to out-perform each other, they try to maximise a unity of command and resistance, strengthen intelligence and communication and maintain flexibility in the selection and deployment of sanctions. The balance of offensive and defensive operations is adjusted to the relative vulnerability and strengths of the protagonists. The dispersion of sanctions, personnel and resources can be reversed for the concentration of sanctions at key points in a critical battle. Objectives, once gained, have to be consolidated.

The group's resources and actions have to be marshalled and deployed against an opponent in such a way to produce the greatest possible shift of power. Two central options from military strategy relevant to nonviolent struggle are 'concentration' and 'strategic withdrawal'. The first promotes the goal of massing sufficient power to decisively defeat the adversary's forces. In nonviolent struggle, this can be translated into the concentration of political power in order to undermine the crucial basis of support for the adversary. Strategic withdrawal (which has a long history in military strategy) can also be considered in a nonviolent struggle faced with mounting costs. On the other hand, shifting strategy risks engendering defeatism (Kruegler, 1992, p. 25).

Tactical decisions govern behaviour in direct engagements with opponents. Particular techniques of direct action such as marches, demonstrations, strikes, sit-ins and boycotts are seen as tactics in a longer term campaign. Decisions at the logistical level are linked to the operations to be performed before and also during the conflict in order to enhance prospects for their success. Capability building entails training nonviolent actors and leaders, preparing propaganda and creating redundant communication capabilities. The efficient use of nonviolent sanctions is supported by establishing a transportation system to support tactical dispersion and concentration. Logistical issues are linked to building support structures with allies (resupply, sanctuary, obtaining external sanctions) and stockpiling resources for endurance and relief (Kruegler, 1992, pp. 28-29).

Nonviolent Direct Action

Popular nonviolent techniques include marches, leafleting, picketing, vigils, fasts, boycotts, strikes, the occupation of government facilities, mass imprisonments and refusals to pay taxes and other similar behaviour. Nonviolent actions can be categorised as methods ranging from symbolic protest through paralytic forms of political and economic non-cooperation to disruptive forms of non-lethal physical and psychological intervention. Nonviolent protest and persuasion are designed to express a position, a grievance, or a claim by symbolic or other means. Symbolism can be delivered through words, music, theatre, gatherings and displays of all kinds. Symbolic nonviolent techniques are also well represented by personal witness, vigils, pickets and marches.

Civil disobedience is a stronger measure than symbolic protest and can be a last resort to open communication. Methods based on refusal to cooperate and interference threaten the normal operations of the system. In noncooperation, there is a large variety of ways in which people turn a refusal to behave as expected into a source of opposition. Strikes, boycotts and legal obstructions can be organised against unacceptable laws. Nonviolent intervention covers techniques of active interference in operation of institutions or undermining an adversary's intentions by such means as nonviolent sabotage, seeking imprisonment, guerrilla theatre, seizure of assets, blockades and sit-ins.

The specific methods of protest, non-cooperation and other nonviolent methods can be found in numerous examples from both Western and Non-Western societies. Many people have conducted conflict by doing, or refusing to do, certain things without using physical violence. German workers refused to produce coal under the direction of French troops in their struggle against French and Belgian occupation of the Ruhr in 1923. Other examples of nonviolent resistance include strikes in labour camps in the Soviet Union in the 1950s, opposition by Norwegian teachers and other professionals to the imposition of a fascist state and collaboration among the Danes to save the lives of the Danish Jews.

Recent examples also include the ongoing Tibetan resistance against the brutal Chinese rule since 1950, the Palestinian Uprising *Intifada* from 1987 to 1990, the democracy movement against the military dictatorship in Burma between 1988 and 1989 and protests in Eastern Europe leading to the overthrow of socialist governments in the late 1980s. Struggle for land reform and other changes in many Latin and Central American countries was also waged in a nonviolent manner supported by liberation theology. These grassroots based movements have been organised without systematic training programmes or a charismatic leadership (McManus and Schlabach, 1991). Economic boycotts and public pressure were exerted to change the exploitative policies of multinational corporations in such cases as the boycott against Nestle in the late 1970s and early 1980s.

Justification of Nonviolent Methods

Nonviolence is often considered not only as an effective means of opposing social evils and/or foreign rule but also as a moral and political alternative to war. Defence of people's lives and ways of life cannot be achieved by violent means that are self-destructive. Nonviolence of the weak has a pragmatic ground as much as a principled, moral one because violent weapons are not available or because their use, in a particular struggle, is judged inexpedient especially when people are outnumbered or overpowered. Thus, the need for nonviolence is often justified by the costs involved in the destruction and suffering caused by resorting to violence.

Means that generate hatred and intolerance will corrupt the goals of social justice. The protection of civilised values is incompatible with inhumane means of destruction. If a struggle for freedom is waged by a military organisation requiring strict hierarchy and unconditional obedience, those principles may be carried over into the organisation of a new political rule. To seize the apparatus of the armed forces, secret police and bureaucracies require a counter-monopoly of violence. It will increase the temptation to crush political opponents after the original goals are obtained. The coercive apparatus of state power was established after violent revolutions in Bolshevik Russia and Communist China. In revolution or national liberation won by violent struggle, groups tend to use violence in an attempt not to lose out politically.

Effectiveness Political conditions explain variations in the overall levels and ways conflict is prosecuted (Vogele and Bond, 1997, p. 366). Nonviolence may work against moderate opponents in countries with some degree of civil and political freedom. However, principled nonviolence is not universally applicable, in particular, against ruthless and dictatorial regimes (e.g., Stalinist Russia and Maoist China). The struggle of Gandhi was successful because its enemy was the British. There was explicit support for Indian independence freely expressed even within Britain itself. Civilian resistance to German occupation in the Second World War occurred in countries where Nazi rule was mildest.

Nonviolent resistance may sometimes not be feasible or take too long a time to be effective even though in theory noncooperation could topple or undermine a system of racial or economic oppression. Sustained nonviolent resistance under extreme political oppression requires impossible levels of heroism. This view is well reflected in the writing of Franz Fanon, a black psychiatrist who became identified with the anti-colonial struggle (1965). In many poor, oppressed societies, violence is part of everyday life 'embedded in the hunger of children and in the humiliating insults of the rich'. Under the intolerable level of violent oppression, nonviolent change, negotiated solutions and gradualism are not seen as the most viable way to future justice (Keefe and Roberts, 1991). For that reason, a campaign, which begins with nonviolent action, may escalate into violence over time because nonviolence is seen to be ineffective. Independent movements in the Third World often moved from nonviolent protest to guerrilla warfare.

It is difficult to ensure that any major campaign remains nonviolent. Violence may be a natural response to anger and frustration and a way of reacting to and denying fear. There is also deep-seated identification of the image of the warrior with courage and pride. Nonviolence is often depicted as passive and acquiescent. It is not always easy to train people for nonviolent action so that they retain a nonviolent discipline. It is difficult to separate the hatred of offences from hatred of the offenders.

During an intense struggle, many different positions exist on the degree to which the use of violence is prohibited. Some people may oppose certain types of violent conflict but not all violence. Others do not participate in violence personally, but they do not interfere with the use of violence under certain conditions such as opposition to injustice or a war of aggression.

Some may also reasonably argue that since nonviolence depends on persuasion of opponents and compromise, it does not pose a radical challenge to vested economic or political interests. Martin Luther King, Jr. tried to work through the Democratic Party and the American political establishment. King was accused by a more militant wing of the African American movement of incorporating black people into the status quo. His Christian principles and apparent dependence on existing elites were consistently challenged.

In response to these criticisms, proponents of nonviolence can say that violent resistance is more ineffective. Indeed, it is easier for a well-armed and ruthless regime to put down some forms of guerrilla warfare or violent uprising than a major strike or mass noncooperation (Carter, 1990, p. 213). The outcome of violent struggles can often be even more savage. Equally importantly, repression of violence is easier to justify than organised mass nonviolent movements.

The advocates of nonviolence strategies also argue that nonviolence avoids the danger of creating a new form of repression even though it is less likely to achieve radical social change than a successful violent revolution. Nonviolent struggle repudiates armed forces for external defence and reliance on a police force. It challenges repressive punishment to maintain internal order. More importantly, transformative nonviolence enhances the ideas of decentralising political and economic power.

18   Peace Movements

Peace movements are fluid and sometimes short-lived social phenomena with the broad participation of ordinary people. Specific peace traditions are often contained in small but prophetic organisational groups that nurture ideas, initiatives and motivation for the wider peace movement. On the other hand, the term 'peace movement' does not simply refer to the organised activities of small groups. It extends far beyond traditional peace organisations to encompass many people from all walks of life committed to the prevention of war or the abolition of the war system. These include physicians who raise public awareness of the dangers of nuclear war by warning of its medical consequences; politicians who work for the legislation of disarmament and arms control; artists who express a moral voice for peace and the environment; scientists who question the wisdom of new weapons; and countless others who contribute to the public outcry against violence and oppression in large or small ways (Cortright, 1993, p. 3).

History of Peace Movements

The history of peace movements is one of discontinuities and divisions (Young, 1987). Peace movements have been more active in certain periods. The movements were more visible from the late 1880s until 1914 and from the 1920s until the mid 1930s. During World War II and the early Cold War period, the traditions of peace movements were kept only in pacifist organisations. One can also talk of mass peace movements in Europe and the U.S. in the late 1960s and in the early 1980s. Until recently, the peace movement has largely been defined as a phenomenon relevant to Western industrial democracies. On the other hand, grassroots challenges to structures of oppression and violence emerged in many Third World countries.

Religious Pacifism   The history of anti-war sentiment or peace ideas is much older than even the first secular peace groups in 1815. Many religious traditions renounced war as a principle or goal of society and opposed military conscription. Some of these groups such as the Society of Friends (also called Quakers), despite their often small numbers, influenced the development of peace movements for more than 300 years. In the tradition of Christian love, since the English Civil War, they have practiced conscientious objection and refused to kill other people.

Peace churches have repudiated participation in war, believing that violence suppresses love, truth and freedom by breeding fear, hatred and prejudice. They saw the connections between violence and an unequal world. The pacifism of these churches did not permit anything that could be construed of as support for state violence.

Most of the noncombatants during the American Independence War came from the peace churches and individual pacifists. During the Civil War, the peace churches repeated the same pattern of opposition and advocated anti-militarism. The general public, not completely but slowly, accepted the pacifist values of peace churches. Most states passed laws exempting from the militia those who could prove membership in a recognised peace church.

Early Secular Peace Groups   The origin of organised secular peace movements can be traced back to the early 19th century. The New York Peace Society was formed in August 1815 by influential merchants and clergymen. The Massachusetts Peace Society emerged a few months later in Boston followed by the creation of other small local peace societies scattered through the U.S. The first peace societies drew upon a commitment to oppose war under the influence of Quakers, Unitarians and other free thinking Protestants. Their members were recruited from the educated elite and an urban middle class who were eager to convert their religious energies to social improvements (DeBenedetti, 1980, pp. 33-34). At the same time, a small group of Quakers founded the British Peace Society, which was strictly committed to pacifist non-resistance. The formation of these first organised groups was a response to the Napoleonic War that brought about a critical change in the nature of a modern war. The ravage of famine, burned and sacked towns and villages generated awareness of the destructiveness and waste of war.

Influenced by the early 19th century liberalism, the first peace societies stressed that differences between states could be settled without recourse to war and granted significance to the role of enlightened public opinion and rational discussion of conflicting interests. Through speaking engagements and publishing activities, they tried to convince the public that war is a waste of resources. Their efforts were mostly aimed at petitioning federal and state governments. They wanted to build support among high placed people, so that they could use their influence to turn the government away from war. In addition, they targeted ministers who were in a position to educate their congregations.

In general, the sentiment of the early peace movement is reflected in their hope that the obsolescence of war is so obvious that a mass change of consciousness could be expected to take place quickly. Some groups recognised the need for and aspired to the transformation of society in preventing total war. Instead of seeking rapid and dramatic reform in hierarchical social structure, however, they envisioned small, incremental, and evenly paced steps to change.

The movement promoted permanent and universal peace. They argued for disarmament and paid great attention to the establishment of the world government. Peace societies criticised the expansionist policies by opposition to the wars of aggression. Many members personally denounced offensive and defensive wars as well as the use of injurious force even in self-defence. The New York Peace Society tended to have an orientation toward a complete pacifist position while the Massachusetts Society put more stress on promoting a world court as an alternative to war. Eventually they were merged with thirty-four groups from other regions to form the American Peace Society in 1828.

The strength in national movements made it possible, by 1843, to hold the first General Peace Convention in London with 324 delegates from Europe and America. The delegates proposed a Congress of Nations and passed resolutions regarding arbitration. However, the momentum began to decline in the early 1850s, due to increasing nationalism, the Crimean War in Europe and the debate over the slavery issues in America (Lewer, 1992, p. 22).

Divisions and Evolution Despite their similar objectives, peace groups had different orientations, strategies and visions for a peaceful world. The division in the early peace movements was evident between positions on denial of all violence and positions on objection only to offensive war. One group called for eradicating all violence – domestic and international. The other group did not oppose all state and personal use of violence and concentrated on the campaign for outlawing only wars of aggression. This position was more readily accepted by the general public.

In 1838, the schisms first appeared at an organisational level with the formation of the New England Non-Resistance Society that had active branches in Michigan, Ohio and Indiana. This bold pacifist organisation was opposed to the conservative tendency of the American Peace Society that increasingly focused only on wars of aggression. Their members were committed to the radical transformation of society and introduced nonviolence to the early development of peace activism. Based on their serious examination of the relationship between pacifism and struggles for freedom from oppression, the Society took a challenge against injustice and denounced all types of violence. Their members refused to participate in the government with the rejection of any role in it. Instead of recognising electoral politics, they directly appealed to individuals and encouraged a revolution of the inner person.

The League of Universal Brotherhood (that existed between 1846 and 1857) is well remembered as the first secular pacifist organisation that sought support among common working people (Cooney and Michalowski, 1977, p. 27). The group was more international and had branches in U.K. as well as the U.S. They recognised the mutual slaughter of workers when governments declare war. In order to promote increased international understanding, they encouraged local communities to set up sister city relationships with their counterparts abroad and to institute exchange programs whereby people could live in another country for a while.

In challenging the injustice of society, the New England Non-Resistance Society and the League of Universal Brotherhood took up such social issues as slavery, prisons, minority rights, women's rights and the causes of oppressed people as well as the problems of war. In contrast with the older organisations which sought to influence professionals and important people, the newer organisations devoted more attention to the common populace. The pacifist organisations in the U.S. declined and disintegrated due to internal and external pressure in the wake of the fast approaching American Civil War.

The secular peace society lost vitality while the American Peace Society continued to rely on the influential and well-to-do. The American Peace Society abandoned a pacifist position. It considered the Civil War as a domestic policing activity and restricted their definition of violence to an international war. On the other hand, the pacifist tradition of the New England Non-Resistance Society (dissolved in 1849) was inherent, to a great extent, in the Universal Peace Union founded in 1865. Based on their belief that neither a government nor an individual should take an inviolable human life, they criticised all forms of violence and encouraged unilateral disarmament (Cooney and Michalowski, 1977, p. 37). The Union was also concerned about oppressed ethnic groups and labour.

Turning Points The first modern popular mass movements against war emerged in the late 19th century. The diverse intellectual trends of the period, including anarchism, socialism, liberalism and internationalism, all affected the direction of peace movements. Compared with liberal reformists, the socialist oriented movement represented by the first Socialist International and the elements of anarchist anti-militarism were aimed at mobilising people for the ideal of creating a new warless world society through the radical transformation of the old social order. The socialists believed that a growing educated and organised working class would lead a campaign against any war caused by their imperial and capitalist masters (Kemp, 1990, p. 183).

In the 19th century we also saw the emergence of more mass based organisational structures. New organisations such as the Red Cross developed an international network. Many peace groups sought to organise public opinion in society and pressure politicians to change the existing structures and introduce new policies. The search for the means of preventing war was sought through instruments to change state behaviour such as negotiation, mediation, arbitration, international treaties and law. Institutional reforms based on liberal Enlightenment traditions were a popular approach in the 1890s. These movements were led by business people, lawyers and other professionals. There was a great surge of support for such initiatives as a world court and international organisations. The lobbying and educational efforts of peace groups contributed to the establishment of the Hague Court (1899), the first permanent tribunal for international arbitration, which paved the way for the League of Nations.

The peace movement between 1890 and 1914 reached the first peak of visible popular support, and it reflected prior origins and foundations built by a range of peace groups and organisations (Young, 1987). Many peace societies in the late 19th century represented an internationalist tradition that stresses a search for war prevention through international cooperation and understanding of different cultures. Pacifist churches and peace sects stressed loyalty to humanity. The rise of popular socialist internationalism further promoted transnationalism beyond states and national borders.

New Organisations In the first half of the 20th century, peace movements had to confront World War I and later concerns about World War II. The popular peace movement was divided in the event of the First World War. Particularly visible was a significant decline in socialist internationalism and anti-militarism. The moral critique of the war and an appeal to transnational allegiance were swamped by the surge of nationalist feelings. Some groups such as the American Peace Society even supported U.S. President Woodrow Wilson's war decision, claiming that peace could not be attained unless Germany and its allies were defeated.

On the other hand, a struggle to keep peace movement traditions coincided with the efforts to acquire a new mass basis. During the first major world war, the silent majority was weary and sceptical of war as an instrument of politics. Anti-war feeling and sentiment in some sectors of society resulted in organised resistance. Though their influence diminished with the intensification of the war, the Anti-Enlistment League formed in 1915 organised events to oppose conscription. Four thousand conscientious objectors existed during World War I. One of the first modern trade union peace movements also took place with an attempt by German locomotive drivers to refuse to drive soldiers to the war front.

A number of key international peace organisations were formed during and immediately following World War I. They drew on all the previous traditions and linked international war resistance and the anti-conscription struggle with schemes for social change. The War Resisters International wanted to thwart war by enlisting people in all countries to pledge resistance to conscription. In Great Britain, the Union of Democratic Control and the No Conscription Fellowship were formed with a democratic and internationalist orientation.

On the other side of the Atlantic, the Fellowship of Reconciliation was given birth as a liberal pacifist group in 1914 by an ecumenical effort to unite and co-ordinate religious pacifists of all faiths. The Fellowship fought against the decision to go to war and represented conscientious objectors. The American Friends Service Committee, created in 1917 by Quakers, initiated a tradition of opposition to military conscription and resistance to taxes for the military. Some groups such as the American Union Against Militarism founded in 1916 and the People's Council of America in 1917 were still comprised of radical pacifists and socialists.

Feminist anti-militarism was an important element in the coalition against war. In agitating opposition to World War I, 1,500 women marched through the streets of New York in August 1914. The Women's Peace Party formed in 1915 urged an early end to the war, and their members met with women from other countries in The Hague and undertook a mediation campaign. Since its existence in 1919, the Women's International League for Peace and Freedom (WILPF) recruited members in support of social justice and pacifism. The Women's Peace Society organised street demonstrations, theatrical events, songs, candle light ceremonies, and prayer services as well as leafleting department stores to protest against the display and sale of warlike toys. In Britain, the Women's Cooperative Guild spoke for working class women's concerns of peace. They condemned the use of militarist material in textbooks and campaigned in the 1920s for an annual peace day in schools (Liddington, 1995).

Prior to World War II In the early 1930s, many groups were active in lobbying for disarmament. In 1932, the U.S. branch of the Women's International League for Peace and Freedom sponsored a Peace Caravan from Hollywood to Washington, D.C. to support the World Disarmament Conference. Based on a long history of using petitions for policy change, in 1932, women collected nine million signatures to urge steps to achieve total and universal disarmament (Vickers, 1993, p. 120). Disarmament issues also drew the attention of labour unions. One of the earliest examples was the initiative by the British Transport and General Workers' Union in 1929 to create a special committee to study the economic effects of disarmament.

However, these and other movements failed to halt the arms race, as their predecessors had failed in the early 20th century. They failed in most of its other stated goals as well and several key peace traditions suffered dramatic discontinuities. The period after the rise of the fascist governments in Germany and Italy and the catastrophe of warfare from 1939 to 1945 created a profound disjuncture in the peace movement (as did the previous periods of major wars). The community of peace organisations and ideas largely remained an isolated island without a peace movement while the silent mass supported the war alliances.

Peace groups were posed with the moral dilemma against pacifist regimes in Europe, though they recognised that violence is no answer to tyranny. Many (e.g., WILPF) accepted the partial legitimisation of war in the face of fascism and, by extension, defended liberal political values against autocracy with force of arms. The anti-fascist front of the 1930s produced the groundwork for supporting the just war theory, which rationalised the Second World War.

Concerns of Nuclear Testing Dropping atomic bombs on Japan in 1945 produced a profound impact on future warfare and the military strategies based on nuclear deterrence. Mutually assured destruction (MAD) provoked great anxiety and fear in the post-World War peace movements. Another wave of activism that arrived by the late 1950s focused on nuclear testing.

Opposition to nuclear weapons, notably atmospheric nuclear testing with its resulting fallout, generated a series of serious protests. The upsurge of public opinion against nuclear arms grew in Europe, North America, Australia and elsewhere, reviving the old peace traditions.

Most importantly, nuclear pacifism was represented by newly founded programmes such as the British Campaign for Nuclear Disarmament (1958), which is well known by its acronym CND. Its innovative forms and new traditions of mass movements for the opposition to nuclear testing reflected the drastically altered character of war and weaponry. On the other side of the Atlantic, the Ban-the-Bomb movement was organised by the Committee for A Sane Nuclear Policy (SANE) and the Committee for Nonviolent Action (CNVA) with the goal of bringing the arms race under control. SANE was structured as an educational membership organisation and employed more traditional techniques to argue for gradual general disarmament. By maintaining the radical pacifist tradition, on the other hand, CNVA was engaged in effective civil disobedience action at nuclear bomb test sites in Nevada and the South Pacific. In 1961, CNVA also urged for unilateral disarmament through a San Francisco to Moscow Walk for Peace joined by peace walkers from nine other countries. Given their pacifist credentials, they were allowed to have an opportunity to deliver a radical pacifist message to the public in the Soviet Union for the first time with a vigil in Moscow (Cooney and Michalowski, 1977, p. 145).

Nuclear testing in the Pacific provoked transnational voyages for peace. In addition, there were international protests against France's nuclear testing programme in the Sahara organised by British and American pacifists along with a group of Africans in December 1959. These experiences helped pacifist activists from many countries build the World Peace Brigade, in 1961, with the creation of a training centre for nonviolent action in Dar-es-Salaam, Tanzania. The movement against nuclear testing achieved its objective with the signing of the Limited Test Ban Treaty by the major powers in 1963. While the movement ended, nuclear testing went underground, and the nuclear arms race continued.

Opposition to the Vietnam War and Social Justice The period between the mid 1960s and early 1970s was represented by popular opposition to the Vietnam War and the civil rights movements. The War Resisters League and the Fellowship of Reconciliation continued to organise mass rallies against American military intervention in Vietnam following their first significant protest in December 1964 in New York. Civil disobedience demonstrators turned the steps of the Pentagon into a 'speak-out' forum, and No Tax for War in Vietnam Committee called for tax resistance. Street demonstrations were common in 1966. The war was also a catalyst for a new international coalition. A world drive for signatures in support of ending the Vietnam War was launched by the Women's International League for Peace and Freedom, in 1965.

Since the first mass anti-draft initiative was taken at a rally at New York's Central Park in April 1967, non-cooperation with the draft became more systematically organised by such groups as The Resistance. Pacifist civil disobedient actions coexisted with street demonstrations and mass rallies. The movement that started with a group of dedicated individuals drew millions of people with various levels of commitment and political orientations (Cooney and Michalowski, 1977, p. 198). Nonviolent pacifist groups played a critical role in agitating the public. They counselled draft resisters and provided safety by finding them places of refuge in Canada and elsewhere, as had the Underground Railroad for runaway slaves during the American civil war. Public anxiety was relieved with the agreement on the withdrawal of U.S. troops between the U.S. and Vietnamese governments in 1972.

In the early 1960s, human and civil rights also came to be seen as integral to peace with the growing discontent of African Americans. The mass protests were triggered by such events as the Montgomery Bus Boycott (1956), the student sit-in movement at a lunch counter in Greensboro, North Carolina, which spread to South Carolina, Tennessee and Virginia (1960) and Freedom Rides (1960) that were organised to protest against segregation. The civil rights movements continued with massive civil rights marches organised by the Southern Christian Leadership Conference and other groups. The protests and demonstrations for social justice depended on the massive use of nonviolent action. These movements led to improvement in the political, economic and social status of minority groups in the U.S.

Resurgence Movements against nuclear weapons surged again in the early 1980s with military bellicosity between the U.S. and the Soviet Union and a perceived growing danger of nuclear war. Many peace groups were engaged in diverse activities such as international marches and camps, nuclear free zones and town twinning. The movements were a direct response to the extremist military policies of the Reagan administration. Many people were concerned about the abandonment of serious negotiation on nuclear arms reduction. In Europe, the NATO decision to deploy new intermediate Range Nuclear Forces in Western Europe provoked fear of another war.

In the context of what appeared to many as a renewed Cold War, the largest mobilisation in the history of the European peace movement was realised in 1981. The demonstrations opposed the U.S. deployment of Cruise and Pershing II missiles and the Soviet deployment of SS-20 missiles with a call for an end to the arms race. The most momentous energy was created by peace movements that came from spontaneously coordinated mass demonstrations in 12 European capitals and other major cities (London, Bonn, Brussels, Paris, Athens, and Rome) in 1981. This upsurge of anti-nuclear activity included between two and three million people who took to the streets from October to December 1981. These demonstrations illustrated a sense of political purpose that had seldom been observed before.

In the U.S., a popular momentum arrived with the nuclear freeze movement that proposed halting research, testing, production and deployment of new nuclear weapons. The Nuclear Weapons Freeze Campaign consolidated in 1981 played a remarkable role in linking autonomous local groups and national organisations and securing official endorsement from new peace organisations of lawyers, educators, nurses and other occupational groups (Chatfield, 1992, p. 154). On June 12, 1982, nearly one million people gathered at New York's Central Park in order to demand an end to the arms race. Rock stars and Hollywood celebrities volunteered their services for this largest political demonstration in U.S. history held at the opening of the Second Special Session of the UN General Assembly on Disarmament. In their official messages, the gathering called for halting the arms race and diversion of military spending to fund human needs development.

The popular reaction eventually had an impact on arms control negotiations between Washington and Moscow. It gave new life to the global peace movement, generating a vision of unity and hope. The movement involved more transnational and massive protests than any event in the 1960s. The political coalition comprised of anti-nuclear, women's and environmental movements was broader than the anti-Vietnam War movement. In addition to their transnational dimensions, these protest movements can also be characterised by new forms of political organising, less reliance on former structure and leadership, and a greater political awareness.

During the 1980s, there was also consistent opposition to military involvement in Central America led by churches, religious and human rights organisations. The movement was concerned to prevent another Vietnam. More than 1,000 organisations both at local and national levels participated in opposition to the U.S.-sponsored war in Central America during the 1980s. In particular, traditional peace groups such as the American Friends Service Committee and the War Resisters League supported the struggle for liberation from oppression in Central America. Over 70,000 U.S. citizens travelled to Nicaragua, deeply troubled by the pain and suffering that U.S. foreign policy inflicted on the country. Whereas some activities were inspired by religious or moral principles, others were motivated by democratic ideals (Cortright, 1993, p. 219).

The Persian Gulf War Peace activism during the Gulf War represented the post-Cold War anti-war sentiment. Peace demonstrations and vigils took place around the world. Half a million people demonstrated in Washington, D.C. In Paris, peace groups demanded a referendum on France's involvement. In Spain, demonstrators called for the shut-down of military bases used as staging points for U.S. troops in the Gulf. More than 20,000 protesters marched through London. Approximately 3,500 people walked from Madrid to U.S. air and naval bases to deliver their demand. In Japan, 1,000 demonstrators formed a human chain near a U.S. naval base.

Building a Popular Base for Nuclear Disarmament

Given their impact on the end of the Cold War, the mass peace movements in the 1980s need to be further examined in the context of their social characteristics. Public consciousness reached a new political climax by exerting pressure for policy changes. The success of the anti-nuclear movement was attributed to the fact that it enjoyed public support in the early 1980s. More than 150 national organisations endorsed the freeze on nuclear weapons, including the U.S. Conference of Mayors, the Young Women's Christian Association and the American Nurses Association as well as the National Council of Churches.

The entertainment community was not exempt from being gripped by nuclear anxiety during the 1980s. The nuclear freeze campaign was supported by many of biggest names in the television, film and music recording industries. The Hollywood committee of SANE was reborn, and the members included the actors Marlon Brando, Kirk Douglas and Henry Fonda (Cortright, 1993, pp. 65-66). The Rolling Stones and others visited

Moscow to improve U.S.-Soviet relations. In the public mind, the backing of media stars gave unprecedented legitimacy and recognition to the anti-nuclear movement. Celebrity involvement in peace activism, hunger, human rights and the environment created an image of acceptability. Activities of the peace movement were supported by news media coverage, too.

The Reagan administration was unable to win support for its nuclear policies. In a 1982 poll, approval of the peace movement in the major NATO countries ranged from a low of 55 percent to a high of 81 percent. Intense public pressure on the withdrawal of NATO and Soviet missiles led to challenging the entire Cold War system of East-West relations. They influenced the social democratic parties in major European countries. Nuclear weapons were delegitimised in some countries. In Britain, anti-nuclear war movements were well represented and supported by the Labour party with its policy on unilateral nuclear disarmament in the 1980s. New Zealand's national defence policy in the 1980s was strongly influenced by a sentiment of peace movements. The result was a ban on all nuclear facilities, including visits by nuclear armed or nuclear powered naval vessels, much to the anger of the U.S. In order to win over public opinion, the U.S. and Soviet governments began to make a compromise on the deployment of cruise, Pershing II, SS-20 and other nuclear missiles.

Religious Groups and Opposition to Nuclear Weapons The engagement of religious leaders cast a mantle of respectability. Pax Christi, the Catholic-based peace organisation, preached the danger of nuclear war and exerted a major influence within the Catholic community during the 1980s. Half of the U.S. Roman Catholic bishops personally endorsed the freeze. In March 1981, seventeen bishops wrote to then archbishop Joseph Bernardin asking that the newly formed committee on War and Peace address a series of fundamental questions on the morality of nuclear weapons policy.

The opposition to the military build-up of the Reagan administration was seriously raised in the pastoral letter entitled 'The Challenge of Peace: God's Promise and Our Response' (Cortright, 1993, p. 47). With the challenge against the very foundation of U.S. nuclear policy, the bishops endorsed a policy of 'no first use'. They condemned nuclear warfare and urged the support for a comprehensive test ban treaty. Retaliatory strikes, which threaten innocent life, were denounced through questioning the fundamental principles of nuclear deterrence. Political justification for the use of limited nuclear warfare was met with scepticism.

The Methodist policy recommendations also endorsed a comprehensive test ban, support for existing arms control treaties, a ban on space weapons, and no-first use of nuclear weapons. The statement 'In Defence of Creation' issued by the United Methodist Church rejected the arms race and the whole concept of deterrence as a national security policy. They also pointed out the economic consequences of the arms race: 'justice is forsaken in the squandering of the arms race while a holocaust of hunger, malnutrition, disease and violent death is destroying the world's poorest peoples'. The United Presbyterian Church was also an early endorser of the nuclear freeze, and they established a Peacemaking Program in 1980 to support peace education both nationally and locally.

Representing nuclear pacifism, the World Council of Churches, in 1983, declared the production, deployment, and use of nuclear weapons as a crime against humanity. The New York based National Council of Churches has sponsored an annual Peace with Justice programme, in hundreds of local churches, which focuses on peace education. The National Council, the United Church of Christ, and other Protestant denominations also established peace advocacy programs in New York or in Washington, D.C. Many of these church offices participated in lobbying efforts and were actively involved in the campaigns for the nuclear freeze, against the MX missiles, and for peace in Central America. The church social action offices were a regular part of the peace movement presence on Capital hill.

Professional Organisations Professional groups were also very active in anti-nuclear movements. Physicians for Social Responsibility, founded in 1961 to deal with the growing concern about the health effects of atmospheric nuclear testing, were actively engaged in raising consciousness against the arms race. The group helped the American public that there would be no winners in a nuclear war. The membership rose from just a few hundred in 1979 to 30,000 in 1984 under the charismatic leadership of Helen Caldicott (Lunardini, 1994, p. 170).

International Physicians for the Prevention of Nuclear War was founded and co-chaired by Russian and American doctors. By sponsoring international forums on the consequences of nuclear war, they tried to educate the public. The mutual trust that was visible with high-level personal contacts between the organisation's leaders helped develop common cause over the vital issues of human survival. By linking scientific authority and professional prestige to the commitment to the prevention of nuclear war, the physicians contributed to the transformation of public opinion and cultural values during the 1980s (Lewer, 1992, p. 79). This group received the Nobel Peace Prize in 1985 with acknowledgement of the physicians' efforts as an important factor in generating public pressure for arms limitation.

Trade Unions As a rule, active and concrete action on international issues has not been frequent among the trade unions, which have preferred to leave these questions mainly to political parties. In general, the conversion of the armaments industry to civilian production is a more familiar issue than nuclear disarmament to the trade union movement. However, there have been sectors of trade unions more actively involved in making policy statements and participating in nonviolent peace activities.

In the early 1980s, United Auto Workers, the International Association of Machinists and other largest U.S. trade unions endorsed a freeze on nuclear weapons. The Trade Union Congress in England has made statements on nuclear disarmament. At its 1979 congress, the federation of German trade unions took a strong stand in support of disarmament. The interest of trade unions in nuclear disarmament was not unusual in considering other earlier organised activities such as a mail strike carried out by the post, telephone and telegraph workers international union in 1973 in protest against French nuclear tests in the atmosphere.

Women's Contributions Women have been at the forefront of struggle for nuclear disarmament in the early 1980s as other times of peace movements. The best known example is the Greenham Common Women who formed camps around nuclear bases in England to protest deployment of U.S. intermediate nuclear missiles. In the U.S., more than a thousand women joined a series of sit-ins, demonstrations and other events -- organised by the Women's Pentagon Action -- that called for an end to the war system.

In feminist peace perspectives, opposition to hierarchy is closely connected to protection of life and disarmament. In several thousand local groups throughout Western Europe and the U.S., women took the lead in educating citizens about the nuclear threat. The women's anti-nuclear movements in the 1980s was built upon their past involvement in disarmament dating back to the European Movement of Women Against Nuclear Armament formed at the end of the 1950s and the demonstration of women at a NATO conference in the Netherlands against plans to set up a multilateral nuclear force in 1964.

Innovations in Anti-Intervention Movements

The 1980s were also characterised by a variety of innovations made in campaigns against U.S. participation in regional wars. Many movements grew out of the dissatisfaction with the policy agendas of foreign policy elite in the national capital. It demonstrates the competence of ordinary citizens in formulating a response to the complicated security issues. Opposition to U.S. intervention in Central America, in particular, El Salvador, Guatemala and Nicaragua stemmed from the awakening of moral sensitivity. The U.S. government supported the right-wing dictatorships that tortured people as they were allies in fighting against the spread of communism in the region.

In opposing U.S. sponsored wars in the region, many peace groups were engaged in direct action as well as lobbying. The overwhelming consensus accepted the legitimacy of massive nonviolent action and other activities in expressing the views of ordinary people. Civil disobedience became a much less divisive issue, as people began to believe that their government policies caused pain and atrocities for people in other countries. They took a variety of actions, including a sanctuary movement.

The sanctuary movement protected El Salvadoran and Guatemalan refugees who escaped from war and torture in a similar manner that the Underground Railroad led slaves to freedom in the North during the American Civil War (Cortright, 1993, p. 219). The sanctuary groups provided safety for the political refugees in the U.S. by resisting attempts of the Immigration and Naturalization Service to deport them. Many U.S. citizens risked jail terms in protecting 'illegal immigrants', mostly landless peasants and other groups. More than 400 churches and religious institutions offered shelter and food, and without their participation, the movement would not have been successful.

It was also a great concern that the Reagan administration would invade Nicaragua to eliminate the Sandinista regime or dispatch troops to support the governments backed by the military in Guatemala and El Salvador. The Pledge of Resistance was a direct response to growing fears of attacks against Nicaragua. The campaign reported, at the end of 1986, the commitment of more than 80,000 American citizens to civil disobedience in the case of the invasion. It is difficult to know the exact impact of these resistance movements on changes in the U.S. policy. However, it is certain that their role in public education about the issues made it difficult for the Reagan administration to launch a military intervention.

Some groups took trips to personally observe conditions related to local struggle. This approach reflects a lack or distrust of information being received from the government and the mass media. A vast number of visits were made to Central America, in particular, Nicaragua, by Americans and Europeans in early and mid-1980s. These visits were provoked by the Reagan administration's policy to overthrow the socialist oriented national governments.

The boldest method of nonviolent civilian intervention was 'Witness for Peace'. Ordinary citizens were recruited to travel to Nicaragua by the Catholic Inter-Faith Task Force on Central America. The volunteers placed themselves in the middle of combat zones that were threatened by attacks from the U.S.-backed Contras guerrilla group. These volunteers, involving 4,000 American citizens, tried to provide a human shield in prevention of armed violence. They documented atrocities committed by the Contras and spoke to the media (Cortright, 1993, p. 220).

Community Peace Activities

For many years local communities have set up educational assistance, refugee and exchange programmes through which they can address their international concerns with peace and justice. At the peak of the peace movement in the 1980s, a multitude of peace action groups, women's peace programs, peace camps and anti-cruise missile campaigns arose spontaneously in many localities inspired by community activists. National and transnational groups working on disarmament, development and human rights also built their community bases to mobilise support and resources for their activities.

With a focus in diverse issue areas, the locally based programmes introduced creative methods for direct action in an attempt to change government policies. The anti-apartheid campaign during the 1980s focused on the withdrawal of investments in corporations doing business in South Africa. Local programmes for the conversion of weaponry production facilities to civilian use involved participatory educational exercises concerning strategies to rebuild a local economy for peace.

It was noticeable during the height of anti-Soviet campaign by the Reagan administration that local governments were increasingly involved in peace related issues. 'Some 4200 towns and cities in 23 countries declared themselves to be nuclear free zones' (Alger, 1995, p. 62). In the summer of

1984, at a conference convened at Hiroshima and Nagasaki, mayors of many cities around the world established a worldwide movement of cities against nuclear weapons. The local level ballot initiatives, as part of the nuclear freeze campaign in the early 1980s, gave people an unprecedented opportunity to express their views on a nuclear policy.

In response to popular concerns, many local governments also adopted anti-apartheid, sanctuary, conversion resolutions and legislation. Projects on twinning cities in foreign countries promoted exchange programmes. Hundreds of municipalities in Europe became part of a network of the towns and the development movement that supported projects benefiting Third World communities.

Politics of Peace Movements

Many realists rely on military superiority and nuclear deterrence in maintaining international order. Though they may agree with measures that reduce the risk of accidental nuclear war or pre-emptive strikes in a crisis, they tend to believe that nuclear capabilities ought to be, if necessary, further enhanced for national security. This view was held by the top U.S. government officials in the early 1980s. President Reagan even believed that a limited nuclear war would be possible. He launched the largest peacetime military build-up in U.S. history. The military budget grew from 130 billion dollars in 1979 to nearly 300 billion in 1985, an increase of more than 50 percent above inflation. Naval forces were deployed near Russian territory and threatened nuclear strikes against its heartland.

The peace movement called for the de-nuclearisation of military policy as well as demilitarisation of defence policies. Peace groups opposed to nuclear arms and to other military policies sought to exert effective pressure to enhance a particular negotiating stance – for example, the Freeze proposals in the early 1980s. Some argued for conditional steps that will eventually lead to bilateral or multilateral negotiations involving missile trade offs. However, a strong voice was also raised for unilateralism as an ideal for nuclear disarmament. In Europe, major peace groups called for major action by each country regardless of what others do. 'Demands for unilateral action can in principle be achieved by popular pressure on one government, and government actions can be monitored by the news media and public opinion' (Carter, 1992, p. 23).

Peace movements lobby for specific policy changes. Demand for an end to nuclear tests, for removal of bases or renunciation of particular weapons is a logical extension of popular pressure on governments for reversing their policies. Peace groups have used debates on disarmament at the UN to mobilise public pressure for progress in cutting arms. 'The UN Special Sessions on Disarmament in 1978 and 1982 were both the focus of petitions and lobbying' (Carter, 1992, p. 23). The role of public opinion and its impact on the legislative process has been an important element in the politics of anti-nuclear movements. Though not successful in getting majority support, in June 1979, Senators Mark Hatfield and George McGovern developed a proposal for U.S.-Soviet Freeze on strategic nuclear weapons deployment.

Peace groups, in general, oppose realism by advocating that conflict is not inevitable among states and that military strength does not guarantee security. International conflict, to a great extent, arises from misperception and unnecessary hostilities. An honest re-examination of adversarial relations would reveal the basis for the misunderstanding and bring about the needed change. Significant reform would occur with the proper realisation by individuals and groups at all levels of societies (Lofland, 1993, p. 89). The atmosphere for mutual understanding and transnational cooperation can be improved by exchanging delegations and organising conferences of professionals as well as mechanisms of mediation and reconciliation.

Issues and Strategies

Different political analyses and approaches coexist among peace activists. These differences can be compared in terms of goals, strategies and values. Some groups believe that peace ought to be achieved through fundamental transformation of the existing system. Others concentrate on changing policies in the narrow domain of issue areas.

Total Rejection of Militarism   Peace movement traditions built on pacifism object to the war system and deny its legitimacy. The orientation of these groups is well represented by the Fellowship of Reconciliation and the War Resisters League. Pacifists oppose all types of wars, believing that killing human beings is morally wrong and is the greatest evil of all. In addition to opposing the military policies of their states, they personally refuse to take part in war, most directly by resisting conscription. The War Resisters League has gained a reputation for its objection to conscription. Many pacifist groups seek reforms through the engagement in campaigns not to pay war taxes spent on military activities.

In full pacifist positions, de-militarisation should go beyond opposition to specific weapons or spots of military conflict in a particular part of the world. In the event of war, they would not join in any wartime hysteria of hatred, revenge and retaliation, nor cooperate with government authority in any capacity to cause injury. If their commitment to opposition to all types of war preparation means breaking the law, then they are ready to practice civil disobedience and to accept the consequences of their beliefs.

Socialist anti-war orientations were further fused and concerned with the struggle to remove the war making society or institutions associated with capitalism and an oppressive state system. They wish to create a nonviolent, just, equitable and harmonious society as a condition for peace. This strategy is sometimes linked with utopian and communitarian ideas. Efforts to banish war altogether are most likely to be associated with educating the public in establishing firm structures of positive peace. Human rights, social justice, struggles for racial equality, trade union rights, women's rights and opposition to colonialism are all related to building a peace system.

Overall, these groups, which oppose the prevailing social economic system and the institution of war itself, have the most consistent and uncompromising position and make more persistent efforts than those opposing only particular wars or specific means of waging war. The groups with an orientation toward anti-militarism always constitute the small core of peace campaigns, both because of the strength of their convictions and their long-term organisational commitment. The absolutism of pacifist positions fails to reconcile with immediate political realities. Faith-based groups have a strong commitment to nonviolent transformation, not just arms control. The scope of their goals is less tangible in the sense that they seek long-term structural changes rather than short-term policy changes (Zisk, 1992, p. 62). Pure pacifists have always been a minority but maintained existence during the downturn of peace movements, coming back to rekindle the consciousness of the public in the next crisis.

Focus on Single Issues It is more difficult to abolish a system of war than to stop specific wars or oppose particular types of weapons. Narrow agendas centred around single issues (rather than challenging militarism, in general) can be a main focus of a peace movement. Peace groups have been created in response to concerns about individual wars or narrow aspects of a war system. Such issues as the Vietnam War, intervention in El Salvador or

Nicaragua drew great public attention. There also has been opposition to an increase in the military budget, chemical weapons and anti-personnel mines as well as nuclear weapons.

Many groups opposed to armaments pay most attention to a reduction in or elimination of particular dimensions of weapons or weapons delivery systems, including cruise missiles, the B1 bomber, neutron bombs, nuclear weapons, or similar items. The Campaign for Nuclear Disarmament, the European Nuclear Disarmament and the Committee for a Sane Nuclear Policy have been active in the opposition to nuclear weapons. Bans on the production, deployment and use of specific weapons have been advocated because they are exceptionally destructive, indiscriminate and inhumane. The Ban-the-Bomb movement in the late 1950s and the early 1960s and the Freeze Movement in the early 1980s opposed, respectively, testing of nuclear weapons and the nuclear arms race. The concerns about nuclear weapons reappeared during nuclear testing in the South Pacific by the French government in 1995. Testing was eventually stopped by international outrage.

Peace movements in Western Europe and the U.S. have long been primarily engaged in direct opposition to a particular war or nuclear weapons, and this trend continued throughout the 1980s and the 1990s. It is easier to achieve a movement's objective with concentration on a specific issue. On the other hand, peace movements that have a narrow focus tend to disband when their issues are (even partially) resolved. For example, anti-war movements lost popular appeal after the resistance to the war in Vietnam pressed the U.S. government to withdraw their troops from Vietnam. European opposition to the deployment of nuclear missiles by NATO sparked a virtual firestorm of anti-nuclear protests during the early 1980s. With the signing of the INF treaty of 1988 banning such missiles on both sides, the European anti-nuclear movement has been dormant.

Organisational Bases and Structure

Acquiring a mass base requires local, grassroots organising. The nuclear freeze movement, in terms of their mobilisation of mass support, was successful due to their orientation toward grassroots activities. Their popular appeal had a revolutionary aspect with radical democratisation of the debate over nuclear weapons, military strategy and national security policies. Ordinary citizens made assertions and demands for their views to be heard in the most vital issue related to the future survival of the human race. The acceptance of direct action influenced the grassroots character of the new movement, rooted in local communities.

The Nuclear Weapons Freeze Campaign grew out of peace movement efforts to link the growing public concern about nuclear power with the escalating dangers of the nuclear arms race. During the early Reagan years, largely in response to the intensification of the Cold War, SANE enjoyed a dramatic membership increase from 4,000 in the late 1970s to 150,000 in the mid-1980s, becoming the largest single organisation dedicated to opposing nuclear weapons (Lunardini, 1994, p. 186). The British CND also experienced unprecedented expansion as a broad, populist organisation. The CND membership jumped from 3,000 in 1979 to 30,000 in 1980, eventually reaching more than 100,000 by 1984. The number of their local branches dramatically rose from 30 in 1979 to 1,000 at the end of 1981 (*New York Times*, 13 November 1981).

While a strong grassroots base is an important element in organisational vitality, the increase in the membership can naturally lead to building a more hierarchical decision making structure. Some groups may favour the development of strong leadership and central authority for other reasons. If an organisation has a focus on lobbying activities rather than direct action, they tend to be more dominated by bureaucratic tendencies and specialists. These characteristics are reflected, to a certain extent, in Physicians for Social Responsibility, the Union of Concerned Scientists and SANE/FREEZE (emerging from the 1987 merger of the former with the Nuclear Freeze Campaign).

Many peace movements have led to the development of an international network whereas some campaigns are limited to purely nationalistic bases. One of the most significant strategic ingredients in Europe's anti-nuclear movements was the creation of a transnational base. The European Nuclear Disarmament (END) established with an appeal drafted by British Historians added a new dimension to the nuclear disarmament movement in their campaigns for a nuclear free Europe. The notion of a nuclear free zone is based on an emphasis on transnational linkage and non-alignment.

The Green movement, influential in Europe, can also be seen in the same context of building grassroots transnational networks. Its underlying philosophy represents a synthesis of ecology, feminism, political decentralisation, community and work place democracy, anti-authoritarianism and anti-militarism. The movement relies on the grassroots coalitions of local groups that remain largely autonomous. The development of transnational organisational links based on grassroots movements in the 1980s is contrasted with the anti-nuclear weapons campaigns of the late 1950s sponsored and created from the top down.

Major Characteristics of Peace Movements

Contemporary mass movements against war and militarism have several interesting characteristics. First of all, peace movements have become pluralistic in their issue orientations, priorities and goals. They have been influenced by a variety of traditions, motivated by a range of concerns and guided by diverse strategies. Many people who have been active in feminism, socialism, religious nonviolence, radical ecological pacifism and so on have been increasingly drawn into peace activities. Those groups that focus primarily on economic justice have found themselves involved in the peace movement agenda through recognition of the economic cost of military expenditures. Some peace movements are closely associated with feminist agendas and their concerns about a patriarchal military system.

Second, occasional coalitions are formed between peace movement activists, environmental movements and opponents of nuclear power. The movements have made efforts to reach out to other groups in order to broaden their appeal and deepen their commitment. The anti-nuclear power movement, with its local bases, strengthened the nuclear freeze movement in the 1980s. Environmental organisations such as Greenpeace and Friends of the Earth have been increasingly involved in anti-nuclear protests. Such groups express their anti-war and particularly anti-nuclear concerns because of the threat of environmental destruction arising from nuclear war and also from ongoing radio active contamination produced by nuclear weapons facilities.

Third, peace movements in the West have been closely connected to the concerns of middle class people. For instance, the nuclear freeze campaign, support for a comprehensive test ban and environmental movements have drawn their support largely from the relatively well-educated sections of society. Religious and professional (such as physicians and lawyers) groups and college students were more actively involved in disarmament, human rights and anti-war movements than other groups. Trade unions, on the other hand, were more concerned with economic conversion.

Fourth, peace movements have been largely motivated by the rise of popular anxiety (Barash, 1991, p. 68). Peace activism has largely been reactive, swelling in response to crises. The movements have typically grown when the threat to peace was great. Ironically, therefore, they have done best in terms of enthusiasm, membership and financial contributions when the situation has seemed darkest. This was particularly evident during the early years of the Reagan administration when anti-communist rhetoric was inflammatory and domestic military build up reached record levels.

Fifth, peace movements shrink when governments successfully modulate their rhetoric (but not their policies) or co-opt the peace movement agenda by showy but relatively trivial concessions. The energy 'quickly subsides, even though the underlying problem remains as serious as ever' (Barash, 1991, p. 68). Peace movements are readily being moderated by limited success such as the partial test ban treaty of 1963 and the INF treaty of 1988. The anti-nuclear movement of 1958-63 diminished rapidly after the partial test ban treaty was signed although the nuclear weapons arms race simply went underground, intensifying rather than diminishing. The anti-war sentiment in the U.S. did not outlast specific crises, and the anti-nuclear movement has become less visible with U.S.-Russian agreements on significant reductions in strategic nuclear forces. Since the end of the 1980s, reduced tension between the U.S. and Russia contributed to diminished concern about nuclear weapons despite their continuing threat to humanity.

Sixth, another important reason for the historical decline in peace movements has been their tendency to focus on too narrow an issue. The European peace movements first gained momentum with the deployment of NATO Euro-missiles; then they were bereft of an issue when the INF treaty on the elimination of these missiles on both sides was negotiated. The ups and downs of peace movements can be explained by political cycles and public reactions to major international crises. It remains to be seen whether the modern peace movements can sustain their momentum when immediate, readily perceived threats do not exist.

Peace Movements in Developing Countries

Various peace groups in non-Western societies have recently devoted time and energy in an effort to become better acquainted with disarmament, development, human rights and other issues. India is one of the developing countries that have local traditions of various types of social movements. In late 1983, a peace ride was completed, with a central focus on disarmament, between Assam and Delhi, India. A movement against foreign military bases in the Philippines was co-ordinated by the national democratic front, and the support came from the middle class. The sentiments of the movement were skilfully orchestrated by anti-government groups. The anti-base coalition became a vehicle for the closure of the U.S. military base.

Despite these noticeable activities, disarmament issues are not strong in many developing countries. In general, anti-war movements in the Third World are disparate, often anonymous and most certainly marginalised. On the other hand, many social movements can be identified in the struggle for a series of basic demands arising from the condition of underdevelopment, a lack of self determination, violation of civil and human rights, absence of ecological protection, militarism and threats to cultural survival. Much of the energy of radical activists is dedicated to a struggle for basic rights that the peace movement in the West has taken for granted.

One area where social movements in the Third World have made a distinct impression is the ecology. The stress on the environment, as is interrelated to a range of development issues, holds a central position in its critique of a modern economic system that is responsible to cultural genocide and industrial pollution. Grassroots associations in Malaysia have successfully encouraged various forms of localised conservation activities. In Kenya and other parts of Africa, women's development groups have been on the forefront of the struggle to reverse deforestation. In Brazil, the movements for social justice and peace have been largely defined by an amalgamation of environmental organisations, trade unions and women's groups.

Overall, the nature of grassroots movements in the Third World is diverse and hard to compartmentalise. Owing to repressive political circumstances and limited resources, it is not easy to develop conscious organisational structures for campaigns. In addition, some movements suffer from a tendency to focus on issues that have narrow local and regional relevance. Groups have yet to learn how to develop agendas beyond their past struggles against neo-colonialism and foreign intervention. The absence of democratic institutions in many Third World countries is considered as an obstacle to the expression of peace issues.

Environmental and development groups have begun to be aware of like-minded groups working outside their particular region and making efforts to establish lateral communication networks within the Third World. Peace activities have also been stimulated by various outposts of Western based multinational organisations such as Friends of the Earth and Quakers. These groups have also attempted to cooperate with home grown groups of a similar complexion and build an international base for the agenda. The World Peace Council has maintained a presence in several Third World countries for many years.

A Comparative Context The broad definition of peace embraces four dimensions, including limiting violence, economic well-being, social justice and ecological balance. In industrialised countries, campaigns have tended to concentrate on limiting violence, and the central core of peace movements has been established by control of nuclear weapons. In order to build broader coalitions, the disarmament agenda has been extended to economic issues such as jobs for peace and conversion of military production to peaceful purposes.

In the 21st century, events, movements and ideas outside the Western and industrial countries will become more significant. Third World peace movements, as well represented in Gandhi's successful struggle to liberate India, have goals of securing autonomy and self-reliance from external dependence through nonviolent struggle. Now people at the grassroots level want to attain greater autonomy from their post-colonial state in the their pursuit of development. Many religious and women's groups in developing countries are now actively engaged in challenging the violation of their basic rights for survival.

Development has remained the central core of peace thinking in the Third World, because the satisfaction of basic needs would help overcome conflict between communities and enhance economic well-being. Human survival is understood more in terms of economic and ecological insecurity caused by challenges from a modern political economy. The concern for the relationship between peace and development has brought a broadened definition of security in the Third World. With the practice of an alternative development paradigm at a community level, it has not been difficult to find a cogent critique of an external development model and industrialisation.

Commitment and Motivation

There are critical factors for personal involvement in change: obligation to act for change, belief in the necessity of change, motivation to help others, conviction in their ability to make difference and understanding of problems (Downton and Wehr, 1997, p. 31). A period of heightened protest (e.g., the civil rights and anti-Vietnam movements in the 1960s and the early 1970s and anti-nuclear movements in the 1980s) exhibits the desire to search for hope. Their action was provoked by fear, anger, frustration and threats caused by government policies in foreign wars and the expansion of the military and nuclear industrial complexes, with ample evidence of their threats to communities. Political and social situations lend opportunities for drawing millions of normally passive citizens to the movements.

People are motivated to participate in peace action not only by fear of violence but also desire for change. A sense of urgency can be generated by deteriorating social conditions, the emergence of violence or ecological decline. Moral responsibility may arise from the perception of crisis. Movements for peace have to be based on the ethical norms of nonviolence, social principles and goals of democracy. Value and ethical imperatives provide a strong commitment to the mission. Since it takes time to see the impact of their action on change, a sense of assurance for contributions to transformation of society can be gradually developed.

Shared discourse within and between the movements, allies and supporters is developed by common ways to frame the issues, though priorities and strategies may not be identical. Long-term commitments are encouraged and supported by solidarity derived from building a sense of community (Downton and Wehr, 1997, p. 44). A sense of belonging with shared principles, targets and goals for action creates a community. The role of a community is crucial when people are engaged in protracted conflict to overcome the overwhelming power of military industrial complexes. Prolonged struggle with militarism entails physical and emotional exhaustion. Commitment stems from a consistent line of action rather than a subjective state of mind especially when faced with the sacrifice of personal comfort. At the same time, an articulated vision of a peaceful world sustains commitment.

A Final Note

Many peace groups were founded as the expression of human faith to carry on the tradition of peace witness in a constructive and diversified manner. They are concerned with the victims of war and injustice on every continent of the world while searching for new ways to remove the causes of war. Some of them house the homeless, set up food pantries and comfort the sick while accepting lives of voluntary poverty among the poor. Some agitated for farm workers rights, labour and environmental movements. They periodically go to jail for resisting the arms race and social injustice. Many peace groups have been engaged in linking social justice to peace. Nonviolence principles provide the backbone of the ongoing struggle.

Contemporary peace movements have developed an alternative foreign policy concept, defence strategies, a positive view of social goals, broader motivation and a workable model of a disarmed economy. A moral responsibility is embedded in the awareness of an interdependent global system and a vision for a shared future. Peace action calls not only for widespread participation but also empowerment on the part of ordinary citizens. The idea of linking the local and the global has often given practical support to peace groups.

Despite the failure of political leaders to cooperate in many important global issues, grassroots movements played an important role in building bridges between different cultures with their universal peace message. They have proven that ordinary people are able to maintain non-cooperation and resistance against militarism. Opposition to war mobilisation on a sustained basis has been maintained by a strong local communal base or an organisation with a social orientation toward a pacifist ideology or religion that provides a transcendental human identity moving beyond national boundaries (Young, 1987).

The course of peace movements may have not run altogether smoothly, nor have peace movements been uni-directional or universally welcomed. During war, peace activities are typically denounced and often attacked or banned as unpatriotic and cowardly. However, the special hope is that peace movements might serve as midwives for a new world, 'providing it with the impetus and the power to be born at last' (Barash, 1991, p. 75). Successful social movements would probably have to achieve a certain level of realism in confronting the power of the state, while also, when possible, breaking out of a strictly state centred model of politics.

The struggle for peace in the new century has a full agenda and has much to learn from the accomplishments of peace movement activists worldwide. Some attributed the end of the Cold War to anti-nuclear movements in the 1980s. The Vietnam War was terminated in a large part because of public discontent fuelled by immense pressure from the domestic peace movement. In the 20th century, conscientious objection has become more widely accepted as a basic human right. In recent history, the institution of slavery was abolished due to persistent struggle. Also successful was support for Women's Suffrage in the early 20th century. The civil rights movements played a big role in reducing discrimination against specific gender and racial groups.

PART IV
INTEGRATION

Non-violence and conflict management skills as well as alternative security mechanisms have been mostly applied to and advocated for the reduction of violent situations. However, there has been a growing consensus that lasting peace can be obtained only through the transformation of social systems that produce economic disparities and political oppression. The foundations for a peaceful world order have to be based on autonomy and economic and social well-being for groups and individuals. These conditions can be achieved by the guarantee of human rights, self-determination and development strategies to reduce economic inequity and unacceptable life conditions. In addition, the realisation of peace could not be seriously considered without protecting the ecological system that sustains human life. Diverse peace strategies need to be integrated in building a holistic peace system that entices not only people from different cultures but also living and non-living species on the planet to a harmonious, non-exploitative and interdependent relationship.

19   Applications and Future Directions

In peace studies, the main themes and analysis arise from the examination of the social, economic and cultural origins of violence. Traditional security paradigms are outdated in meeting new challenges in the 21st century, and there are different priorities and paths toward peace. Changes in personal motivations and value systems are commensurate with structural transformation. Future research for conflict and peace research has to focus on reweaving relations.

Challenges and Paradigm Shift

The traditional paradigm dependent on military power and elite diplomacy does not pay much attention to the security needs of individuals and groups. A typical national security paradigm neglects social and economic inequities arising from an asymmetric, hierarchical relationship in the existing system. Social erosion following discrimination and disparities has been the main cause of violent conflict, but a neo-liberal political order proved inadequate to meeting the concerns of diverse groups. In particular, the prescription of a free market economy along with a pluralistic political order has not contributed to resolving conflict in many divided societies.

It is often argued that problems of national security are so complex that they have to be left to the experts in the government (Fischer, 1984, p 190). In a traditional national security paradigm, high priority is given to the management of war and crisis situations. Strong military power and an alliance system are designed to deter any challenges to the existing order. No question is raised about an elite dominant system that perpetuates social and economic hierarchies.

Traditional security is anchored in the myth of an orderly national space in need of protection from outside danger through military means (Tickner, 1994). Exclusionary state identities and national boundaries as well as the zero-sum pursuit of national interest are counterproductive to common security. The limitation of old security paradigms (that still regard war as a legitimised policy tool) is illustrated in the form of recurring violence and the costs to maintain coercive mechanisms. National military preparedness is incompatible with global dimensions of security for all human beings on the planet. 'In today's global village, the fortress image of national defense seems anachronistic and dangerously out of step with the realities of transnational corporatism and subnational conflict' (Hempel, 1996, p. 217).

The first step toward peace on the planet is to replace state-centric security paradigms with the concept of common security that stresses a shared interest in survival. There exists a delicate balance between community self-sufficiency and global interdependence. Human security focuses on non-military deterrence, economic and social well-being and autonomy for groups and individuals. Alternative visions of security also have to put priority on the well-being of all living species on the planet. Ecological security not only helps to prevent conflict between human societies arising from environmental degradation but also redress unbalanced relations between humans and nature.

Designing a Peace System

Diagnosis   A relatively small number of people are in command of the political and military machinery of internal and international violence. Those who are victimised by dominant systems have a deep sense of powerlessness. An oppressive system is sustained by the capacity to reproduce order through fear and threats. Monopolies of political power and economic disparities have been a prevalent source of violence in many societies. In particular, coercive state institutions and dominant economic interests have threatened the cultural and physical survival of many marginalised communities. 'Furthermore, our continued commitment to violence threatens to kill the life-sustaining capabilities of Mother Earth' (Paige, 1993, p. 136). The tasks for building peace need to be assessed not only in terms of visible manifestations of violence (e.g., war, genocide) but also in relation to systems responsible for the elimination of indigenous cultures and the destruction of nature.

Goals   The ultimate goal of peace is to achieve conditions for human development with social change supported by new institutional arrangements

(Woodward, 1983, p. 271). Realising peace, in a more fundamental sense, constitutes both individual and social transformation. Nurturing positive relationships is not separable from the constellation of new cultural norms for peace and a communal base for political and economic democracy. The elements for both positive and negative peace can mutually reinforce each other in overcoming the dominant forms of social and economic conditions associated with militarism and oppression.

Priorities Peace can be most appropriately applied to almost everything that happens, and it is least effective when limited only to anti-war applications. As peace issues touch upon human well-being in everyday life situations, 'military answers continue to ignore fundamental spiritual and humanistic concerns' (Eldrige, 1994, p. 9). Different priorities arise in thinking about strategies for peace since the desire and aspirations for peace as well as the perception of threats are not the same across societies. In impoverished countries, daily physical survival is the immediate concern while ecological destruction threatens future prosperity in affluent societies. On the other hand, individual and collective levels of self-realisation, autonomy and freedom are considered important regardless of cultural differences.

Paths Different steps and paths exist toward institutional and social transformation. In response to emerging signs of crisis, problem-solving approaches attempt to find remedies for a malfunctioning system. Reformed methods, procedures or mechanisms are introduced within the existing system boundaries. In the end, critical approaches are needed for structural rearrangements that go beyond partial reform. Removing an asymmetric relationship takes a longer time than technical solutions to a narrow set of problems.

Growing complexities of global problems challenge the effectiveness of simple remedies. New institutional mechanisms could be established, but the success of their operations depends on specific social and psychological environments. Development of particular norms for change is related to the process of learning and forming consensual knowledge to deal with ecological destruction, social disharmony, uncontrolled proliferation of violence and other signals of stress.

The immediate measures to control physical violence include peacekeeping and enforcement functions. Peace making has been defined in terms of promoting mutual understanding in managing and resolving differences in critical issues through dialogue. Community building with social reconstruction and reconciliation is critical to de-linking a continuing cycle of violence (Lumsden, 1999). The elimination of social oppression is closely interconnected to personal growth and maximisation of inner propensities and potentialities.

World federalists place a major responsibility for controlling violent behaviour on the supra-national organisations with the capacity to settle disputes and enforce law. It is important to mention, however, that functional networks and informal arrangements across cultural boundaries are not provided by centralised institutional mechanisms. There has been a strong support for the view that community based organisations serve the local social and economic needs better than bureaucratic agencies at the federal level. While allowing a functionally interdependent relationship between groups, a decentralised order maximises group autonomy that does not exist in a state-centric system. Multilateralism would bridge distinct units and identities in developing common perceptions of reality without imposing a hegemonic value system. Multiculturalism, unlike fundamentalism, promotes cultural diversity and non-discrimination (Cox, 1997, p. 253).

Structural Change

If the origins of social ills are traced to dominant institutions and values, creating a nonviolent world would depend on the elimination of social and economic injustice and ecological abuse. Personal growth is hampered by hierarchical structures at all social levels (Galtung, 1980). Self-realisation, value transformation and fulfilment are more likely to occur in symmetric but interdependent relations between social, ethnic and religious groups.

Since no actor exists in a social vacuum, identities and roles of individuals need to be reinterpreted in terms of their relationship to others. The marginalised and the dispossessed are put at the centre of security and development activities in order to end oppression. Since social justice and nonviolent societies cannot be imposed from the outside, they have to be generated internally. In addition, since peace affirms positive life experiences, life preserving values and principles have to be further extended to recognise the intrinsic value of the non-human world.

Human Needs and Institutional Values Institutions are, in general, designed to preserve society in its existing forms and do not favour change. There is a dialectic interplay between individual needs and societal values and interests.

In the micro-macro relationship, individuals are aggregated into groups and social networks, thus accounting for structural relationships; at the same time, local, regional and global relationships can be disaggregated back to individuals (Rosatie, et al., 1990, p. 173)

Social networks and groups have different structural and functional orientations toward meeting individual needs. The institutional logic of a free market system is not geared toward the consideration of individual human needs for the reason that the market has been manipulated by those who have monopoly over resources, information and capital. Political and social institutions adhering to a neo-liberal economic model have not provided a material or psychological environment for needs satisfaction.

The requirement for structural transformation at a macro-level arises from the failure of existing institutions to address the needs of individuals and groups. The incompatibilities between institutional requirements and individual needs are illustrated in arms build-up at the sacrifice of development. Non-hierarchical systems and societal values support the pursuit of individual human needs. In interacting with others, individuals can be organised to create groups that fulfil their needs and values.

Personal Transformation

Some religious traditions view peace in personal terms by stressing a tranquil inner state of mind and unity with the universe. On the other hand, making one's own inner peace may not change the world dramatically. Personal peace would not solve the problems of poverty around the world and human rights abuse. Peace can be made internally, but violence in the outside world may destroy conditions for personal tranquillity. Internal peace does not seem to be sufficient to bring about harmony in the outside world. Then, why and how should we discuss personal transformation?

It can be well noted that improving the world would proceed from the individual realisation of peace values in our own lives. Fighting social injustice may require breaking out of oppression in interpersonal relations. The elimination of oppressive personal relationships helps alleviate the pain and suffering of others. If politics are to be altered to change society, then people's views must also be changed. Changes in our life can be consistent with our own beliefs. Only change in people can bring about cultures that 'cultivate the values of the society' (Reardon, 1989, p. 25).

If we consider that individual well-being is affected by social systems, the achievement of peace at a social level can be a necessary condition for peace at the personal level. On the other hand, personal behavioural patterns have an impact on the legitimisation of certain social values and mechanisms. Individuals can personally participate in nonviolent transformation in life style, for instance, by reducing unnecessary consumption, which contributes to economic disparity and ecological degradation. It is imperative that our self-interest has to be extended to embrace the whole.

A society consists of actors of various kinds who are equipped with different intentions and capabilities and who pursue their goals. It takes time to find value consensus and common goals at a collective level. Personal transformation may have to precede changes in major social values. Personal motivation for peace derives from hopes for contributing to constructing a better world. People can be more conscious of the causes of violence and oppression when they are better informed. The vision of peace and happiness suggested by the Dalai Lama and other spiritual leaders suggests that 'changes from destructive, adversarial behaviour to that of compassion, mutuality, love' can result from 'sustained and gratifying disciplines of examining the inner self and outer reality' (Fellman, 1998, p. 209).

Personal development evolves with changes in personal orientations from self-interest to collective well-being. Feelings of fulfilment and accomplishment are encouraged by peace action. Individuals can be considered as active participants in creating reality and giving it meaning (Snare, 1994, p. 6). At the same time, the sense of solidarity and interdependence reinforces a personal belief in responsibility for action. Individual action is spiritual to the extent that it explores the meaning of life; it is political given that people work for change to take place; and it is also relational since feelings of satisfaction arise from commitment to others.

Personal change, if it is to be sustained over time and not subject to repeated manipulation of outside forces, must be autonomously and intentionally embraced and integrated into the self. Self-respect is strengthened by confidence in one's own ability to bring about changes. Personal transformation contributes to empowerment if the goals are pursued with one's own self-sufficient means. It also relates to an ethical commitment to a nonviolent relationship. Moral conviction based on pacifism and ecological thinking raises a sense of outraged humanism. A transformative experience is often gained by personal witness or experiences of the misery of others and emotional reactions to injustice.

The emphasis on equality and liberation requires the will to respond to problems in a constructive way. Courage and discipline are needed for any meaningful change to occur. One difficult question to answer remains how one can find a feasible and desirable balance between relative personal privilege and selfless devotion to peace.   *Balance*

Reweaving Relations

Peace in interpersonal terms is achieved by realising harmonious social relationships (Wenden, 1995, p. 5). The experience of all phenomena in the world as manifestations of a basic oneness relies on the awareness of the unity and mutual interrelations of all things and interdependence of events. Holistic views of relationships are gained by the ability to acknowledge the suffering of others. Peace cannot be achieved without mending relationships that produce injustice, pain and fear.

Peace making and building are the art and science of weaving and reweaving oneself with others into a social fabric of mutual love, respect and concern. In that sense, they are reflected in the language and symbols of Native Americans, ecologists and other marginalised groups (Pepinsky, 1995, p. 40). Peaceful relations can be enhanced by non-aggression and care for the welfare of others. New relations arise from the experience of trust and happiness that are alien to the concept of national security.

Transformation of social order is as much a matter of emotional maturity as structural change. 'The crisis that threatens our planet, whether seen from its military, ecological, or social aspect, derives from a dysfunctional and pathological notion of the self' (Macy, 1991, p. 187). Reweaving victims, offenders and bystanders into a trustworthy social fabric is an important first step in rebuilding balanced relationships among all components of the planetary system.

Future Directions

Reassessment   Systems of violence have been the direct result of the acceptance of the survival-of-the-fittest system. In order to win wars, enemies have to be identified, isolated and subdued for the sake of one's own safety. The war system represents an all-embracing structure of mutually interlocking organisational and behavioural variables that legitimise violence at all levels of human society. From this perspective, the conclusion deduced is that war within the present world system can be eliminated by the systemic transformation of economic, social, political and psychological interactions.

Compared with wars between states in an international system, inter-group conflict represents a struggle for power associated with competing claims for identity, security and autonomy along the lines of class, ethnicity, religion, or any combination of these. Many uprisings, peasant revolts and religious rebellions in human history are examples of social conflicts seeking change. It is obvious that threats and other types of deterrence strategies based on elite control serve the imperatives for the maintenance of a hierarchical system that benefits a privileged class.

Technocratic solutions to human misery caused by structural conditions are not adequate to overcome the experiences of hundreds of years of oppression and hostilities. The analysis of human elements is ignored in economic rationalism. Narrowly interpreted problem solving approaches encourage the development of techniques by which the problems are redirected and temporarily managed. Critical theory is different from technical problem solving based on the method of controlling human behaviour. A critical approach is oriented toward revealing the experiences of emancipation that reconnect knowledge to everyday practice. It enhances the possibilities of transformation by calling the practice and power of existing institutions into question.

Prescriptive aspects of peace building parallel analytical dimensions. If the primary task of building peace requires envisioning and embracing new relations, we shall overcome the fear and feelings of insecurity derived from uncertainty. Peace building should be viewed as more than a means to re-establish the status quo. Lasting solutions would not be found through an instrumental application of knowledge and skills. Theories and tools for resolving conflict and waging nonviolent struggle are made more meaningful by exploring the holistic meanings of peace that entice adversaries in a common destiny. Participatory democracy has to be supported by the desire for autonomy and self-fulfilment.

Globalisation Context Globalisation generates movements for the lateral extension of social connectedness across time and space. Local happenings are more likely to be shaped by events occurring many miles away. Over the last several centuries, 'global making' has been celebrated by modernity that represents the type of social life and organisational forms originating in the 17th century Europe (Giddens, 1990). An interesting feature of globalisation is the prevalence of rationalistic modern culture along with hegemonic political and economic order supported by a neoliberal ideology. Global culture is equated with the spread of consumerism, communication and other technological innovations.

In a monolithic vision of history (e.g., *The End of History* by Fukuyama, 1992), modernity is the triumph of neoliberalism and Western democracy. Capitalism and pluralistic democracies have become a civilising project on a global scale especially with the demise of socialist states at the end of the 20th century. What is ignored in this type of discourse is the role of violence implicated in the modernisation project. Cultural conflict arises from the perception of threats to tradition and identity by a modernisation process that imposes social and economic hegemony.

The continuing trend toward globalisation is reflected in the domination of all pervading international economic and cultural networks over local social traditions. The tension often results in oppression and internalisation of violence in many communities. At another level, economic penetration to the remote corners of the world along with modern instrumental logic and technology destroys the very foundations for interdependent, organic relationships between humans and nature built into the practices of indigenous cultures such as Buddhist and other holistic religious traditions.

In the margins of the global political economy, deep-seated contradictions are found in the relationship of dependence and domination. Ethnic demands are largely 'a product of the failure to build a national state in the periphery of the capitalist system' and the failure to provide a liable means for economic survival (Amin, 1993, p. 95). Through capitalist expansion, indigenous populations are evicted from communal land, becoming wage workers (Comacho, 1993, p. 42). 'Crises sparked by acute inequities resulting from the development process generally impact on the internal political process and democracy' (Wignaraja, 1993, p. 30).

Grassroots Challenges Social movements arising from resistance to the modernisation project have many sided manifestations in challenging bureaucratic, technocratic states as the main sources of violence. In looking back at the history of the past several hundred years, despite their seemingly unchallenged status, the modernisation projects have met resistance from the thrust of early protests against industrialisation, anti-colonial struggles, working class movements and contemporary religious and fundamentalist reactions (Rupesinghe, 1994, pp. 15-24). The imposition of external power has been challenged by ethnic and other types of social movements in the periphery.

Resistance to the process of homogenisation has been made in the form of re-energising indigenous culture as well as localisation and adaptation of an external knowledge base. Grassroots struggles, often spontaneous, have been directed against a centralised bureaucratic system that articulates the oppressive nature of a modern state. Many of these resistance movements opposing the hegemony of state bureaucracies and corporations may not have been able to alter the course of events that have a major impact on their life. However, they have bred the seed for solidarity among the marginalised communities and sustained the hope for their future survival.

The creative energies of people are released by their struggle to respond to multifaceted crises (Wignaraja, 1993, p. 5). People in many Asian, African and Latin American countries showed dramatic responses to military dictatorships. Ecological movements against deforestation have mobilised women's groups whose lives were devastated by logging industries and state bureaucrats. In local communities, the knowledge system evolves by practice based on experience, and the mediation of tensions between old forms of life and new challenges can be managed by indigenous cultural institutions. The seeds of hope germinate and multiply in expanding the economic and political space for struggle.

Post-Modern Cultural Politics The critical movements around the world are part of on-going struggles in an inter-dependent world. At the same time, they also represent the articulation of many different experiences and aspirations and are not confined in one particular meaning of reality. Many local movements defy grand strategies for revolution but demonstrate 'creative, innovative resistance, carried out in specific sites of struggle' (George, 1996, p. 67). These movements do not pursue abstract ideals but rather are engaged in a process of local politics for change.

The protest movements are less motivated by the economic calculation of costs and benefits than by the pursuit of clear moral and political goals. New social movements represented by environmental and anti-war agendas responded to social strain arising from post-industrial society. The value oriented movements brought new issues to the forefront of politics (e.g., green parties). Despite their limited base in the educated middle class, they nonetheless challenged the moral tenets of state hegemony and their related phenomena, war, environmental abuse and economic inequality. Its common cultural experiences are forged by shared values and identities embedded in civil society. Commitments and values attached to the goals of the movements are reproduced in everyday life through the visions for a new political order.

Hope for the Future In the Hegelian notion of dialectics, the movement of history and progress is based on challenge to the dominant system. The hegemonic system has not silenced the demand for an alternative order. The relevance of modernity to peace research is its relationship to violence. The application of violence has been impersonalised in high tech wars such as the U.S. bombing in Iraq and Serbia while ethnic wars are still waged by personal killings and assault. Peace research raises moral and political challenges to the instrumental use of violence ranging from ethnic cleansing to bombing of innocent civilians. Understanding various aspects of violence and social oppression will remain a key aspect of peace research in forthcoming centuries.

In dealing with threats to security, the global community needs to take a fresh look at the range of collaborative actions, which are desirable and plausible. The participation of groups affected by the causes of conflict is the key to solutions for the problems. In considering that social relations that link distant localities will be more likely to be intensified, challenges remain to encompass cultural diversity and decentralised political forms. There are different social circumstances providing opportunities for change. Indigenous norms and practices can be reinterpreted and reapplied to a contemporary context.

Concluding Remarks The quest for peace will be a never ending process. Truth can be sought through purposeful acts and visionary thinking for the future that does not marginalise any component of a web of various relations. The path toward a peaceful world will require overcoming the instrumental logic of a modern, industrial society that converts everything into an object to be experimented upon, controlled and eventually remolded for the purpose of those who have power. It is based on a process to deconstruct the dichotomy imposed on marginalised others. Obstacles to dialogue need to be removed by a profound love for the world.

Bibliography

Ackerman, P. and Kruegler, C. (1994), *Strategic Nonviolent Conflict: The Dynamics of People Power in the Twentieth Century*, Praeger, Westport, CT.

Alecio, R. (1995), 'Uncovering the Truth: Political Violence and Indigenous Organizations', in M. Sinclair (ed.), *The New Politics of Survival: Grassroots Movements in Central America*, Monthly Review Press, New York.

Alfredsson, G. (1996), 'Different Forms of and Claims to the Right of Self-Determination', in D. Clark and R. Williamson (eds), *Self-Determination: International Perspectives*, Macmillan, Houndsmills, Basingstoke, Hampshire, pp. 58-86.

Alger, C. (1987), 'A Grassroots Approach to Life in Peace', *Bulletin of Peace Proposals*, vol. 18, no. 3, pp. 375-91.

Alger, C. (1989), 'Peace Studies at the Crossroads', *The Annals*, no. 504, pp. 117-27.

Alger, C. (1990), 'Grassroots Perspectives on Global Policies for Development', *Journal of Peace Research*, vol. 27, no. 2, May, pp. 155-68.

Alger, C. (1995), 'Peace Building in the Post-Cold War Era', in H. Jeong (ed.), *Peace Research: Past and Future*, The Network of Peace and Conflict Studies, Columbus.

Alger, C. (1999a), 'The Quest for Peace: What Are We Learning?' *International Journal of Peace Studies*, vol. 4, no.1, January, pp. 21-46.

Alger, C. (1999b), 'The Expanding Parading Tool Chest for Peacebuilding', in H. Jeong (ed.), *The New Agenda for Peace Research*, Ashgate, Aldershot, pp. 13-42.

Alger, C. (2000), 'Challenges for Peace Researchers and Peace Builders in the Twenty-First Century', *International Journal of Peace Studies*, vol. 5, no. 1, Spring.

Amin, S. (1990), *Delinking: Towards a Polycentric World*, translated by M. Wolfers, Zed Books, London.

Amin, S. (1993), 'Social Movements at the Periphery', in P. Wignaraja (ed), *New Social Movements in the South: Empowering the People*, Zed Books, London, pp. 76-100.

Anaya, S. J. (1996), *Indigenous Peoples in International Law*, Oxford University Press, New York.

Anderson, B. (1993), *Imagined Communities: Reflections on the Origin and Spread of Nationalism*, Verso Publications, London.

Arend, A.C. and Beck, R.J. (1993), *International Law and the Use of Force: Beyond the UN Charter Paradigm*, Routledge, London, pp. 112-38.

Arendt, H. (1969), *On Violence*, Harcourt, Brace & World, Inc., New York.

Arnold, G. (1994), *The Third World Handbook*, St. James Press, Chicago.

Asian and Pacific Women's Resource Collection Network (1992), *Environment*, Asian and Pacific Women's Resource and Action Series, Asia and Pacific Development Centre, Kuala Lumpur.

Avruch, K. (1998), *Culture and Conflict Resolution*, United States Institute of Peace Press, Washington, DC.

Ayres, R. (1998), 'Eco-restructuring: The Transition to an Ecologically Sustainable Development', in R. Ayres (ed.), *Eco-restructuring: Implications for Sustainable Development*, United Nations University Press, Tokyo, pp. 1-52.

Azar, E. E. (1990), *The Management of Protracted Social Conflict: Theory and Cases*, Dartmouth Publishing, Aldershot.

Barash, David P. (1991), *Introduction to Peace Studies*, Wadsworth, Belmont, CA.

Bennett, A. L. (1991), *International Organizations: Principles and Issues*, Prentice-Hall, Englewood Cliffs.

Bercovitch, J. (1992), 'The Structure and Diversity of Mediation in International Relations', in J. Bercovitch and J..Z. Rubin (eds), *Mediation in International Relations: Multiple Approaches to Conflict Management* , St. Martin's Press, New York, pp. 1-29.

Bercovitch, J. and Houston, A (1996), 'The Study of International Mediation', in J. Bercovitch (ed.), *Resolving International Conflicts*, Lynn Rienner, Boulder, pp. 11-35.

Berridge, G. (1994), *Talking to the Enemy: How States without Diplomatic Relations Communicate*, St. Martin's Press, New York.

Birkenbach, H. (1997), 'The Role of Fact-Finding in Preventive Diplomacy', *International Journal of Peace Studies*, vol. 2, no. 2, pp. 21-36.

Bischak, G. (ed.) (1991), *Towards a Peace Economy in the United States: Essays on Military Industry, Disarmament and Economic Conversion*, Macmillan, London.

Bose, A. (1987), *Dimensions of Peace and Nonviolence: The Gandhian Perspective*, Gian Publishing House, Delhi.

Boulding, E. (1976), *The Underside of History: A View of Women through Time*, 2 vols, Westview Press, Boulder.

Boulding, E. (1992), 'The Concept of Peace Culture', in UNESCO, *Peace and Conflict Studies after the Cold War*, UNESCO, Paris, pp. 107-34.

Boulding, K. E. (1978), 'Future Directions in Conflict and Peace Studies', *Journal of Conflict Resolution*, vol. 22, no. 2.

Boutros-Ghali, B. (1992), *An Agenda for Peace, Preventive Diplomacy, Peacemaking and Peacekeeping*, Report of the Secretary-General pursuant to the statement adopted by the summit meeting of the Security Council on 31 January 1992, The United Nations, New York.

Boutros-Ghali, B. (1995), *An Agenda for Peace,* United Nations, New York.

Boutros-Ghali, B. (1998), 'Peacemaking and Peacekeeping for the New Century', in Olara A. Otunnu and Michael W. Doyle (eds), *Peacemaking and Peacekeeping for the New Century,* Rowman & Littlefield Publishers, Lanham, MD, pp. 21-6.

Boyce, J. (1996), *Economic Policy for Building Peace: The Lessons of El Salvador,* Lynn Rienner Publishers, Boulder, CO.

Brock-Utne, B. (1989), *Feminist Perspectives on Peace and Peace Education*, Pergamon Press, New York.

Brock-Utne, B. (1990), 'Feminist Perspectives on Peace', in P. Smoker, R. Davis, and B. Munske (eds), *Introduction to Peace Studies*, Pergamon Press, Oxford, pp. 144-50.

Brohman, J. (1996), *Popular Development*, Blackwell Publishers, Oxford.

Brown, L. (1977), 'Redefining National Security', *Worldwatch Paper*, October, vol. 14, Washington, D.C.

Brown, M. et al (eds.) (1996), *Debating the Democratic Peace*, MIT Press, Cambridge.

Brown, S., et al. (1977), *Regimes for the Ocean, Outer Space and Weather*, Brookings Institution, Washington, DC.

Buchanan, L. (1991), *Secession*, Westview Press, Boulder, CO.

Bulhan, H. A. (1985), *Franz Fanon and Psychology of Oppression*, Plenum Press, New York.

Bunch, Charlotte and Carillo, Roxanna (1998), 'Global Violence Against Women: The Challenge to Human Rights and Development' in Michael T. Klare and Yogesh Chandrani (eds), *World Security: Challenges for a New Century*, St. Martin's Press, New York, pp. 229-48.

Burrowes, R. (1996), *The Strategy of Nonviolent Defense: A Gandhian Approach*, State University of New York Press, Albany.

Burton, J.W. (1984), *Global Conflict: The Domestic Sources of International Crisis*, Wheatsheaf Books, Brighton.

Burton, J.W. (1987), *Resolving Deep-Rooted Conflict: A Handbook*, University Press of America, Lanham, MD.

Burton, J.W. (ed.) (1990a), *Conflict: Human Needs Theory*, Macmillan, London.

Burton, J.W. (1990b), *Conflict: Resolution and Provention*, Macmillan, London.

Burton, J.W. (1996), *Conflict Resolution: Its Language and Processes*, The Scarecrow Press, Lanham.

Burton, J.W. (1997), *Violence Explained*, Manchester University Press, Manchester, UK.

Burton, J.W. and Dukes, Frank (1990), *Conflict: Practices in Management, Settlement, and Resolution*, St. Martin's Press, New York.

Butfoy, A. (1997), *Common Security and Strategic Reform: A Critical Analysis*, Macmillan, London.

Cahill, K.M. (ed.) (1996), *Preventive Diplomacy : Stopping Wars Before They Start*, BasicBooks and the Center for International Health and Cooperation, New York.

Camilleri, J.A. (1995), 'State, Civil Society, and Economy', in J. Camilleri, A.P. Jarvis, and A.J. Paolini (eds), *The State in Transition: Reimagining Political Space*, Lynne Rienner Publishers, Boulder, CO, pp. 209-28.

Cammack, P., et al. (1993), *Third World Politics*, The Johns Hopkins University Press, Baltimore, MD.

Caputi, J. (1996), 'Unthinkable Fathering: Connecting Incest and Nuclearism', in K.J. Warren and D.L. Cady (eds), *Bringing Peace Home: Feminism, Violence and Nature*, Indiana University Press, Bloomington, IN, pp. 133-51.

Cardoso, F. (1972), 'Dependency and Development in Latin America', *New Left Review*, July-August.

Carley, M. and Christie, I. (1993), *Managing Sustainable Development*, University of Minnesota Press, Minneapolis.

Carroll, B. (1987), 'Feminism and Pacifism: Historical and Theoretical Connections', in R.R. Pierson (ed.), *Women and Peace,* Croom Helm, London, pp. 2-28.

Carter, A. (1990), 'Nonviolence as a Strategy for Change', in P. Smoker, et al. (eds.), *A Reader in Peace Studies*, Pergamon Press, Oxford, pp. 210-16.

382   *Peace and Conflict Studies*

Carter, A. (1992), *Peace Movements: International Protest and World Politics Since 1945,* Longman, London.

Chadwick, E. (1996), '"Rights" and International Humanitarian Law', in C. Gearty and A. Tomkins (eds), *Understanding Human Rights,* Mansell, London, pp. 573-95.

Chatfield, C. (1992), *The American Peace Movement: Ideals and Activism,* Twayne, New York.

Chatfield, C. and Ilukhina, R. (1994), *Peace: An Anthology of Historic Alternatives to War,* Syracuse University Press, Syracuse.

Chigas, D., et al. (1996), 'Preventive Diplomacy and the Organization for Security and Cooperation in Europe: Creating Incentives for Dialogue and Cooperation', in A.and H. Chayes (eds), *Preventing Conflict in the Post-Communist World,* Brookings Institute, Washington, D.C., pp. 25-98.

Choucri, N. and North, R.C. (1975), *Nations in Conflict: National Growth and International Violence,* W. H. Freeman, San Francisco.

Churchill, R. and Lowe, A. V. (1988), *The Law of the Sea,* Manchester University Press, Manchester.

Clark, M. (1994), 'Unconventional Solutions to Environmental Problems', in *Peace and Conflict Studies,* vol. 1, no. 1, pp. 2-24.

Clark, M. (1998), 'Aggressivity and Violence: An Alternative Theory of Human Nature', *Peace and Conflict Studies,* vol. 5, no. 2, June, pp. 2-7.

Clark, G. and Sohn, L. (1966), *World Peace Through World Law,* 3rd enlarged, Harvard University Press, Cambridge.

Clark, G. and Sohn, L. (1973), *Introduction to World Peace through World Law,* World Without War Publications, Chicago.

Claude, I.L. (1971), *Swords into Plowshares: the Problems and Progress of International Organizations,* 4th ed., Random House, New York.

Comacho, D. (1993), 'Latin America: A Society in Motion', in P. Wignaraja (ed.), *New Social Movements in the South: Empowering the People,* Zed Books, London, pp. 36-58.

Conca, K. (1994), 'In the Name of Sustainability: Peace Studies and Environmental Discourse', *Peace and Change,* vol. 19, no. 2, April, pp. 91-113.

Cooney, R. and Michalowski, H. (1977), *Active Nonviolence in the United States,* Peace Press, Culver City.

Cortright, D. (1993), *Peace Works: The Citizen's Role in Ending the Cold War,* Westview Press, Boulder, CO.

Coser, L. (1956), *The Functions of Social Conflict,* The Free Press, New York.

Cox, R. (1996), *Approaches to World Order,* Cambridge University Press, Cambridge.

Cox, R. (1997), 'Reconsiderations', in R. Cox (ed), *The New Realism: Perspectives on Multilateralism and World Order,* United Nations University Press, Tokyo, pp. 245-62.

Crane, B. (1994), 'International Population Institutions', in P. Haas et al. (eds), *Institutions for the Earth, MIT Press,* Cambridge, pp. 351-93.

Crosby, J. and Van Soest, D. (1997), *Challenges of Violence Worldwide,* National Association of Social Workers, Washington, D.C.

Cultural Survival (1993), *State of the Peoples: A Global Human Rights Report on Societies in Danger,* Beacon Press, Boston.

Curle, A. (1986), *In the Middle: Non-Official Mediation in Violent Situations*, Berg, New York.

Curtin, D. (1996), 'Making Peace with the Earth: Indigenous Agriculture and the Green Revolution', in K.J. Warren and D.L. Cady (eds), *Bringing Peace Home: Feminism, Violence and Nature*, Indiana University Press, Bloomington, pp. 54-67.

Daes, E. (1996), 'The Right of Indigenous Peoples to "Self-Determination" in the Contemporary World Order', in D. Clark and R. Williamson (eds), *Self-Determination: International Perspectives*, Macmillan, Houndmills, Basingstoke, Hampshire, pp. 47-57.

Dahrendorf, R. (1959), *Class and Class Conflict in Industrial Society*, Stanford University Press, Stanford.

Damrosch, L. (1993), *Enforcing Restraint: Collective Intervention in Internal Conflicts*, Council on Foreign Relations Press, New York.

Daugherty, W.H. (1993), 'System Management and the Endurance of the Concert of Europe,' in J. Snyder and R. Jervis (eds), *Coping with Complexity in the International System*, Westview Press, Boulder, pp. 71-106.

Davies, J. (1971), 'Toward a Theory of Revolution', in J.C. Davies (ed.), *When Men Revolt and Why*, The Free Press, New York, pp. 134-48.

Davinic, P. (1993), *Regional Approaches to Confidence and Security Building Measures*, Opening Statement by the Director of the United Nations Office for Disarmament Affairs, United Nations Office for Disarmament Affairs, United Nations, New York, pp. 3-5.

de la Court, Thijs (1992), 'Critique of the Dominant Development Paradigm', *Development*, no. 2.

De Mello, S.V. (1995), 'Humanitarian Aspects of Peacekeeping', in D. Warner (ed.), *New Dimensions of Peacekeeping*, Martinus Nijhoff Publishers, Dordrecht, pp. 137-146.

de Silva, K.M. (1996), 'Ethnicity and Nationalism', in de Goor, et al (eds), *Between Development and Destruction: An Enquiry into the Causes of Conflict in Post-Colonial States*, Macmillan, London, pp. 109-25.

DeBenedetti, C. (1980), *The Peace Reform in American History*, Indiana University Press, Bloomington.

Dedring, J. (1999), 'On Peace in Times of War: Resolving Violent Conflicts by Peaceful Means', *International Journal of Peace Studies*, vol. 4, no. 2, June, pp. 1-26.

Destexhe, A. (1996), 'Humanitarian Neutrality: Myth or Reality?' in K.M. Cahill (ed.), *Preventive Diplomacy : Stopping Wars Before They Start*, BasicBooks and the Center for International Health and Cooperation, New York.

Deutsch, K., et al. (1957), *Political Community and the North Atlantic Area: International Organization in the Light of Historical, Experience*, Princeton University Press, Princeton, NJ.

Dinstein, Y. (1994), *War, Aggression and Self-Defence*, Cambridge University Press, Cambridge.

Dollard, J. et al. (1939), *Frustration and Aggression*, Yale University Press, New Haven.

Donnelly, J. (1995), 'The Past, the Present, and the Future Prospects', in M.E. Easman, and S. Telhami (eds), *International Organizations and Ethnic Conflict*, Cornell University Press, Ithaca, pp. 48-71.

Douzinas, C. (1996), 'Justice and Human Rights in Postmodernity', in C. Gearty and A. Tomkins (eds), *Understanding Human Rights*, Mansell, London, pp. 115-37.

Downton Jr., J. and Wehr, P. (1997), *The Persistent Activist: How Peace Commitment Develops and Survives*, Westview Press, Boulder.

Doyle, M.W. (1994), 'Balancing Power Classically: An Alternative to Collective Security?', in G. Downs (ed.), *Collective Security beyond the Cold War*, University of Michigan Press, Ann Arbor, pp. 133-68.

Druckman, D., et al. (1999), 'Conflict Resolution Roles in International Peacekeeping Missions', in H. Jeong (ed.), *The New Agenda for Peace Research*, Ashgate, Aldershot.

Dupont, C. (1993), 'The Rhine: A Study of Inland Water Negotiations', in G. Sjöstedt (ed.), *International Environmental Negotiation*, Sage Publications, Newbury Park, pp. 135-48.

Eastby, John (1985), *Functionalism and Interdependence*, University Press of America, Lanham.

Eckhardt, W. (1974), 'Changing Concerns in Peace Research and Education', *Bulletin of Peace Proposals*, vol. 5, no. 3, pp. 280-84.

Ekins, P. (1992), *A New World Order: Grassroots Movements for Global Change*, Routledge, London.

Eldrige, W. (1994), 'Community and World Harmony: New Citizen Peacemaking Roles for a Changing Global Culture', *Peace and Conflict Studies*, vol. 1, no. 1, December, pp. 9-13.

Elshtain, J.B. (1987), *Women and War*, Basic Books, New York.

Esman, M.J. (1990a), 'Political and Psychological Factors in Ethnic Conflict', in J.V. Montville (ed.), *Conflict and Peacemaking in Multiethnic Societies*, Lexington Books, Lexington, pp. 53-64.

Esman, M.J. (1990b), 'Economic Performance and Ethnic Conflict', in J.V. Montville (ed.), *Conflict and Peacemaking in Multiethnic Societies*, Lexington Books, Lexington, pp. 477-90.

Evans, G. (1993), *Cooperating for Peace*, Allen & Unwin, St. Leonards.

Fanon, Franz (1965), *The Wretched of the Earth*, Grove Press, New York.

Fellman, G. (1998), Rambo and the Dalai Lama: The Compulsion to Win and Its Threat to Human Survival, State University of New York, Albany.

Findlay, T. (1994), 'Mulilateral Conflict Prevention, Management and Resolution', in *SIPRI Yearbook 1994*, Oxford University Press, Oxford.

Fischer, D. (1993), *Nonmilitary Aspects of Security: A Systems Approach*, United Nations Institute for Disarmament Research in association with Dartmouth, Aldershot.

Fischer, D. (1984), *Preventing War in the Nuclear Age*, Rowman and Allanheld, Totowa, New Jersey, pp. 108, 113.

Fisher, R. and Ury, W. (1991), *Getting to Yes*, 2nd Ed., Penguin Books, New York.

Forcey, L. (1989), 'Introduction to Peace Studies', in L. Forcey (ed.), *Peace: Meanings, Politics, Strategies*, Praeger, New York, pp. 3-14.

Foucault, M. (1971), *The Archaeology of Knowledge*, Harper and Row, New York.

Foucault, M. (1977), *Discipline and Punish: The Birth of the Prison*, translated by A. Sheridan (1975), Penguin, London.

Freire, P. (1998), *Pedagogy of the Oppressed*, Continuum, New York.

French, M. (1985), *Beyond Power*, Summit Books, New York.

Freud, S. (1959), 'Why War? A Reply to a Letter from Einstein', in J. Strachey, (ed.), *Collected Papers*, vol. 5, Basic Books, New York.

Freud, S. (1961), *Civilization and Its Discontents*, translated by J. Strachey, Norton, New York.

Fukuyama, F. (1992), *The end of history and the last man*, Free Press, New York.

Galtung, J. (1969), 'Violence, Peace and Peace Research', *Journal of Peace Research*, vol. 6, no. 3, pp. 166-92.

Galtung, J. (1973), 'World Indicators Program', *Bulletin of Peace Proposals*, vol. 4, no. 4, pp. 354-8.

Galtung, J. (1975), *Essays in Peace Research*, Christian Ejlers, Copenhagen.

Galtung, J. (1980), *The True World: A Transnational Perspective*, Free Press, New York.

Galtung, J. (1985), *Self-Reliance and Global Interdependence*, University of Oslo, mimeo.

Galtung, J. (1988), *Transarmament and the Cold War*, Christian Ejlers, Copenhagen.

Galtung, J. (1990), 'Cultural Violence', *Journal of Peace Research*, vol. 27, no. 3, pp. 291-305.

Galtung, J. (1996), *Peace By Peaceful Means: Peace and Conflict, Development and Civilization*, Sage Publications, London.

Gandhi, M. K. (1951), *Non-Violent Resistance*, Schocken Books, New York.

Gashaw, S. (1993), 'Nationalism and Ethnic Conflict in Ethiopia', in C. Young (ed.), *The Rising Tide of Pluralism: The Nation-State at Bay*, University of Wisconsin Press, Madison, WI, pp. 138-58.

George, J. (1996), 'Understanding International Relations after the Cold War: Problems beyond the Cold War', in M. Shapiro and H.R. Alker (eds), *Challenging Boundaries: Global Flows, Territorial Identities*, University of Minnesota Press, Minneapolis, pp. 33-80.

Ghai, D., et al. (1992), 'Ethnicity, Development and Democracy', in UNESCO, *Peace and Conflict Issues after the Cold War*, UNESCO, Paris, pp. 79-103.

Giddens, A. (1990), *The Consequences of Modernity*, Polity Press in association with Basil Blackwell, Oxford, UK, pp. 63-78.

Glossop, R.J. (1993), *Confronting War*, McFarland, Jefferson, NC.

Gochman, C. and Maoz, Z. (1984), 'Militarized Interstate Disputes, 1816-1976', *Journal of Conflict Resolution*, vol. 18, December, pp. 588-615.

Goldsmith, E., et al. (1972), *Blueprint for Survival*, Penguin, Harmondsworth.

Gordenker, L. and Weiss, T.G. (1993), 'The Collective Security Idea and Changing World Politics', in T. Weiss (ed.), *Collective Security in a Changing World*, Lynne Rienner Publishers, Boulder, CO.

Goulding, M. (1993), 'The Evolution of United Nations Peacekeeping', *International Affairs*, vol. 69, pp. 451-65.

Gramsci, Antonio (1971), *Selections from the Prison Notebooks of Antonio Gramsci*, translated and edited by Q. Hoare and G. Smith, International Publishers, New York.

Gregg, Richard B. (1966), *The Power of Nonviolence*, Schocken Books, New York.

Groom, A.J.R. (1990), 'Paradigms in Conflict: the Strategists, the Conflict Researcher and Peace Researcher', in F. Dukes and J. Burton (eds), *Conflict: Readings in Management and Resolution*, Macmillan, London, pp. 71-98.

Grubb, M., et al. (1993), *The Earth Summit Agreements: A Guide and Assessment*, Earthscan, London.

Gurr, T. (1970), *Why Men Rebel*, Princeton University Press, Princeton.

Gurr, T. (1996), 'Early-Warning Systems: From Surveillance to Assessment to Action', in K.M. Cahill (ed.), *Preventive Diplomacy : Stopping Wars Before They Start*, BasicBooks and the Center for International Health and Cooperation, New York.

Haas, Ernst B. (1958), *The Uniting of Europe*, Stanford University Press, Stanford.

Haas, Ernest (1964), *Beyond the Nation-State: Functionalism and International Organization*, Stanford University Press, Stanford, CA.

Hammarskjöld, D. (1960), *Annual Report of the Secretary General on the Work of the Organization*, United Nations General Assembly, 15th session, 16 June 1959-15 June 1960, supplement 1A.

Hampson, F. O. (1995), *Multilateral Negotiations*, The Johns Hopkins University Press, Baltimore.

Hampson, F.O. (1996), *Nurturing Peace: Why Peace Settlements Succeed or Fail*, United States Institute of Peace, Washington, DC, p. 3.

Handelman, H. (1996), *The Challenge of Third World Development*, Prentice Hall, Upper Saddle River, N.J.

Hannum, H. (1990), *Autonomy, Sovereignty and Self-Determination*, University of Pennsylvania Press, Philadelphia.

Hannum, H. (1996), 'Self-Determination in the Post-Colonial Era', in D. Clark and R. Williamson (eds), *Self-Determination: International Perspectives*, Macmillan, London, pp. 12-42.

Harcourt, A. H. (1991), 'Help, cooperation and trust in animals', in R. Grinde and J.Groebel (eds.), *Cooperation and Prosocial Behaviour*, Cambridge University Press, Cambridge, pp. 15-26.

Hardin, G. (1968), 'The Tragedy of the Commons', *Science*, vol. 168, no. 3859, 13 December, pp. 1243-48.

Hartshorn, G. (1991), 'Key Environmental Issues for Developing Countries', *Journal of International Affairs*, vol. 44, no. 2, pp. 393-402.

Häusler, S. (1992), 'Reformulating Social, Cultural and Ecological Sustainability', *Development*, no. 2.

Hempel, L.C. (1996), *Environmental Governance: The Global Challenge*, Island Press, Washington, D.C.

Henderson, H. (1994), 'Ethical Implications of Agenda 21', in N.J. Brown and P. Quiblier (eds), *Moral Implications of a Global Consensus*, United Nations Environment Programme, New York, pp. 27-34.

Henderson, M. (1996), *The Forgiveness Factor*, Grosvenor Books, London.

Herman, J.L. (1992), Trauma and Recovery: The Aftermath of Violence from Domestic Abuse to Political Terror, Basic Books, New York.

Hinde, R. (1990), 'Human Aggression: Biological Propensities and Social Forces', in P. Smoker, et al. (eds.), *A Reader in Peace Studies*, Pergamon Press, Oxford, pp. 172-81.

Hobson, J. (1988), *Imperialism: A Study*, Unwin Hyman, London.

Hoffman, M. (1992), 'Third-Party Mediation and Conflict-Resolution in the Post-Cold War World', in J. Baylis and N.J. Rengger (eds), *Dilemmas of World Politics*, Clarendon Press, Oxford, pp. 261-86.

Hollins, H., et al. (1989), *The Conquest of War*, Westview Press, Boulder.

Homer-Dixon, T.F. (1994), 'Environmental Scarcities and Violent Conflict', *International Security*, vol. 19, no. 1, pp. 5-40.

Horowitz, D. L. (1985), *Ethnic Groups in Conflict*, University of California Press, Berkeley.

Houweling, H.W. (1996), 'Destabilizing Consequences of Sequential Development', in L. van de Goor, et al. (eds), *Between Development and Destruction: An Enquiry into the Causes of Conflict in Post-Colonial States*, Macmillan, London, pp. 143-70.

Howard, M. (1979), '*Temperamenta Belli*: Can War be Controlled?' in M. Howard (ed.), *Restraints on War*, Oxford University Press, Oxford, pp. 1-16.

Hughes, B. (1997), *Continuity and Change in World Politics: Competing Perspectives*, 3rd Ed., Prentice Hall, Upper Saddle River, N.J.

Human Rights Watch (1995), *Playing the 'Communal Card'*, Human Rights Watch, New York.

Huntington, S. (1993), 'The Clash of Civilizations?' *Foreign Affairs*, vol. 72, no. 3., pp. 22-49.

Hutchinson, F. (1992), 'Making Peace with People and the Planet', *Peace, Environment, and Education*, vol. 3, no. 3, pp. 3-14.

International Institute for Strategic Studies (IISS) (1992), *The Military Balance 1992-1993*, Brassey's, London.

International Labor Organization (1976), *Employment, Growth, and Basic Needs: A One-World Problem*, ILO, Geneva.

Irwin, R. (1988), *Building a Peace System*, Expro Press, Washington, D.C.

Isard, W. (1992), *Understanding Conflict and the Science of Peace*, Blackwell, Cambridge, Mass.

Jenkins, R. (1997), *Rethinking Ethnicity: Arguments and Explorations*, Sage, London.

Jeong, H. (2000), 'Evaluating Strategies for Building Peace', *Development and Policy Studies*, vol. 6, no. 2, pp. 8-18.

Jeong, H. (1999a), 'Research on Conflict Resolution', in H. Jeong (ed.), *Conflict Resolution: Dynamics, Process and Structure*, Ashgate, Aldershot, pp. 3-34.

Jeong, H. (1999b), 'Peace Research and International Relations', in H. Jeong (ed.), *The New Agenda for Peace Research*, Ashgate, Aldershot, pp. 3-11.

Jeong, H. (1999c), 'Environmental Security and Social Conflict', *Peace and Security*, Vol. XXXI, March, pp. 21-9.

Jeong, H. (1995a), 'Political Economy of Structural Adjustment', *The Journal of International Studies*, no. 36, pp. 77-94.

Jeong, H. (1995b), 'Alternative Development Strategies and Regeneration of Social Space for Human Development', *Peace and Change*, vol. 20, no. 3, July, pp. 329-47.

Jeong, H. and Väyrynen, T. (1999), 'Identity Formation and Reconstruction', in H. Jeong (ed.), Conflict Resolution, Ashgate, Aldershot, pp. 59-78.

Juda, L. (1996), *International Law and Ocean Use Management: The Evolution of Ocean Governance*, Routledge, London.

Kamieniecki, S. (1991), 'Political Mobilization, Agenda Building and International Environmental Policy', *Journal of International Affairs*, vol. 44, no. 2, Winter, pp. 339-58.

Kant, I. (1903), 'Perpetual Peace: A Philosophical Essay' (1795), translated by M. Smith, Allen & Unwin, London.

Keefe, T. and Roberts, R.E. (1991), *Realizing Peace : an Introduction to Peace Studies*, Iowa State University Press, Ames.

Kegley Jr., C. and Wittkopf, E. (1995), *World Politics: Trend and Transformation*, 5th ed., St. Martin's, New York.

Kelman, H. (1981), 'Reflections on the History and Status of Peace Resaerch', *Conflict Management and Peace Science*, vol. 5, no. 2, Spring.

Kemp, G. (1990), 'The Art of War', in Smoker, P., et al.(eds.), *A Reader in Peace Studies*, Pergamon Press, Oxford, pp. 182-90.

Kemp, G. (1988), 'Nonviolence: A Biological Perspective', in C. Alger and M. Stohl (eds), *A Just Peace through Transformation*, Westview Press, Boulder, pp. 112-126.

King, Jr., M.L. (1963), *Why We Can't Wait*, Harper & Row.

Kirk, G. (1989), 'Our Greenham Common: Feminism and Nonviolence', in A. Harris and Y. King (eds), *Rocking the Ship of State: Toward a Feminist Peace Politics*, Westview Press, Boulder, CO, pp. 115-30.

Kleidman, R. (1993), *Organizing for Peace: Neutrality, the Test Ban, and the Freeze*, Syracuse University Press, Syracuse, NY.

Krasner, S. (1982), 'Structural Causes and Regime Consequences: Regimes as Intervening Variables', *International Organization*, Spring, p.186.

Kriesberg, L. (1982), *Social conflicts*, 2nd ed., Prentice-Hall, Englewood Cliffs, N.J.

Kriesberg, L. (1998), *Constructive Conflicts*, Rowman & Littlefield Publishers, Lanham.

Kriesberg, L. (1999), 'Paths to Varieties of Intercommunal Reconciliation', in Jeong, H. (ed.), *Conflict Resolution: Dynamics, Process and Structure*, Ashgate, Aldershot, pp. 105-29.

Krippendorff, E. (1973), 'Peace Research and the Industrial Revolution', *Journal of Peace Research*, Spring, no. 3.

Kruegler, C.(1992a), 'Strategy and Nonviolent Action', *Transforming Struggle*, Program on Nonviolent Sanctions in Conflict and Defense, Center for International Affairs, Harvard University, Boston.

Kruegler, C. (1992b), 'Why Strategy Matters', *Transforming Struggle*, Program on Nonviolent Sanctions in Conflict and Defense, Center for International Affairs, Harvard University, Boston.

Kruzel, J. (1991), 'Arms Control, Disarmament, and the Stability of the Postwar Era', in C.W. Kegley Jr. (ed.), *The Long Postwar Peace*, Harper Collins, New York.

Kupchan, C.A. (1994), 'The Case for Collective Security', in G. Downs (ed.), *Collective Security beyond the Cold War*, University of Michigan Press, Ann Arbor, pp. 41-68.

Lakey, G. (1987), *Powerful Peacemaking: A Strategy for a Living Revolution*, New York Society Publishers, Philadelphia.

Lawson, S. (1995), 'The Authentic State: History and Tradition in the Ideology of Ethnonationalism', in J. Camilleri, et al. (eds), *The State in Transition: Reimagining Political Space*, Lynne Rienner, Boulder, CO, pp. 77-90.

Lebow, R.N. (1996), *The Art of Bargaining*, The Johns Hopkins University Press, Baltimore, MD.

Lederach, J.P. (1994), *Building Peace: Sustainable Reconciliation in Divided Societies*, UN University Press, Tokyo.

Lenin, V. I. (1939), *Imperialism*, International Publishers, New York.

Lentz, T,F. (1961), Towards a Science of Peace: Turning Point in Human Destiny, Bookman Associates, New York.

Lerche III, C. (1998), ''The Conflicts of Globalization', in *International Journal of Peace Studies*, January, vol. 3, no. 1, pp. 47-66.

Levine, A. (1996), 'Political Accommodation and the Prevention of Secessionist Violence', in M. Brown (ed.), *The International Dimensions of Internal Conflict*, The MIT Press, Cambridge.

Lewer, N. (1992), *Physicians and the Peace Movement*, Frank Cass, London.

Liddington, J. (1995), '"Wars will cease when ...": Feminism and Anti-Militarism in Britain, 1918-1939', in Grünewald, G. and P. van der Dungen. Twenty-Century Peace Movements, The Edwin Mellen Press, Lewiston, pp. 81-100.

Lijphart, A. (1984), *Democracies: Patterns of Majoritarian and Consensus Government in Twenty-One Countries* , Yale University Press, New Haven, CT.

Lijphart, A. (1990), 'The Power-Sharing Approach', in J. V. Montville (ed.), *Conflict and Peacemaking in Multiethnic Societies*, Lexington Books, Lexington, pp. 491-510.

Lindroos, R. (1980), 'Disarmament, Employment and the Western Trade Unions', *Current Research on Peace and Violence*, vol. 2, pp. 85-92.

Lipson, C. (1994), 'Is the Future of Collective Security Like the Past?', in G. Downs (ed.), *Collective Security beyond the Cold War*, University of Michigan Press, Ann Arbor, pp. 105-32.

Litvinoff, M. (1990), *The Earthscan Action Handbook for People and Planet*, Earthscan Publications, London.

Lodgaard, S. (1991), 'Security through Enhanced Regional and Global Cooperation', in United Nations Department for Disarmament Affairs (ed.), *Challenges to Multilateral Disarmament in the Post-Cold War and Post-Gulf-War Period* , United Nations, New York, pp. 78-93.

Lofland, J. (1993), *Polite Protesters: The American Peace Movement of the 1980s*, Syracuse University Press, Syracuse, NY.

Lorenz, K. (1966), *On Aggression*, Harcourt, Brace and World, Inc., New York.

Lovelock, J.E. (1987), *Gaia: A New Look at Life on Earth*, Oxford University Press, Oxford.

Lumsden, M. (1999), 'Breaking the Cycle of Violence', in H. Jeong (ed.), *Conflict Resolution: Dynamics, Process and Structure*, Ashgate, Aldershot, pp. 131-52.

Lunardini, C. A. (1994), *The American Peace Movement in the Twentieth Century*, ABC-CLIO, Santa Barbara.

Lund, M. (1996), *Preventing Violent Conflicts: A Strategy for Preventive Diplomacy*, U.S. Institute of Peace Press, Washington, D.C.

MacGregor, F.E. and Rubio, M.C. (1994), 'Rejoinder to the Theory of Structural Violence', in K. Rupesinghe and M. Rubio (eds), *The Culture of Violence*, The United Nations University Press, Tokyo, pp. 42-58.

Mack, J.E. (1990), 'The Enemy System', in V. Volkan, et al (eds), *The Psychodynamics of International Relationships*, Lexington Books, Lexington, pp. 57-70.

Macrae, J. and Zwi, A., et al. (eds)(1994), *War and hunger: Rethinking International Responses to Complex Emergencies*, Zed Books, London.

Macy, J. (1985), *Dharma and Development: Religion as a Resource in the Sarvodaya Self-Help Movement*, Kumarian Press, West Hartford, CT.

Macy, J. (1991), *World as Lover, World as Self*, Parallax Press, Berkeley.

Manshard, W. (1998), 'The Biophysical Basis of Eco-restructuring', in R. Ayres (ed.), *Eco-restructuring: Implications for Sustainable Development*, United Nations University Press, Tokyo, pp. 55-76.

Mather, A.S. and Chapman, K. (1995), *Environmental Resources*, Longman Scientific and Technical, New York.

Max-Neef, M., (1986), 'Human Scale Economics: the Challenges Ahead', in P. Ekins (ed.), *The Living Economy: A New Economics in the Making* , Routledge, London, pp. 43-54.

McCully, P. (1996), *Silenced Rivers: The Ecology and Politics of Large Dams*, Zed Books, London.

McGarry, J. and O'Leary, B. (1993), *The Politics of Ethnic Conflict Regulation*, Routledge, London.

McGrew, A. (1992), 'Conceptualizing Global Politics', in A. McGrew et al. (eds), *Global Politics*, Polity Press, Cambridge, pp. 1-28.

McIntosh, S. (1994), 'The International Court of Justice,' K. Clements and R. Ward (eds), *Building International Community: Cooperating for Peace*, Allen & Unwin, St Leonards, Australia, pp. 207-10.

McManus, P. and Schlabach, G. (1991), *Relentless Persistence: Nonviolent Action in Latin America*, New Society Publishers, Philadelphia.

McRae, K. (1990), 'Theories of Power-Sharing and Conflict Management', in J. V. Montville (ed.), *Conflict and Peacemaking in Multiethnic Societies*, Lexington Books, Lexington, pp.93-106.

Meadows, D.H., et al. (1972), *The Limits to Growth. A Report for the Club of Rome's Project on the Predicament of Mankind*, Universe Books, New York.

Mehrota, S. (1997), *Development with a Human Face*, Oxford University Press, London.

Merchant, C. (1996), *Earthcare: Women and the Environment*, Routledge, New York.

Merrills, J.G. (1998), *International Dispute Settlement*, Cambridge University Press, Cambridge, UK.

Miall, H. (1992), *The Peacemakers: Peaceful Settlement of Disputes since 1945*, St. Martin's Press, New York.

Mies, M. (1986), *Patriarchy and Accumulation on a World Scale*, Zed Press, London.

Milburn, T. (1996), 'What Can We Learn from Comparing Mediation Across Levels', in *Peace and Conflict Studies*, vol. 3, no. 1, pp. 40-52.

Miller, B. (1992), 'A New World Order: From Balancing to Hegemony, Concert or Collective Security', *International Interactions*, vol. 18, no. 1, pp. 1-33.

Mingst, K. A. (1995), 'Economic Cooperation', in Merry M. Merryfield and Richard C. Remy (eds), *Teaching about International Conflict and Peace*, State University of New York Press, Albany, pp. 217-42.

Mingst, K.A. and Karns, M.P. (1995), *The United Nations in the Post-Cold War Era*, Westview Press, Boulder, CO.

Mitchell, C.R. (1981), *The Structure of International Conflict*, St. Martin's Press, New York.

Mitchell, C.R. (1999), 'The Anatomy of De-Escalation', in H. Jeong (ed.), *Conflict Resolution: Dynamics, Process and Structure*, Ashgate, Aldershot, pp. 37-58.

Mitchell, C.R. and Banks, M. (1996), *Handbook of Conflict Resolution: The Analytical Problem-Solving Approach*, Pinter, London.

Mitrany, D. (1966), *A Working Peace System*, Quadrangle Books, Chicago.

Mitrany, D. (1975), *The Functional Theory of Politics*, Martin Robertson, London.

Mittelman, J.H. (1997), *Out from Underdevelopment Revisited: Changing Global Structures and the Remaking of the Third World*, St. Martin's Press, New York.

Møller, B. (1993), 'Transarmament and conversion', in J. Balazs and H. Wiberg (eds), *Peace Research for the 1990s,* Akademiai Kiado, Budapest, pp. 61-78.

Møller, B. (1996), 'UN Military Demands and Non-Offensive Security', *Peace and Conflict Studies*, vol. 3, no. 2, December, pp. 1-20.

Molitor, M.R. (1999), 'The United Nations Climate Change Agreements', in N.J. Vig and R. Axelrod (eds), *The Global Environment: Institutions, Law and Policy,* Congressional Quarterly Press, Washington, DC, pp. 210-35.

Montville, J. (1987), 'The Arrow and the Oliver Branch: A Case for Track Two Diplomacy', in J. McDonald and D. Bendahmane (eds.), *Conflict Resolution: Track Two Diplomacy*, Foreign Service Institute, U.S. Department of State, Washington, D.C.

Montville, J. (ed.) (1990), *Conflict and Peacemaking in Multiethnic Societies*, Lexington Books, Lexington.

Morgenthau, H.J. (1959), *Politics Among Nations: the Struggle for Power and Peace*, 2nd ed., rev. and enl., Alfred A. Knopf, New York.

Mortimer, E. (1998), 'Under What Circumstances Should the UN Intervene Militarily in a "Domestic" Crisis?' in O. Otunnu and M. Doyle (eds), *Peacemaking and Peacekeeping for the New Century*, Rowman & Littlefield Publishers, Lanham, pp. 111-44.

Moss, R.H. (1993), 'Resource Scarcity and Environmental Security', in Stockholm International Peace Research Institute, *SIPRI Yearbook, World Armaments and Disarmaments*, Oxford University Press, Oxford, pp. 27-36.

Murphy, A.B. (1996), 'The Sovereign State System as Political-Territorial Ideal: Historical and Contemporary Considerations', in T. Biersteker and C. Weber (eds), *State Sovereignty as Social Construct*, Cambridge University Press, Cambridge, pp. 81-120.

Murphy, C. and Augelli, E. (1993), 'International Institutions, Decolonization, and Development', *International Political Science Review*, vol. 14, no. 1, pp. 71-85.

Myers, N. (1993), *Ultimate Security*, W.W. Norton, New York.

Naess, A. (1989), *Ecology, Community and Lifestyle*, Cambridge University Press, Cambridge.

Nagler, M. (1997), 'Peacemaking through Nonviolence', *Peace and Conflict Studies*, vol. 4, no. 2, pp. 56-63.

Nagler, M. (1999), 'What is Peace Culture?' in H. Jeong (ed.), *The New Agenda for Peace Research*, Ashgate, Aldershot, pp. 233-58.

Naidu, M.V. (1996), *Dimensions of Peace, Multi-Disciplinary Investigative and Teaching Association*, Brandon, Canada.

Nayar, R. J. (1996), 'Not Another Theory of Human Rights!', in C. Bearty and A. Tomkins (eds), *Understanding Human Rights*, Mansell, London, pp. 170-94.

Neufeld, Mark A. (1995), *The Restructuring of International Relations Theory*, Cambridge University Press, Cambridge.

Nicholson, M. (1992), *Rationality and the Analysis of International Conflict*, Cambridge University Press, Cambridge.

Nicholson, M. (1996), *Causes and Consequences in International Relations: A Conceptual Study*, Pinter, New York.

Nieburg, H. (1989), 'Problems of War and Peace Are Inseparable', in L. Forcey (ed.), *Peace: Meanings, Politics, Strategies*, Praeger, New York, pp. 27-38.

Norris, R. et al. (1991), 'Nuclear Weapons', in Stockholm International Peace Research Institute, *SIPRI Yearbook 1991: World Disarmament and Disarmament*, Oxford University Press, Oxford.

Nussbaum, M. (1997), 'Kant and Cosmopolitanism', in J. Bohman and M. Lutz-Bachmann (eds.), *Perpetual Peace: Essays on Kant's Cosmopolitan Ideal*, The MIT Press, Cambridge, pp. 25-58.

Oberthür, S. (1998), 'The International Convention for the Regulation of Whaling: From Over-Exploitation to Total Prohibition', in H.O. Bergesen, et al (eds), *Yearbook of International Cooperation on Environment and Development, 1998/99*, Earthscan Publications Ltd., London.

Osgood, C. (1962), 'Reciprocal Initiative', in J. Roosevelt (ed.), *The Liberal Papers*, Doubleday, Garden City, pp. 155-228.

Ostergaard, G. (1986), 'A Gandhian Perspective on Development', in G. Chester and A. Rigby (eds.), *Articles of Peace*, Prism Press, Bridport, pp. 142-68.

Paige, G. (1993), *To Nonviolent Political Science: Four Seasons of Violence*, Center for Global Nonviolence Planning Project, University of Hawai'i.

Paige, G. (1997), 'To Leap beyond Yet Nearer Bearing: From War, to Peace, to Nonviolence, to Nonkilling', *International Journal of Peace Studies*, vol. 2, no. 1, pp. 97-108.

Parajon, F., et al. (1996), 'The UNESCO Culture of Peace Programme in El Salvador', *International Journal of Peace Studies*, vol. 1., no. 2, pp. 1-20.

Parekh, B. (1989), *Colonialism, Tradition, and Reform: An Analysis of Gandhi's Political Discourse*, Sage Publications, Newbury Park, CA.

Parson, E. (1994), 'Protecting the Ozone Layer', in P. Haas et al. (eds), *Institutions for the Earth, MIT Press*, Cambridge, pp. 27-74.

Payer, Cheryl (1982), *The World Bank: A Critical Analysis*, Monthly Review Press, New York.

Peach, L.J. (1996), 'An Alternative to Pacifism? Feminism and Just-War Theory', in K.J. Warren and D.L. Cady (eds), *Bringing Peace Home: Feminism, Violence and Nature*, Indiana University Press, Bloomington, pp. 192-210.

Peck, C. (1996), *The United Nations System as a Dispute Settlement System: Improving Mechanisms for the Preventive and Resolution of Conflict*, Kluwer Law International, The Hague.

Peck, C. (1998), *Sustainable Peace: The Role of the UN and Regional Organizations in Preventing Conflict*, Rowman & Littlefield Publishers, Lanham, MD.

Pepinksy, H. (1995), 'Peacemaking Primer', *Peace and Conflict Studies*, vol. 2, no. 2, December, pp. 32-53.

Peterson, V.S. and Runyan, A.S. (1993),*Global Gender Issues*, Westview Press, Boulder, CO.

Pettman, R. (1996), *Understanding International Political Economy: With Readings for the Fatigued*, Lynne Rienner, Boulder, CO.

Pinder, J. (1998), *The Building of the European Union*, 3rd Ed., Oxford University Press, Oxford.

Porter, G. and Brown, J.W. (1996), *Global Environmental Studies*, Westview Press, Boulder, CO.

Preston, P.W. (1986), *Making Sense of Development*, Routledge & Kegan Paul, New York.

Princen, T. (1992), *Intermediaries in International Conflict*, Princeton University Press, Princeton, NJ.

Pruitt, D. and Carnevale, P. J. (1993), *Negotiation in Social Conflict*, Brooks/Cole Publishing Company, Pacific Grove.

Pugh, M. (1998), 'Post-Conflict Rehabilitation: Social and Civil Dimensions', *Journal of Humanitarian Assistance*.

Pye-Smith, C. (1994), *The Wealth of Communities: Stories of Success in Local Environmental Management*, Kumarian Press, West Hartford, CT.

Raiffa, H. (1982), *The Art and Science of Negotiation*, Harvard University Press, Cambridge.

Rapoport, A. (1960), *Fights, Games, and Debates*, The University of Michigan Press, Ann Arbor.

Rapoport, A. and Chammah, A. (1965), *Prisoner's Dilemma: A Study in Conflict and Cooperation*, University of Michigan, Ann Arbor.

Ratner, S. (1995), *The New UN Peacekeeping: Building Peace in Lands of Conflict After the Cold War*, St. Martin's Press, New York.

Reardon, B. (1985), *Sexism and the War System*, Teachers College, New York.

Reardon, B. (1989), 'Toward a Paradigm of Peace', in L.R. Forcey (ed.), *Peace: Meanings, Politics, Strategies*, Praeger, New York, pp. 15-26.

Reardon, B. (1990), 'Feminist Concepts of Peace and Security', in P. Smoker, R. Davis, and B. Munske (eds), *Introduction to Peace Studies*, Pergamon Press, Oxford, pp. 136-43.

Redclift, M. (1992), 'Sustainable Development and Popular Participation: A Framework for Analysis', in D. Ghai and J. Vivian (eds), *Grassroots Environmental Action*, Routledge, New York.

Renner, M. (1994), *Budgeting for Disarmament: The Costs of War and Peace*, World Watch Paper No. 122, Worldwatch Institute, Washington, DC.

Reychler, L. (1994), 'The Art of Conflict Prevention: Theory and Practice', in W. Bauwens and L. Reychler (eds), *The Art of Conflict Prevention*, Brassey's, London, pp. 1-21.

Richardson, L. (1960), *Statistics of Deadly Quarrels*, Boxwood, Pittsburgh.

Riggs, R. and Plano, J. (1994), *The United Nations: International Organization and World Politics*, 2nd ed., Wadsworth, Belmont.

Riggs, R. and Plano, J. (1988), *The United Nations: International Organization and World Politics*, Dorsey Press, Homewood.

Roberts, A. (ed.) (1967), *The Strategy of Civilian Defense: Civilian Resistance as a NationalDefense, Nonviolent Resistance to Aggression*, Stackpole Books, Harrisburg, PA.

Roberts, A. (1993), 'Humanitarian War: Military Intervention and Human Rights', *International Affairs*, vol. 69, no. 3, pp. 429-49.

Robertson, A. H. and Merrills, J. G. (1996), *Human Rights in the World*, Manchester University Press, Manchester.

Ronen, D. (1998), 'Can There Be a Just Resolution of Conflict?' *Peace and Conflict Studies*, vol. 5, no. 1, June, pp. 8-25.

Rosati, J., et al. (1990), 'A Critical Assessment of the Power of Human Needs in World Society', in J.W. Burton and F. Dukes (eds.), *Conflict: Readings in Management and Resolution*, Macmillan, London, pp. 156-80.

Rosenau, J. (1997), 'The Person, the Household, the Community, and the Globe', in R. Cox (ed), *The New Realism: Perspectives on Multilateralism and World Order*, United Nations University Press, Tokyo, pp. 57-80.

Rousseau, J. (1927), *A Project of Perpetual Peace* (1761), translated by E. Nuttall, Richard Cobden-Sanderson, London.

Rubenstein, R. (1999), 'Conflict Resolution and the Structural Sources of Conflict', in H. Jeong (ed.), *Conflict Resolution: Dynamics, Process and Structure*, Ashgate, Aldershot, pp. 173-96.

Ruddick, S. (1989), 'Mothers and Men's Wars', in A. Harris and Y. King (eds), *Rocking the Ship of State: Toward a Feminist Peace Politics*, Westview Press, Boulder, CO, pp. 75-92.

Rupesinghe, K. (1994), 'Forms of Violence and Its Transformation', in K. Rupesinghe and M. Rubio (eds), *The Culture of Violence*, The United Nations University Press, Tokyo, pp. 14-41.

Sachs, A. (1996), 'Upholding Human Rights and Environmental Justice', in L. Brown (ed.), *State of the World*, W.W. Norton, New York, pp. 133-51.

Sachs, W. (ed.) (1992), *The Development Dictionary: A Guide to Knowledge as Power*, Zed Books, Atlantic Highlands, New Jersey.

Salim, S.A (1996), 'Localizing Outbreaks: The Role of Regional Organization in Preventive Action', in K.M. Cahill (ed.), *Preventive Diplomacy : Stopping Wars*

Before They Start,   BasicBooks and the Center for International Health and Cooperation, New York.

Sandole, D. J. D. (1993), 'Paradigms, Theories, and Metaphors in Conflict and Conflict Resolution: Coherence or Confusion?', in D.J.D. Sandole and H. van der Merwe (eds), *Conflict Resolution Theory and Practice: Integration and Application*, Manchester University Press, Manchester, pp. 3-22.

Schirmer, J. (1993), 'The Seeking of Truth and the Gendering of Consciousness: The Comadres of El Salvador and the Conavigua Widows of Guatemala', in S.A. Radcliffe and S. Westwood (eds), *'Viva': Women and Popular Protest in Latin America*, Routledge, New York.

Schofield, S. (1994), 'Militarism, the UK Economy and Conversion Policies in the North', in G. and K. Tansey and P. Rogers (eds), *A World Divided: Militarism and Development after the Cold War*, St. Martin's Press, New York, pp. 67-82.

Schrijvers, J. (1993), *The Violence of Development: A Choice for Intellectuals*, INDRA, The Netherlands.

Schumacher, E. (1973), 'Buddhist Economics', in H. Daly (ed.), *Toward a Steady-State Economy*, W. H. Freeman, San Francisco.

Scimecca, J. A. (1991), 'Conflict Resolution in the United States: The Emergence of a Profession', in K. Avruch, P. Black, and J. A. Scimecca (eds), *Conflict Resolution: Cross Cultural Perspectives*, Greenwood Press, Westport, pp. 19-40.

Scott, J.C. (1990), *Domination and the Arts of Resistance: Hidden Transcripts*, Yale University Press, New Haven.

Sen, G. and Grown, C. (1987), *Development, Crises and Alternative Visions: Third World Women's Perspectives*, Monthly Review Press, New York.

Senghaas, D. (1974), 'Peace Research and the Third World', *Bulletin of Peace Proposals*, vol. 5, no. 2, pp. 158-72.

Sharp, G. (1973), *The Politics of Nonviolent Action*, Porter Sargent, Boston.

Sharp, G. (1990), *Civilian-Based Defense: A Post-Military Weapons System*, Princeton University Press, Princeton, NJ.

Sheehan, M. (1996), *The Balance of Power: History & Theory*, Routledge, London.

Shehadi, K. S. (1993), 'Ethnic Self-Determination and the Break-Up of States', *Adelphi Papers*, no. 283, pp. 3-90.

Shiva, V. (1991), *The Violence of the Green Revolution: Third World Agriculture, Ecology and Politics*, Zed Books, London.

Shore, W. (1970), *Fact-Finding in the Maintenance of International Peace*, Oceana Publications, New York.

Sibley, M. (ed.) (1963), *The Quiet Battle: Writings on the Theory and Practice of Nonviolent Resistance*, Doubleday, Garden City, N.Y.

Simard, G. (1996), 'The Case of Mauritania: Women's Productive Activities in Urban Areas – a Process of Empowerment', in P. Ghorayshi and C. Belanger (eds), *Women, Work and Gender Relations in Developing Countries*, Greenwood Press, Westport, pp. 151-66.

Sinclair, M. (ed.) (1995), *The New Politics of Survival: Grassroots Movements in Central America*, Monthly Review Press, New York.

Singer, D. (ed.) (1979), *The Correlates of War I*, Free Press, New York.

Singer, M. and Wildavsky, A. (1993), *The Real World Order: Zones of Peace, Zones of Turmoil*, Chatham House Publishers, Chatham, N.J.

Sites, P. (1990), 'Legitimacy and Human Needs', in Burton, J. and Dukes, F. (eds), *Conflict: Readings in Management and Resolution*, Macmillan, London, pp. 117-44.

Sivard, R.L. (1991), *World Military and Social Expenditures*, 13th ed., World Priorities, Washington, D.C.

Sivard, R.L. (1993), *World Military and Social Expenditures*, 15th ed., World Priorities, Washington, D.C.

Skidelsky, Lord R. and Mortimer, E. (1996), 'Economic Sanctions as a Means to International "Health"', in K.M. Cahill (ed.), *Preventive Diplomacy : Stopping Wars Before They Start*, BasicBooks and the Center for International Health and Cooperation, New York.

Small, M. and Singer, D. (1982), *Resort to Arms: International Civil Wars, 1816-1980*, Sage Publications, Beverly Hills.

Smith, A. (1991), *National Identity*, University of Nevada Press, Reno.

Smith, Anthony (1986), 'Conflict and Conflict Identity', in E. Azar and J.W. Burton (eds), *International Conflict Resolution, Theory and Practice*, Lynne Rienner Publishers, Inc., Boulder, CO.

Smith, D. (1997), *The State of War and Peace Atlas*, London, Penguin.

Smith, K., et al. (1991), *Growing our Future: Food Security and the Environment*, Kumarian Press, West Hartford, CT.

Smith, R.C. (1993), 'Indians, Forest Rights, and Lumber Mills', *Cultural Survival Quarterly*, Spring.

Smoker, P. (1972), 'Anarchism, Peace and Control: Some Ideas for Future Experiment', *Peace Research Reviews*, vol. IV, no. 4, February, pp. 52-69.

Smoker, P. (1992), 'Possible Roles for Social Movements', in M. and K. Tehranian, *Restructuring for World Peace*, Hampton Press, Cresskill, pp. 90-110.

Smoker, P. (1994), 'The Evolution of Peace Research', *Peace and Conflict Studies*, vol. 1, no. 1, December, pp. 3-5.

Smoker, P. and Groff, L. (1996), 'Sprituality, Religion, Culture and Peace: Exploring the Foundations for Inner-Outer Peace in the Twentieth Century', *International Journal of Peace Studies*, vol. 1, no. 1, pp. 77-113.

Snare, C. (1994), 'Defining Others and Situations: Peace, Conflict and Cooperation', *Peace and Conflict Studies*, vol. 1, no. 1, December, pp. 6-8.

Snyder, J. (1993), 'Introduction: New Thinking about the New International System', in J. Snyder and R. Jervis (eds), *Coping with Complexity in the International System*, Westview Press, Boulder, CO, pp. 1-24.

Soroos, M.S. (1995), 'Resolving Conflict Over the Global Environment', in M.M. Merryfield and R.C. Remy (eds), *Teaching about International Conflict and Peace*, State University of New York, Albany, pp. 293-320.

The South Commission (1990), *The Challenge to the South,* the Report of the South Commission, Oxford University Press, Oxford.

Stavenhagen, R. (1996), 'Self-Determination: Right or Demon?' in D. Clark and R. Williamson (eds), *Self-Determination: International Perspectives*, Macmillan, Houndsmills, Basingstoke, Hampshire, pp. 1-11.

Stockholm International Peace Research Institute (SIPRI) (1994), *SIPRI Yearbook*, Oxford University Press, London.

Stokke, O.S. (1997), 'Regime as Governance System', in O.R. Young (ed.), *Global Governance: Drawing Insights from the Environmental Experience*, The MIT Press, Cambridge, pp. 27-64.

Switzer, J.V. (1994), *Environmental Politics: Domestic and Global Dimensions*, St. Martin's Press, New York.

Sylvester, C. (1990), 'The Emperor's Theories and Transformations', in D. Pirages and C. Sylvester (eds), *Transformations in the Global Political Economy*, St. Martin's, New York.

Symonides, J. (1998), 'New Human Rights Dimensions, Obstacles and Challenges', in Symonides, J. (ed.), Human Rights: New Dimensions and Challenges, Ashgate, Alershot, pp. 1-44.

Terchek, R. (1998), *Gandhi: struggling for autonomy*, Rowman & Littlefield Publishers, Lanham, MD.

Thacher, P. (1991), 'Multilateral Cooperation and Global Change', *Journal of International Affairs*, vol. 44, no. 2, Winter, pp. 421-32.

Thakur, R. (1996), 'Towards a Nuclear-Weapon-Free World', *Peace and Conflict Studies*, vol. 3, no. 2, December, pp. 33-51.

Thomas, C. (1992), *The Environment in International Relations*, Royal Institute of Affairs, London.

Thompson, M. (1995), 'Repopulated Communities in El Salvador', in M. Sinclair (ed.), *The New Politics of Survival: Grassroots Movements in Central America*, Monthly Review Press, New York.

Tickner, J.A. (1994), 'Feminist Perspectives on Peace and World Security in the Post-Cold War Era', in M. Klare (ed.), *Peace*, pp. 43-54.

Tilly, C. (1978), *From mobilization to revolution*, Random House, New York.

Tolstoy, L. (1967), *Writings on Civil Disobedience and Nonviolence*, The New American Library, NewYork.

Tomasevski, K. (1995), 'Human Rights – Fundamental Freedom for All', in E. Childers (ed.), *Challenges to the United Nations: Building a Safer World*, St. Martin's Press, New York, pp. 82-112.

Townsend, J.G., et al (1995), *Women's Voices from the Rainforest*, Routledge, New York.

Trolldalen, J.M. (1992), *International Environmental Conflict Resolution: The Role of the United Nations*, The United Nations Institute for Training and Research, Geneva.

True, M. (1992), *To Construct Peace*, Twenty-Third Publications, Mystic.

Uclés, M.L. (1995), 'Building an Alternative: The Formation of a Popular Project', in M. Sinclair (ed.), *The New Politics of Survival: Grassroots Movements in Central America*, Monthly Review Press, New York.

The United Methodists Council of Bishops (1986*)*, *In Defense of Creation: The Nuclear Crisis and a Just Peace*, Graded Press, Nashville.

The United Nations (1948), *Universal Declaration of Human Rights*.

The United Nations (1972*)*, *Report of the United Nations Conference on the Human Environment*, UN Document, A CONF, 48/14 and Corr. 1.

The United Nations (1990), *The Blue Helmets: A Review of United Nations Peace-Keeping*, United Nations, New York.

The United Nations (1995), *The United Nations and Human Rights, 1945-1995*, The United Nations Blue Book Series, Volume VII, United Nations, New York.

The United Nations (1996), *The United Nations and the Advancement of Women 1945-1996*, Document No. 84, United Nations, New York.

The United Nations Children's Fund (UNICEF) (1998), *State of the World's Children*, Oxford University Press, New York.

The UN Chronicle (1992), 'The Earth Summit', *The UN Chronicle*, vol. xxix, no. 2, June, pp. 40-63.

The United Nations Development and Cooperation (1994), *Focus on Population*, no. 1, New York.

United Nations Development Programme (UNDP) (1992), *Human Development Report, 1992*, Oxford University Press, New York.

United Nations Environment Programme (1992), 'The State of the Global Environment', *Our Planet*, vol. 4, no. 2, pp. 4-9.

United Nations Research Institute for Social Development (UNRISD) (1980), *The Quest for a Unified Approach to Development*, UNRISD, Geneva.

Vasqeuz, J.A. (1993), *The War Puzzle*, Cambridge University Press, New York.

Veit-Brause, I. (1995), 'Rethinking the State of the Nation', in J. Camilleri, et al. (eds), *The State in Transition: Reimagining Political Space*, Lynne Rienner Publishers, Boulder, CO, pp. 59-76.

Vickers, J. (1993), *Women and War*, Zed Books, Atlantic Highlands, N.J.

Vogele, W.B. (1992), 'Defense, Difference and Nonviolent Action', *Transforming Struggle*, Program on Nonviolent Sanctions in Conflict and Defense, Center for International Affairs, Harvard University, pp. 31-6.

Vogele, W. and Bond, D. (1997), 'Nonviolent Struggle: The Contemporary Practice of Nonviolent Action', in R. Powers and W. Vogele (eds.), *Protest, Power, and Change: An Encyclopedia of Nonviolent Action from ACT-UP to Women's Suffrage*, Garland Publishing, New York, pp. 365-68.

Vogler, J. and Imber, M.F. (1996), *The Environment and International Relations*, Routledge, London.

Volkan, V.D. (1990), 'Psychoanalytic Aspects of Ethnic Conflict', in J.V. Montville (ed.), *Conflict and Peacemaking in Multiethnic Societies*, Lexington Books, Lexington.

von Clausewitz, C. (1977), *On War*, Princeton University Press, Princeton, NJ.

Wagner, R.H. (1993), 'The Causes of Peace', in R. Licklider (ed.), *Stopping the Killing*, New York University Press, New York, pp. 235-68.

Walton, J. and Seddon, D. (1994), *Free Markets & Food Riots: The Politics of Global Adjustment*, Blackwell, Cambridge, MA.

Waltz, K. (1979), *Theory of International Politics*, Random House, New York.

Wapner, P. (1996), *Environmental Activism and World Civic Politics*, State University of New York, Albany.

Warren, K.J. and D.L. Cady (1996), 'Feminism and Peace: Seeing Connections', in K.J. Warren and D.L. Cady (eds), *Bringing Peace Home: Feminism, Violence and Nature*, Indiana University Press, Bloomington, IN.

Waters, M. (1995), *Globalization*, Routledge, New York.

Wedge, B. (1990), 'The Individuals, the Group and War', in J. Burton and F. Dukes (eds.), *Conflict: Readings in Management and Resolution*, Macmillan, London, pp. 101-16.

Weinberg, B. (1991), *War on the Land: Ecology and Politics in Central America*, Zed Books, London.

Weiss, T.W., et al. (1994), *The United Nations and Changing World Politics*, Westview Press, Boulder, CO.

Wells, D. (1996), *Environmental Policy: A Global Perspectives for the Twenty-First Century*, Prentice-Hall.

Wenden, A. (1995), 'Defining Peace: Perspectives from Peace Research', in Schäffner and A. Wenden (eds), *Language and Peace*, Dartmouth, Aldershot, pp. 3-16.

Wiener, M. (1996), 'Bad Neighbours, Bad Neighbourhoods: An Inquiry into the Causes into the Causes of Refugee Flows', *International Security*, vol. 21, no. 1, Summer.

Wignaraja, P. (1993), 'Rethinking Development and Democracy', in P. Wignaraja (ed.), *New Social Movements in the South: Empowering the People*, Zed Books, London, pp. 4-38.

Williams, M. (1994), *International Economic Organizations and the Third World*, Harvester Wheaster, New York.

Wilmer, F. (1993), *The Indigenous Voice in World Politics*, Sage Publications, Newbury Park, Calif.

Woito, R.S. (1982), *To End War: A New Approach to International Conflict*, The Pilgrim Press, New York.

Wolf, E. (1997), *Europe and the People without History: With a New Preface*, University of California Press, Berkeley.

Women's Feature Service (1993), *The Power to Change: Women in the Third World Redefine Their Environment*, Zed Books, London.

Woodcock, G. (1944), *Anarchy or Chaos*, Freedom Press, London,

Woodward, B. (1983), 'The Abolition of War,' *Crosscurrents*, vol. 33, no. 3, Fall.

World Bank (1991), *World Development Report, 1991,* The World Bank, Washington, DC.

World Commission on Environment and Development (WCED) (1987), *Our Common Future*, Oxford University Press, Oxford.

Wright, Q. (1942), *A Study of War*, University of Chicago Press, Chicago.

Young, C. (1993), 'The Dialectics of Cultural Pluralism', in C. Young (ed.), *The Rising Tide of Pluralism: The Nation-State at Bay*, University of Wisconsin Press, Madison, WI, pp. 33-5.

Young, M. C. (1991), 'Self-Determination Revisited: Has Decolonization Closed the Question?', in G. Nzongola-Ntalaja (ed.), *Conflict in the Horn of Africa*, African Studies Association, Atlanta, GA, pp. 41-66.

Young, N. (1987), 'Peace Movements in History', in S. Mendlovitz and R. Walker (eds), *Towards a Just World Peace*, Butterworths, London.

Zacher, M. (1990), 'Toward a Theory of International Regimes', *Journal of International Affairs*, vol. 44, no. 1, September, pp. 139-75.

Zebich-Knos, M. (1998), 'Global Environmental Conflict in the Post-Cold War Era: Linkage to an Extended Security Paradigm', *Peace and Conflict Studies*, vol. 5, no. 1, June, pp. 26-40.

Zisk, B. (1992), *The Politics of Transformation: Local Activism in the Peace and Environmental Movements*, Praeger, Westport.

Zohar, D. (1991), *The Quantum Self*, Flamingo/Harper Collins, London.

Index